COLLECTION TECHNIQUES FOR A SMALL BUSINESS

By Gini Graham Scott, Ph.D.

and John J. Harrison

Published by The Oasis Press
Grants Pass, Oregon

Published by The Oasis Press®
© 1994 by Gini Graham Scott and John J. Harrison

All rights reserved. No part of this publication may be reproduced or used in any form or by any means, graphic, electronic or mechanical, including photocopying, recording, taping, or information storage and retrieval systems without written permission of the publishers.

This publication is designed to provide accurate and authoritative information in regard to the subject matter covered. It is sold with the understanding that the publisher is not engaged in rendering legal, accounting, or other professional service. If legal advice or other expert assistance is required, the services of a competent professional person should be sought.

— *from a declaration of principles jointly adopted by a committee of the American Bar Association and a committee of publishers*

Please direct any comments, questions, or suggestions regarding this book to:
    Editorial Department
    The Oasis Press®/PSI Research
    P.O. Box 3727
    Central Point, OR 97502
    (541) 479-9464
    info@psi-research.com *email*

The Oasis Press® is a Registered Trademark of Publishing Services, Inc., an Oregon corporation doing business as PSI Research.

ISBN: 1-55571-312-2 (binder)
       1-55571-171-5 (paperback)

Printed in the United States of America
First edition 10 9 8 7 6 5

 Printed on recycled paper when available.

Table of Contents

Introduction xi
How This Book Will Help You.. xii

PART I — How to Protect Yourself from Bad Debts

Chapter 1 — Establishing a Credit Policy 1
What to Consider in Establishing a Credit Policy 2
Determining the Right Policy for Your Business 5

Chapter 2 — Protecting Yourself..9
Accepting Checks..10
Taking Credit Cards 13
Working Out Billing Policies 16
Promissory Notes 19
Written Contracts...19
Getting Collateral...23
Obtaining Co-Signers 25
Arranging for Conditional Sales and Consignment, and Using Inventory
   As Security..26

Chapter 3 — Dealing With Credit As You Expand Your Business........29
Creating Your Own Credit Rating 30
Doing an Extensive Credit Check for Large Accounts 31
Checking the Seven Sources 33
Making Your Decision 38
Why Do All This Checking?...41

PART II — How to Get Your Money and Keep Good Will

Chapter 4 — Strategies for Collecting..45
Getting Set to Collect 45
Keeping Track of Overdue Accounts 48
The Do's and Don'ts of Debt Collecting 51

Chapter 5 — Motivating the Debtor to Pay 55
Stage 1: Notifying and Reminding the Debtor 55
Stage 2: The Appeals Phase 66
Suggesting Alternatives 75

Chapter 6 — Communicating Effectively with the Debtor 79
Discussing the Bill 79
Handling Stalls and Objections 85
Dealing With Disputes and Negotiating Settlements 105

PART III — How to Get Tough and Go To Court

Chapter 7 — Getting Tough 119
Making the Final Demand 119
Types of Demands 120
Getting Outside Assistance 126

Chapter 8 — Pre-Collection Letters, Attorneys, and Collection Agencies 137
Using Pre-Collection Letters 137
Using An Attorney 144
Using a Collection Agency 149

Chapter 9 — Deciding to Go to a Small Claims Court 161
The Advantages of Going to a Small Claims Court 161
An Overview of the Small Claims Court Process 162

Chapter 10 — Preparing Your Case and Appearing in a Small Claims Court 189
Preparing Your Case 189
Appearing in Court 194

PART IV — How to Collect What You Win at Court

Chapter 11 — What To Do After You Win — Your Alternatives 203
Deciding to Collect On Your Own 204
Getting the Debtor to Pay Voluntarily 211

Chapter 12 — Finding the Debtor and Any Assets Through Public and Private Records 217
What to Look For and How to Find It 217
The Major Sources of Information 219
When to Use the Different Sources 222
Using Public and Private Records for Information 222
Examining the Debtor Through the Courts 233

Chapter 13 — Using the Legal Process to Collect 247
The Tools to Collect Your Judgment...248
Getting the Debtor's Assets...256

Chapter 14 — Dealing With Complications...........................285
Dealing With a Bankruptcy...285
Dealing With a Divorce...288
Collecting Assets From Another State......................................289
Dealing With a Debtor Who Gives Property to Someone Else 289
Dealing With a Name Change 290
Dealing With the Death of the Debtor 291
Renewing or Reviving a Judgment..292

Chapter 15 — A Few Final Words 293

APPENDIXES

Appendix A — Bibliography..295

Appendix B — Reproducibles of Forms, Worksheets
Form 1, New Client Questionnaire..297
Form 2, Check Deposit Record..298
Form 3, Promissory Note 299
Credit Rating Scoring System...300
Collections System Time Line 301
Form 4, List of Debtors Who Owe Debtor Form......................302
Form 5, Information on the Debtor And Any Assets...............303
Form 6, Real Estate Inquiry Form 304
Form 7, Examination in Supplementary Proceedings Example 305
Verification to Tax Assessor 306
Form B-10 Bank Verification Form..307

FORMS AND EXAMPLES

Form 1, New Client Questionnaire..3
Form 2, Check Deposit Record..14
Form 3, Promissory Note 20
Credit Rating Scoring System...32
Collections System Time Line 50
Sample Collection Letter 150
Form 4, List of Debtors Who Owe Debtor Form......................153
Plaintiff's Statement Example 172
Claim of Plaintiff Example 174
Civil Subpoena Example 192
Sample Reminder Letter After Judgment.................................213
Form 5, Information on the Debtor And Any Assets...............220

Checklist of Sources for Locating Debtor And Any Assets 221
Example of Post Office Form 225
Example of Request Form From Motor Vehicle Dept. 227
Form 6, Real Estate Inquiry Form 231
Subpoena Duces Tecum Example 237
Example of Judgment of Debtor's Statement of Assets 238
Order to Appear For Examination Example 240
Form 7, Examination in Supplementary Proceedings Example 241
Writ of Execution Example 249
Example of Memorandum of Credits, Accrued Interest, and Costs After Judgment 253
Sample Letter of Instructions 255
Example of Notice of Levy 258
Example of Abstract of Judgment 259
Example of Earnings Withholding Order 269
Example of Claim of Exemption (Enforcement of Judgment) 274
Example of Notice of Opposition of Claim of Exemption 275
Example of Claim of Exemption (Wage Garnishment) 276
Example of Financial Statement 277
Example of Memorandum of Garnishee 279
Example of Notice of Hearing on Claim of Exemption 281
Example of Employer's Return 282

Acknowledgments

This book is dedicated to all the people who owe or have owed me money, and who I can't name here, because of current libel laws:

M.M. (collected $280 — May 12, 1984, suit dismissed)
S.T. (judgment for $110 — June 6, 1984; judgment satisfied)
R.G. (judgments for $548 — May 24, 1984, and $712 — Sept. 28, 1984)
R.K. (judgment for $1,500 — June 6, 1984)
H.N. (judgment for $1,261 — June 6, 1984)
A.R. (judgment for $155 — June 17, 1984, judgment satisfied)
T.K. (judgment for $575 — July 17, 1984)
E.R. (judgment for $1,500 — August 30, 1984, judgment satisfied)
R.H. (judgment for $295 — September 18, 1985, judgment satisfied)
D.E. (judgment for $540 — August 25, 1986)

and a dozen others, with unpaid bills and bounced checks too small to file suit.

They got me interested in the techniques of collecting money as I went through the frustrations of trying to collect from them.

Also, on a more serious note, I want to give special thanks to the various people who helped me with this book:

Michael W. Perna, a collections attorney in Oakland, California, who gave me invaluable information on collecting judgments;

Stefan A. Riesenfeld, a law professor at Boalt Hall in Berkeley, California, whose class on Creditors' Remedies and Debtors' Protections proved extremely helpful;

Mike Markowitz, a bill collector in Daly City, California, whose class on bill collecting showed me some insider strategies for finding and collecting from an unwilling debtor;

Tim Schooley, a lawyer and one-time Small Claims Legal Advisor in Alameda County, who reviewed my materials on the small claims process and made some suggestions;

Michael Coleman, of Coleman & Coleman, who gives seminars on collecting internationally, and provided me with some help in promoting my book; and many others, too numerous to mention.

Dedication

My work into this project is dedicated to my father, Floyd D. Harrison, Sr., who lives and works in Lansing, Michigan.

John J. Harrison

Foreword

As a practicing attorney specializing in creditor-debtor law, I am often astounded at how little the small-business community, and individuals generally, know about their rights with respect to debt collection. Often debts that would otherwise be collectable escape payment because the creditor either was not aware of his rights, or did not take appropriate actions to protect them.

While it can be said that experience is a great teacher, it is often an expensive one. Many more individuals are engaged in small enterprises than ever before; it is essential that they have some understanding of what the legal system can—and cannot—do for them in the enforcement of money obligations of others. Such information is not only useful after a debt turns sour, but can also reduce the incidence of bad (uncollectable) debt in the first place.

Therefore, Gini Graham Scott's book, *Collection Techniques For A Small Business*, should be an important resource for anyone who has credit dealings with others. Even if one is not now in the process of attempting to collect a debt, this volume will be extremely useful in the management of credit transactions and in enhancing the enforceability of obligations to pay money.

Michael W. Perna, Esq.
Oakland, California

Introduction

Almost everyone is owed money or owes money to someone. A person makes a loan to a friend who doesn't pay it back. A customer can't obtain a refund on defective merchandise she wants to return. An investor takes a chance, and the company has problems. A business sells a product on credit, and the buyer doesn't pay or sends a bad check.

For many people, especially those in small business, the psychology and process of collecting debts is a real mystery. You ask for the money, people give you an excuse, and then you don't know how to counter that. In fact, many small businesses give up on collecting debts before they should.

The reasons are many: They fear the debtor's ill will if they have been good customers or business associates. They simply do not know the strategies for motivating the debtor to pay while maintaining good relations. They also stop trying because they mistakenly conclude the debtor simply won't pay, and the creditors are unaware of the legal remedies available to them. And, some become so emotionally involved and pursue their debt so energetically (and, sometimes, even illegally) that they may find themselves owing the debtor money when the debtor sues them for libel, slander, harassment, theft, assault, extortion, or other illegal collection practices.

In short, if you want to collect the money owed to you, you have to know the rules of the collection game. Then, within these general guidelines, you can be creative. Indeed, in many instances, you have to be resourceful to get your money because you are competing with other creditors to get paid by a debtor who doesn't have enough to pay everyone, or uses a priority system to pay the more important creditors first. So, you have to find a way to make your claim come to the top of the pile—or perhaps look for non-monetary alternatives for getting paid.

However, collecting what you are owed is only half the story. The other half involves taking preventive measures in advance to protect yourself from collection problems. Depending on the circumstances, these measures can range from writing up effective loan agreements to making decisions about when to extend credit and to whom. In other words, you need to create a credit policy whereby you decide under what circumstances you will extend credit and how much you will risk.

You also need to understand how to tailor the debt collection approach to the needs and personality of the debtor, to maximize the possibilities of collection while keeping the debtor's good will or continued business. And, of course, you have to learn when and how to get tough.

How This Book Will Help You

This book is designed to help you collect this money in two ways:
(1) By establishing a good credit policy, so you can make the best decision about whether to extend credit.
(2) By knowing what to do when you have problems collecting extended credit.

While this book is designed especially for the small business person owed a small amount of money (up to $2,000), individuals or business people owed much more should find the basic principles and strategies discussed in this book useful, too.

Note, however, that many of the forms, fees, and regulations for collecting, which are described in this book, may vary from state to state. It is recommended to check with the proper authorities in your state when you begin collecting the money owed you.

Also in the back of the book in the appendix you'll find useful reproducibles of forms and worksheets found in the book. If you need a specific form, such as a New Client Questionnaire, all you have to do is remove that page from the book and make the appropriate number of copies. It's that simple. This should save you valuable time and money.

If your major problem is locating your debtor, see Chapter 12. We have placed this chapter following the discussion on what to do after a favorable court decision. However, you may not need to pursue action in a court—you may merely need to find the debtor.

Part I

How To Protect Yourself From Bad Debts

Chapter 1

Establishing A Credit Policy

Whenever you aren't paid in full in cash immediately, you are extending credit, which always involves some risk. The check may not clear; the account may be closed; the debtor won't pay your bill or will take ages to pay.

Thus, to protect yourself and reduce risks, you need to create a preventive financial policy, with guidelines on when you can give credit, under what conditions, and to whom.

In creating this policy, you should also determine your answers to the following questions in advance:

(1) Do I expect all payments to be in cash, money order, or C.O.D. (Cash On Delivery), or will I extend credit?

(2) How much deposit do I want before doing any work or shipping the product? And, when the job is completed or the product shipped, do I want cash only? Will I accept C.O.D? Or will I bill?

(3) Will I accept checks, and if so, for how much? And, what identifications or verifications will I need?

(4) Will I accept credit cards? And, if so, which ones? What kind of credit checks will I make to protect myself?

(5) What contract forms do I need to cover the situations likely to occur in my business? What kind of protective clauses do I want in these contracts to cover me if I am not paid?

(6) When I bill, what kind of terms will I offer? What sort of discounts, if any, will I give for early payments? What charges for interest or penalties will I add if payments are late? And, when will these charges start?

By the same token, determine when you will start charging for your products and services, and make sure that your customer or client knows this. For example, some lawyers and consultants offer their first hour or half-hour of consulting free, so the client can decide whether he or she wants their services.

Others charge immediately—and some want payment in cash or check right after the consultation. Others even ask for full payment before the session starts.

What to Consider in Establishing a Credit Policy

Any policy can work for you, depending upon the kind of business you're in and other factors. The point is to think out your policy beforehand; don't create it on the spur of the moment. Then, you have your customer or client know what it is.

The reason policies may differ so widely is because situations, customers, clients, and the products or services offered differ extensively, too. Also, you may want to have alternate policies to cover different situations.

You can also have alternate credit policies for different customers, depending on your assessment of their ability and willingness to pay. Should they ask for credit, get information about them, and use that to make your assessment. To be diplomatic, you might call this a New Client or New Customer Questionnaire, (See Form 1) which you use to provide better service, rather than saying it's a Credit Application, which may put people on the defensive. Then, without much ado, ask them to fill it out, saying something like "It's for our records," or "It's so we have a better idea of who our customers (clients) are, so we're better able to help." Then, once this is filled out, you can use the information to decide how much credit to extend, and later if you have trouble getting paid, this data can help you collect.

If you have any customers or clients who balk at filling out this form, tell them they don't have to fill it out if they pay cash or give you a deposit in advance. (Again, you can always say this is what your accountant wants you to do.) Or you can try some gentle persuasion, such as "Well, this is normal procedure." If the person still doesn't want to fill out the form, make sure that the person has a good reason.

Having a more rigorous financial policy may result in losing some customers or clients. But, then, it may be to your advantage to lose these people who don't like to sign contracts and make firm commitments. For the bottom line is not just how much you sell or what work you do, but how successfully you can collect, as well.

The link between credit and sales

In setting your financial policy, consider the link between credit and sales. Sometimes they can conflict, since a tough credit policy can discourage sales. Or you can use a more liberal policy as a competitive tool to promote and get people to buy your products or services. For example, many businesses have signed on as merchants with MasterCard or Visa, because they have found many customers don't want to pay cash, don't have their checkbooks, or don't want to write a check. But if they can buy on credit, they will.

FORM 1

NEW CLIENT QUESTIONNAIRE

Name _____

Home Address _____

City _____ State _____ Zip _____

Business (if own business) _____

Employer (if employed) _____

Address _____

City _____ State _____ Zip _____

Phone _____ Can we call you at work? _____

Nearest relative for emergencies:

Name _____

Address _____

City _____ State ____ Zip _____ Phone _____

Nearest friend for emergencies:

Name _____

Address _____

City _____ State ____ Zip _____ Phone _____

Who referred you to us:

Name _____

City _____ State ____ Zip _____ Phone _____

Do you: ❏ Own Home ❏ Rent Other _____

How long at last address? _____

Previous address if there less than 2 years: _____

City _____ State _____ Zip _____

Bank Name: _____ Account # _____

If paying by charge card:

Charge Account Name _____ Account # _____

As one successful businessperson says, "You've got to take advantage of that impulse sale. Make it as easy as possible for people to buy, and you'll make that sale."

Similarly, many suppliers know they'll get more clients and make more sales if they extend credit. For example, a start-up company may choose a printer for its brochures because the printer doesn't require a deposit up front, agrees to take less down, or gives the company longer to pay. Since the company is strapped for cash in the beginning, the credit the printer extends is a sales incentive to choose that printer over another, even if the bid is the same or a little more. Then if the new business goes well, the printer's decision may lead to more work from that customer in the future.

However, in extending any credit, there's always a risk, and you have to weigh that against increasing sales. It's a problem that faces every business that offers credit.

In turn, every loss means that much more you have to work or sell to make up, depending upon your average profit margin. For example, if you've got a margin of 10%, for every $100 loss you suffer, you have to sell another $1,000 in products or services to catch up.

The risks of extending credit

The risks of extending credit take various forms. For example, a customer who buys your product or service on MasterCard or Visa can always return them or dispute the bill, and if successful, the purchase will be charged back to you. Another risk is the company to whom you extend credit can go "belly up."

Thus, you've always got to weigh the advantage of increased business and sales against the risk you won't get paid, and set your credit policy accordingly, based on how the pluses and minuses shape up and how much of a risk you are willing and able to take. But in any case, your overall rating should be more positive than negative; for if your negative credit balance exceeds your sales or popularity by too much, you'll go out of business or become personally bankrupt.

If you're in a company that's big enough to have different people handling credit and sales, realize the two should ideally be coordinated together. For example, your salesperson can casually pick up credit information in the course of making a sale, the reason being the salesperson already has the customer's good will, and the customer will be more receptive to offering information to the salesperson. But when someone else calls for a credit check, the person might get suspicious and defensive. On the other hand, the sales people do need a tight leash to make sure they don't offer too much credit to make the sale, resulting in a customer who can't pay, or end up losing too many sales because of restrictive credit arrangements.

In short, whatever your situation, you should have a credit policy already worked out. You should coordinate it with any sales efforts. Pre-planning is the sensible way to survive and flourish in business. The following sections will discuss some specific elements to include in your policy. Then, you decide on the specifics that are right for you.

Determining the Right Policy for Your Business

There's no right credit policy for everyone—it depends on your business, your customer, current economic conditions, the size of your bank account or company, how much credit you can afford to risk, and the likelihood you will get paid.

In general, establish overall guidelines that are best suited to your current situation; then adapt them according to your assessment of the prospective debtor. We will start with some basics here, and look more closely at how to assess your client or customer in the following sections. The major areas where you need to make decisions are as follows: (1) Cash, C.O.D., or credit?, (2) Checks, (3) Credit cards, (4) Collateral, (5) Written contracts, (6) Deposits and billing, and (7) Promissory notes.

Various factors, outlined below, will affect whether you take a harder or more liberal line in each of the areas listed above—most notably, the general economic climate, the area where you do business, the nature of your business, your personal financial strength, the stability of your clientele (though you may vary your policy for different customers), and your emphasis on expanding sales, versus reducing credit risks.

Taking a hard or soft line

A more hard-nosed approach to credit involves taking cash or C.O.D. (Cash on Delivery) payments only, accepting checks only under limited circumstances and requiring plenty of identification, avoiding credit cards or carefully checking every card that you get, working up binding contracts, asking for large deposits, or getting payments in advance. This conservative approach may tend to restrict your sales, but you'll have more protection against poor credit risks—and, in some situations, you need this.

Conversely, with a more liberal policy, you'll offer plenty of credit to qualified customers, take checks with only minimal identification, accept credit cards with a signature only, use informal contracts if any, and do work or ship products based on only a promise to pay.

Both approaches can work very effectively depending on your situation and the factors previously listed. Then, as circumstances change, so can your approach, for you want to keep adjusting your policy to your current situation or market.

General economic climate

When economic conditions are good and booming, you can afford to be more liberal with credit, because you are in a more solid financial position yourself to extend it—and the people to whom you lend funds will be in a better position to pay. At the same time, when times are good, people may be more demanding about expecting credit. They find that other individuals and businesses are extending credit more freely so they expect you to do so, too.

Conversely, when times become difficult, extending credit becomes more risky. You may have more financial problems yourself, so you need more cash up front to keep up with day to day expenses. Concurrently, you face more risks since individuals and companies may have more difficulty making payments; the reason is that people are more likely to lose jobs or get less pay, while businesses are apt to have less business and more payment problems themselves.

Thus, adapt your policies to the times. In times of economic upturn, be more willing to give credit in various ways; and when things get tough, become tougher in offering credit.

The nature of your business

The kind of business you are in also influences your policies, since different businesses attract different types of customers. Some are more stable and likely to pay than others. Then, too, different businesses have different payment and credit traditions. Also, the size of your average transaction and whether you expect continuing business with the same customer or client should affect your policies, too.

(1) Be aware of what others in your field are doing. For example, if you are a small printer, it may be traditional for printers in your area to get 50% of the estimated cost of the job down and the rest on delivery. On the other hand, a doctor or lawyer commonly sends a bill, while a locksmith who goes out on a job normally receives a full payment after completing the work with a check or in cash. Unless you have a good reason for creating different credit-payment arrangements, it's probably to your benefit to look to others in your industry to set your general approach. Many businesses today ask for payment in full after services.

(2) Look to transaction size as a guide. If your sales are usually for small amounts, it makes more sense to get it all in cash, and perhaps selectively take small checks. On the other hand, if you have large sales, you have a reason to accept credit cards or checks (with the appropriate credit checks, of course.

(3) Extend more credit if your business has continuing clients or customers. For example, at gas stations, most business is of the pass-through variety, where motorists stop by on their way to somewhere else, and relatively little business actually comes from the area. Thus, gas stations

rarely accept checks; it's usually pay as you go, sometimes in advance, with cash or credit cards. On the other hand, a corner drug store which depends on regular customers typically takes checks without checking anyone's ID.

As you continue to do business with the same customer, you can extend more credit. For example, a printer may start off with 50% down and cash on delivery for everyone. After a few months, however, the printer may take small jobs with nothing down and bills with payment due in 30 days. For bigger jobs, the arrangement is 50% down and the rest 30 days after billing.

(4) Keep your antennae attuned for changing conditions. Even with customers you have learned to trust, you should be aware of sudden changes. Take new information into consideration, such as a business being in trouble, a customer losing a job, or even the economy going soft. Of course you may want to give the person a break if the signs point to recovery, but if the client is in a hole which he or she can't climb out of, be careful. You want to balance your compassion with an assessment of the hard, cold economic facts. Ask yourself whether you will win a continued customer by your help in time of need, or whether you will lose your customer as well as your own shirt.

Your own financial strength

The amount of credit you can extend also depends on how strong you are financially. As you'll notice in looking around the marketplace, the larger the company, the more likely it is to have credit arrangements. The bigger companies are more able to afford extended payments, and more likely to promote credit to make sales.

These large companies, in turn, can better afford it when a customer is a "slow pay" or defaults, because they have a much larger customer base and can more easily work the cost of credit into the cost of other sales. But if you're small and struggling, you don't have that reserve; so a few wrong credit choices can put you under.

Thus, you have to base the credit you extend on your own cash flow. If you need your income almost immediately to balance the books and stay afloat, it's probably better not to extend any credit. Just work on a cash and carry arrangement, and perhaps permit C.O.D.'s, checks, and a partial deposit down. Then, as you get stronger, you can think about billing and credit cards, if your type of business and clientele warrants this.

Expanding sales versus reducing credit risks

You might also consider how your credit policy is affecting sales. Is it interfering with sales in any way, and if so, how much? Would the increased profit from greater sales balance out the risk of losses due to giving more credit?

To answer these questions, track your sales for awhile, and notice if you lose any sales because you won't extend credit. For example, if you have a store or a booth in a trade show, make a note each time anyone asks to make a purchase on a credit card and then doesn't buy because you don't offer this kind of credit. If only a few people ask and don't buy, you may not need this kind of service. Or ask yourself if people might walk by without stopping at all, because you don't prominently advertise that you offer credit. If you don't know, check it out, perhaps by looking at what the businesses around you do. If they take cards, perhaps you should, too.

Also consider the costs of offering credit when people pay. For example, at some banks which offer MasterCard or Visa, you have to pay the bank a minimum of $15 a month in discounts on sales (which is the percentage the bank deducts from each credit card sale you make when it pays you for the transaction) or you must make up the difference from your own account. If most of your customers aren't buying on credit, it may be costing you too much to keep the service. Or if you offer some service and your clients normally pay up at once, ask yourself if you have lost any clients because they would prefer to receive bills.

To find out, you might monitor calls about fees and services. Notice if any callers seem concerned about your billing arrangements, and if any decline your services when you say you don't send bills and expect payment by cash or check. If so, figure out your costs in lost clients versus possible losses if the clients you bill don't pay.

Chapter 2

Protecting Yourself

To be in the best possible position to collect later, if things go wrong, you have to do all you can to protect yourself in advance. This includes the following:

- Getting the proper identification so you can find the debtor or any assets later;

- Writing up a good agreement or contract, so you have an airtight claim on which to collect and can pass your collection costs on to the debtor.

Having a serious approach has several benefits:

(1) It puts your prospective customer, client, or loanee on notice that you are serious in expecting to be paid so you are less likely to have debtors who think they can take advantage of you.

(2) You have a firm basis for reminding the debtor of his or her obligations if you do have problems—It's all in black in white.

(3) You will also have a better chance of tracking down the debtor and getting your money back if you do go to court.

Many people don't take such steps when they extend credit. They depend on oral agreements or take checks and credit card payments on little more than faith. But that's not what you want to do. You may realize a few months later when you have a collection problem that it's like locking the barn after the horse is gone. You suddenly have to search for the horse; then when you find him, you may find you don't have the proper equipment to bring him in. Or you may find the horse is safely on the other side of a canyon; so again, you have lost.

Thus, the solution is to prepare yourself before the collection problem begins. In this way, you either avoid the problem or confront it better when it occurs. The key areas to consider are as follows:

Accepting checks

What to Look For

Whenever you accept a check, review the check to make sure it is filled out properly and get a minimal amount of information to protect yourself.

The basics to check for include making sure of the following:

- The check is signed;
- The correct amount is filled out in two places;
- The check is made out to the right person or left blank so the payee can fill it in;
- There's a pre-printed address and phone number (no "starter" checks);
- You should also ask for the customer's driver's license as an ID and possibly one credit card number.
- There should be no unusual writing on the reverse side (endorsement section). Written comments such as "paid in full" may legally bind you to consider the account closed if you accept the check.

Article 3 of the Uniform Commercial Code (UCC) provides some guidelines on accepting or rejecting checks. However, laws may vary from state to state, so the more you know about your state laws, the better.

Checks from Corporations

Accepting checks from a corporation is different than accepting checks from an individual. Asking for the payee's driver's license number as identification may be inappropriate, since the corporation is comprised of more than just that individual. Obtaining information on an account's "rating" may be a wise alternative. Call the bank on which the check is drawn and ask for a rating of the checking account. The bank should tell you the account has a medium 3 figure average balance; this means there is usually at least $500 in the account. You can also call the secretary of state, corporations section (generally in the capital of the state where the business is located) to obtain additional information about the corporation, such as how long it has been in existence and the names of its principal officers.

NSF Checks

Non-Sufficient Funds (NSF) checks can be a problem. Do not be surprised when you receive notification of a bad check—it happens. Call the bank where the check is drawn and ask if there are now sufficient funds to cover the check.

If there are, redeposit the check immediately, or go directly to the bank that day and cash the check.

Deposit clients' checks immediately upon receipt. Some companies wait several days before depositing a quantity of checks; every day that goes by increases the risk that the check will be returned to you stamped NSF.

Before deposit, examine the check itself. Also, look at the endorsement. Be wary of any writing—other than the endorsement—on the reverse side of the check. The words "paid in full" might be construed as "consider any acceptance as payment in full on the account should you decide to deposit it." While some companies simply cross out the markings and deposit the check, it is best to send such checks back to the customer when the amount is not payment in full.

A pre-printed address on the check indicates that the payee has had the account for at least a few weeks and is more likely to be a responsible person. A phone number on the check gives you a possible way to contact the payee in the event the check is bad. Asking for the driver's license number is important because the Department of Motor Vehicles is one source for obtaining the payee's address, since people are supposed to keep their address current when they move or renew their license.

If it's a relatively large check from a person you don't know or if you have any reason for concern, you may also want to call the person's bank before you turn over the merchandise or perform a service just to be sure there is enough money in the account.

What Can Go Wrong and How to Protect Yourself

Many things can make it difficult to collect your money:

(1) **A payee stops payment on a check.** This is perfectly legal, if the payee has a good reason to do so. If you have any reason to suspect that payment may be stopped—for example, a customer has complained about high prices or has talked about making returns—have some kind of agreement form to use as back-up (such as one stating that all claims for adjustment must be made in writing within 15 days), so you can later support your claims for payment if necessary.

(2) **The payee moves.** Approximately 20% of the U.S. population changes address each year. Still, some people will continue using old checks which show the previous address. Confirm that the address on the check is still current by cross-checking it against the address on the person's driver's license or other ID, making sure that the identification itself is current. You should also make every effort to verify the phone number shown on the check.

When you take a little extra time to verify a check, you are less likely to be stuck with a bad check and no way to locate the payee.

(3) **A checking account may have insufficient funds to cover the check, or the account may be closed.** Again, be careful.

Extra Precautions You Can Take

When you're uncertain about whether to take a check, there are a few other things you can do besides collecting the usual information:

- If you belong to a merchant's association or check cashing service which collects the names of bad check writers, you can call to verify whether the person is listed as a "no-pay."

- If it's during banking hours, you can call the person's bank to verify the account and the balance. Simply call the bookkeeping department, say you are holding a check for a certain amount, give the name and account number, and ask if the check is good.

- If you have doubts about whether the money will be in the bank in the morning or whether the person might stop payment on the check, you can deposit the check immediately. Obviously, you can't do this with every check, and sometimes it's better not to take such a check, but at times the gain can outweigh the risk.

- If you get the check on an evening or weekend when you can't call the bank for verification, you can tell the customer that you will hold the merchandise until you have a chance to verify the check.

Waiting for Checks to Clear

An alternate strategy if you are selling mail order, or expect payment in advance for your services, is to wait a week or two for the check to clear before you turn over any merchandise or engage in any work for the person. If you use this approach, simply advise your customers or clients that if they pay by check, rather than by money order or certified funds (certified check, money order, or official bank check), you will hold their merchandise or wait on doing any work until the check clears. (Usually this is about 10 days for out-of-area or out-of-state checks, and 2 to 3 days on local checks) Code any mailing labels or work orders to reflect the date on which you deposited the check or the date on which you can freely ship or perform services.

Then, if the check comes back in the meantime, you simply cancel the order and don't ship the product or do the work. Send a note to the person about the situation—it's always possible he or she will send you another check or tell you to put through the first check again.

This approach is particularly wise for out-of-town checks, where everyday check verification is more time consuming and follow-up on bad checks more difficult.

Keeping Records of the Checks You Deposit

Another good strategy if you are accepting a check as a deposit and intend to bill for the balance is to make a photocopy of the check. You won't see the check again unless it is no good. Then, if you have any problems later in getting paid and need to locate the person's account, you have a copy of the account number, which is useful as long as the person keeps the same account. Also, any notations on the check (such as "payment on account" or "down payment, $500 balance due") will help bolster your case should it end up in court.

A good way to protect yourself is to keep a Check Deposit Record (Form 2) which includes these major items from the check.

There are two major advantages to keeping this record. First, as with the photocopy method, if this check is a deposit or first payment and the person subsequently doesn't pay your bills, you have a source of information you can use for follow-up. Also, if this person later gives you a bad check and doesn't make it good, you have an additional source of information besides what is written on the returned check, and this information may be more valid.

Secondly, you have a backup record when you deposit your checks at your bank, in the unlikely event the bank loses your deposit. Thus, you can track down each check writer and get another check.

Taking credit cards

Setting Up a Credit Card Account

To accept credit cards, you need the appropriate merchant discount agreements with each of the companies whose cards you are going to take. In the case of MasterCard or Visa, you can work out arrangements through a commercial bank, though some banks have stricter policies than others for opening new accounts.

For example, larger banks commonly require that you actually have a store or retail business before they will even consider giving you an account, and they don't want to deal with people operating businesses from their home. Your bank may make an exception if you have been with the bank for a long time (say 10 years or more). But, otherwise, these larger banks believe your volume of business won't be large enough to justify having an account. Also, they are afraid if you are in a small home-based or mail order business, you may have more problems than usual with bad cards, charge backs, or returned charges, and too little volume to warrant the hassle.

FORM 2
CHECK DEPOSIT RECORD

Date Deposited	Name on Check	Address	Phone Number	Bank Acct. #	Driver's License #	Credit Card #

As a result, you'll probably do better making arrangements through a smaller bank. Even if you don't have an account there, these banks may be receptive, because they are more eager to get your business. They may also open up an account for you provisionally, pending approval of your application.

At a bare minimum, you'll need a business name (from the county clerk's office) showing that you are legitimately a business, because the bank will want to open up a business account for you. Be aware, however, that a business account will cost more than a personal bank account. Thus, if you're just getting started taking credit cards, the small bank route is one way to go.

The Major Problems With Credit Cards

The pitfalls to watch once your application to use credit cards is approved are as follows:

- The card is invalid because it has expired, someone has reported it lost or stolen, or it has been altered or counterfeited.

- The person may return the merchandise or dispute the charge, and you'll get a chargeback on your account.

How to Protect Yourself

If you have any reason to question the card or the person's satisfaction with the transaction, do a little checking to protect yourself. Here are a few things you can do:

- **Check the name of the person on the card against other ID.** Make sure signatures match.

- **Check the "invalid card" list sent to merchant account holders.** The list is regularly updated, and if you accept a card on the list, you are responsible for the total charged. Conversely, if you discover a person has a "hot card" on the list, you are supposed to take it away, for which you will be rewarded. (But use your own judgment in confiscating cards. Typically, when you do a careful check, the customer, if guilty, will run off. However, if it looks like you will be in a battle, you may be safer returning the card and saying, "There seems to be some problem; you better to talk to your bank about this." Then call the police.)

- **Call a credit card service to check the status of a card.** The service will not only use a computer to check the card's validity against a list of invalid cards, but the company also has the latest updates a few days before you get them. Then, whenever you get any large or questionable purchases, call them in.

- **Write down additional information on the credit invoice.** This will help you track the person down later—like the customer's driver's license number, current address, and phone number.

- **Have the person sign an agreement or release form for any merchandise received.** This indicates he or she is satisfied with the purchase and agrees to your procedures for collecting disputed funds. (See the discussion about signing agreements.) Then, should you find yourself in a charge back dispute, you have more clout to back up your side, when the credit card people contact you about the dispute in trying to resolve it and determine whether they should put the transaction through or charge it back to you.

Working out billing policies

If you decide to bill anyone for anything, you need to be even more careful, since you are one step further from getting paid. A bill is only a signed or verbal agreement that the debtor will pay you; and when he or she does, you may still not have cash in hand because the customer might pay with a check or a credit card.

Also, between making the agreement and getting paid, much can go wrong. For example, a customer might claim the merchandise didn't arrive or come in good order, say the wrong items were shipped, dispute the amount of your bill, suffer some financial reverses, or decide your services didn't help after all. It's important to develop a policy to protect yourself whenever you bill customers or clients.

There is a solution to this dilemma. Three days after the product or service is delivered, call the customer. State that you are calling to see if the customer is satisfied. Get the full name of the person you speak to.

Ways to Protect Yourself

You can get prepared in some of the following ways:

- Consider getting a substantial deposit in advance. A deposit of half of the total amount would be fair. This will cover part of the bill or at least get your out-of-pocket costs for doing the job. The deposit not only gives you some financial protection, but it also shows the other person really wants the product or your service.

- Have a formal written contract. This contract should describe specifically what you are providing in terms of services, product, or both, and indicates clearly how much is being paid for what, by whom, and when.

- Do a preliminary credit check on the person. This way you get the information you need to be sure he or she can afford to pay and to find the person or his or her assets if there is a payment problem later.

This check-up can include information about where the person banks, people he or she has done business with before, who to contact in case of an emergency, etc. Then, if the debtor doesn't pay, you have some information to help you follow-up and collect later.

Keeping Your Customers and Clients While Checking Credit

If you do a credit check, you might want to call it something else to be more diplomatic. In many traditional buyer-seller situations, the buyer will expect to fill out a credit application and give references, so there is no problem calling it exactly what it is. (For instance, when a retail store buys from a manufacturer, a typical arrangement is for the retailer to supply credit information for approval before the order is shipped.)

However, in other situations, such as where a professional person is dealing with a client, the buyer-seller relationship is still there, but it is covered over by an expert/teacher/helper/therapist or client relationship, so any sales transaction is downplayed, and a formal credit application is usually avoided since it might be taken as an insult. You still need the information, but the way around this problem is to call the form you use something else, such as "New Client Data Form," "Client Background Information," or "Personal Background and Skills Questionnaire."

You might also sprinkle in a variety of questions which give a well-rounded picture of the client to dispel concerns about the more sensitive financial questions, such as hobbies or interests. Or say the information will be used for a demographic profile, which you might want to use for this purpose later.

Having Alternate Policies

You might also consider having several alternative policies, depending on how willing the customer/client is to sign a contract or supply credit information. For example, a lawyer explains her financial policy this way: She tells her clients her fee schedule and if they ask her to bill them, she gives them a credit application, called a "New Client Information Form" to fill out. If they balk at filling it out, she tells them they don't have to do so, but then she will have to ask them to pay by check, credit card, or cash at the end of each consultation. Most of the time, she reports, her clients fill out the form when she gives them the choice. By letting them choose, they the customer or client feels better about giving the information.

Another arrangement which works for many people is to break down a total job into stages, and bill for payment at the end of each stage. The advantage of this approach is that you don't get too far out on a limb in doing a project, only to find out that the client is dissatisfied with the results and doesn't want to pay. For example, a writer might divide up the work at logical break-points, such as:

(1) collecting materials, doing preliminary research, and writing an outline;

(2) doing interviews and preparing transcripts;

(3) writing the introduction; and

(4) writing individual chapters. Then, the writer would ask for a 50% deposit before each phase and bills for the balance when that particular phase is completed.

Conveying Your Terms to Your Customer or Client

When you bill, you should determine in advance when you expect to receive payments or be paid in full, and convey this expectation clearly to your customer or client. In setting your terms, check common practices in your area for your industry and for companies of your size. Then, you can be competitive by employing a similar policy. Or if you want to use your credit arrangements to give you a sales edge, be a little more liberal in offering credit. But whatever you decide, state this clearly on any contract you write and on any bills.

Common Billing Practices

By having firm arrangements, you can easily tell when there are payment delays, so you can follow up accordingly. Some common arrangements might be the following:

- A 50% deposit down and full payment when the work is done;
- Out-of-pocket expenses in advance and full payment due within 30 days of receiving the bill;
- Full payment due within 5 (10 or 30) days of receipt of the bill with a 2% discount for full payment within 5 days.

You might also want to include penalties for late payments to spur people to pay on time. If so, specify these penalties in your billing agreement and on your invoice. Example: "Late payments subject to an 18% per annum interest charge."

Usually, your best protection of these late charges is a signed agreement. Having a notice of such charges included on your invoice may not be sufficient to allow you to collect such late charges.

If you are dealing with larger companies or with the government, you may have to extend your terms to accommodate longer billing cycles of 45 to 90 days, though you may be able to negotiate shorter terms.

Whatever your arrangements, the key is to establish your billing terms in advance and get your customer or client to agree to them. Then, you have a basis for determining when the account is delinquent and can act accordingly. Otherwise, your client or customer can always come back to you claiming: "I am planning to pay." But the issue is when? Next month? Next year? You have to be clear when your bills become due—or you may end up in the loans or investment business besides your own business, too.

Promissory notes

Whenever you extend credit, you can use a promissory note in which you outline the money owed, when any payments will be made, and when the entire balance comes due. The promissory note also indicates any money paid down, the amount loaned or financed, any finance charges, and the terms of payment— how much is payable, how often, starting when, and the grand total. For an example, see Form 3.

A note commonly states, too, that if a payment is missed, the creditor may demand the whole balance, and that if the creditor accepts a late payment, the remaining balance is still due. It may further include a small late charge (perhaps $5), and may state that the debtor is responsible for paying any costs of collection and attorney's fees. Then, you and the debtor sign it.

Besides using a promissory note to firm up your initial agreement to extend credit, you can seek one later on, as will be discussed, to reaffirm a debt where there is a verbal agreement or any possibility of dispute.

Written contracts

Contracts are useful whatever your financial policies for clarifying your agreements—and it gives you documentation should you go to court. Although verbal contracts are valid, written contracts more accurately and precisely spell out what is agreed.

Advantages of a Written Contract

A contract, effectively written, does two things:

- It makes it clear what services or products you are offering or receiving in return for what payment.

- It gives you evidence you can use if you have collection problems to: remind the other party what was agreed and what is owed; and present your case in court, if necessary.

```
                         FORM 3
                     PROMISSORY NOTE

Amount of Note: $ _____    Date: _____

For value received, the undersigned promise(s) to pay to the order of
_____ the sum of

    (1) $ _____ (amount of note) as follows: paid  herewith
    (2) $ _____ (down payment) leaving a balance of
    (3) $ _____ (total financed) plus finance charge of
    (4) $ _____ (finance charge) for a total of payments of
    (5) $ _____ (total you will pay)

The annual percentage rate is _____ per cent simple interest.

TERMS OF PAYMENT: $ _____ payable on ___/___/___, and $ _____
each thereafter, beginning on ___/___/___ with a final installment of
$ _____ for a total of _____ payments.

DEFAULT in the payment of any installment shall, at the option of
_____, and without notice or demand, render the
entire balance at once due and payable. Acceptance of any late
payment shall not constitute a waiver of any subsequent payment when
due.

IF SUIT is instituted to collect on this note, the undersigned
promise(s) and agree(s) to pay the cost of such action, together with
attorney fees in such amount as may be fixed by the court.

CONSIDERATION for this promissory note is: Forbearance of legal
action in the matter of: _____ vs. _____ .

Signer:        Co-Signer:

             x_____     x_____

Print names:

             _____      _____

Address:

             _____      _____
             _____      _____

This note signed at _____, (city) _____ (state)
on this date: _____ we received a copy of
this note: _____ (initial) _____ (initial)

Sign and return this note immediately upon receipt. Make all payments
promptly. Payments are due in our office on the due dates indicated
above. Late payments are subject to a $25.00 late charge. No
statements will be sent. Your check is your receipt.

Payment is posted on the received business day, not the date mailed.

In addition to the late charge, interest will incur after late
charge.
```

The problem with verbal agreements is that people often have different understandings or different memories about what was agreed. Then, when a dispute develops, it can be difficult to prove that there was a contract or what it was.

On the other hand, a written contract is solid proof of the agreement. In fact, account receivables backed up by contracts can be sold or factored to a third party, because they represent assets you are legally owed.

Items to Include in a Contract

When you write a contract about a sale, loan, work project, or other creditor/debtor arrangement, the contract should minimally contain the following information:

- A description of the service, or loan;
- The amount of payment expected, and when due; (If there are installments, the contract can indicate the penalties if a payment is missed—such as interest on the balance or an option for the creditor to demand the entire amount.)
- The length of time the agreement will last, if ongoing transactions are involved (such as when you hire a consultant on a monthly retainer);
- Under what circumstances, if any, the contract may be terminated and by whom;
- How the customer or client might act if he or she has any complaint about the product or service; (For example, a contract might indicate that a customer has up to 30 days to return the merchandise for a full refund, or for a refund less a 10% service charge; otherwise, it is assumed the customer has received the merchandise in satisfactory condition.)
- What recourse the creditor has if the customer or client fails to pay, such as the ability to collect interest, collection costs, attorney's fees, court costs, and other expenses;

You should also clarify your contract with specifics, so both you, the debtor, and an objective third party can understand exactly what you mean. There are too many examples when one or the other party in a contract agreement misunderstood the actual meaning of the contract.

Inserting a Collection Costs Clause in Your Contracts

Because of the high cost of collecting, include a clause in any contract or loan agreement that the debtor will be responsible for the costs of collection if the debt isn't paid when due. This way, you can get back your reasonable collection expenses and interest. Without such a clause, you usually can't charge overdue interest or add on your collection expenses, other than those incurred through the courts.

An example of such a statement is as follows:

> "If the amount due in this agreement is not paid by the date indicated, and it is necessary to take steps to collect on this debt, then the client (customer, borrower) agrees to pay all reasonable collection costs, including attorney fees, which are necessary to collect the debt."

Should your prospective customer or client raise any objections to this clause, you can downplay its significance in the interests of good will. For example, you might say, "Oh, that's just a routine clause our accountant requires us to have on every agreement."

Then, if the person continues to resist signing, it may be a danger signal to you that you may have some problems down the road.

Making Sure Your Client/Customer Understands the Contract

Once you have an airtight contract, be sure your customer or client reads and signs it, so everything is completely understood and there are no recriminations later. If appropriate, read it over with your customer or client on the spot and answer any questions.

If a careful on-the-spot reading and signing won't work for you, an alternative approach might be to do one of the following:

- Invite your client/customer to take a contract form home to review, sign, and send in.

- Go over the major points in the contract, explain this is your standard policy, and ask your client or customer to sign, and read over the contract in detail within the next three days. Then he or she can call if necessary to cancel the contract.

Getting a Commitment From Your Customer or Client

If possible, get a down payment as a show of commitment, even if you have to take a postdated check for a contract that won't go into effect for several months. Requiring a deposit shows you the person is serious—and he or she realizes you are, too. For example, if you are setting up a retainer arrangement for a month or two hence, get part of it now to "hold the space" or "reserve the commitment." Or perhaps get a post-dated check and establish a notification date up to when the postdated check will be returned. This way, the obligation to cancel or change the agreement is on the customer or client, and not on you to reconfirm that you still have an agreement.

Getting collateral

When you are extending a small amount of credit, it may not make sense to ask for collateral. But as the monetary stakes increase, getting some security for your credit makes sense. Then, if the person doesn't pay up, you can take their collateral. If, however, the person declares bankruptcy, you are more protected because the secured creditors are paid off first, and if you have rights to that collateral free and clear, you will get it all.

Making Arrangements for Collateral

All sorts of things can be considered collateral: objects, rights to property, accounts receivable, cars, furniture, even merchandise in a store or consignment items placed in that store by you. Sometimes, a debtor will say there isn't anything to put up for collateral (because he or she is thinking about the traditional things people usually use, such as the car, wedding ring, or the house). But if you're creative, you can come up with all sorts of things.

To get collateral, you have to ask for it, since the debtor isn't likely to volunteer it. However, when you ask, most will go along with your offer, particularly if you present it in two ways. First, make your request sound like your regular policy, and if you are dealing with a business associate who might be miffed at the implication you don't trust him or her, blame it on your accountant as usual. (e.g., "Yeah, I know we don't really need it in your case, but our accountant has told us to do it, so that's our policy.")

Secondly, make the debtor see that it is to his or her advantage to make this arrangement. For example, point out that since you have collateral, you can extend more credit or extend it for a longer time. Also, if you're in a competitive selling situation, you can explain that this collateral enables you to give the person better terms than he or she might get from someone else: You can be more liberal, because you've got the collateral for security.

Having collateral can be a psychological tool to help you collect since, in most instances, the debtor would rather make good on his promise to pay than to give up the pledged property.

Making Sure Your Collateral Protects You

If you are going to get collateral, make sure that it's only pledged to you or that your rights in a shared item or set of items are clearly specified, so you know there's enough collateral there to satisfy your interests. Also, check up from time to time to make sure your collateral is still on hand.

This prevents problems such as when a person uses the same item or items as collateral with more than one person or when the person specifies the order in which collateral holders get to exercise their right, you find after a sale of the collateral there isn't enough left for you. Then, too, if the person isn't honest, there's a risk he or she may sell off your collateral, so when you are ready to collect it, it isn't there.

To further protect yourself, observe these points:

- Make sure the amount of collateral you receive is equal to the amount of credit you offer. You don't want to end up with collateral that's worth much less than the debt—then the debtor doesn't care.

- Make sure you have a repayment agreement, if you expect the debtor to pay you back over time. In this agreement, indicate that the payments must be made when due, or you have the right to require payment of the entire amount—or get your collateral at that time if they can't pay.

- Value the collateral properly, so it really is worth what you think. To do this, assume that you will have to sell the collateral yourself either directly or at an auction, and estimate what this sale value would be. (Remember, this sale value can vary according to a number of circumstances, including whether you're selling an individual item or whether it's part of the assets of a business being liquidated, where this sale is occurring, what time of year, and the market demand for that kind of item.)

- Find out if there are other claims against the asset (for example, another creditor has already placed a lien on a car, or there is an existing mortgage on a house), and subtract the value of these claims to determine what you have left. You can get a general idea about other claims by asking your customer or client. However, if a sizable amount is involved, it's worth doing some extra checking to be sure. You can check various public records, such as the Department of Motor Vehicles to find out about a lien on a car or the Tax Assessor's Office to find out about any liens on a house.

- Write up a clear and effective security agreement to protect your collateral, containing these elements:
    - date, name and address of the debtor, and name of the creditor;
    - a statement about what is pledged;
    - a statement that the security will include similar property the debtor acquires. (For example, if a debtor has put up some tools as security and trades them in for a better set of tools, the new tools become part of your collateral.)
    - a statement that the collateral will be kept at the debtor's address and will be adequately insured, if the creditor requests this;
    - a statement that the debtor owns the collateral free and clear and so is able to pledge it as security;
    - a statement that if the debtor defaults on any payment or otherwise breaches this agreement, the creditor can declare the whole balance due;
    - a clause indicating that the debtor will be responsible for any reasonable costs of collections and attorneys' fees in the event of a default or breach of contract;
    - the signature of the debtor and creditor.

For an even stronger security agreement, you can add a clause stating that the value of the collateral must at least remain at the value of the debt. This way, if you work out an agreement giving you some general category of property as security (such as inventory on hand or the debtor's accounts receivables) which had a certain value when you signed the agreement, the debtor can't start selling off part of this property to reduce it below the value of your security. If so, you can immediately call for your cash.

Another strategy is to include a comprehensive clause that expands your collateral to include other assets if the collateral originally pledged isn't enough to satisfy your debt. For example, don't just ask for inventory as security, but ask for other assets that the business or individual owns. Then, if there are problems later, you have more leverage to collect.

Continue to monitor the amount of collateral on hand. Don't just take your debtor's word for it. If the individual or business doesn't pay, the debtor may be having many other financial problems, too, and might start selling off inventory or assets, which represent your collateral. So check up from time to time yourself or have a sales person do it. Similarly, if your collateral includes receivables, ask for a list of these every few months to make sure you are still protected.

If you decide to extend more credit, write up another security agreement, or add a clause to your first one stating that your collateral balance is increased to cover the new debt, too. Alternatively, if you are going to be extending credit on an ongoing basis, include a clause stating that collateral worth the value of the debt will be applied to cover both present and future debts.

Obtaining co-signers

Sometimes, you may want to close a sale, but aren't sure the prospective debtor has enough financial power to handle that much credit. That's the time to suggest the individual consider getting a co-signer or guarantor.

One likely situation where you might want to do this is when someone is just starting a business, and he or she seems obviously undercapitalized. Yet with some credit the venture might make it. To reduce your risk, you might ask the new owner to get a co-signer, like a relative, business associate, or close friend. Similarly, if someone wants a loan who doesn't have much of a credit history, you might offer to make the loan if someone else will guarantee it.

Another common situation is where you feel extending credit to a small company set up as a corporation is too risky. In this case, ask the owner or key officers or stockholders to personally guarantee any credit or loan. If the company is a partnership or proprietorship, you don't need a special agreement, since the owners are automatically liable.

If you do get a guarantor or co-signer, be sure that (1) the guarantor is a good credit risk if the original signer isn't, and (2) the guarantor is locked into securing the agreement.

Since an individual is not legally liable for another person's debt (unless he or she specifically assumes the debt in writing), you should draw up a firm guarantee or co-signer agreement. Specifically, the guarantee agreement should state the following:

- The guarantor understands he or she has an absolute and unconditional responsibility to pay, and cannot make any counter-claims against the creditor.

- The guarantor agrees to cover any and all debts due from the debtor, including any interest or other charges. (If you expect an ongoing credit relationship, try to get the guarantor to agree to both debts which are due now and those which the debtor subsequently makes. Alternatively, you can limit the guarantee to a specific debt, and limit the credit you extend accordingly.)

- The guarantor agrees to remain bound by the agreement, even if the terms are changed or extended in some way, or if another guarantor or party to the loan is released from the agreement. Also, the guarantor agrees to remain bound if there should be any substitution in the collateral used to secure the loan.

- The guarantor should understand he or she is assuming primary liability, and if there are two or more guarantors, they understand they are assuming joint liability. Otherwise, if you don't state this, you have to do everything you can to collect from the original debtor first; and, whether you have done your best can be open to much interpretation.

- The guarantor should agree that there is no time limit on how long his guarantee lasts, but that it will continue as long as the debt.

- Finally, the guarantor should agree to pay all collection costs and attorney fees necessary to collect on this agreement.

Arranging for conditional sales and consignment, and using inventory as security

If you are in the business of selling a product, there are several creative ways of promoting your business and protecting yourself, too. These include making a conditional sale, selling your merchandise on consignment, or releasing your inventory to the buyer on a gradual basis until the buyer pays for all of it.

Conditional Sales

If the debtor wants to buy something you own but can't pay in full, you can protect yourself through a conditional sale. This way, you still have title to the item until the debtor pays you in full; if he or she doesn't, you take it back. The debtor only gets title after paying in full.

This approach is ideal for larger, more expensive items, like a boat or car. You transfer the registration to the debtor when you make the sale, but you keep the title until he or she pays.

When you make a conditional sale arrangement, your agreement should include these points:

- A clear indication that this is a conditional sale, in which the seller retains full title to the goods until they have been paid for in full;
- A description of the items being sold;
- The basic price, and any additional charges, such as sales tax, finance charge, and insurance;
- The amount paid down and any other credits;
- The balance for which the seller is extending credit, and any interest charged on this;
- The amount of payment expected each week or month, and when this payment starts;
- An agreement by the buyer that he or she will keep the goods safely at the address indicated on the agreement and will not permit any other liens to be put upon them;
- A statement that the full balance will be due if the debtor defaults, and that the debtor will pay any reasonable costs of collection and attorney fees. In addition, the seller can take the goods back and sell them to secure payment and can add on any expenses to the amount due.
- The name, address, and signature of the buyer and the seller.

Consignments

Another effective approach, which some manufacturers and publishers use to extend credit to retailers, is selling on consignment. In some cases, sellers use a formal consignment agreement, which states that the retailer has received the items in good condition; will display them and use his or her best efforts to sell them; will give the seller an accounting within a certain period after the sale; and will return the items on demand if unsold.

Others, however, use the informal method when only small amounts of merchandise are involved. In this arrangement, the merchant makes an inventory of the items on a letterhead or purchase order, indicates the commission or discount from the retail sales price, notes the final date for the seller to pick up the items if not sold, signs it, and gives a copy to the seller.

Then, the seller checks back sporadically to see if the merchant needs more or arranges to pick up the items if they do not move.

If you can, get the merchant to assume responsibilities for any damages, so if your merchandise is damaged while on consignment, you have an understanding of what you are entitled to collect.

In short, when you do consignment selling, you are extending credit, and you should get the same sort of protections any creditor gets. Thus, ask for an agreement; in fact, say it's your usual policy. Point out also to the merchant that it is to his or her advantage since he or she will have a continuous supply of goods. Present the credit you are offering as something of value; and the merchant will be more receptive to your request for security.

Using Inventory as Security

If you are doing business with someone who is short of cash, needs the products or services you offer, and seems honest and likely to succeed, you can use inventory or work you do as a security. Under this arrangement, the person gives you an order for what he or she needs—but you only deliver a small part of it at intervals. Then, the person pays you on each delivery, or as you complete another phase of the work.

It's a calculated risk that the debtor will stay in business; but if it works, you'll probably not only get paid, but will also end up with a long-term mutually beneficial business relationship.

Make several copies of the note

Have your note signed and copied immediately. Place the original in a safe place, such as a company safe or a bank safety deposit box, or give to your accountant or attorney for safekeeping. Give one copy to the customer. Keep another copy in your office for quick reference.

Chapter 3

Dealing With Credit As You Expand Your Business

If you are just starting out in a business, you won't need to make the extensive credit checks discussed in this chapter. But as you get larger you will, when you extend large amounts of credit to many customers or to a few large accounts.

In fact, in some businesses, you may have to give extensive credit to the people you deal with to stay in business; it's part of the accepted way of doing things. For example, large manufacturers frequently work with suppliers this way, as do retail stores buying from manufacturers and wholesalers. In turn, retail stores need this credit, because they don't get paid until they sell the merchandise. There's a whole credit chain and any bad decisions made along the way can echo along the chain. You can see how this process works on the chart on the following page. Payments flow in from one direction; credit in the other.

For instance, if the products don't sell, the stores can end up short of cash and delay paying the wholesalers or manufacturers. If they have the product on consignment, they can simply send the merchandise back. Then, if the wholesalers or manufacturers don't get their money on time, they can hold up paying their suppliers, who in turn, may have subcontractors or employees they can't pay right away.

So, whenever you are in the chain and if the business ahead of you has problems, you may, too, particularly, when you extend a lot of credit. Thus, as you become a big time creditor, you have to not only evaluate the debtor's present situation, but his or her future prospects.

30 Collection Techniques For Small Business

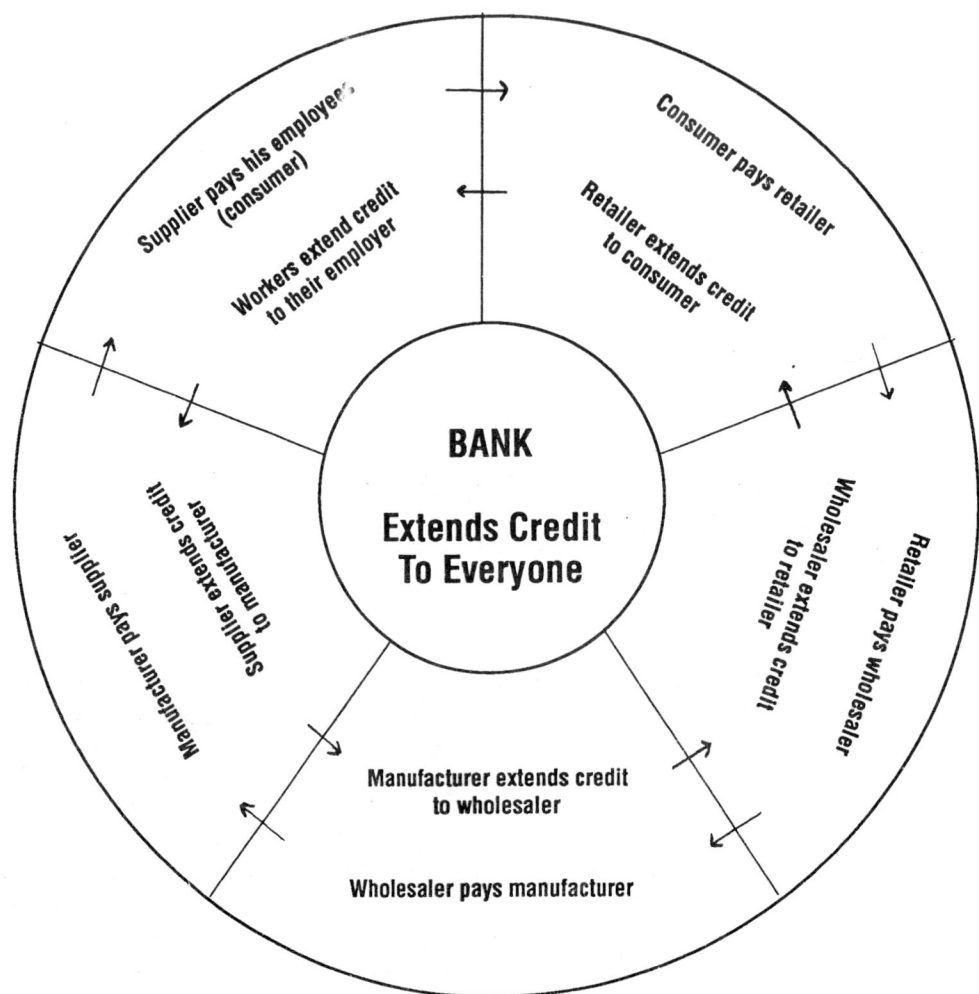

Creating Your Own Credit Rating

If you are in a business with a large number of clients or customers, you can speed up your credit checking. Use a credit rating system based on what your customer or client tells you to determine whether to offer credit. The idea is to make sure the individual has a minimal level of credit worthiness by scoring various bits of information and combining these for a single score. This information is based on characteristics which are predictive of a customer's ability and willingness to pay.

Many creditors, including credit card companies, retailers, oil companies, banks, and loan companies, use such a system.[1] Whoever is doing the checking merely feeds the ratings for various characteristics into a computer and the computer does the rest. A clerical worker can easily do the job and a trained credit person is not needed to review the application. Also, using this system avoids any biases a credit manager might bring to the job.

Because of the discrimination provisions of the Equal Credit Opportunity Act, the companies using this rating approach don't use data on marital status and sex, though they generally update their systems periodically to reflect other current demographic patterns related to credit. You can further adjust the system to reflect good credit risks in your industry and to reflect changing economic conditions and geographic factors.

A sample chart showing how this system works for one creditor is shown on the following page.

The highest points are awarded for signs of stability, high occupational status, and limited financial obligations to other lenders. According to Cathy Clark, who discusses this system in *Credit!*[2], a person would need about 15 to 18 points based on this list to get a loan. If you feel other categories are important, add them; or adapt the numbering system and scoring to suit your own needs in extending credit.

Banks use a credit scoring system, and they still occasionally make bad loans. Further, even with a credit scoring system, a subjective evaluation is needed. Use your instincts. Get the facts. Then make your credit decision based on a combination of the two.

Doing an Extensive Credit Check for Large Accounts

When extending credit to large accounts, you need to do some checking in depth. For an excellent discussion about how to set up an extensive credit checking program, see *Getting Paid* by Arnold S. Goldstein. He suggests using information from seven credit sources, rating them in terms of priority, and cross-checking the information from each source, to get a complete and accurate credit picture for making a good decision.[3]

The reason for not relying on only one credit source is that one source might give an excellent rating, while others are picking up the problems. Also, it is important to keep monitoring the situation with an information update, since the financial condition of each company is constantly changing—sometimes gradually, sometimes rapidly. As a result, if you extend credit based on old information, you may be in for a rude shock, when you suddenly discover a company formerly in excellent shape is having financial problems. So, you may not get an expected check.

> **SAMPLE CREDIT RATING SCORING SYSTEM**
>
> | Subject | Points |
> |---|---|
> | Telephone at home | 2 |
> | Time on job | 4 |
> | Years at residence | 2 |
> | Checking/Savings | 1 |
> | Total | 9 |
>
> Note: Financial institutions also use the "5 C's"— Character, Capacity, Capital, Conditions and Collateral to make a credit determination.
>
> Source: *It's A New Day For Consumers*, by John J. Harrison

Goldstein suggests using these seven sources of information:

(1) Reports from credit reporting agencies, like TRW, Trans Union, CBI (Equifax) or Dun and Bradstreet;

(2) Information from the customer, including financial statements, and history on the company and its market;

(3) Bank references;

(4) Evaluations from credit associations and interchange clubs made up of others in your industry;

(5) Reports from your sales people in the field about the company and industry trends;

(6) References from other creditors, including your competitors; and

(7) Other sources, including public records, court records, customers of your customer, and your own attorney or accountant.

Using this program, you can work up an appropriate credit mix, depending upon the size of the order and the credit risks you are taking. This way you avoid the risks many companies take when they automatically ship or do the work if the order is small enough (say under $300 or $500) and outwardly, the company looks solid. Unfortunately, one problem with automatic shipping is that companies which have problems and don't want you to check too much usually start with small orders, because they figure, usually correctly, that you won't take the time for a regular credit check. Some may even give you two small orders a few weeks apart, instead of one large order you might check.

But, according to Goldstein, you should check even the smallest order you ship on credit—at least by calling Dun and Bradstreet or TRW. Then, at the next level of checking, add in bank references, and as the credit risk increases, include other information sources. Afterwards, monitor the results of your credit checking by category, and if you have a higher than average loss rate in a particular category—say 9% or more, then tighten up and do more checking.[4]

The rationale behind doing all this checking is that it's cheaper to spend a few extra dollars investigating before you ship or do the work, than trying to collect afterwards. It may be too late.

Checking the Seven Sources

Checking credit ratings

At the minimum, use a credit rating service, and preferably two. Most companies checking credit use Dun and Bradstreet (D & B), which not only provides ratings, but also has reference books with background information on each rated firm. This includes data on the company's organizational structure, age, history, sales, profitability, principals, and some financials.

According to Goldstein, D & B ratings are fine for large firms, with sales of several million dollars or more, because D & B does its own research on these. But, it falls down on rating the smaller firms, since it relies on what the owner of the business says or what D & B can obtain quickly from a few other sources.[5]

Thus, to rate a smaller company, use another source, like TRW Credit, which receives information from companies all over the country, and which describes the payment histories of their customers. The TRW system isn't fully comprehensive, since TRW only gets the information its own suppliers provide, and you may want a rating for a company that doesn't do much business with TRW firms, or pays off the TRW subscribers promptly, but pays everyone else slowly. According to Goldstein, if you combine TRW with D & B, you are usually covered.[6] Or if you are rating individual customers, you can use a service like CBI.

Besides these national sources, you can also get credit ratings through rating agencies associated with particular industries. For instance, there are special agencies in the furniture business and jewelry business. Check your own industry for such agencies.

Getting financial statements and other information from your customer

Once it appears that your customer wants to place a large order, or that a continuing relationship with an account could become a large customer, you should get more detailed information. Depending on circumstances, use a credit application, personal meeting, or phone interview, but however you do it, you will be more apt to get complete and accurate information if you do the following:

- Keep the credit information you request as short as possible.
- Make the request seem routine by using a preprinted or form letter.
- Give the customer a reason why he or she should give you this information. (For example, it will help him or her get maximum credit, or you will hold the order until you have received and accepted any credit information).
- Be sure the customer knows you'll keep all information in confidence.

You should also ask the following questions, according to Goldstein:[7]

- How long has the company been in business (which would be a sign of stability)?
- Have the principal officers been in other firms that have had problems?
- Have the owners or stockholders (if the company is small) been in other firms that have had problems?
- Which state was the company incorporated in (this you need, if it ever comes to a suit)?
- What bank does it use (so you can check credit references)?
- Who are its present suppliers (or its reason for changing suppliers or adding a new one—a warning sign if it's switching because of credit problems)?
- How much does the company expect to buy from you each year (so you can estimate your profit potential compared to your risk of making the sale)?
- What are the company's plan for growth (another indicator of your potential profit and possible risk)?
- Have other retail firms similar to the company located at the same place (signaling a poor location and possible future problems for the company)?
- What are the other trade and business names used by the company, including its affiliates, divisions, and parent firms (so you can put them all through your credit tests)?

When large distances are involved, some companies use the mail or phone to get such information. However, if you do have the opportunity, try to meet so you can establish a personal relationship, thus increasing your chances for future collection. In a personal meeting, you are in a better position to go over expectations and terms, as well as obtain the credit information you need in a more casual, friendly way. Additionally, you can use this personal meeting to not only check credit, but to sell more, if the credit risk warrants this. By contrast, when you only use the mails or phone, your contact can seem cold and impersonal.

There are also some advantages to visiting the customer in his own place of business, where he or she can show you around and feel more comfortable opening up, a strategy Goldstein recommends.[8] Or if you can't visit yourself, have a salesperson visit. Although you want to be sure the company's credit checks out (which is the bottom line), you also want to build good will and promote a mutually beneficial long-term relationship.

Another advantage to visiting the business is that you can gain some insight into the company. For example, if it is a retail store, are the shelves full? How do the employees act? How do they treat you? Is this a business where you would feel comfortable as a customer?

Using banks

Banks are another source of credit information. Since bankers are fairly conservative and cautious, you won't get much directly from your customer's bank. But if you have a good relationship with your own banker, you can occasionally ask him or her to obtain some information for you. You don't want to ask too frequently, since your banker is doing you a favor in getting the information. But if the account is a large one, or if you are having trouble deciding, your banker, when called on occasionally, can help you decide.

Goldstein suggests asking about the following kinds of information:[9]

- The average cash balance in the account;
- The company's history of returned or bounced checks;
- The number and status of outstanding loans with the bank;
- The liens or encumbrances, if any, against the customer's assets;
- The problems, if any, experienced by the firm;

The bank may also have information that gives an indication of the general condition and stability of the firm, and its prospects for growth.

Exchanging information

Another way to get credit data, when you get serious about checking on someone, is through the credit interchange associations serving your industry.

There's an umbrella association of credit managers called the National Association of Credit Management, which collects data nationally. The organization is made up of local bureaus which obtain credit information from their members on their customers and then send it to the national association. In turn, the association compiles and makes this information available to all its bureaus.

There are also numerous local interchange groups, made up of suppliers in a particular industry. These groups have meetings a few times a month, where members get together to talk about experiences with selected customers.

Usually, the customers to be discussed are announced in advance, so members can bring in any information they have on that account. Then, at the meeting, each supplier reports in turn on that customer. To find out about the clubs in your area, contact the National Association of Credit Managers at the following address:

National Association of Credit Managers
520 Eighth Ave.
New York, NY 10018

Another source of information is the Better Business Bureau. Although the Better Business Bureau will not give out credit information, it will provide a list of comments or complaints against the prospective client. If a company has a history of complaints against it, you may not want to do business with it.

Generally, the best time to use these services is when you check out a first order or an unusually large order. Also, if a customer asks you to increase his or her credit or suddenly starts having problems paying you, that's another good time to check.

Getting information from your salespeople

When you have salespeople working with specific customers, they are in an excellent position to collect credit information for you. And this includes both in-house people (such as a salesperson selling a computer) and people out in the field (such as a person calling on prospective customers for a pepper box company).

Salespeople are in such a good position, because they are developing rapport with the customer in order to make a sale. Then, once that rapport is established, it's easy to use it to get the customer to talk about credit, particularly if the customer realizes that this is necessary to get the product he or she wants. Also, when salespeople do the credit checking, this makes giving the information seem more casual and easier to give.

Salespeople can help, too, by doing some behind-the-scenes checking for you. They can learn the names of other suppliers from the customer's inventory—and later you can use these for references. Also, the salesperson can see what the customer's business looks like physically and report back if he or she notices any problems. Or if things are getting better, the salesperson can note this, too. This kind of information won't normally be available through regular credit services and agencies, but your salespeople can find it out.

To help them discover what you want, you can give them a New Account Form to fill out listing the basic credit information you need. For example, Goldstein recommends that his clients get the following data:[10]

- Name of company, address, and phone number
- Principal's name

- Years at location
- Size of location
- Affiliated or parent companies
- Estimated sales volume
- Physical appearance of company
- Description of area
- Amount of inventory
- Current suppliers
- Prior suppliers
- Reason for change
- Have previous suppliers been paid
- Estimated purchases
- Credit line and terms requested
- Bank references
- Recommendation for credit

Getting credit references

Credit references from your customer are probably your least valuable source for checking credit, since any company can supply at least a few good references, and won't volunteer the bad ones. You'll get a somewhat more objective appraisal if you ask for a half-dozen or so references rather than the traditional three, and check the last few references listed, since the company is probably not as close to these. You might also ask specifically for the name of the company's landlord and insurance agency; they usually have a close look at what is going on.

It's also ideal if you locate a few references on your own. Often, you can get these through your salespeople. Another approach some big time creditors use is to call suppliers the customer is likely to deal with in the area. It may take a little more time to do this extra checking, but you'll end up with less biased, more accurate references. And, if you've got a substantial amount of money at stake in the transaction, it's worth it. In turn, you can offer to cooperate if the people you call want references—for if they have something to gain from you, they are more likely to give you accurate and comprehensive information.

When you call these references, ask the following questions:

- How long have you been working with the company?
- How much credit do you extend and on what terms?
- What does the company owe you now?

- Has the company ever been overdue and for how long?
- What kind of credit record has the company established generally?

Another approach, suggested by Goldstein, is checking the customer's invoices with some suppliers. You let the customer think he or she is likely to get a better deal from you. But then, you look at the payment record, to see how well the customer pays the bills.[11]

Checking other sources

You can't spend all your time checking, of course. However, if the size of the order warrants it and you aren't sure, there are a few more sources you can use: public records, court records, and your prospective customer's relationship with major customers.

Public Records. The public records to check are in the recording office for the state, city, or county where the customer is located. You can check if the customer has any tax liens or attachments recorded against him or has any mortgages requiring payments.

Court Records. You can also check the court records in most of the larger courts, since they have been computerizing their records. Simply look up your prospective customer's name (either the company or its chief officers) in the list of defendants for small claims and civil actions. If you find one or two actions, don't worry, since these are probably about disputed bills. But if you find a string of lawsuits over collections, that's the time to be concerned—because the next lawsuit filed may be by you.

Customers of the Business. Finally, the customers of your customer can be a good source of information about whether the company you are considering doing business with has a good relationship with its own customers. If there are any reports of late deliveries or out-of-stock problems, you may want to do some more checking because if your customer loses customers and hence money, that can create payment problems for you.

Making Your Decision

After you have made all the checks you want, you can analyze the results by combining all the information together in a single file. A good systematic way is to summarize the information on a Customer Credit Information Record, and keep the other reports and materials there for back-up. Then, review the record to decide whether to give credit and how much credit to risk.

For details on the decision-making process, I again recommend Goldstein's book. But, in brief, the main factors to consider are the following:

(1) **What is the customer's past paying record like, and what are the reasons?** The customer may have had some occasional problems, but if there was a good reason for them, he or she is probably still a good risk. Some danger signals to watch for are the following:

- Does the customer pay certain suppliers on time, but not others? That may mean the customer might have a cash flow problem, so he or she pays the more important suppliers first. If you will be a primary supplier, you may not need to worry, but otherwise, there could be risky waters ahead. On the other hand, if the company is doing financially better now, this may mean everyone will get paid.

- Is the customer chronically late with everyone? That can mean serious cash flow problems or the customer is simply negligent. In this case, you should never offer much credit or require all orders C.O.D.

- Are there occasional delinquencies with a few suppliers? That could be done to a dispute. If so, you probably don't have to be concerned. But before you breathe free, check out the situation to be sure, determining the nature of the dispute. After all, you want to be certain that kind of problem is not likely to happen between you and your customer.

(2) **Is the company a seasonal business?** This may become a factor if the company is likely to experience seasonal or cyclical problems in making payment. For example, selling sailboats or arranging vacation cruises are seasonal businesses in this category. Another related question is whether the company has recently suffered an unusual problem (such as a labor strike or fire). In either situation, you need to make your evaluation on a case by case basis. In the cyclical situation, decide if you are willing to wait until the season when most accounts get paid; and, in the case of an unusual problem, decide if the company is likely to pull out. (Then, if it does, and you've shown your support, usually you'll find that your faith will be well compensated.)

(3) **Is the company likely to continue to pay in the future?** According to Goldstein, too many credit decisions are made based on a company's past track record. But because circumstances change so much, it's important to assess the future, too. Thus, he recommends looking at each company much like an investor would, taking the following factors into account:[12]

- What is the background of the company and its owners? If there is a pattern of prior Chapter 11 or bankruptcy proceedings, several lawsuits, or one large pending lawsuit, this suggests there could be problems up ahead.

- How is the management ability of the company officers? If the management team is new or inexperienced, that's another sign for caution; and a further personal credit report on the principals signing the checks may be in order.

- What is the market position of the company? If the business is growing and its growth is properly funded, that's fine. But when growth is too rapid and out of control, that can be a danger sign.

On the other hand, if the business is stagnant or declining, that also suggests danger ahead.

The strength of the industry as a whole and whether the company has a good customer base affects the company's market position, too. If the company is too dependent on a few key customers or has a lot of business with the government, you could easily have a problem if the customer's customer goes out of business, cancels the contract, or takes a long time to pay, because then your customer has trouble paying you.

Then, too, take the competition into consideration and watch for signs that the company's business is being threatened by a competitor (which means less business for you) and again possible payment problems. Information on the company's physical plant and the surrounding area will give you feedback on the market position, too.

- What is the company's financial strength, based on its solvency, profitability, and liquidity? The first factor to look at is solvency, since a firm has to be solvent to pay its bills. There are three key elements to look at to determine solvency:

What is the company's average aging of its payables? In other words, how long does it generally take to pay its current suppliers and how does this compare with the industry standard? For example, if the industry averages is 30 days, and it takes a company about 60 to 90 days to pay, that's a possible sign of danger ahead.

What is the company's current ratio? This indicates how adequate its current capital is to meet current obligations. You find this out by dividing the company's total assets by its total current liabilities.

What is the company's ratio of total debt to net worth? In other words, how do the debts of the company stack up against the owner's equity in the company?

To test profitability, there are two measures to look at:

What is the company's net profit on sales? (Divide net profit by net sales to learn this.)

What is the company's return on investment if it is a large company? (To find out, divide the net profit by the company's net worth.)

Finally, to examine liquidity, look at the company's immediate situation and long term prospects. The factors to look at here are the following:

Does the business have enough working capital to keep going successfully? (To get the working capital ratio, divide cash on hand by total sales.)

Is the business likely to have a long-term cash flow? (You'll have to look at the business more closely to get the answer to this one, but if you're going to be a long-term creditor, you need to know, since the vast majority of business failures are due to businesses that seem to be solvent and profitable. But then, a long-term loan comes due, and they just can't make it.)

Why Do All This Checking?

In summary, as your own business expands, you may have to extend more and more credit, and as you do, you have to look more seriously at when and how much to extend, and to whom. In extending large amounts of credit, you are, in effect, becoming an investor in the success of your customer. You may not have stocks; you may not get dividends. But you are an investor all the same, and you get your profits by increasing your sales, and most importantly, getting paid.

To make sure you do, you have to check—and continue checking—to be certain the credit risks you are taking are worthwhile, for the business world out there is continually changing. If you want to get paid, you have to stay on top of things. It's like being in a continual competition—you are competing to get your money, and not just make sales, along with everyone else.

Footnotes

[1] Cathy Clark, *Credit!*, Fountain Valley, California: Eden Press, 1982

[2] *Ibid.*

[3] Arnold S. Goldstein, *Getting Paid*, New York: John Wiley & Sons, 1984, p. 20.

[4] *Ibid.*

[5] *Ibid*, p. 27.

[6] *Ibid*, p. 28.

[7] *Ibid*, p. 23.

[8] *Ibid*, p. 22.

[9] *Ibid*, p. 26.

[10] *Ibid*, p. 32.

[11] *Ibid*, p. 36.

[12] *Ibid*, p. 45-60.

Part II

How To Get Your Money And Keep Good Will

Chapter 4

Strategies For Collecting

Getting Set to Collect

In order to collect any debt effectively—whether small or large, there are several key principles:

(1) Follow-up within five (5) days after the payment is due. Whenever possible, check the day's mail for payment before calling your client.

(2) Be consistent in your collection work. This will prevent you from hearing, "you didn't call me last month when I was late."

(3) Start with the assumption the debtor is an honorable, responsible person who only needs to be reminded about the debt to pay. Therefore, treat the debtor in a friendly, respectful way at first.

(4) Be careful to follow the legal and ethical guidelines for debt collecting.

(5) Always ask for payment in full (or payments when due). But be flexible enough to accept alternate arrangements.

(6) See yourself as someone who seeks to work with the debtor to help him or her to pay the debt. Work on motivating the debtor to pay through appeals to basic human needs such as pride, honor and integrity

(7) Work out your own system for following up to collect debts in a timely fashion.

(8) Unless things appear hopeless, try to maintain your customer's or client's good will while you work on getting your money. This way you can continue to work together when the collection process is over.

The four stages

When you set up a collection system, the time line for various types of collection activities can vary depending on the size of the debt and other factors. Once a debt becomes overdue, the collection process goes through these four phases, which can end anytime (once the debt is paid or turned over to a collection agency).

The four basic stages are as follows:

(1) The notification or polite reminder stage (sometimes referred to as the "nudge");

(2) The discussion stage;

(3) The push or firm demand stage;

(4) The "squeeze" or "bitter end" stage, where there are several alternatives: a collection agency; an attorney (if the account is large enough); or a small claims or municipal court

This stage may involve a single alternative, or perhaps a combination of them, depending on the difficulty of collection and the size of the debt.

Determining a time line

A good way to set up a system is to use these stages as a guideline and establish a time line indicating when you will move from stage to stage. You can use the same time line for all of your debts or vary it for different types of debts (i.e., from individual customers; from suppliers; and from associates) or for debts of different sizes (say under $100; from $100 to $1,500; from $1,500 to $5,000; and over $5,000).

One reason for establishing different procedures based on the debt's size is that you will handle them differently if there are serious problems. For example, for accounts under $100, you might turn over to a collection agency; those from $100 to $1,500, you might take to a small claims court; those from $1,500 to $5,000, you might file in municipal court yourself (you won't need an attorney if the case is clear-cut or with a firm contract or promissory note); and those over $5,000, you might take to an attorney.

Plan to start your time line running within five (5) days to a maximum of 30 days after the payment is due. Usually, the sooner you start, the better. Some individuals and companies prefer a longer grace period. However, getting started early is a more powerful reminder that you are serious and the debtor has less time to file and forget.

The Maturity Date. The date that an account is due, sometimes called the "maturity date," can be established in a number of ways—verbally or by a promissory note, contract, or bill or sale. (For example, the promissory note or contract may specify that payment is due by March 15, 1996; or a bill of sale may state that payment is due within 5, 10, 15, or 30 days after delivery. If you can, go for a shorter payment date after delivery.)

Many creditors wait 30 days to send out their first notification that the account is due. If you wait, you simply give the debtor a longer period in which to stall. Thus, it's better to get started right away. Five days to a week is normally enough. If the debtor has put a check in the mail, you should have received it by then.

Putting the four-stage process to work

The Notification/Reminder Stage

Your assumption at this stage should be that the debtor has made a mistake and has forgotten about the bill. Typically, you can plan on sending out a brief notification letter, reminder note, or perhaps make a short phone call to remind the debtor.

The Discussion Stage

After the Notification/Reminder Stage, the second stage begins. The creditor has to do more than merely remind the debtor. Now the creditor has to motivate the debtor to pay, and discover if there is any problem why he or she hasn't paid. Your assumption now should be that the debtor knows about the debt, but can't or won't pay.

You should focus in this phase on assisting and working things out with the debtor. Since brief reminders haven't worked, you now need to make one or more appeals using individually written letters, telephone calls, or in some cases personal visits. Although seeing the debtor in person is usually the most effective way to deal with the problem, it may not be economically feasible. So more typically, creditors rely on phone calls and letters. Also, if there is an ongoing business relationship, this is usually the time when creditors cut off additional credit. Depending on the situation, this stage can range from about 15 to 45 days.

The Push or Firm Demand Stage

Once it appears that discussion hasn't worked, it's time for the third stage (commonly about 45 to 90 days after starting the collection process). Your assumption is still that the debtor can't or won't pay. If you haven't collected the money now, turn the account over to someone else at the company. Tell your customer you are turning the account over to the "credit manager" or the "credit committee." Let someone else call and try a different approach.

The Bitter End Stage

If the debtor still doesn't pay, it's time to move to the final stage. Each action has some advantages and disadvantages. A lawyer will typically send out one or two demand letters or make a call or two before filing suit. A collection agency will try to motivate the debtor through letters and persuasion. If you go to court yourself, you can speed up the process of initiating litigation.

Then, if you do win at court, you still have to collect, which is a whole other process that can take much time and effort, if the debtor still doesn't pay.

The chart on the following page will give you an overview of the process. The time frame is one commonly used by individuals and companies trying to collect from customers, clients, and other businesses. But you can shorten or lengthen the process as is best for you, setting up general guidelines for moving from one phase in the collection process to another. Then, adapt your timeline to the circumstances and nature of the debt.

Keeping Track of Overdue Accounts

Once you have established when accounts become overdue and set up a time line for follow-up, you need a system to advise you about these times so you can swing into action with letters, phone calls, or personal contact. You will still treat each debtor individually, since you have to find ways to motivate the debtor and work out any payment problems on a case-by-case basis. But your system will let you know when it's time to act, as you gradually increase the pressure from simple reminders to firmer efforts to collect.

Essentially, this system keeps a record of all past due bills on a daily basis, so you know exactly how long each account is overdue. Then, when you review the records for that account, you can readily tell what you have done so far to collect.

There are three common follow-up methods, and you can either set up a manual system or put the whole process on a computer. These systems are as follows:

The Ledger System

This is based on your daily books, which list the sales made and indicate which ones have payments due. You use succeeding columns in the ledger to indicate when you take steps to collect past due funds. It's an excellent, simple system if you are a small businessperson, retailer, or professional, and only have a small number of accounts, since you can keep all of the records in one place. Then, you review the records from time to time to find out which accounts are overdue and take the appropriate action.

If you decide to use this system, you have to check through the books regularly (at least once a week) to keep current with your accounts.

The Card Tickler System

This is good when you have a large number of accounts, whether clients, suppliers, or customers. The system involves using a special file in which you make a card for each overdue account, listing information about the bill—amount, terms, when due, and what you've done to collect so far. You divide up the file into a number of compartments—31 if you plan to review the cards for delinquencies each day, 10 or 15 if you expect to do your review every two or three days.

Also, date each compartment to indicate when to take action on the cards in that section. When you do your review, check each card against the ledger. If it's still unpaid, take some action, note this on the card, and move the card ahead in the file to your next review period—commonly 15 days later. Or if the bill is paid, as noted in the ledger, remove the card and destroy it or put it in a back file—just in case the debtor gets into debt again.

The advantage of this system is it systematically calls the delinquent files to your attention, so you can handle them in a regular fashion. The one disadvantage when you use a ledger book is you end up with two sets of records on overdue accounts and have to check back and forth between the cards and the ledger.

However, one way around this might be to use cards in place of a ledger to record all payments. Then, you file the cards for paid-up accounts in chronological order, just like you might record payments in a ledger, while unpaid account cards go into the tickler system. Should a customer, client, or supplier run up additional bills, you use another card to record these and clip together all cards for a single individual or company in both files.

The Duplicate Invoice System

This system is most appropriate when you send out bills to your customers or clients in addition to recording payments and when you have a large number of accounts that become overdue. Whenever you send out a bill, keep an extra copy in the duplicate files, which you can arrange like a card tickler system. Then, when the bill is paid, you pull the duplicate invoice from the file, and destroy it.

The system makes sense when many of your bills are overdue, since it's efficient to make duplicate invoices. If not, you are creating double work.

However, if you have so many overdue accounts that you need a double system, maybe you should ask yourself what the problem is that so many people don't pay right away and perhaps tighten things up.

COLLECTIONS SYSTEM TIME LINE

Name of Stage	Length of Time for Stage	Time Elapsed Since Money First Due at Start of Process
Balance of Payment Becomes Due	--	0
Notification/Reminder Stage	30 days	5-30 days
First notification		5-30 days
Discussion Stage	15-45 days	35-60 days
Push or Firm Demand Stage	10 days	50-105 days
The Bitter End Stage	30-180 days	60-115 days
Going to a collection agency before you get the case back or the agency files suit	30 days-6 mo.	2-4 months
Hiring an attorney before filing suit	30-60 days	2-4 months
Filing for a Small Claims Court appearance and having a hearing	30-60 days	2-4 months
Filing a Municipal Court Action and getting a default judgment if the debtor doesn't answer (a contested case can take much longer)	30-60 days	2-4 months

Using a manual or computer system

You can use these systems manually, or you can put your collections program on the computer so the computer does everything. It can record your sales or receipts, type out bills, keep track of overdue accounts, print out collection letters, let you know when to make a collection call, or keep notes of everything that happened. Whether you use your computer as a ledger, card-tickler/ledger system, or duplicate invoice system, your computer can streamline everything you do. It's particularly efficient when you have numerous accounts.

You can find software out there to help you do most everything. For example, the software can keep your ledger, follow-up on your receivables, and print up automatic billing statements for past due accounts. Check with your local computer software dealer for recommendations on an accounts receivables system.

The Do's and Don'ts of Debt Collecting

Before you actively launch into a debt collecting campaign, be aware of what you can and cannot do. When you are trying to collect your own debts, you have more freedom in what you can do, since many restrictions on debt collection apply to the actions of third parties (like business credit departments or collection agencies, which are heavily regulated by both federal and state laws). But even so, there are many restrictions designed to protect the debtor from undue harassment and public embarrassment.

In the beginning stages of the collection process, you aren't likely to run afoul of regulations. You should know what they are, for one stage can rapidly move into another, particularly if you call or personally meet with the debtor. For example, you might start off the meeting with a simple reminder, and then things quickly escalate to an appeal, a discussion, a dispute, and perhaps a threat to go to court.

Collecting some debts can be so frustrating that creditors may be tempted to use some of the old and illegal standbys of the collection field—for example, calling the debtor at all hours of the night, telling the debtor's friends he or she is a "deadbeat," making threatening calls to the debtor's boss, or even warning the debtor "to pay up . . . or else."

Remember, all those tactics are illegal and can get you sued. In the long run, the approach of motivating and assisting the debtor to pay works better, because for the most part, debtors want to pay if they can, once they acknowledge and accept the debt. Your role is to motivate them in a legal, dignified way.

So what can't you do to collect a debt? In general, you have to avoid any of the following:

No Falsehoods, Misrepresentation, or Deceptive Practices

This is provided by two federal laws—the Federal Trade Commission Act and the Fair Debt Collection Act. Also, many state laws are very tough, permitting both damages and attorney's fees for unfair or deceptive collection activities. Under these provisions, some of the things you can't do are the following:

- Pretend you are someone other than who you are or use other deceptive means to collect a debt unless you are involved in skip tracing. However, some people do use aliases.

- Use a fake identity on a letterhead or in a phone call; as an individual, however, you have more leeway than the third party collector. (After all, your "new identity" could be a side business you have created.)

- Imply that you are an attorney or a federal or state government agent, or that you work for a credit reporting bureau or collection agency when you do not.

- Send out collection notices that look like official court summonses or documents. You can buy these notices in some stationery supply stores—but don't. If your debtor actually believes the document is real, he or she will probably turn it over to an attorney, and you're likely to face a countersuit in court.

- Suggest the debtor has committed a crime by not paying the debt.

- Threaten to turn the account over to your "legal department for collection" if you don't have a legal department;

- Threaten to do anything other than turn the case over to a collection agency, attorney, or file suit, or make this threat unless you're going to do it. If you threaten to take a specific collection action and don't do it, that's misrepresentation. And if you threaten certain actions (like notifying other creditors, telling the debtor's employer or friends, or publishing the debtor's name on a list of debtors), you might be involved in extortion, and you definitely don't want to do that.

- Charge excessive interest on the debt, because then you're committing usury.

- Inflate the debt so the debtor thinks he or she owes more than the actual debt. You can always try to get a bit extra when you take the debtor to court and want to sue for damages, interest, or emotional distress. But if you make your bill excessive and provoke a response, it could be your debtor suing you.

You also can't plead you didn't intend to deceive if you are caught by your debtor in one of these practices and he or she decides to sue.

No Harassment and Abuse

In the old days, creditors could do just about everything (and did) to make life miserable for the debtor, including threatening to hurt the debtor and his or her property or reputation. But now any sort of harassment and abuse are out. However, since there is a fine line between contacting and harassing or abusing someone, the courts often require that the debtor warn you to stop doing something before they will consider it harassment. More specifically, the kinds of activities to avoid here are the following:

- **Do not make repeated phone calls.** You can only call once a day if you reach the person you want. You can call a business back until you reach the person who writes the check, unless someone tells you that person is away or will be busy for some time. Then, you have to wait a reasonable time before calling again.

- **Do not call before 8 a.m. or after 9 p.m.** If calling a different time zone, be careful. It is the debtor's local time that counts. Also, do not call on Sundays.

- **Try to contact the debtor at his/her home telephone number.** Be careful when contacting the debtor at his/her place of employment (it is best to ask on the New Client Questionnaire if they can be called at work). If you must call the debtor at work, do not be aggressive. Ask if it is all right for him or her to speak on the phone. If they say it is not all right, promptly end the conversation.

- **Do not pretend you're someone else, so you can call again and again.**

- **Do not make obscene phone calls.**

- **Do not make threats of violence or harm to the debtor's property, person, or reputation.**

- **Do not make threats to members of the debtor's family.**

- **Do not make any physical threats.** Of course, no physical action, or you're liable for assault. Sometimes this happens and many debtors don't dare to complain. But, again, you have been warned.

- **Do not visit the consumer or businessperson and refuse to leave when asked.** Of course, you can go and visit; but if the debtor tells you to go away, do so. Otherwise, you're trespassing and harassing the debtor.

No Ruining the Debtor's Reputation

The libel and slander laws can be devastating. All the debtor has to show is that you made a defamatory statement to a third person who either heard or read your remark. Some of the libelous or slanderous activities to avoid are as follows:

You can't publish the names of debtors to show they owe you money.

You can't send the debtor a postcard mentioning an overdue debt (although you can send one for a regular payment notice), and you can't indicate anything on the envelope suggesting this is a dunning notice. You can't do this because then you are, in effect, publishing or making a public statement about the debt. In fact, even a sealed letter addressed to the debtor can open you up for a libel action, if it is likely that your communication might be opened by a third person, such as a secretary. In general, do not write to a person at his/her business.

Likewise, you can't send or pass around telegrams, pictures, photographs, cartoons, tapes, or other materials you have prepared to embarrass the debtor.

You can't talk to anybody where the debtor works about the debt.

You can't call the debtor names, like "deadbeat" or "crook." Unless the debtor has been actually charged as such and convicted, you're committing libel. Likewise, you can't imply the debtor is such things by using suggestive statements, such as, "I don't think he's honest." And you can't make unfounded conclusions you can't prove, such as: "He doesn't have very good credit."

No Invasion of Privacy

You also have to avoid, at all costs, intruding unreasonably into the debtor's private affairs when you try to collect the debt. This means the following:

- You can't use the debtor's name or furnish information about him or her without receiving permission. There are certain exceptions, since you do have the right to give credit or financial information to individuals and groups with a specific interest in obtaining this information—such as credit reporting agencies, credit interchange clubs, other creditors, prospective suppliers, and the customer's bank or other lending institutions, unless a customer has specifically asked you not to disclose this information. (However, you can still tell the credit reporting bureaus.)

- You can't look through records, reports, and letters which belong to the debtor to gain information on his financial situation unless you have permission to do so.

However, creditors have been known to surreptitiously seek to locate records about the debtor to get the information they need to effect service or find assets. But, this is a risk. And, if caught, the creditor can be sued by the debtor.

Conversely, you may want to give other creditors or credit services information in return for the information they give. In this case, you can legally do so, as long as the person is an interested party with a right to know, and you state only the facts without drawing your own conclusions. (For example, you can talk about the credit line you have offered, the unpaid balance, the usual rate at which the customer pays, and the like without any problem. Then, let the person to whom you give this information decide whether to give credit or not.)

Final thoughts

Telephone calls generally yield better results than letters. Effective telephone techniques are discussed later in this book.

Personal visits are a good way to make contact, especially if the telephone number is unpublished or unlisted. If you are owed money by a company or corporation, visiting the location during business hours should not pose a problem.

Paying a visit to the debtor's home can be risky business. Make certain you are bonded by an insurance company.

Chapter 5

Motivating The Debtor To Pay

Stage 1: Notifying and Reminding the Debtor

Once the loan or credit you have extended becomes overdue, the first stage of the collection process begins. Usually, creditors allow a few days as a "grace period." Some loans have no grace period.

The assumption at this stage is that the debtor has overlooked paying the debt. Once notified or reminded, will pay. Thus, the first notification is typically very gentle, with each reminder getting a little stronger. The emphasis is on treating the debtor as a well-intentioned, responsible person or company, and maintaining good will.

Commonly, this stage lasts about 30 days, and creditors generally use notes, letters, or notices stamped on bills to let the debtor know the account is overdue, though some may phone. Commonly, too, creditors make up to two or three contacts at this stage, before stepping up the pressure by moving on to stage two.

However, some creditors don't believe in extending the process, so after one or two contacts without getting paid, they move directly to the appeals or final demand stage and plan to take the whole matter quickly to court if they must.

There is no single correct formula. Use the approach that best fits your personal style and seems best suited to the particular situation and debtor.

The first notification

When you first discover a bill or loan is overdue, there are several notification strategies. Whichever you use, clearly indicate the amount due. If the debtor has any question or dispute about the balance owing, he or she will let you know. These notification strategies include the following:

- If you are using a monthly statement or billing system, send a duplicate copy of the unpaid statement or invoice to the customer, and stamp it "PAST DUE!" Or use this popular variation: "PAST DUE! PLEASE SEND CHECK BY RETURN MAIL." The advantage of this method in some situations is it is impersonal, so the debtor won't feel any personal slight.

- If the statement or bill is only a few days overdue, you might write a few brief words on the invoice such as "JUST DUE" or "PLEASE," "URGENT," or "FINAL NOTICE." Again, the advantage is the impersonal touch, although you can use handwriting to give your statement a more personal flavor, and you can adapt your comment to specific situations.

- For a little more personal touch, combine a stamped or handwritten notice with a brief note. This works well if you already know the debtor. For example, to a business owner you have previously met, you might say something like: "Hi, Joe. This probably fell through the cracks. Can you take care of this?"

- Send out a brief letter announcing the bill is due. Some creditors use a form letter and fill in the amount; others type out a new copy each time. An example follows below:

```
Dear Ms. Smith:
Your bill for $100 was due on June 15, and is now 5
days overdue. Can you please send your check by
return mail? Thanks for your cooperation.
Sincerely . . .
```

- Make a phone call to notify the debtor. This usually works best if you are calling a small company, where you speak personally to the owner. For example:

    Speak to the client as if you were conducting an ordinary conversation. Then, just before concluding the conversation, say "by the way, it was brought up that your last invoice wasn't paid."

Sending out reminders

After your first notification, wait about 10 to 15 days to see if you get paid. If not, it's time to send out reminders. Most creditors still use a letter or other written notice at this stage—though some phone—indicating the balance due and any account number.

There may be other reasons why an account has not been paid: someone goes on vacation; their accounts payable system works slowly; or they may be experiencing a "cash flow problem." Only by contacting the debtor can you find out why payment has not been made.

As with the notification, at this stage, the assumption is still that the debtor has forgotten about the bill, accepts the balance, and will pay it once reminded. Accordingly, your communications about the bill should still be routine, and there is no need yet to initiate a discussion about payment or make appeals to the debtor. If the debtor has any questions with the amount, it's his or her responsibility to raise that objection.

While some creditors send up to six or seven reminders, most send only one or two to speed up the collection process. Another reason for sending only a few reminders is, if these don't work, it's likely there is some problem why the person won't pay (generally a dispute or cash flow problem) and often debtors don't volunteer these explanations. They simply continue to ignore the reminders, until the creditor raises the issue.

Types of reminders

There are three written types of reminders—plus you can always make a follow-up phone call. In each, you quickly describe the situation or problem (payment is overdue), suggest that the debtor probably overlooked this, propose what the debtor should do (pay the bill), and ask for action now (send in your check). Some creditors add a brief tag line that the debtor should excuse the reminder if he or she has already sent in their payment. But that's not necessary—if the debtor has sent in a recent payment, he or she will be aware your correspondence has probably crossed in the mail.

The four reminders are as follows:

(1) **The Personal Letter.** This is probably the most effective reminder, because it shows you have singled out the account or bill for personal attention. You should keep the letter brief, to the point, and suggest that the debtor probably forgot about the bill (which is why you're sending a personal reminder to make payment.) A good strategy at this point is to emphasize the importance of the request by saying you need the payment to get your books in order at the end of the month or have to update your records. Then, if you have to get tough later, you can always blame your accountant to preserve good will as long as possible.

If you have a lot of these letters, you can cut down costs by using a computer. Feed in a basic letter, insert the debtor's name, amount, date due, and account number, if any, in the appropriate places, and the letter comes out looking like a personal letter. For example:

```
Dear Mr. Smith:
Probably you overlooked this, but your bill for
$300 from June is still overdue. We sent you a
notice about this 10 days ago.
Can you please send in your check so we can close
our books on this matter? Or if your check is
already in the mail, please excuse this notice.
Sincerely,
```

Another good technique for personal letters is to give the debtor a way to save face by suggesting you understand he or she is busy and probably didn't have time to pay. Also, you can make it more convenient for the debtor to send in the money by enclosing an envelope. For example:

```
Dear Ms. Allen:
You're usually very busy, and that's probably why
you have forgotten to pay us the $300 overdue on
your account. To make it easy for you to take care
of this, I've enclosed a self-addressed envelope.
Won't you please send in your check today, so we
can keep your account up to date.
Sincerely,
```

The Impersonal Form Letter

This is a variation of the personal letter. It says much the same thing ("this is a reminder, the account is overdue, please send in your payment"), but it is obviously a form letter, since you fill in the blanks with the correct amount.

With some debtors, using a form letter is an advantage, because they don't have to take your requests for payment personally; rather your billing seems to be coming from your accounting department.

A typical form letter might look something like this:

```
Dear _____ :
A friendly reminder to let you know your account
# _____ for $ _____ is now
overdue.
You may have overlooked our previous notice to you,
so here's a second notice for your convenience. Can
you please put your check in the mail today.
```

Or, you might use this format, recommended by T. Frank Hardesty in his seminars for in-house business collections.[1] The amount due is prominently featured before the body of the letter, and a photocopy of the invoice is included with the letter to further remind the debtor of the amount owed.

```
(Date)
(Name and Address of debtor)
          PAST DUE BALANCE: ($000.00)
Dear Mr./Mrs./Ms.:
A statement was mailed to you, showing your recent
past due balance. It may have merely been
overlooked, so ... here is another copy.
Please mail in your check today, so that we may
keep your account the way you want it to be:
current.
Thank you.
```

The Stamped Reminder or Printed Sticker

Another approach is to send the debtor the original bill with another "past due" notification stamp. But in contrast to the initial notification, this notice is a little more urgent, and the repetition serves as a follow-up reminder. For example, the stamp might announce something like the following:

PAST DUE!
PLEASE REMIT TODAY!

Or it might go into somewhat more detail, such as this stamp:

A FRIENDLY REMINDER:
YOUR ACCOUNT IS OVERDUE.
WE'VE BEEN EXPECTING YOUR CHECK
WON'T YOU PLEASE SEND IT TODAY?

You can obtain preprinted stamps in a stationery supply store or have them made with your own message.

The Reminder Phone Call

These calls can be used for two major purposes:

- As an immediate follow-up to your initial notification if the amount due is particularly large and you seek quick action;
- As an interim reminder between sending reminder letters or statements.

What to Do if You Receive Collection Calls

Up to this point, the emphasis of this book has been on techniques for collecting money owed to you. Occasionally, though, a business or individual may find itself on the receiving end of a collection call from a creditor or bill collector.

The easiest way to avoid receiving such a call is to keep in touch with the creditor. Contact the creditor any time you are unable to make a scheduled payment. Explain your circumstances and let the creditor know when you will make the payment.

Above all, be honest. While lying may buy you some extra time, it will also buy you a lot of trouble in the form of more aggressive collection action once the creditor discovers the lie. And if you lie your credibility will be lost, which could jeopardize your chances of obtaining a credit extension or future credit.

What do you do if you receive a collection call? Here are some helpful tips.

- **Make the payment as soon as possible.** If the failure to pay was due to a simple oversight, explain this to the caller. Tell him or her that you will mail the payment that same day, and do so.

    If you cannot pay the bill in full, do not just send in a partial payment without first asking the creditor. Write down the name, title and telephone number of the individual you talk to.

- **Tell the truth.** Again, honesty is essential. If you are experiencing a cash flow problem, let the caller know this. Do not feel embarrassed or ashamed.

- **Do not avoid the collection call.** They will only keep calling and may even come out to your home or business. Do not tell them your accountant is handling this, unless this is fact.

- **Remain calm.** Don't let the caller intimidate you. If the collector is overly aggressive or rude, do not lose your temper. The worst thing you can do is to allow the call to deteriorate into a shouting match. The collector will remember—and may make note of—any argument that occurs during the course of a call. Ask to speak to his or her supervisor. Tell the supervisor that you simply forgot about the payment and will mail it today ... and be sure to do so.

- **Take notes.** As with calls you make in your collection effort, it is important to document any collection calls you receive. Write down the date and time of the call; the name, title and phone number of the person who calls; and the result of the call, e.g., "Promised to make payment by the November 10."

One example: An accountant or accounts payable person calls a customer service representative. The customer service representative may agree to an extension of time; however, he or she may not relay that information to the appropriate department. Then, unless you have the name of the customer service representative who granted the extension, the collection manager may not believe you spoke to anyone. In his or her mind, he would have had to personally receive such a call or had the message passed on to him.

Asking for an extension

Many consumers and businesses order products or services on credit, with the honest intention of paying when payment is due. They are also hopeful that the economy will improve or sales will increase, allowing them to pay their bills sooner. There is an old saying, "He who lives on hope, dies fasting." We are not stating do not have hope—be optimistic. At the same time, however, have a realistic picture of what your cash flow is: Can you really expect to pay for this product or service within 30 days if nothing changes to improve your situation? If not, perhaps it would be best not to get an extension of credit. But for many, asking for an extension is an appropriate action.

Remember the tools in the prior chapters. If a creditor is calling you and you do not have the money, attempt to work out an extension arrangement. The creditor usually does not want to turn the account over to an attorney or a collection agency because of the increased cost. If they turn the account over to another agent they will lose at least a third of the dollar amount owed. Mention this to them. Do not threaten to file bankruptcy or sue for harassment unless you actually intend to do so.

Remember, you want to have the creditor work the account—not a collection agency or attorney. As discussed earlier, having an account turned over to a third party has many negative factors: the third party is generally more aggressive; your credit may be damaged; and they will take other action sooner than the original credit grantor.

Offering a settlement

If your account has been turned over to an attorney or collection agency, you can offer to pay off the majority of the claim as an offer to settle.

For example, let's say you owe $1,000. If you can pay $750 in good funds (cashier's check) in 30 days, offer that. Say something like, "I may be able to borrow $750. I would be willing to do this if you would consider this payment in full."

Third parties will often settle because of the commission and because a settlement will save both time and expensive legal fees. If the settlement is agreed to, ask for a letter indicating agreement with the terms of the settlement, and send a letter formalizing the offer. Keep copies of all documents sent and received. Again, write down the names and phone numbers of everyone to whom you speak. And be sure to make the payment by the date agreed to. In addition, request in writing that this account will not leave a bad mark on your credit rating. All the creditor has to do to remove a bad mark is to contact the credit reporting companies.

Be careful of any collateralized loans you have, especially with finance companies or other financial institutions. For example, if you have a car loan and it falls past due, the institution holding the loan can repossess the vehicle.

Disputing an account

If you dispute an account, pay that portion of the account you agree with. Then contact the company and explain the nature of your dispute. State only the facts—don't let your emotions take over. Ask the creditor to make an adjustment in your favor. If you know you are right, be persistent. If you are uncertain, ask another creditor if he or she feels that you owe this bill. As always, keep notes of all phone calls and make photocopies of all written correspondence.

If the creditor refuses to acknowledge your dispute or make an adjustment to your account based on your dispute, contact the Better Business Bureau. Inquire as to whether others have had similar problems with that creditor. The Better Business Bureau may even be able to mediate your claim—this could result in a significant savings in time and money, especially if such mediation helps you avoid going to court.

Additional Reminders

Sending Out More Intense Personal Letters

Some creditors use a series of reminder letters which are still polite and courteous, on the assumption the debtor is basically an honorable person who only needs to be prodded. But increasingly, these reminders become more firm and insistent as the emphasis shifts from gently prodding to urging the debtor to take care of the matter now and send in the money that's due.

The reminder letter also helps establish the validity of the debt, should the debtor subsequently dispute it: The letter has this power because if the debt isn't valid, the debtor should not ignore the letter, but should call the debt into question. If he or she doesn't, this helps support your case.

Some Examples of Follow-Up Personal Letters

One type of polite and courteous reminder letter tells the debtor you are sending another reminder. He or she hasn't responded to a previous reminder and may have misplaced the earlier bill. This letter may also urge the debtor to act now to avoid further reminders. For example, here are two letters in a series which are still reminders, although the second is a little more firm and insistent than the first:

```
Dear Ms. Wyatt:

This is a second reminder about the $100 you owe us
for the books we sent you in June. You can avoid us
bothering you with any more reminders by sending in
your check today.
Sincerely,
```

```
Dear Ms. Wyatt:

You have not responded to our previous statement
and notices about the $100 due for the books we
sent you in June. Since we know you are busy and
may have easily misplaced or overlooked our bill,
we're sending you this last reminder. So, please,
since this bill has been unpaid for two months,
let's get this matter settled now. Please send in
your check today.
```

Another strategy for a follow-up letter is to combine a reminder with a statement of what you, as the creditor, have done to help the debtor, and to emphasize that you believe you have done everything to carry out your part of the agreement. Also, you might mention your hope to continue to work together for mutual benefit, implying that this will end if the debtor doesn't pay. Finally, you might remind the debtor he or she can always phone if there is any problem, so you can discuss it and try to resolve it.

For example, Hardesty recommends this approach in the following two letters which form a series of increasing intensity. While the past due balance is prominently featured in these letters, in many collection letters the balance is included in the text.

```
(Date)
(Name and Address of debtor)
          PAST DUE BALANCE: ($000.00)
Dear Mr./Ms.     :
Why have you not replied to our many friendly
reminders of your past due balance?
Did we not bill you properly? We believe we did.
Did you not receive the merchandise you ordered? We
feel certain you did.
The above past due balance has reached an advanced
stage. Do mail your check today to clear that
balance ...
... Or, if there is a problem ... phone. Let us
work with you to clear your balance quickly. Today,
please. Thank you.
Sincerely,
```

```
(Date)
(Name and Address of debtor)
          PAST DUE BALANCE: ($000.00)
Dear Mr./Ms.       :
With deep concern, we again remind you of your past
due balance with us.
In providing you with quality products, we help
your success. When you do not pay ... then there
can be no success for you or for us.
It is our wish to work with you, toward profit ...
for many years. To that end, we'll keep doing our
part ... in providing quality products.
Please ... do your part ... mail your check in full
today ... please.
Sincerely,
```

Making Follow-Up Calls

While many creditors use the two-step reminder approach with personal letters, some combine a reminder letter with a follow-up phone call, or reverse the process and call first. Then, if that doesn't work, they send a letter 10 to 15 days later.

Whenever you call, you should say much the same thing you would in a letter. Keep it casual and polite, though firm, with the intensity based on when you call.

If your call is a follow-up to your first notification, then your tone should be relatively supportive and gentle, such as the first letter below. But if you've already sent out one reminder, then sound more urgent and intense.

A follow-up call after a notification letter:

> *Hello . . . This is _____*
>
> *I just wanted to be sure you got our letter notifying you that your account for $200 is overdue.*
>
> *Well, this is just another friendly reminder to ask you to send in your check, so we can close our books on this matter.*

A follow-up call after a previous reminder letter:

> *Hello . . . This is _____*
>
> *I'm surprised we didn't hear from you, since we've sent you two previous letters about your account. The current balance of $200 has been overdue for about two months, and I wanted to remind you about this matter.*
>
> *We certainly value you as a customer, and we would like to get your account up to date. So won't you send in your payment today?*

Sending Mailgrams or Telegrams

Another approach used by some creditors[2] is following up the first reminder letter with a telegram or mailgram. The advantage of this type of reminder is it conveys more urgency than a personal letter, and it's particularly good if a substantial amount of money is at stake—say over $200, since on small amounts, a telegram reminder may seem like overkill, and it may not be cost effective to send one out.

If you use a telegram, keep it short and snappy, since people expect this when they get a telegram. Also, brevity conveys urgency. For example, you might say something like the following:

```
                    SECOND REMINDER:
YOUR ACCOUNT FOR $200 IS SERIOUSLY OVERDUE, AND YOU
MAY HAVE OVERLOOKED OUR PREVIOUS NOTICE. SO PLEASE
     SEND IN YOUR CHECK TODAY, SO WE CAN KEEP
                YOUR ACCOUNT CURRENT.
```

Alternatively, you can send out a longer mailgram. This service is provided by Western Union and enables you to send a full-length collection letter for the price of an ordinary telegram. You include what you might say in an ordinary reminder letter. But the letter is transmitted by wire and comes in an envelope like a telegram, so it appears more urgent than an ordinary letter.

Moving on

In sum, the notification/reminder phase is designed to prod the debtor to pay on the assumption that he or she can and will. However, if after several reminders, you still haven't been paid, it's time to up the ante and start using psychological appeals to motivate the debtor to pay. If the reminders haven't worked, it's time to bring out the stick or the carrots.

Stage 2: The Appeals Phase

After the debtor has ignored your reminders to pay for a month or two, you have to change your assumption that the debtor has merely overlooked or forgotten the debt because you know he or she knows. Now, you have to assume there is some problem, and you must overcome it to get paid. Thus, much like a salesperson persuades a customer to act, you must appeal to the debtor, overcome any objections, and convince him or her to pay.

You'll encounter three basic problems, and dozens of variations on each theme.

(1) The debtor acknowledges the debt but claims he or she can't pay you because of not having enough money. Your task accordingly is to work with the debtor to (a) help him or her get the money, (b) realize he or she has resources to pay of which he or she may not be aware, (c) put a higher priority on paying you, or (d) work out a payment arrangement to pay over time.

(2) The debtor honestly disputes the debt and won't pay until the dispute is resolved. Now, your task is to work out a solution to the debt, and, if possible, get payment for the undisputed amount, while you work out a solution for the rest.

(3) The debtor does not want to pay, and may claim a lack of money or a dispute. Because the debtor has no intention to pay if he or she can evade the debt, your job is to get through any smoke screens the debtor puts up, show you mean business, and appeal to the debtor's self-interest or to a fear of what will happen if the debt isn't paid.

A key part of the appeals process is finding out exactly what is wrong and why so you can appropriately confront the problem and determine the best way to solve it. Thus, you must become something of a problem solver and psychologist to figure out the best way to write, call, or meet with the debtor to resolve the problem.

Some creditors use letters as much as possible in this phase since it generally takes less time and costs less to follow up in writing, particularly if the debtor lives or works far away. But frequently, you have to personally talk to the debtor to work things out. Adapt your approach to the circumstances and size of the debt. The appeals phase may last longer than any other part of the collection process.

Going to court and trying to collect at the end

Commonly, it starts after a month of reminders, and lasts about 30 to 60 days. In some cases, however, it can drag on for many months, even a year or more, if the debtor is particularly good in coming up with excuses and the creditor is especially patient.

Plan on keeping the process as short as possible. Get to the heart of the problem. Appeal to the debtor with increasing firmness. Work on finding a solution that is mutually agreeable to you and the debtor. If the debtor has no intention of paying, move quickly into the final demand stage. Lastly, take whatever action you have threatened.

By moving quickly, you'll avoid the common trap of many creditors—getting stuck in an endless appeals process. Usually, when you know how to target your appeals appropriately, and overcome any problems standing in the way of payment, you'll get your money from a debtor who is basically honest. If you don't get paid, why waste time treading water with people who won't pay. Catch a wave and get tough.

Initiating the appeals process

You can initiate the appeals process in several ways:

The Letter. Probably, this is the all-around best approach for routine business matters. The first letter is typically fairly warm, polite, and respectful, since you still hope to keep the customer or client's good will. But now, you are appealing to the debtor to pay and asking him or her to advise you if there is any problem. However, initially it's best to state your appeal in a broad general way, since until you talk to the debtor and find out why he or she hasn't paid, you aren't sure how to proceed.

The letter has several advantages. First, it is a fairly low-cost and diplomatic way to motivate the debtor and uncover any problems. Also, if the matter should end up in court, you have another document you can use to support your claims. With some debtors you know personally, the objectivity of the letter can be an advantage in keeping your relationship on a friendly footing because you can make it appear like you're not directly bugging someone to pay—it's your office or accountant who's doing it. On the other hand, some associates might be put off by the objectivity, since they would prefer to hear about any problems directly from you. So, use your own judgment in this matter.

The Phone Call. This is a common approach when a debt involves a close business associate. If you are used to communicating regularly by phone, it might make sense to continue to do so, and get directly to the heart of the problem. The call is also good with people or companies that are local and relatively easy to reach by phone.

The advantage of using the phone is you don't have to appeal in broad generalities as is common in a first appeals letter. Instead, you can ask the debtor directly for a reason for non-payment, and immediately seek to work out a solution.

The disadvantage is that a verbal discussion can sometimes create more room for misunderstanding, and verbal agreements are less compelling in court. However, if you already have a written agreement, or if you follow up your call with a letter reconfirming what you both have said, you can avoid building on misunderstandings. Also, your summary letter, if not contradicted by the debtor, will have some weight in court.

The Personal Meeting. This is ideal if the debt is a substantial amount and involves someone in the area with whom you have an ongoing business relationship. Also, if you don't already have a written agreement, this is a good time to extract a promissory note reaffirming the debt and the debtor's intention to pay. With a large amount, it's probably best to go to the debtor's business location. For example, if the business is in trouble, you'll be able to notice it by a walk through the plant or office. If you see many machines idle or desks empty; that suggests a recent layoff.

After the initial contact

After your first appeals letter, call, or meeting, follow up if the debtor doesn't follow through as agreed. Some creditors, particularly if the debt is large and not disputed, now move immediately to the final demand stage. Others may try a few more appeals.

Since circumstances vary so widely—the size of the debt, the debtor's reasons for non-payment, your assessment of the debtor's financial circumstances and intention to pay, your relationship to the debtor (business associate, customer, etc.), your desire to continue working with the debtor, and your own style (conciliatory or tough?)—use your own judgment on the best approach for you.

While some creditors use a series of letters or phone calls, you might consider varying the mix. For example, if your first letter doesn't produce results, try the phone. Or, if you have worked out an agreement on the phone and the debtor doesn't fulfill this, mention this in a follow-up letter. Similarly, use letters or calls to follow up after a meeting; or set up a meeting if your letters or calls don't work.

A common arrangement is two or, at most, three appeals; then go on to the final demand if the matter is still unresolved. Most honest debtors who value their reputation or a continued relationship with you will pay at this point. But with the others, I recommend getting tough.

Motivating the debtor

The appeals process is much like selling, except you're not selling a product or service. Rather, you're selling the debtor that it's in his or her best interest to pay the debt.

The Principles of Motivating the Debtor. The five basic principles of selling have been widely noted in books on sales techniques. These steps, modified a little to suit your purposes as a creditor, are the following:

(1) **Attracting the debtor's attention.** You want the debtor to listen to what you have to say, so start off your letter, phone call, or meeting, with something interesting or attention getting, like "You don't want to lose your excellent credit rating with our store, do you?"

Questions or strong statements are good attention-getters. You want to avoid rambling introductions like "In reviewing our records, it has come to our attention that ... ." Similarly, when you call, don't sound unsure of yourself or take too long to make an introduction. Get right to the point to get the debtor's attention.

Your initial approach is extremely important. You have about 4 to 10 seconds to make your first impression and get the person's attention. In this short time, the person decides if he or she wants to listen to what you say next and develops a mental set about how to receive this information.

When you make the right approach, the person is receptive or, in the case of a debt collection situation, at least willing to seriously consider what you say. By contrast, when your approach is wrong, the person will tune you out or think that what you are saying is not very important. Then, to continue any communication effectively, you have to struggle to reverse the first impression.

Thus, it is critical to gain the right kind of attention from the beginning in collecting, just like in sales.

(2) **Building the debtor's interest in what you say.** Face it. In collecting a bill, you are not "selling" a very popular product or service. But you still have to build the debtor's interest by stressing the benefits he or she will receive in paying your bill.

Thus, don't only restate how much is due—the debtor probably knows that very well already after getting your reminders. Instead, give reasons why the debtor will benefit. This process is much like explaining the advantages a buyer will gain from a product or service, rather than explaining how the product works and why. All good salespeople will tell you stress benefits, not product functions, and it's exactly the same when you try to collect.

For example, say the following:

> *"You'll be able to clear up this credit rating problem in just a few minutes, if we can settle your overdue bill of $200."*

Do not, however, say:

> *"We've already sent you several reminders about the $200 you owe and you still owe it."*

Also, to be effective in collecting, as in sales, find out about the person's motives and interests, so you can direct your appeals to these. Thus, when you call or meet with the debtor, ask questions and listen to find out what he or she wants. Or in a letter, urge the debtor to phone or write you about any problems. Not only will the information you get be crucial for your appeals strategy, but letting the debtor react is valuable because it gets him or her involved in resolving the collection problem, so he or she feels you are working together—it's not me against you.

(3) **Developing the debtor conviction that the situation is serious and must be resolved immediately.** After you've attracted attention and interest, you want to convince the debtor you are worth listening to and your message is an important one that requires a positive response very soon. (This is like convincing a prospect you have a valuable product and selling yourself along with the product.)

Your first impression starts the process. During the rest of your presentation letter, continue to back that up.

For example, if you are calling, sound forceful and assertive. Send a letter that looks good on an impressive letterhead. If you have a personal meeting, dress in a stylish business-like way to show that you consider this a serious matter.

Besides making a good first impression, convey to the debtor your own conviction, belief, and assurance that the debtor will and should pay, just as if you were a salesperson promoting a product you believe is good. To be convincing, you must appear confident, and to appear this way, you must believe in your ability to collect and the debtor's ability to pay. Then, when you write or talk to the debtor, the style or tone of your communication will convey this message.

(4) **Encouraging the debtor's desire to pay.** To spark desire, you need to combine interest and conviction with an appeal to the emotions. It's just like selling a product. You can make a person interested in listening or convince him or her that what you say has merit by appealing to his or her intellect. But to make a person truly desire something—including wanting to pay a debt—you have to engage the emotions, too.

This is the purpose of using the major appeals following this section. In addition, you can make your appeals even more powerful by the language you use when you talk or write to the debtor.

(5) **Making the close and getting the debtor to make a payment.** The final step in a collections contact is making the close where you ask the person to take some action, as in sales. When you write a letter, you assume the person has been convinced and is ready to act at the end. But if you are talking to the debtor, you have to be sensitive about when he or she is ready to act; so you must watch for the appropriate "buy" signals, indicating the person has been sold by what you have said. Accordingly, when the debtor seems ready to respond and is agreeable, it's time to close by asking for some action.

As in sales, you can ask for this action directly:

> "Why don't we close this matter by having you pay me $100 now? Then, we'll write up a promissory note stating you will pay me $100 each month for the next three months."

Or, for a more subtle close, do as many salespeople do: Assume the person has already agreed to what you are selling or stating, and you act on that basis. This is what is called the "assumptive close," where you pull out an agreement form and say the following:

> "Okay, would you prefer to give me the first payment in cash or write a check? Just sign here to confirm our agreement."

The major appeals

When the debtor owes the debt and believes he or she owes at least part of it, appeals to his or her honor, pride, self-interest, and other motivators can be effective; though different approaches are needed when the debtor disputes the debt or is intentionally trying to avoid it.

Assuming the debtor accepts the validity of the debt, your object is to find ways to get the debtor to pay—and claims of no money are no excuse. You've got to motivate the debtor to FIND the money. And, if the debtor has other debts competing for attention, which many do, you're in a competitive sales situation. So, you've got to work even harder to motivate the debtor to pay YOU!, rather than someone else.

There are five basic motivators or appeals. Just as salespeople use them to promote attention, interest, conviction, and desire, and to close a sale, so you'll find them effective in trying to collect, since collecting is another form of sales.

The five major appeals are directed to the following key needs of the debtor:

(1) **Physical needs** ... for self-preservation and protection

(2) **Security needs** ... for comfort and ease

(3) **Social needs** ... for belonging, friendship, affection, and love

(4) **Ego needs** ... for self-esteem, reputation, status, recognition, pride, respect, self-confidence, achievement, and independence

(5) **Self-fulfillment needs** ... for realizing one's potential, being creative, or achieving a high degree of financial gain or profit.

Collecting is a unique profession. For example, successful salespeople stress the positive aspects of buying the product or service. A collector has to emphasize the negative or loss side of the appeal to make the debtor feel anxious or nervous to get the person to pay. From this perspective, these five major appeals might be restated as follows to let the debtor know the negative consequences if he or she doesn't pay:

(1) Difficulties with self-preservation and protection, i.e., loss of home or car (provided you can legally do this).

(2) Discomfort and everyday activities (i.e., more annoying phone calls and collection letters; loss of a secured property like a TV or stereo; difficulty in getting credit or loss of a good credit rating.

(3) Shame, dishonor (the implication being that it's shameful or dishonorable not to pay your debts' when upstanding, respectful members of the community make a commitment to pay and do.)

(4) A failure in achieving personal or business goals (i.e., you won't have credit when you need it for your business, or you may lose out on future business deals if you can't pay a debt now.)

Deciding What Appeals to Use

You can decide on the best appeal or appeals based on the information you have or learn about the debtor. You can use data on the debtor's income level, lifestyle, community involvement, and nature of debt (purchase, business loan, or personal loan) to give you cues. Also, if you talk to the debtor, ask questions to gain more information. Or, if the debtor responds to you with a letter, look at it closely for clues.

In choosing which appeal to use, you are like a salesperson sizing up the prospect or an ad copywriter trying to find the right approach to make the customer buy. In a sales situation, successful salespeople learn to listen and probe to find out what motivates a customer—the person's so-called "hot button." When you speak to the debtor, you should do the same.

In advertising, copywriters similarly use a variety of themes in an ad campaign to motivate action. You might think of writing a series of appeal letters that way. If one hot button doesn't work, try another, each time stepping up the pressure a little more to be persuasive.

(1) **People concerned about survival or about losing the security they have.** These people are especially concerned with taking care of monthly bills. They often have trouble paying debts, because they have difficulty getting by and managing money.

Thus, a key way to appeal to them is to reassure them that paying the debt will give them less to worry about. They won't have to worry about losing essential property or services which they might if the matter ends up in court; and they will avoid hassles with the big institutions they often fear, like the banks, police, and courts.

Appeals to the need for self-preservation and safety:

- "You won't have to worry about this unpaid bill anymore."
- "You'll feel more secure after you've taken care of your debts."
- "You might not get the credit you need in the future if you don't pay this bill."

- "If you don't pay your bills, this could endanger your credit and cause other problems. For example, some employers look at their employees' credit ratings, and this can affect your future promotion or your chances of securing another job."

- "You wouldn't want your employer to think you didn't pay your bills, would you? They would find out if we have to go to court and garnish your wages. That could cause you a lot of problems in the future."

- "If we don't get your payment today, we'll have to take further action which could result in an inconvenience for you in the future."

- "You'll save money by paying this now. If not, we'll have to add interest and other charges."

- "It will be much more expensive for you in the long run if you do not pay."

(2) **People who want comfort and ease.** These people are especially concerned about losing the income or property that gives them a comfortable lifestyle. They want to do more than just "make it" and pay the bills; they want a comfortable life, where they can take it easy and relax.

They might be especially interested in a nice home in the suburbs, car, and the usual conveniences, or they might be satisfied with a modest apartment or condominium in the city. Frequently, these people are blue collar and office workers with middle level jobs, who see themselves as part of the mainstream and feel they need the appropriate material items and income to keep up.

Appeals to the need for comfort and ease:

- "You'll feel relieved when this is over, and you won't have to worry about us contacting you again."

- "We'd like to be able to continue to extend you credit, so you can continue to take advantage of our special sales and layaway purchase plan that is designed to make everything easy for you as one of our valued customers."

(3) **People who seek belonging, love, and affection.** These people are especially concerned about anything that affects their ability to gain this. They are very interested in being with others and feeling acceptance and social approval. They want to be thought of as good, honest, trustworthy people.

Those with a more settled middle income lifestyle are particularly concerned that they fit into their community and are accepted. Others, meanwhile, especially the young and single, may crave travel, adventure, and fun and interesting friends. They see money as a way to satisfy their need to fit in, often taking on debts they can't afford because they are trying to keep pace with others in the community or in their social set.

Appeals to the need for belonging, love, and affection:

- "Don't miss out on the fun activities our group has planned. Get your membership renewal in today."

- "Don't let your money problems interfere with your marriage or relationship with your family. When you take care of your bills, everything will be much smoother for you at home."
- "Your family will appreciate you for taking care of this matter now. You wouldn't want to put them in a situation where you can't get credit when you need it, would you?"
- "You want the other members of your family to respect you, don't you? When you pay your bills, you set a good example for your children."

(4) **People who seek recognition.** These people fear anything that damages their self-esteem, pride, or reputation; they want power, prestige, or respect from others. They are especially interested in proving their self-worth through their achievement or trappings of success.

Typically, you'll find such people among those on the way up who are trying hard to make it in some field or among those who have already attained a position of power in business, politics, or the arts. Often, they end up spending too much because of trying to impress others, and the appeal that particularly motivates them is any threat to their power, prestige, or self-respect.

Appeals to the need for recognition and self-esteem:

- "We presume you are an honest person who wants to take care of this debt."
- "You are a responsible, trustworthy person, aren't you? Then, pay this bill as you agreed."
- "I know you face your obligations and responsibilities. Well, this is your responsibility, and you should take care of it."
- "I'm sure you can understand the difficulties your non-payment has caused our company. So, we appeal to your sense of responsibility and concern for others. Please pay us the money that is due."
- "I'm sure if you look to your own conscience, it'll tell you that it's only right to pay the bill, and it's wrong not to pay."
- "We extended credit to you in good faith, and we have been fair to you. You want to be fair with us and show good faith, too, don't you?"
- "You already have a good payment record with us. We hope you'll want to keep your good credit record."

(5) **People who seek self-fulfillment.** These people are especially concerned about anything that limits their freedom for creative expression or accomplishing personal goals. They are a little out of the ordinary and can be found in all walks of life, though they are unlikely to be among those who are just making it—except for the rare person who struggles very hard and makes it by the bootstraps.

Essentially, these people are very inner directed and want to achieve goals or ideals they have set for themselves. Often they may end up in debt because they have a vision they were not able to achieve, and they may remain in debt because desire to achieve and continue to be creative.

Appeals to the need for self-fulfillment:

- "You can't gain true success in the long run if you don't live up to your personal obligations."
- "We'd like to continue to help you meet your personal goals with our program. But we can't unless you pay us the balance due."

To an extent, all of us share these characteristics just listed, and therefore, may respond to any number of appeals. But the advantage of categorizing the debtor is that some people respond more to certain appeals than to others. Thus, if you can assess the debtor appropriately, you can emphasize the corresponding appeal and be more effective in selling the debtor on paying.

However, if you have limited information, rely on the broad general appeals that are widely applicable to everyone—such as having a good reputation; being an honorable, responsible person; maintaining comfort and security; and being liked.

Suggesting Alternatives

Although it's preferable to request immediate payment in full in your first appeals and leave it up to the debtor to request other terms, sometimes a debtor may not because he or she is embarrassed to admit to financial problems.

If you suspect this might be the case, then in your last appeals letter or call, you might suggest you are open to an alternate payment arrangement if the person has problems paying. Or, if you think the debtor might have some question or complaint about the debt, perhaps mention this, too. Example:

"Since you haven't responded to any of our reminders or previous appeals, is there some problem we can discuss? We'd like to work it out with you if there is."

"If you have any difficulty paying the requested amount in full, we might be able to work out a special arrangement with you. And, if you have any question or complaint about the bill, now is the time to let us know."

Place a time limit on suggesting a payment plan. For example:

"If you contact us within 14 days of the date of this letter, we can place you into a special program."

If you do not place this time limit, the debtor may feel he can put this matter off.

If the debtor responds with a grievance, methods of handling this are discussed later. But assuming the problem is the person's ability to pay the bill, there are four major arrangements you can suggest:

(1) **Extending the Account Through a Deferred Payment.** In effect, you are suggesting the debtor continue doing what he or she is already doing—extending the date when the account is supposed to be paid. However, by formally extending the account, you are taking pressure off the debtor and thereby promoting good will. A common arrangement is for 30 days. But make this suggestion only if you feel the debtor realistically can and will pay at this time. Otherwise, you are simply giving the debtor a free ride for the extension period, and at the end, he or she may simply not pay again. Thus, when you enter into this agreement, ask for some formal assurance that the debtor will pay you then (like a signed letter of agreement). Also, be sure the debtor has a good explanation of why he or she missed the original payment date.

(2) **Accepting a Postdated Check.** This approach is like extending the account, except you have the promised payment in hand, assuming the check is good. If it isn't, at least you're in a stronger legal position to collect.

Accepting such a check makes the most sense in a situation where the debtor currently doesn't have the money, but is expecting some money in soon. Assuming the money arrives, the check will be good. Under the circumstances, make sure the debtor really is likely to get this money and is not just giving you some hopeful story.

Have the customer deliver the check directly to you, or have it mailed to your attention. Some will mail a predated check and risk having the check cashed prematurely.

(3) **Accepting a Series of Partial Payments.** In this fairly common arrangement, you suggest the debtor makes a series of payments, and you work out something reasonable the debtor can pay. For example, you might divide up the total into four to six payments to be paid over a like period of months and ask for the first payment immediately. Then, each month the debtor makes another payment.

In some cases, creditors don't charge interest to show good will. But it's fair to add on a reasonable interest, if you want to propose this.

Never agree to weekly payments. A week goes by too quickly, and weekly arrangements rarely, if ever, work out.

(4) **Writing Up a Promissory Note Payable By the Bank.** If the amount due is substantial, perhaps ask the debtor to pay you via a promissory note for the full amount of the debt, plus interest for the amount of time over which he or she will pay off the note. The key difference from other promissory notes which are just promises (and sometimes quite empty ones) is this note is not made out to you, but to a third party (usually a bank) to whom the debtor makes the payment, and the third party pays you. In effect, the debtor is taking out a loan to pay you in full. The promissory note is his or her agreement to pay off the lender.

Getting paid on the continued business plan

If the debtor hasn't been able to pay and you have a product or service he or she still wants, you can promote continued business and get paid. You offer to continue doing business with the debtor on a C.O.D. plus basis. According to this arrangement, the debtor can still buy your products or services, but pays C.O.D., plus a little extra to retire the old debt.

The best time to use this strategy is when you see the debtor struggling and you know he needs what you offer to stay in business (even though he could possibly get it from a competitor). You might continue to be a good paying customer if you help him or her get back on his or her feet.

Just tell the debtor you can't extend any more credit, but you'll be glad to provide what he or she needs at the usual rates, if he or she pays up front and is willing to work off the debt. The result is a win-win situation. The debtor gets what he or she needs for business; and you gradually get your money, while maintaining the debtor's business and good will.

Taking extra steps to get your money

In making your appeal, you normally want to relay on the usual channels for the debtor paying you, such as mailing you the money or stopping by with a check. Preferably, you don't want to offer to make a special trip to the debtor's business or home, because you can end up spending a lot of time and gas money driving around to collect debts. Professional collectors call this "setting up a bread run," and ideally, you don't want to do that.

However, if the sum is substantial, and if you are beginning to doubt the debtor's promises and feel a personal appearance by you or your messenger will give you the extra push you need, by all means do it.

Even if you don't feel comfortable playing the "tough guy" role, you can still convey firmness with your personal appearance to give your appeal extra clout. For example, offer to wait until you get to see the debtor and resolve the matter. Suggest that you will be going directly from your visit to the courthouse, if you cannot sit down and talk about the matter now. Or make a remark using one of the appeals already described such as "I know you value your reputation and want to be fair in paying your debts. So, let's discuss this and get this matter resolved."

Footnotes

[1] T. Frank Hardesty, *Collection Techniques for Accounts Receivable*, Fairfax, California, Dible Management Institute, 1982, p. 19-20.

[2] Goldstein, *Getting Paid*, 1984.

Chapter 6

Communicating Effectively With The Debtor

Discussing the Bill

After you've made several appeals to the debtor, and the debtor still hasn't paid, you know you have a problem.

At this time you must begin to deal with the debtor directly to determine the real cause for the debtor not paying the bill. Since it's to your advantage to settle without getting tough and involving a lawyer, collection agency, or the courts, now's the time to get some dialogue going, and find out the real cause for the debtor not paying the bill. Then, by dealing with that cause, you are likely to get the debtor to pay.

The five major reasons for non-payment

Once you find out the real reason the debtor isn't paying, you can work on resolving the situation and find a more compelling appeal to motivate payment. In order to make the debtor's motive to pay more compelling than the debtor's resistance to paying, you must first understand why the debtor has been resisting or why you haven't been able to motivate him or her. Then you can more effectively appeal to the person's needs and overcome resistance. In short, you have to be both a problem-solver and salesperson.

There are five main reasons for non-payment:

(1) The debtor acknowledges the debt, but can't (or believes he or she can't) pay the whole amount, but is open to working out payment agreements.

(2) The debtor wants to stall, because he or she is uncertain whether to acknowledge responsibility for the debt. Or if the debtor accepts the debt, he or she isn't ready to pay.

(3) The debtor has a real grievance or dispute, so he or she believes that either all or part of the debt is not owed.

(4) The debtor is intentionally trying to avoid paying the debt by avoiding the creditor or making up excuses.

(5) The debtor has become handicapped or destitute, or due to other mitigating circumstances truly can't pay anything now. He or she may be able to pay later.

When you understand the debtor, you can respond accordingly. But realize the debtor can shift from one category to another depending on circumstances and your own response. For example, if you come down too hard on a debtor who acknowledges the debt, can't pay in full, and is open to payment arrangements, you can alienate the debtor. As a result, the debtor may decide he or she has a real grievance, and so it's appropriate not to pay. Likewise, if you wait too long to get paid by a debtor who is having trouble paying, he or she may turn into a real hardship case with no money.

So, once you assess the situation, act fairly and quickly to get the money that's due as soon as you can.

Finding out about the debtor

To determine the real reason for non-payment and find out how to motivate the debtor or reduce resistance, you have to learn to listen and develop rapport with the debtor. Then, when you talk to the debtor, say what you mean, so the debtor understands and you aren't misunderstood. Bill collectors are trained in such communication techniques when they learn to collect bills professionally, and the same sort of techniques will work for you.

The main keys to communicating effectively with the debtor to find out problems and seek solutions are the following:

(1) **Keep Your Message Simple and Brief.** Do this so the debtor easily understands what you are trying to say. Avoid using long words to impress the debtor—you will only confuse or alienate him or her from telling you how he or she really feels and working with you.

For example, when you state the problem, say something like the following:

> *"You promised to pay us for the furniture when you bought it, and now you have to pay the bill."*

Not:

> *"I'm sure you understood that the contract you signed when you purchased the merchandise committed you to a definite obligation to make regular payments. Now, you are required to make payment in keeping with the agreement you signed."*

(2) **Try Establishing Rapport With the Debtor Immediately.** From the first moment you start to talk about the debt, you should try to establish rapport. If you don't know the debtor, be courteous and polite, yet firm and business-like. You want to treat the debtor with respect, yet show you are serious about getting paid. You should also call the debtor by his or her last name (preceded by Mr., Mrs., or Ms.) and show you are sincerely concerned about helping the debtor solve any problems. But don't let yourself get emotionally involved and let the debtor's excuse deflect your determination from getting back the debt. For example, don't let a hard luck story throw you, even if true. Remember, the debtor still owes the money, and normally has other alternatives for finding a way to pay you other than making you wait. Even though there are occasions where establishing rapport will not help, it is wise to try this approach first.

If you do know the debtor, be friendly, yet firm. You want to preserve good feelings but still show this is a serious call about the money that's due. It's important to establish this rapport from the beginning of the conversation, because you only have a few seconds to make a good first impression and set the tone for the conversation. If you have never talked to the debtor before, your opening is especially important, because you don't get a second chance to make a good first impression.

One way to establish rapport as you talk is to indicate you have had similar experiences, so you can understand and sympathize. In turn, the debtor is more likely to identify with you or be receptive to what you say, since he or she will see you as someone who has had similar problems or is sincerely trying to help.

For example, if you are a businessperson talking to another businessperson, you can discuss how you had to overcome debts yourself when you started out. Or, if you are talking to someone having problems making ends meet, talk about your struggles, too. Whatever the situation, come in on the same wave length as the debtor and show you sincerely understand.

The following sample conversation illustrates the approach:

> Debtor: *"I'm afraid I can't pay right now, since my debts have been so high the last few months. The factory I worked at closed a few months ago and I'm still unemployed."*
>
> Creditor: *"Sure. I understand what it's like to be without a job, when you've worked at it so long. I had that experience, too, a few years ago, when my office closed, and I was out of work. But I found something part time, and even though it wasn't exactly what I wanted, it made me feel really good to know I had a job and someone believed in me enough to give me another chance. I'll bet you could find something, too, while you're looking for another regular job."*

(3) **Stay In Control of the Conversation.** Since you took the initiative in calling or in leaving a message to call you back, you're in charge. So it's up to you to direct the call by having a goal for where you want the discussion to go, and setting the tone for the conversation. In particular,

since you want to get paid as soon as possible and eliminate any barriers to that goal, concentrate on achieving that end. Should the debtor try to deflect you from this goal, get the conversation back on track.

Avoid losing control by asking the wrong questions which give control of the conversation to the debtor. For example, if the debtor expresses concern that he or she can't pay the whole thing, don't suddenly ask: "Well, how much can you pay?" because then the debtor is likely to come back with a low unreasonable figure, which he or she thinks shows good faith. Then, the problem is you're negotiating from a low figure, and it's hard to get back to what you want.

Rather, ask questions to establish what the debtor can pay if he or she acknowledges the debt. For example: "How much time do you need to pay off the debt?" or "How much are you short?" When the debtor responds, you are in a position to make an offer yourself, if the debtor can't pay in full.

(4) **Don't Let Yourself Get Emotional and Lose Control.** It can be easy to get frustrated, when you feel the debtor is delaying or giving you excuses. But stay cool. You'll only make the situation worse if you get mad, for you'll make the debtor more resistant to paying, and if you get abusive or threatening, you're treading on shaky legal ground. Also, if you let yourself get emotional, it's harder to think clearly and keep the conversation on track.

Conversely, if the debtor gets mad and yells at you, it's to your advantage to stay calm and collected, for the debtor will sense your confidence and control and will usually calm down.

(5) **Allow the Debtor to Let Off Steam.** Sometimes debtors will get upset when you press them about the money they owe. But try not to take this personally because often they are mad about their situation and are feeling generally frustrated, rather than being angry at you.

When you call, the debtor may want to express these feelings, and it is often advantageous to let the debtor get emotional, if necessary, and get out any anger or hostility. So just listen quietly. Then, when the anger is out, you can have a calm conversation. Otherwise, if you go into combat with the debtor or refuse to listen, it's likely you'll get the debtor madder, possibly turning his or her anger toward you.

(6) **Listen Carefully to the Debtor and Respond Accordingly.** When you listen, you have a chance to find out what the real problem is, learn about the debtor's true motivations, and understand what alternatives might be appropriate for resolving the situation.

One of the worse things to do is to jump to conclusions and act on unwarranted assumptions about why the debtor can't or won't pay. Your risk is further alienating the debtor and further reducing your chances the debtor will pay.

For example, in the following conversation, it is obvious the creditor hasn't listened:

> Debtor: *"I wish I could pay you for the TV I bought, but I don't have it now. I can barely pay the rent, and I've got lots of other bills."*
>
> Creditor: *"I'm sorry. I've been waiting long enough. I can't wait any longer."*
>
> Debtor: *"But I already told you. I don't have the money..."*

Instead, the creditor should try to show he or she understands the debtor and would like to help find a solution. For example, after the debtor states the problem, the creditor might say the following:

> Creditor: *"Well, I appreciate your concern in wanting to get this bill paid, and I realize you're having problems with your other bills. So I'd like to try to help you find a solution, and it's also to your advantage to get this bill paid. You know, you might take out a loan so you can consolidate your debts, pay them all off, and then make a smaller payment each month on the loan. Or maybe, we can work out a reasonable payment plan, if you can tell me how much time you need to pay off the balance."*

(7) **Use Pauses Effectively.** After you make a statement, pause to give the debtor a chance to think and react. The reason for pausing is that people feel uncomfortable with silences, so your silence puts pressure on the debtor to respond. You've said your piece, and now it's up to the debtor to make the next move. If the debtor hesitates or responds uncertainly, you may be tempted to fill in the pauses and help out the debtor. But don't. Let the debtor respond and listen. For example, suppose you say:

> *"You've received several reminders from us already, but we still haven't received your payment for the $200 balance. What seems to be the problem?"*

Then, even though the debtor stumbles, like so ...

> *"Oh ... uh ... well ... I'm not really sure ... I thought it was paid ... Uh, well ... perhaps, you're right ... Maybe I did forget to pay it after all."*

... wait until the debtor is clearly finished speaking.

(8) **Ask Your Questions in a Positive Way.** The underlying psychology is to get the debtor used to agreeing with you. Then, he or she is more conditioned to continue agreeing when you ask for payment and will be more receptive if you suggest a few alternatives. By this time, you have gotten the debtor in a "yes" frame of mind with your questions. An example of this line of questioning follows below:

> Creditor: *Well, you do think of yourself as a responsible person, don't you?*
>
> Debtor: *Yes.*
>
> Creditor: *And, you do value your reputation in the community, don't you?*

Debtor: *Yes.*

Creditor: *Then, don't you agree that it would be a good idea to pay off the money you owe our store, so you can keep your good credit record?*

Debtor: *Well, yes ...*

As you ask these questions, assume the debtor will answer positively, and your confidence will shine through. In turn, your confidence will make the debtor even more likely to say "yes."

(9) **Speak Confidently.** Show you are positive and confident when you speak to let the debtor know that you are sure the debt is owed, and you can work out any problems that stand in the way of the debtor paying you. The advantage of this approach is the debtor feels your certainty, and this puts the burden on the debtor to dispute the debt. At the same time, you show you are convinced you can help the debtor solve any problems. Thus, you are in a better position to overcome any of the debtor's objections, excuses, or stalls.

For example, if the debtor tries to put you off with a comment like the following:

"Well, I'm sure this debt was already paid ... "

Say with confidence:

"I'm sorry, but my records don't show any payment. If you have a canceled check you can send me to support your claim, please send it along today. If not, I'll have to assume my records are valid, and I'll look forward to getting your payment by Friday."

(10) **Help the Debtor Find a Solution.** Invite the debtor to get involved in finding a solution to the problem. This way you get his or her cooperation, and the debtor may think of solutions he or she hadn't thought of before.

The advantage of getting the debtor involved is he or she doesn't feel you have imposed the payment arrangement yourself, and doesn't agree to something he or she resents and therefore won't keep. Instead, if the debtor helps to come up with the solution, he or she has more of a commitment to keeping the bargain.

One way to get the debtor involved is to ask questions about what he or she thinks he should do. For example:

"Since we're agreed on the balance that's due, how do you think you can get the money to pay this amount?"

If the debtor gets stuck, you can suggest several alternatives, which the debtor may not have been aware of before. Then, let the debtor select the alternative he or she prefers. For example:

"Well, perhaps you could talk to your boss about an advance, or maybe your credit union might loan you some money. Then, too,

your bank might give you a loan, or if you already have one, you can probably make arrangements with your bank to refinance it."

If the debtor says one alternative won't work, suggest another or ask the debtor for ideas.

(11) **Be Prepared to Overcome Stalls, Objections, Etc.** If the debtor comes up with a stall, objection, grievance, or apparently phony excuse, be prepared to overcome it. You should have a rough idea of the kinds of responses you might get, so you can immediately counter an excuse with the proper response.

- If the debtor stalls because he or she is uncertain about whether to acknowledge the debt or pay it, you want to reassure the debtor the debt is due and he or she should pay.

- If the debtor raises an objection, be prepared to counter that objection and resell the debtor on paying the debt.

- If there is a real grievance, be prepared to work out a way to resolve the complaint.

- If the debtor seems to be seeking to evade the debt with a phony excuse, be prepared to call the debtor on his or her actions and get to the real reasons the debtor wants to evade the debt (he or she might think you'll eventually go away if he or she stalls long enough). Then, when you talk, reaffirm what you expect the debtor to pay.

(12) **End Your Conversations with a Specific Action.** Unless you decide that you need to take legal action or write the matter off, conclude your conversation with the debtor's agreement to do something. To get this agreement, emphasize that it's urgent for the debtor to act now, preferably the minute he or she hangs up the phone.

Though you may get a broken promise, and many bill collectors do, end the conversation on a positive note with an expectation the debtor will act. Then, if the promise is broken, you can deal with that later.

However, for now, assume the debtor is agreeing to act in good faith, and ask the debtor to make that a firm commitment.

(13) **Reinforce the Action.** Once you have a commitment to act, go one step further to emphasize and reinforce it for the debtor. The practice effective bill collectors use, as recommended by the American Collectors Association, is asking the debtor to write down what he or she has agreed to do and repeat it back.

For example, you might conclude your conversation thus with the following:

"Well, perhaps you could talk to your boss about an advance; or Okay, then, Mrs. Allen, you've agreed to send us that check for $200 today. I'll be looking for it in the mail on Wednesday. So now, if you'll write down our address and the amount of the check ... And now if you'll repeat that address and amount back to me, so you know you've got it right ... ."

Handling Stalls and Objections

Stalls and objections occur when the debtor isn't ready or able to pay the bill, or when he or she isn't sure whether to accept responsibility. The *stall* is basically an attempt to gain more time by delaying the date when the debtor has to assume responsibility for the bill or pay it. The *objection* is an excuse or reason why the debtor can't or won't pay. Sometimes the objection is based on a real dispute or grievance, and we'll deal with that later. But often the debtor raises an objection to get out of paying the bill if the creditor buys the objection.

Since an individual with a real grievance is likely to respond as soon as the problem occurs (for example, if a recently purchased TV doesn't work, the person will call the store right away; if an order arrives damaged, the person will call to complain), you should treat objections involving a complaint with a good dose of skepticism. Say you aren't sure the dispute is really justified or comment that it's unusually late to raise this argument. Often the debtor will respond by dropping the complaint, and you can treat the matter like a regular stall or objection. But if the debtor continues to complain, then deal with the matter as a real complaint.

Getting prepared to respond

To respond effectively to a stall or objection, be prepared in advance by knowing (1) the kinds of objections people are likely to raise and (2) how to answer them.

The types of objections will differ depending on whether you are dealing with an individual customer, or business; on the type of debt (purchase or loan), and other factors (such as the size of debt or business). But there are common objections that come up regularly. Thus, one good way to get prepared is to make a list of common excuses and how to respond. (For example, sit down with a sheet of paper and brainstorm a list of excuses you have heard or are likely to hear. Or keep a list of new excuses as you speak to debtors, so you'll be ready to respond when you hear that excuse again.)

Secondly, since a likely objection is having no money, be aware of the various sources where the debtor can go to raise money. This way, you can turn someone else into the debtor's banker—not you.

Dealing with specific stalls

The strategy for dealing with stalls is a little different from dealing with objections, since the stall is essentially a delaying tactic to put off acknowledging responsibility for the bill or to avoid paying it. The debtor isn't disputing the bill; instead he or she is biding for extra time. Thus, you have to reassure the debtor that he or she is responsible, and the problem can and must be handled now.

A good way to deal with any stall is to counter with an alternative, showing why the stall isn't an important barrier to paying. For example, a debtor says he can't pay today, because ... "My car is broken," "I can't get out of the office." So you come back with an alternative to derail the stall, such as: "You can send in your check by mail," "I'll be glad to stop by your office this afternoon."

In some cases, the stall is a way to cover up or avoid expressing an objection, and if so, uncover that. For example, after you overcome a stall with an alternative, the debtor may suddenly reveal there is another "real" reason that he or she doesn't want to pay or doesn't feel he or she should.

As an example, say you tell a debtor she can send in a check if she can't stop by to see you, or you indicate you are willing to accept part of the balance if she doesn't have the whole thing. But the debtor really doesn't want to accept the responsibility for the bill and comes back with: "Well, to tell the truth, I don't think I owe the debt. I've had problems with the stereo ever since I bought it ..." Now you know the real reason the debtor is resisting and must deal with that. Additionally, you can suggest that the customer contact the manufacturer for repair or replacement if under warranty.

The following are some frequent stalls and good responses. You can create your own list of stalls and responses, too.

(1) **The debtor can't meet you to bring you the money.**

   The debtor may come up with all kinds of reasons why he or she can't meet you, such as the following: "I'm having trouble with the car," "I'm waiting for a package," or "I'm expecting someone to stop by."

   The most effective response is to offer an alternative, so the debtor doesn't have to meet you, such as:

   - "You can put your check in the mail today."
   - "I'll stop by to pick it up."
   - "I'll have someone from the office drop over."

(2) **The debtor has to check with someone else to see if the debt is valid or has already been paid.**

   Typically, the individual consumer will say he or she has to check with a spouse, while the business debtor will have to go to a bookkeeper or accountant or attorney. But if your own records are up to date, you know when this is a stall.

   A good strategy here is to either reassure the person the debt is due (e.g., "We keep careful records, and we know we haven't received your payment"), or offer to call the person who needs to be contacted yourself, so the debtor can't delay making the contact or use the excuse, when untrue, that this person says the bill is paid. Frequently, when you do offer to call, the debtor will realize the excuse won't work, won't want you to call yourself, and may counter with another reason, which might be the real one. For example:

"Well, perhaps you're right and we didn't pay it. But this month, we're a little slow with our payments, because we're short of cash."

(3) **The debtor has already sent you a check or money order, though it hasn't arrived.**

This is the old "the check is in the mail" or "you should have received the check" ploy. The debtor's strategy of trying to blame the mails may be good for a little time, but after a few days to give the debtor the benefit of the doubt, follow up if the check doesn't arrive. Ask questions to verify the check was actually sent and suggest some of the following alternatives, so you don't end up waiting for days for a check that doesn't come:

- *"When did you send your payment? Where did you send it from? Was it by check or money order? What was your check or money order number?"*

- *"When was the envelope postmarked?"* (A typical response might be, "I mailed it on Friday, but the postman didn't pick it up. It should be postmarked today.")

- *"Please send us another check. You can stop the first one, or we'll be glad to send it back."*

- *"We'll need a copy of the money order or canceled check you sent. We'll be glad to help you trace it, if it's lost."*

- *"Perhaps you think you mailed the check or money order. Please look around your office while we talk, and if you don't see it there, we'll need another check."*

- *"We'll wait until tomorrow, and if it doesn't arrive, we'll need you to make out another check and stop the first."*

(4) **The debtor offers to put out a tracer to find out what happened to the payment he or she sent.**

This is another common ploy to buy time, akin to the check is in the mail story. If you go along with it, the debtor can go through the motions of tracing and have a few more weeks to play with your money. Commonly, the debtor will claim he or she has to trace it through the post office, which takes about 30 days to trace, and then if the debtor wants to stall a little longer, it's easy to add on a few more days.

When you get a tracer story, don't get fooled. If you have any doubts, immediately put the burden on the debtor to show you documentation or give you a replacement, or be ready to take further action. You can even graciously offer to help the debtor with the trace. For example:

- *"We'll need to have a copy of the money order or canceled check you say you sent us for our records within the next three days, so we can verify this as a trace."*

- *"We are not responsible for the mail."*

- *"Even if you did send the money, we'll have to have a replacement money order or check while you trace it, and then when it turns up (... we'll be glad to send you a refund ... we'll return your original check ... you'll get a refund from the company that issued the money order ... etc.)"*

- *"We'll be glad to help you trace down these funds, if you send us a copy of your money order or canceled check ... In the meantime, we'll need to have you issue another to us."*

Always insist on getting a photocopy of both sides of the canceled check. This is the only way the check can be traced.

(5) **The debtor has sent you part of the money owed but owes more, and you have not agreed to partial payments.**

In this ploy to buy time, the debtor is hoping you'll let the matter slide, since he or she has sent in a partial payment suggesting good faith. Or the debtor may hope you make a mistake and think the bill is paid in full.

You should respond by writing or calling the debtor immediately. Thank him or her for the partial payment and restate your agreement about what the total amount due should be. Some companies choose to send the partial payment back to the debtor.

Then, if the debtor explains he or she doesn't have enough money, deal with this as you would any claim for not enough funds.

(6) **The debtor claims that some business problem has prevented checking if the debt is valid or paid or that there has been a breakdown in the usual system for making payments.**

This is often a convenient fiction for a business that is having cash flow problems and wants to buy time. Or it suggests the company may be hopelessly disorganized, and you can expect to have continuing problems collecting. Some typical claims might be:

- *"The computer is down."*

- *"We're short handed."*

- *"We're changing over our accounting system, and we have some bugs in the new system."*

When you get an excuse about administrative difficulties, you should expect any problem to be a short-term one, lasting only a few days at most. And computer problems usually last only a few hours. There is no good reason these administrative foul-ups should affect a payment that is long overdue (probably about 6 to 8 weeks at this point). And if the debtor talks about a confused record system, this suggests a deeper problem.

Thus, show you are not willing to accept any of these excuses for continued delay, and counter with questions like the following so you can deal with the real problem:

- *"Is there any reason why you can't cut a special check?"*

- *"Is this a cash flow problem or a computer problem?"*
- *"How long has the computer been down? When is it going to be fixed? Why should a computer breakdown which only lasts a few hours or days delay payment by several weeks (or months)? If you are having so many problems with your computer, why can't you handle this by hand?"*
- *"How short-handed are you? What sort of employees do you need? What are you doing to correct this problem? Why should the absence of these workers* (if they have nothing to do with making payments) *affect you paying the money you owe?"*
- *"How are you changing your system? What kind of bugs? Why can't you pay me using the old system and use the new system when you get it organized?"*
- *"How long have you been having these problems with your records? What are you doing to get them straightened up? If you have such serious problems with your records, you may not be able to find out the information you want; so you can go by our records instead, and these show you haven't paid."*

(7) **The debtor claims the person who pays the bills is unavailable.**

This is a common business excuse. Some variations on the theme include:

- *"Our bookkeeper is on vacation."*
- *"We're waiting for a signature."*
- *"The person who usually pays the bills is sick."*

Again, check out the information to make sure this isn't a convenient excuse to delay. Sometimes, when you put pressure on the debtor, you'll find that someone else can fill in for the bookkeeper or that the needed signature can easily be found. And if the debtor says someone is sick, your reaction depends on whether it's a serious matter like a heart attack or something routine like a cold.

To get the answers you need, you might ask questions like the following:

- *"When is the bookkeeper* (or other person who pays the bills) *returning? Can someone else take care of this matter in the meantime?"*
- *"Whose signature is needed? Can you take care of this matter without that signature? Why not?"*
- *"What's wrong with the person who is sick? Can someone else do his or her job?"*

Or perhaps make this offer:

- *"I'll be glad to speak to the person whose signature is needed myself."*

(8) **The debtor claims the bill was turned over to someone else to pay and that person should have sent it.**

Perhaps the debtor did, believes he or she did, or is just making an excuse. To find out, ask for more information about who is supposed to pay; then offer to check up to make sure this person knows he or she is supposed to pay and will do it. For example:

- *"Who did you give the bill to? ... When did you do this? ... When did they say they would pay it?"*

- *"If this other person is going to be paying us, let me call and check myself."*

Often, if this is a stall, the debtor will immediately stop you from asking more questions, admit he or she may not have referred the bill after all, or agree to personally send you the money; for when you ask your questions, the debtor realizes you are not put off easily and so responds to face the real problem.

(9) **The debtor claims he or she has been too busy to get around to paying you and is still very busy.**

Perhaps the debtor is busy, but this is no excuse. If he or she thought the debt was important enough, he or she would take care of it. Thus, you want to make the debtor understand that the debt is a matter of priority. Also, point out that he or she can take care of the matter in short order. For example:

- *"Sure, we're very busy here, too. But we make sure we get everything that's important done. And this debt is important, because* (and give a few reasons, e.g., the debtor could lose his or her good credit status, you will hold up an order, etc.)*"*

- *"I'm sure if your car broke down, you would get it fixed right away, even though you're busy. Well, this matter is just as important, because ..."*

- *"I can understand how this could be an oversight. But you can take care of this in a few minutes. For example, while we're on the phone, all you have to do is take out your checkbook, write us a check, and put it in the mail."*

(10) **The debtor claims there is no time to pay the bills now because of special circumstances.**

This is a variation on the "I'm too busy to pay" theme, though in this case, the debtor is claiming company-wide circumstances are responsible. For example, some common excuses might be:

- *"It's time for our fiscal year audit, and we don't have time to pay our bills now."*

- *"The auditors are in."*

- *"We're involved in a legal battle, and that's taking all of our time."*

Here, the best response again is to stress the urgency of the situation and show that it's to the debtor's benefit to pay you, even though the company may be very busy now. For example, if the firm wants to keep doing business with you, that gives you some clout. Or perhaps you can come up with a suggestion to reduce the company's time problem.

(11) **The debtor is experiencing some major changes in his or her business—a change in partners; new officers or managers; a purchase by another company, etc.**

When a business change has occurred or is expected to occur soon, a business person will frequently delay making payments, because then the debt may be taken over by the future owners or because the changeover is a good excuse to put off paying bills and thereby improve cash flow.

In this situation, act quickly to determine who really is responsible for the debt: the individual or the business; then decide what to do on that basis.

For example, if the person has signed a personal note guaranteeing your credit, both that person and the business are responsible, and even if he or she leaves, he or she remains responsible if the new owner doesn't pay. Conversely, if the person leaving has no responsibility, perhaps you can convince him or her that it's an advantage to get past obligations paid to promote a smooth transition. Or if you can't do this, speak to the new owners or management as soon as possible to introduce yourself as someone they will want to continue working with, and hence it is to their advantage to pay the bill.

In any case, when a business is transferred from one party to another and there are some past debts in the name of the business, the obligation remains with the business. Sometimes the new owners may try to get out of this; and if they do, simply tell them you know the law.

Don't allow someone to pass the buck. Find out at once who is responsible and let the debtor know you know. Then, try to work out arrangements to maintain good will, though be ready to get tough, if necessary, to assert your rights.

(12) **The debtor has had an illness, accident, or family problems interfering with his or her ability to pay.**

In some cases, personal excuses are used as a delaying tactic; in other cases, they are real difficulties resulting in a serious financial problem. So ask more questions to find out if this is a real objection or another excuse. For example, if the debtor is ill or if someone else in the family is having the problem, why should this interfere with the debtor paying you? Ask questions like the following:

- *"Who is ill? Your spouse? Your children? If you're not ill yourself, why is this creating problems for you in paying the bill?"*

If the debtor is ill, find out how serious the problem is, i.e.:

- *"How long have you been out of work? ... How has this illness affected your business? ... How much longer do you expect to be off work ... or away from your business? ... Are you getting any sick pay or disability insurance? ... Do you have accident or health insurance? ... Have you filed a claim? ... Do you need any help in knowing how to file?"*

- *"When can you pay the balance due?" or ... "When can you start making regular payments again?"*

If it looks like the debtor really has had a serious problem due to illness or a major business calamity (like a fire, flood, or very large decline in business), be sympathetic and agree to delay. But at the same time, make sure the debtor still acknowledges owing the money and will keep in touch with you regularly about when he or she can start paying again. After all, you do want to be understanding ... but you don't want the debtor to think of your debt as a charity contribution. You expect the debtor to get back on his or her feet or get the business going again; then you expect to start receiving your money.

(13) **The debtor is going through a separation or a divorce.**

Sometimes a debtor experiencing marital problems will seek delay, due to feelings of emotional turmoil. In other cases, the debtor may be having financial difficulties because of the situation or expect the other spouse to pay, especially if he or she took on this debt because of the other spouse.

If you encounter this situation, first get more information about the legal status of the relationship and the debt. If the debtor signed an agreement or made the arrangement with you, he or she is still responsible, and you should mention that fact. On the other hand, an ex-spouse will no longer be responsible for the individual debts of the other.

As in the case of illness, accident, or family problems, be sympathetic and supportive, but remember, the debtor owes you the money and you're not to blame for the divorce. You shouldn't have to wait an excessive amount of time for your money or have the debtor try to escape the debt.

If you can, when you talk to the debtor, get any current information on new addresses or new jobs, etc., so if you have to follow up legally later, you will have this data. Some of the questions to ask in this situation are the following:

- *"When did the legal separation occur? Where? Who are the attorneys handling the case?"*

- *"Is there any change in your current employer or business situation? If so, where can you be reached? Where does your wife work?"*

- *"Do you need some help in finding other sources of money now?"*

(14) **The debtor makes a promise and then breaks it.**

Generally, when the debtor makes a promise to send you money and breaks it, he or she isn't fully sold on paying the debt or feels he or she can't afford it. So your job is to reconvince the person to pay or suggest alternate sources of money.

If you have to persuade the debtor, you might stress that: the debtor made an agreement with you; you accepted his or her word or were trying to do a favor in accepting the payment arrangements you did; and you feel it is important to keep promises because they represent a commitment. You might also ask why the debtor didn't let you know if he or she couldn't keep the commitment, and say you are willing to make one last agreement. But stress that you want to be sure the debtor can handle it, and expect him or her to keep the bargain or that's it—you're going to get tough. (Then, if necessary, do.)

If you don't already have a promissory note, this is a good time to ask for one to get the debtor to reaffirm the debt.

More specifically, some of the questions or points to bring up in this situation are as follows:

- *"Why didn't you let me know if you couldn't pay me like you promised?"*

- *"I thought you were going to send me your check, but I never received it. Why didn't you send it as agreed?"*

- *"I trusted you to keep your commitment when we made our agreement. Don't you want me to continue to think of you as a trustworthy person?"*

- *"If I make another agreement with you, I want to be sure you understand this is the last one I will make, before I take further action."*

- *"I'd like to work out another arrangement, but I want to be sure it's a promise you can keep, because I'm going to take further action if you don't."*

- *"Just to be sure there aren't any more misunderstandings, I'd like to sign a promissory note with you indicating the total amount due and how much you are going to pay me each month."*

- *"In the future, I want to be sure you understand our agreement."* (Then you set the payment date; amount; whether it's check, money order or cash; and whether the person is going to mail in the money or give it to you in person.)

- *"Since you weren't willing to make the payments we agreed on, I'd like to get the full payment that's due today."*

- *"You do intend to pay us, don't you?"*

There are all sorts of possibilities after a broken promise, depending on the nature and size of the debt and your relationship to the debtor (customer, client, or business associate). What's important is to be firm in setting up a new agreement, reestablish the person's agreement to pay the debt, and if you can, get the new agreement in writing. Should the debtor break the promise again without an acceptable explanation, it's time to get tough.

(15) **The debtor is trying to avoid talking to you or is avoiding your correspondence.**

If the debtor is trying to avoid you, things are a bit more serious than you probably thought. Typically, when this happens, the debtor is trying to avoid other people, too, because he or she has financial problems and either can't afford to pay or doesn't want to. In some cases, the debtor wants to avoid you because he or she is embarrassed to discuss the situation, or may want to wait to surface until after the problem is resolved. Then, too, a debtor may hope that if the avoidance game goes on long enough, you will forget about the whole situation.

If the debt is small enough, you may want to write it off as more trouble than it's worth; although some creditors, as a matter of principle, don't give up.

In any case, look for early warning signs that the debtor is avoiding you, and be ready to act quickly to deal with the situation, before the debtor disappears permanently and your chances of getting paid diminish.

Some early warning signs include the following:

- Your mail is returned marked "not here" or "moved" (or it's forwarded to an address which isn't any good and then returned) and you don't think the debtor has moved. (Sometimes the debtor will forward his or her own mail in this way to persuade creditors he or she has gone—but may still be there—usually for just a little longer.)

- The debtor doesn't return your calls, although you leave many messages.

- The debtor suddenly starts screening his or her own calls or has people in the office do the same. In some large companies secretaries screen calls as a matter of course, so their boss only speaks to the people he or she wants. But in a small company, where things are more informal and people usually answer their own calls, this screening is often a warning, particularly if the debtor also won't take or return your calls. It suggests he or she is trying to avoid creditors.

- The debtor never seems to answer a personal phone though you call often at different times of the day, and at times get a busy signal. This usually means the debtor has decided not to answer the phone, though he or she may still be using it. If the situation worsens, the debtor may soon have the phone disconnected.

- The debtor is always out or in conference when you call, and doesn't call you back. Some business people are very busy or want to give that impression to seem important. But debtors can use this excuse conveniently, as well, to evade and delay creditors.

- The debtor won't accept certified letters and they come back to you. People with financial problems typically do this, because they imagine these letters probably threaten legal action or include court appearance documents—and often these beliefs are justified.

- The debtor has recently taken some actions that suggest he or she is getting ready to move or go out of business—such as leaving an apartment, selling furniture, getting rid of an answering service, closing a business, or reducing the employee ranks to a skeleton staff. Another sign of impending doom is that the debtor has been very unsuccessful in some important effort—ranging from getting a job to selling a product line or staging a successful event.

- You discover that the debtor is suddenly being hit with a number of complaints or legal suits from other creditors.

If a company or corporation is responsible for the debt, ask management for payment or, if calling, ask for the Accounts Payable department.

As soon as you realize you have this problem, you need to act quickly to either (1) find a way to personally confront the debtor at once to learn what is going on or (2) take some immediate action to file suit and serve the debtor while he or she is still around, for the debtor may be on the verge of giving up and disappearing, because things have gotten so bad, he or she doesn't know what else to do.

Dealing with specific objections

The objection differs from the stall, since it represents a real reason the debtor thinks he or she can't pay. He or she is not trying to delay giving you the reason and is not trying to avoid the issue. Rather, the debtor accepts the debt or at least part of it, but objects to paying it now for some reason.

Commonly, this reason is some variation on the problem of not having enough money, although the debtor may also claim that someone else has assumed the responsibility to pay. As in the stall, your job is to counter each objection, and if the problem is money, learn more about the situation, continue to press for payment, and suggest some sources of funds the debtor can use, so you don't continue to play banker.

In some cases, the debtor may express a grievance to conceal an objection, just as he or she may use a stall this way. And again, your strategy should be the same—probe to find out more about the grievance. Then, if it doesn't have real substance, look for the underlying objection and deal with that.

Reason No. 1 — "We Have Financial Problems ..."

There are numerous variations on this theme; but basically the core problem is the debtor claims to be having financial difficulties. It is important to understand why, because then you can find out if the debtor's claims are true, how serious the problem is, what options the debtor has to raise money, and whether you can help. The answer will also help you to decide whether to agree to wait, arrange a payment plan, or press for your money now.

Certainly, if the situation warrants, be sympathetic and supportive; but don't let the debtor's pleas for patience or sympathy blind you to the fact that he or she owes you money. Some of the common claims involving money problems and suggested ways to react to them are the following:

- **The Debtor Claims To Owe Many Other People Money, Too**

    Frequently, debtors with financial problems will complain about all the other people they owe, hoping you will become more docile in seeking your money, since you are one of the crowd. Or they may use the ploy: "The other creditors are being understanding and waiting. Why can't you?" A good response is: "We are talking about this debt."

    The main question to ask yourself before deciding how to respond, is: Why are there so many other creditors? And why are they willing to wait, if this is true? If this is a special calamity case (such as a business or individual encountering some unusual and unexpected reverses), pull back and be patient. The "patient" will pay when he or she recovers—and will appreciate your understanding and concern.

    But if the debtor has been irresponsible, or if a business has been taking unwarranted risks, or is being run into the ground by incompetent managers, consider the excuse a ploy to buy time, and take action now before it is too late.

    If you discover you are in a rapidly deteriorating situation of diminishing resources, you have to act fast, because it's likely that only some of the creditors, if any, are going to be paid. So you want to step up the pressure to be one of the first in line.

    To decide what to do, here are some questions to raise:

    - *Why does the debtor owe other creditors? Who are they and how much are they owed?* (You can ask the debtor for a list of outstanding bills and income.)
    - *How long has the debtor had a problem in paying off creditors? Has there been any unexpected problem—like a personal tragedy or business disaster—that warrants sympathy and support for the debtor?*
    - *What does the debtor plan to do to pay off creditors? Does the debtor seem to be sincere in proposing this plan?*
    - *Is there anything you can do to encourage the debtor to pay you off first—or to pay you more than the other creditors? For example, can you do something to help the debtor, or do you have anything the debtor might want?*
    - *Has the debtor considered other sources of funding to get the money to pay off his creditors—including you!*

- **The Debtor Claims To Be Only Making Enough to Pay Basic Expenses—But Not Enough to Pay Off Debts**

  You are most likely to get this type of excuse from an entrepreneur who is trying to make it or from a person who likes to live a little beyond his or her means.

  The question to raise here is whether the debtor is ever likely to make more than this basic budget, for perhaps he or she has unrealistic expectations of success and should be willing to cut back on some so-called "basics" to pay the bills.

  To find out, confront the debtor. Ask questions to learn if he or she really intends or is likely to pay in the near future, and decide if further action is needed based on the debtor's response. For example, ask the following questions:

  - *What are the debtor's basic expenses? What can the debtor do to increase his or her income to pay off debts? How likely is this? How soon is this apt to happen?*

  - *Can the debtor reduce some expenses to pay you back? If not, why not? After all, why should you subsidize the debtor's business or lifestyle?*

  - *Is there any way you can help the debtor make more money? What other sources of funds has the debtor considered to raise money? Is he or she willing to use them?*

- **The Debtor Claims He or She Can't Pay Because of Losing a Job or Business Difficulties**

  Sometimes this argument is a delaying tactic, but in other cases, the debtor has intended to pay, but now feels he or she can't. Your approach here should be to determine how serious the problem is, whether the debtor is sincerely trying to resolve it or using it to discourage creditors, and how the problem affects the debtor's ability to pay. For example, the debtor might have other sources of income, be able to borrow, or have likely prospects for a new job or business. Then, use this information to determine if the debtor can pay you now and how much.

  Some questions to ask in this situation include the following:

  - *Why has the debtor left his job and where was he or she working? Or why has the debtor had these business problems, and where is the debtor's business?*

  - *How long has this situation been going on?*

  - *What has the debtor been doing to find work or resolve the business problem? (Perhaps suggest ideas yourself to help the debtor or if the debtor isn't responsive, he or she may have a bad attitude or have become discouraged.)*

  - *What other sources of income does the debtor have?*

- *Does the debtor have any unemployment insurance coming, and can he or she pay you anything out of this? How much and when? Will the debtor be getting any back pay?*

- *What are the debtor's prospects for a new job or getting another business going? How soon is this likely to be a source of income to pay off your debt?*

- *Can the debtor get some financial assistance from relatives or friends?*

- *Does the debtor's spouse work and where? If so, you can tap this source of income.*

If all these questions seem to lead to a dead end, suggest some sources of money.

If you conclude the debtor really can't pay you back now, get him or her to promise to let you know when things change. But also plan to follow up yourself, since many debtors with job or business problems won't call.

- **The Debtor Claims He or She Can't Pay Because of an Illness or Personal Family Problems**

  Again, this argument may be a delaying tactic, as described earlier, or it may be a real objection. If so, determine how seriously this problem affects the debtor's ability to pay. For example, if the debtor is ill, his or her income may be seriously curtailed; but if a spouse, child, or other relative is ill, the debtor may be worried about paying medical bills, but still have enough to pay you—or perhaps the doctor bills can wait. Then, too, the debtor may have enough insurance to cover any medical bills and pay you besides.

  So, again, ask questions to assess the situation and decide if the debtor can and should pay. For example, ask the following:

  - *Is the debtor ill or someone else in the family? If someone else, why should this hold up the debtor's payments to you? And is the debtor justified in not paying your debt now under the circumstances?*

  - *If the debtor is ill, how serious is the illness? How long has he or she been away from work, and how much longer is this likely to continue? And where does the debtor work?*

  - *Does the debtor receive payments while ill, like sick pay or disability insurance? Or is the debtor likely to receive a lump sum settlement later on through medical or accident insurance? (And if necessary, advise the debtor how to file a claim.)*

  If it seems like the debtor can't pay for awhile, perhaps suggest sources of money or ask the debtor to agree to start paying you by a certain date. In any case, ask the debtor to call you to let you know how things are going, and if you don't hear from the debtor, call the debtor yourself every few weeks.

- **The Debtor is Considering Bankruptcy**

    Sometimes a debtor may claim to be near bankruptcy to buy time or persuade a creditor to disappear. In other cases, the situation really is close to terminal, and further pressure from you could send the debtor over the brink.

    Even an offer on your part to work with the debtor is not likely to dissuade him or her from filing for bankruptcy protection. Explain to the debtor that he or she is not protected from creditors until the filing has actually taken place, and that bankruptcy will remain on his or her credit report for up to 10 years. Do not let a debtor or the debtor's attorney intimidate you by threatening to file bankruptcy.

    However, you can try to make your situation more secure if the debtor files as an individual or for a business by having the debtor give you a secured note against some personal or business property. The advantage of doing this is that if the debtor merely owes you money, you will be treated like all the other creditors, and any unsecured assets, over and above those that are exempt, will be distributed among all creditors on an equal proportional basis. However, if you have a written agreement giving you certain items of property not assigned to anyone else, you will usually end up with them as long as you receive the note over three months before the debtor files. (If you get the note within this three month period, you may run into problems because the bankruptcy laws state that a person planning a bankruptcy cannot give away assets in such a way as to favor one creditor over another.)

    If the debtor has a struggling business and wants to keep doing business with you in the hope of saving the business, another strategy is to persuade the owner to sign a personal note to guarantee any money due to you—including both past and future credit.

    Still another possibility, if you are dealing with a business, is to contact the other creditors to see if you can collectively hold off forcing the debtor into bankruptcy, so the debtor can sell the business. Then, even if the resources of the business are liquidated to pay off creditors, you'll get more from the sale of a going business than one where the business has gone bankrupt.

    The kinds of questions to ask in assessing a near bankruptcy situation include the following:

    - *Have you actually filed bankruptcy?*
    - *Have you already paid your attorney's retainer in full?*
    - *What is the name and telephone number of your attorney?*
    - *Will you give me a secured note for some of your property (merchandise, inventory, etc.) if I offer you additional credit?* (This may sound like a terrible idea, because you are giving the person more money—like throwing good money after bad, but you are in a better position with a $2,000 secured note than with $1,000 in unsecured credit. In the first case, you'll get it all, if the individual or business goes under. In the latter case, you'll probably only receive a tiny percentage on the dollar, if this collapse occurs.

■ The Debtor Claims He or She Has Filed for Bankruptcy

If the debtor does file, stop all collection activity. Contact your attorney.

Then, depending on the advice of your attorney, verify that the individual or business has filed by obtaining the date of the bankruptcy and the case number. If not, treat the matter as a "considering bankruptcy" situation. Further, check to make certain that the debt owed to you is included.

Next, if this is an individual bankruptcy, find out why the individual went bankrupt and what's likely to be left after the individual deducts the exemptions allowed by federal or state law—usually about $8,000. Also, find out how much is owed to all the claimed creditors, and ask if the debtor has listed you as a creditor. If the debtor has listed you, you can get a rough idea of how much you will receive on the dollar owed, by dividing the total amount available by the amount owed to all creditors. However, if the debtor hasn't listed you, he or she still owes you the full debt—though you probably shouldn't expect payment for some time, while the debtor gets back on his or her feet.

If you've got a secured note, verify that the secured property is still available. Remind the debtor that he or she has to keep this property because it belongs to you. If you can, get a new note restating this obligation to further remind the debtor.

If you don't have a secured note, try to get the debtor to reaffirm your debt, which means that even if you have been listed as a creditor, the debtor has agreed to pay and can't discharge your debt. Not all debtors are going to want to do this—after all, the purpose of a bankruptcy is to get rid of debts. But you may be able to convince the debtor it's to his or her advantage. For example, you might suggest ways you can help the debtor (such as providing new credit after the bankruptcy; or giving a good reference or referral to a job). Or if you can't get the debtor to reaffirm the whole debt, perhaps you can compromise on a partial figure.

If the debtor is involved in a business bankruptcy, you should similarly try to find out the reason for the bankruptcy. Learn how much is likely to be left after liabilities are deducted from assets. In this case, be sure you are listed as a creditor, and if not, apply to the courts by filing a Proof of Claim. Otherwise, if you're not listed and your debt is with a business (and is not guaranteed by the owners), when the business is liquidated, you're out of luck.

As in the individual case, verify that any secured property owed to you is on hand and make sure the owner doesn't dispose of it.

Also, if you have had a good relationship with the owner or think he or she might start a new business and want to do business with you, you might try to get the owner to personally agree to pay your debt. This approach is often a long shot—it's like trying to find the horse after it's left the barn. But if what you offer is valuable enough to the debtor (e.g., special contacts; products the debtor will want but can't easily get elsewhere), the owner just may do it. At least it doesn't hurt to try.

Creditors should make every effort to learn about bankruptcy laws as they apply to their state, as well as other states where debtors reside. In addition, competent legal counsel can provide valuable advice on what creditors can and cannot do should a debtor file for bankruptcy protection.

Once a debtor files bankruptcy there is little, if anything, a creditor can do to recover the debt owed.

One example: A produce company calls a collection agency to pick up an account. The collection agency representative was given a Chapter 7 bankruptcy petition. There is nothing a collection agency can do once a debtor files bankruptcy.

In another example, a company provided a service to a customer. The customer then filed bankruptcy and the bill was included on the listing of debt. The company called the customer and asked him to pay, but since the debtor had filed bankruptcy, collection was impossible.

Reason No. 2 — "There Must Be Some Misunderstanding ... "

In this situation, the debtor claims to have longer payment arrangements than you expected or agreed upon. This kind of objection shouldn't come up if your financial policies and agreements with customers or clients are already established, clearly stated, and mutually agreed upon in the first place. But sometimes this problem arises if you haven't made your own policy clear, if it is different from traditional payment standards in your industry, or if there has been a misunderstanding about payment terms.

For example:

- You expect your customer to pay when you deliver the work; your customer expects to pay after you send your bill.

- You expect to get paid as soon as your client gets the invoice, but your client thinks he or she has 30 days.

- Your terms are payment in 30 days; but your customer usually has a 45 to 60 day arrangement.

- You expect to get paid based on the date you receive the order; but your customer counts the time from when he or she receives the goods.

To deal with a length of payment objection, you have to go back to your original written agreement. Check to see what you agreed to. Also, before insisting on your own terms for payment, consider the risks of antagonizing the customer or client and decide how much you want to continue to deal with this person. For example, if your terms aren't clearly stated in a contract or invoice signed by your customer, you are probably stuck with your client's or customer's usual payment schedule, which may be longer than your expected terms. Or even if you do have a contract stating that your terms are payment within 30 days, you may want to make an exception for a big company which pays in 45 to 60 days. (Typically, big companies do take longer to pay, but you can usually count on them paying you.)

Alternatively, when your agreement is clear and you feel your customer or client needs you, you can take a stronger position and say something like: "Even if your company usually pays other creditors between 45 to 60 days, our agreement was for 30 days, and that's when we expect to be paid."

It's a good idea to work out your own policies for dealing with this claim in advance. Then, you are better prepared to negotiate terms.

Reason No. 3 — "There Must Be An Error in Processing ... ."

In this situation, the debtor claims there has been some error in processing your bill that has delayed payment. This is a common objection made by business. It can be a real objection due to some goof, or it might be a stall. If it seems to be a real objection, deal with the problem in good faith to get it corrected, then follow up to make sure the matter is being taken care of. But, if after a week or so, you see nothing is happening, you can suspect a stall, probably because the business is having cash flow problems.

Some typical difficulties delaying payment might be the following:

- "The purchase order has the incorrect number and doesn't match the shipment bill."
- "We need a proof of delivery."
- "The invoice was kept by the purchasing department and wasn't sent over for payment."
- "The original invoice was misplaced, and we didn't know it until you called."
- "There was a pricing discrepancy, so we were holding the invoice until we could find out the correct price."

In response to any of these objections, ask additional questions to find out what the debtor needs. If the request is reasonable, supply it. For example, send a new purchase order or invoice, or send a duplicate contract listing the agreed upon price. Include a request for immediate payment with whatever you send.

Then, if the debtor doesn't respond in the next week or two, unless he or she has apparently legitimate reasons (such as having to send requests for payment through the usual channels in a large company), treat the matter as a stall and look for the real objection, so you can act accordingly.

Reason No. 4 — "Someone Else is Responsible for Paying ... "

An individual debtor who owes money is apt to make the claim that someone else is responsible when he or she thinks some institution or organization is picking up his bill. For example, he or she may claim it's up to the insurance company, credit union, or employer to pay.

With a business, this claim may occur when there are internal problems and chains of command aren't clear, so that someone makes an unauthorized purchase and later tries to pass the responsibility to someone else. Or a new owner may try to claim no responsibility for what went on before.

To deal with this objection, you have to first pinpoint who really is responsible and ask the right questions to find out. For example, in some cases, if arrangements have been made, an individual simply has to sign for something; the company's insurance company, credit union, or employer will pick up the bill. But often, the individual has to pay first and afterwards file the necessary forms to get reimbursed, but does not know this. Or the debtor may forget or may not want to be bothered. So, when the bills arrive, he or she may get mad and won't pay.

You can avoid getting stuck by an attempt to incorrectly pass along the responsibility by finding out as soon as a debtor makes this claim who really is responsible. If you don't already have an agreement with the organization the debtor claims is responsible, probably the debtor is supposed to pay and get reimbursed.

Ideally, clarify this situation with the debtor before you make any arrangements to provide services or extend credit, so you can, if necessary, make your agreement with a different, responsible party. However, if you haven't done this, act as soon as there is a payment problem to reaffirm that your agreement is with the debtor, and the debtor has to collect from the other party. If the debtor isn't sure what to do, help, if you can, by suggesting where the debtor can get forms or perhaps even assist the debtor in filling them out.

If you are dealing with a business, do some research to determine who is responsible and talk to that person yourself. Don't leave it up to the debtor only or you may be waiting a long time. For example, if you are in the classic buck-passing situation where the person who made a purchase or arranged for a service claims the boss or department head is responsible, talk to the boss or department head. Then, if the department head returns the buck to the employee, saying the employee made the agreement on his or her own, you may have to go to the next level to find out what company policies pertain in a case like this. If so, tell the employee or boss, or both, what you intend to do, for at this point, they may want to work out some agreement themselves to resolve the matter, before you get the whole company involved and jobs possibly end up on the line.

If you encounter a new owner situation, in most cases, your debt with the old company will be passed along to him, unless you had a special personal deal with the prior owner, since all business liabilities and assets go with the business.

Thus, contact the new owner about the debt, and if he or she resists, use the stick and carrot approach. On the one hand, point out that you would like to continue doing business together and that you can be helpful to the new owner. But on the other, point out that he or she is responsible for the debt in taking over the business.

If the old owner guaranteed the debt personally, responsibility for the debt still falls on him or her, too. But only use that for back up, if you have to go to court to collect. It's more appropriate to try to collect from the new owner, who has taken over what, presumably, will continue to be an ongoing, successful enterprise.

Make certain you collect all essential customer information at the time an order is placed for your product or service. Get the specific name, title and telephone number of the individual placing the order. Most importantly, get a Purchase Order (P.O.) number.

Reason No. 5 — "Oh, the Person Who Owes You Just Died ... . "

When you call or write and someone tells you this, your first response should be sympathetic and understanding. However, realize that some debtors trying to avoid creditors may use this as a story, hoping the creditor will go away.

In any case, ask for the date and place of death. Then, if the death occurred within the past two weeks (and you have no reason to believe you are being given a line), simply thank the person who gave you this information and ask who will be handling the debtor's affairs. You can also call the health or human services department (or the agency that handles vital statistics) of the county government to verify the death.

If your bill is a personal matter, you want the name and address of the administrator or attorney for the estate. If there is no estate, ask if there is life insurance and the name of the company handling this policy, so you can find out how much insurance there is and who are the beneficiaries. By getting this information, you can file a *Creditor's Claim* form against the estate or seek payment from the beneficiaries. The only other possibility to collect if a debtor dies without any money or policy is to look for a relative who might feel a moral obligation to pay off the debts.

If your bill is based on a business arrangement, find out who is taking over the debtor's business affairs. (Usually, these will be passed on to the debtor's partners or anyone taking over the business.) If the debtor has made the agreement on behalf of a large business, you may get paid as you normally would, since business is apt to continue as usual. However, if the agreement was made recently, you may have to struggle to get the debtor's successor to accept the agreement and therefore the debt. If you think there might be any problem of this sort, act quickly to firm things up.

Once you have the name of the appropriate person to contact, use your judgment and sensitivity in deciding how and when to follow up. For example, it's usually fitting to wait until two weeks after the death to ask for payment. This way, you show the proper respect and won't offend the debtor's relatives or business associates as a heartless creditor. And if you hope for continued business with the debtor's firm, you want to be diplomatic.

Dealing with disputes and negotiating settlements

If the debtor raises a real grievance when you appeal for payment, you normally have to resolve the dispute before you get paid. And this involves some negotiation to work out a settlement.

There are two major types of grievances:

(1) The debtor doesn't agree with the amount due because of a mistake in the billing;

(2) The debtor has an objection to the product or service received, and as a result thinks he or she should pay less or nothing

It's important to work out any grievance to speed up the payment process and increase your chance of keeping the debtor's good will. If you ignore the grievance, the debtor will probably continue to ignore the bill, and if you end up in court and the debtor defends the case, you will have to deal with the dispute.

Thus, as soon as the debtor indicates holding back payment because of some grievance, acknowledge the grievance and deal with it. Although some debtors throw out a complaint as a red herring to stall or conceal a lack of money to pay, (until you know or suspect this is probably so) treat any grievance as real. Even if you don't agree the debtor has a valid grievance (because you feel you have done your part), treat it as real as long as the debtor believes the grievance is valid and feels a sense of injustice or is upset over whatever happened.

You need to settle the matter by showing the debtor why he or she should pay all (or at least some of) the bill. Five key reasons to pay are as follows:

(1) There is no real grievance; you have done nothing wrong.

(2) The grievance isn't as serious as the debtor thinks.

(3) In spite of the problem the debtor raises, you have done your best and everything you agreed to do.

(4) You will do everything you can to rectify the situation.

(5) Despite the grievance, whether or not valid, and no matter how serious or not, the debtor will benefit in continuing to work with you.

Your first step in working out the grievance is finding out about the debtor's view of the situation, to determine if there is a real problem, how serious, and what you or your company has done to create it and can do, if anything, to solve it.

To get this information, let the debtor know you are concerned about finding out what happened and want to work with the debtor to resolve this situation. In fact, as soon as you hear the complaint, perhaps tell the debtor, "I'm glad you said that," to show you want to help. Then, if there are specific procedures to get the matter resolved (for example, the debtor should write the complaint in a letter and send it to a certain person), tell the debtor what to do. Or, if you can handle the matter yourself, ask for the information you need or make a proposal on how you will deal with the complaint.

Sometimes you can work things out with a series of letters in which you refer to your records and any agreements you and the debtor made. But often you will have to talk about the matter on the phone or perhaps arrange a personal meeting. And maybe several calls or meetings will be necessary.

In any case, the process of resolving a dispute can go on for some time. Try to resolve it as soon and as favorably as you can. You might think of yourself as a negotiator trying to define a problem and work it out. Like any negotiator, you'll do best if you try to find a win-win solution, where you and the other person both feel you are getting some benefit from the deal, and therefore both feel good about the final resolution. Conversely, if you come on too strong, thinking of the negotiation as an "I win-you lose" situation, the whole process will break down.

So consider the debtor's wants and needs as you go into the process. Listen to what he or she says; assume, unless you have reason to believe otherwise, that he or she is sincere. Then, use your common sense and judgment in cooperating with the debtor to work things out.

Guidelines for Discussing the Problem with the Debtor

When the debtor calls to complain or expresses a complaint when you call, there are certain procedures to follow in each conversation to increase your chances of coming to an agreement about the bill. These, in sequence, include the following:

(1) **Listen to What the Debtor Has to Say Without Interrupting.** When the debtor expresses a complaint, listen. Even if he or she gets angry, let the debtor get it out of his or her system before you start speaking.

(2) **Take Notes on the Debtor's Position.** As you listen to the debtor complain, take notes about his or her position. You can use phonetic shorthand or jot down key words, so you can easily recall what the debtor claims.

(3) **Ask the Debtor for More Information as Necessary.** If you don't completely understand the grievance or the debtor has left out important gaps, ask for more information and explain you need it because you want to help. For example, some things you may want to ask about are as follows:

- What was the original agreement?
- When was it made?
- Who was supposed to carry it out?
- If the debtor wasn't satisfied at the time, why didn't he or she say something then?
- What kind of evidence does the debtor have about the problem? (i.e., invoices, packing slips, letters about damages, etc.)

(4) **Restate the Debtor's Point of View.** Put the debtor's position in your own words in a calm, neutral way to show the debtor you understand what his or her position is, and ask the debtor to confirm if you understand it correctly.

The advantage of making this restatement is now you are both talking about the same thing and the debtor knows you understand. Also, you have defused the emotion from the situation by being calm. Finally, you have gotten the debtor to at least agree with you on some point, for he or she has said "yes" when you correctly repeated his or her position. Then, if you use that yes to build on to develop a series of yes's, you get the debtor in the habit of saying yes, so he or she is apt to be more positive when you advance you own proposal for settlement.

(5) **State Your Own Position or Offer.** After listening to the debtor, you can state your own position or make an offer in light of the debtor's complaint. Depending on what the debtor has said, you may want to advance your original claim for payment again or make a counterproposal. But whichever you do, tell the debtor why it's to his or her benefit to pay you based on what he or she just said; otherwise you're back in square one. For instance, you might say something like:

> *"Well, Mr. Jones, normally we would expect you to pay in full right now. But since the stereo isn't working, we feel it is our obligation to fix it or replace it. Since you did make the purchase and still have the equipment, you do owe us the money—but we will make sure you have the stereo you purchased in good working order within a week or will give you a new one."*

(6) **Repeat the Process.** You should continue the process until you come to an agreement or set up a time when you'll discuss the issue again if you or the debtor need to get more information.

(7) **Be Firm, Yet Flexible in Changing Your Position or Offer.** As you continue to discuss the matter, show you are firmly committed to get the money you feel you are fairly due. Yet, if the debtor presents good arguments to support his or her case, be flexible and willing to change your position. If you can, imagine yourself in the role of an objective judge, listening to the evidence on both sides, and think what a judge might decide. (After all, if you don't work something out, you might be in this situation.)

(8) **Restate Any New Agreement Clearly, Preferably Get It in Writing, and Follow-Up.** If you can get the debtor to reaffirm the original agreement or make a new one, restate your understanding clearly, and ask if the debtor agrees with that. Then, tactfully suggest you would like to reaffirm this arrangement in writing, so everything is clearly understood.

For example, you might offer to write up the new agreement. Then send it to the debtor for signature or arrange for the debtor to stop by to pick it up. Or, if the debtor resists signing, you can protect yourself to some extent by sending a confirming letter, saying that this states what you and the debtor agreed to, and you will assume this accurately reflects the agreement, unless you hear to the contrary from the debtor. This letter is not as strong as a document with the debtor's signature, but if necessary, you can use it to back up your position in court.

In any event, however you reach this new agreement, follow up afterwards to be sure the agreement is kept. For example, if the debtor has promised to resume sending in payments, since you have agreed on a reduced amount due, write or call if any payment is missed.

(9) **If the Debtor Fails to Keep the New Agreement, Consider the Possibility that the Debtor is Using the Grievance to Delay and If So, Get Tough.** Usually, when you work out a new agreement in response to a complaint, the debtor will pay, because your agreement has resolved the grievance. In some cases, a new grievance may arise creating new payment

problems (for example, you fix the debtor's stereo and set up a new payment plan; but the stereo breaks down again). If so, you have to settle the new grievance. However, it's also possible the debtor is raising a new grievance to delay—or wasn't sincere in complaining in the first place.

Thus, if an agreement breaks down, be suspicious. Ask the debtor some hard questions, such as:

- Why didn't he or she call you if there was a problem, rather than withholding payment (for example, if the stereo broke down again, why didn't he or she bring it in for a replacement?)
- Is some other problem causing the debtor to withhold payment, such as a financial problem?
- Didn't the debtor agree to the new arrangement? If so, why didn't he or she keep this commitment?

If you feel the debtor is trying to play games with you, you've got to get tough. You know you have exhausted your appeals in working with the debtor, and now it is time for the final demand. Tell the debtor you can't agree to any more delays; you have already been very patient; you have tried to work with the debtor fairly; and now you will have to take action.

Resolving Specific Complaints and Grievances

Depending on your business or credit arrangements, you are likely to hear certain types of complaints from debtors. Also, your own situation and policies will influence how you respond in settling disputes.

Generally, though, expect that you'll have to settle the grievance before you get paid. A third party bill collector will try to get the debtor to pay the bill first and work out any problems with the creditor later by arguing that: "You made an agreement to pay and it's not fair to expect the creditor to make any special arrangements with you until this bill is paid."

However, when you're still dealing with the debtor yourself, it may be difficult to make this kind of argument on your own behalf. So you'll probably do better if you try to resolve the dispute first, preserve good will, and also get full payment. If you can't get everything resolved in the same transaction, one possibility is to work out a staged arrangement, where you take some action to settle the problem and get some money; take a further action and get paid a little more; and so on, until the matter is resolved. Then, too, be prepared that you might have to settle for a little less than the full amount to preserve good will and work out the dispute.

To work out any dispute, first find out what the grievance involves, how serious it is, and why the person didn't tell you about it sooner. Also, note points of agreement, because at a minimum the person should pay you for this. After you feel you understand the problem, make a proposal to the debtor about what you think would be a good way to resolve the problem. And be prepared for the debtor to disagree and come back with another proposal. In turn, you can reply with a counter-proposal and arguments supporting your position. The process can go on for some time, depending on the complexity of the problem and how far apart you and the debtor are.

But whatever the situation, the key to finding a solution is to remain open and flexible, so you come up with some arrangement that satisfies you while motivating the debtor to pay.

A good way to get prepared to deal with any issues that arise is to make up a list of common complaints and list some ways you might handle them. For convenience, list each complaint and possible responses on a large index card. If you work with other people who handle complaints, suggest they make up a list of complaints and responses, too, or share your list with them. By having this list, you will better know what to expect, say, and do, and this will be better able to work out favorable agreements with you customers and clients.

Following are some common complaints and possible ways to handle them. Use them to get ideas that apply to you; then develop your own approaches.

- **You Overcharged Me for Merchandise or Services**

    An overcharge is a valid complaint, if true, but it's no excuse for ignoring your whole bill.

    One strategy is reviewing the original agreement with the debtor by phone or in person to determine what was actually agreed to in pricing and the items or services to be provided. During this discussion, determine if there were any simple errors in computation or misunderstandings about the cost of the transaction or what was being offered. Then, try to come to an understanding or possibly settle the matter with a compromise, and request full payment for the adjusted bill. Within a few days, follow up with a letter recapping your discussion and include an adjusted bill, so there will be no further misunderstanding. Later, if necessary, you can always use this letter and bill as evidence in court.

    Another approach, if it may take some time to resolve the problem, is to ask the debtor to send you the amount which is not in dispute; then you will do some research on the disputed overcharges. Sometimes a debtor will resist this approach on the grounds that he or she wants to completely settle the matter before paying anything. But try to avoid this complete settlement first technique. This argument is often used as a way to stall, though legally, there is no reason why a person should withhold payment on an undisputed amount. Yet, even so, debtors use this ploy anyway to wear down the creditor, and thus get you to settle for less than they owe.

    Thus, seek to convince the debtor to pay first. For example, mention that the big credit card companies handle disputed debts this way—by collecting what's undisputed right up front from the cardholder while the rest is under discussion. Or maybe appeal to the debtor's sense of fairness or interest in continuing to do business with you.

- **There's a Discrepancy in Your Billing and Our Records**

    This is a variation on the "you overcharged me" theme, since if the discrepancy was in the debtor's favor, he or she would probably hope you didn't see it.

    Often debtors use this discrepancy claim as a stall. But assuming the debtor is raising a legitimate concern, both you and the debtor should go back to your billing or shipping records, and try to reconcile the discrepancy at this point. Or if you can't, one possibility, particularly if there isn't too much at stake, is to offer to split the discrepancy down the middle, and ask the debtor to pay that. Or you may have to base your case on who has better records.

    As in the overcharge claim, work for a complete settlement and immediate payment; or if it will take some time to resolve the discrepancy, urge the debtor to send you the undisputed amount. Then, work on making an agreement about the difference.

- **There Were Some Damages or Shortages in the Product Received**

    Maybe the debtor's claim of damages is true and some adjustments are in order. But then, this is no reason for the debtor to withhold payment for what was received in good condition. And if there was a problem, why didn't he or she advise you right away?

    In some cases, you may decide the debtor waited too long for you to make adjustments for damages or shortages. Then you will have to convince the person why he or she must pay the full amount regardless. (For example, you might argue: "You didn't tell us anything was wrong, so we already paid the shipper for the product.")

    Other responses to damage or shortage claims might include offering to replace the damaged or missing merchandise, or deducting the cost of the claimed items from the cost of the bill. However, if you consider any adjustments, do some investigating first and involve the debtor in the process. Show that you want to work out a mutually fair and satisfying solution, and that you hope the debtor will want to do so, too.

    Some questions to ask in researching the situation to decide how to respond include the following:

    What was damaged or missing?

    Who received this merchandise? When?

    What records do you have, if any, of what was received? Do these records show if anything was missing or damaged?

    Who is at fault for the damage? The shipping company for problems in shipping? The shipper for problems in packing the items?

    Then, depending on what your research turns up and your situation, you can make any number of responses, such as asking or telling the debtor:

> *"Can you please send us a copy of our original invoice, indicating the merchandise that was damaged or missing, and we'll be glad to replace it. Please also include your payment for the amount due with this invoice."*
>
> *"We'll be glad to send you a replacement shipment for what was damaged or missing. We'll send it to you C.O.D. for the total amount of the bill."*
>
> *"Okay, go ahead and deduct the cost of the merchandise that's missing from the total bill."*

However, avoid a response such as this below, where you send additional merchandise and afterwards get payment.

> *"Sure. We'll go ahead and send you the merchandise you say was damaged or missing. Then, as soon as you receive it, please send us the full amount due."*

This helpful response doesn't make too much sense at this point, since the debtor has already delayed a few months to pay the first bill—so why send anything else without getting paid?

As stated earlier, a telephone call placed three days after the sale will help. Just call and ask the customer if everything related to the sale is okay. Document the call.

Another method is to insert a flier with every purchase. Ask that the customer call or write within a month of the purchase should there be any problem.

- **The Merchandise Arrived Later Than You Promised; You Didn't Complete the Project in Time**

At times a delay can mean the difference between whether a product or service is useful to the debtor; and sometimes, you have an airtight contract specifying delivery by a certain time. But other times, a debtor can use a delay as a convenient excuse to evade payment.

Thus, determine the real nature of the situation by asking the debtor questions like the following:

> *Did an agreement state the merchandise had to arrive by a certain time or the service had to be completed by a certain date?*
>
> *Even if there was a delay, is the product or work still useful to you?*
>
> *Do you want to return the item in question? Why haven't you returned it already if there was a problem?*
>
> *Who was responsible for causing the delay? Is it the creditor's fault? Is it due to the shipping company? Or did the debtor do something to contribute to the delay?*

Then, depending on what your investigation turns up and your own policies, some possible responses might be as follows:

If you want to return the merchandise, we'll be glad to credit you and deduct that from your bill. Your new total will therefore be _____ . Now can you send your payment for that amount?

It's only a few days late, and you can still use the merchandise. Also, we only said we would try to ship it to you by that date. So the delay is no reason to withhold payment on your bill. Can you please send it at once?

It took us a little longer than we expected to complete the work for you. Accordingly, we're willing to deduct the cost of the work which we did for you after the date we said we would try to complete everything. But we still expect payment for all the work completed before that time.

■ **Your Product or Service Wasn't Satisfactory**

Product or service satisfaction is another very subjective situation, which raises many questions. By what standards is the debtor claiming the product or service wasn't satisfactory? What did the debtor expect? What did you provide? Why didn't the debtor express any dissatisfaction right away? How serious was this dissatisfaction? Would someone else receiving the same product or service be satisfied? And what is a fair way of resolving this problem?

In short, you and the debtor can have a field day discussing these and many other issues raised by this common complaint. In determining your position, decide how much you want to continue to do business with the debtor and consider how much the debtor is likely to want to continue to deal with you.

Start by asking some questions to find out why the debtor feels dissatisfied, and try to look at the matter from the debtor's point of view. Does the debtor really have some grounds for complaint. Or is he or she being unjustifiably picky? For example, ask some of the following questions:

What didn't you like about the product or service?

What was the original agreement, if any? (For example, is there a written warranty attached to the product, or is an implied warranty involved? Or what kind of service was promised? And is there a contract stating what would be provided?)

When did you feel dissatisfied, and why didn't you say something then?

Would you like to return the item or get a replacement? If so, why did you wait so long to say something?

How much use did you get out of this product or service?

Do you want to continue to do business together if this matter can be resolved satisfactorily? Were you satisfied with the products or services previously provided?

And so on ...

In short, imagine yourself as some outside arbiter or judge trying to get the facts of the case, and imagine what this person would do.

Then, come up with a proposal, trying to be fair to both the debtor and you, based on the debtor's stated reasons for not paying, how strongly he or she feels, whether you or your company are at fault and other circumstances. For example, you might offer to do the following:

Replace or fix the product, and the debtor will pay you the full amount.

Perform the original service again, at your expense, and the debtor will pay in full.

Deduct a part of the bill to cover the costs of fixing the product or getting someone else to complete the project.

Send the debtor a copy of the contract, since the debtor was expecting more that wasn't in the contract, and you did what was stated.

Agree to do some extra work for the debtor (after they pay) or ship some extra goods to compensate for the problems he or she has had.

■ You or Someone Else Was Very Rude or Insulting to Me.

Sometimes a debtor takes offense and won't pay because of the way you presented your bill or tried to collect. Or perhaps you did something after your bill arrived to anger the debtor which had nothing to do with the debt. For example, you argue with the debtor about something else, or maybe the debtor thinks you are responsible for doing something you didn't do.

All sorts of things can happen, and a debtor with financial problems may be especially eager to latch onto almost any incident as an excuse for not paying. Though such conflicts shouldn't have anything to do with the debtor paying a prior bill, they often do.

Although hard feelings shouldn't affect whether the bill is owed (unless, of course, you've used some damaging or harassing collection techniques, that can subject you to a damage claim from the debtor), in practice you will usually need to clear up such feelings to collect the debt, short of getting tough and going to court.

Thus, get a discussion going on the problem, and as necessary, try to resolve any hurt feelings with apologies, explanations, or assurances the problem won't happen again. Yet, at the same time, tactfully point out that the debt is still due—and that any problem since then shouldn't affect this prior obligation.

Accordingly, when you discuss the situation, begin with some questions to find out what occurred and why the debtor feels angry. Also ask what the debtor would like to do to feel better about the situation.

What happened? When did it occur?

Who did or didn't do something?

Why didn't the debtor tell you how he or she felt?

What can you or your company do to help solve the problem or make the debtor feel better?

Then, respond as appropriate, with an apology, explanation, offer to make amends, etc. For instance:

"I'm sorry one of our people was rude to you. I'll talk to him and make sure it doesn't happen again."

"I'm sorry, we had a computer foul-up, and that's why the salesman didn't call on you when he was supposed to do so. But we've gotten our scheduling fixed up now. So I hope you'll accept my apologies, and we can work together without any problems in the future."

Finally, after the debtor's feelings appear to be soothed, diplomatically ask for your money.

"Well, now that we have that resolved, will you need another statement, so you can take care of the account?"

"I'm glad we've been able to take care of that problem. Now, if we can resolve one more thing, everything will run more smoothly in the future. If you can get your check in the mail in the next couple of days, we can close the books on this matter."

Coming Up With Solutions to Possible Problems

The above complaints are only some of the common ones you'll encounter. Undoubtedly, you'll hear many other sorts of grievances and will have your own ways of resolving them.

So start brainstorming. List complaints; come up with questions to ask about them and develop proposed solutions.

The debtor won't necessarily agree with all your suggestions—particularly since you're already involved in a dispute. But by thinking through likely problems and solutions, you can better direct and control the confrontation to end up with a solution that gets you paid.

If you feel you are getting nowhere, let someone else within your company look at the account. A fresh perspective can really help and may open your eyes to a solution you may not have previously considered.

Part III

Getting Tough And Going To Court

Chapter 7

Getting Tough

Making the Final Demand

Normally, you only need to read the first two parts of this book to settle with most of the people who owe you money. Reminders, appeals, and discussing the matter with the debtor will usually get your money back.

But then there are the "hard core" accounts who continue to claim they have no money and aren't interested in settling a dispute, or they're using it as an excuse not to pay. Such people want to do all they can so they don't have to pay.

Once you have given up on using reminders and firm, yet friendly appeals, it's time to switch gears and move on to the final demand. This is Stage 3 of the 4-stage collection process, the "Push" or Firm Demand Stage, when you're no longer interested in maintaining good will.

The final demand stage occurs when you have given up on trying to be friendly and understanding. You want to give the debtor one last chance to pay you—or else you'll take some further serious action, such as turning the account over for collections, going to a lawyer, or filing in small claims court.

If the account is small enough (say under $50) you may want to write it off, if the debtor doesn't respond to this last demand. The reason is that it will probably cost you too much to collect. But whatever the outcome, make your last demand convey a feeling of urgency—that the debtor better act now or suffer the consequences.

Remember, also, that once you make your final demand, there is no going back unless the debtor makes you a counter-offer. Otherwise, if you make a demand and retreat from it to try reminders or appeals again, it would have defeated its original purpose.

Types of Demands

Although I prefer a single "this is your last chance" letter or phone call, some creditors use a series of letters or calls. Each one gets a little tougher, but only the last sets the date when the debtor must settle up "or else".

In either case, your letter or call will typically contain these elements:

(1) A serious tone, stressing the urgency that the debtor act now, before you take action;

(2) A brief statement of the problem(s) you face because of the uncollected debt. In some cases, creditors write up a brief objective overview to review the situation for the debtor and have a summary document they can use if the case goes to court;

(3) A proposal to take further action that will have negative effects on the debtor (though creditors often temper this by saying they regret having to take this action, but feel they have no choice because of the debtor's lack of response);

(4) An offer that the debtor can avoid this action by paying you or contacting you now to discuss the matter;

(5) A date when you plan to take any action if this is expected to be your last communication—otherwise, just talk about the coming action. Once you state a date, you're committed; and

(6) Notice to the customer that you are turning over the account to management. (And do so.)

Preliminary Demands

The Demand Letter. A few examples of representative preliminary demand letters follow. All of them can readily be turned into final demands by adding a statement about when you plan to take action and what you will do.

The example on the following page is one T. Frank Hardesty recommends in his collection seminars.

Note the demand still involves an appeal, but this time the appeal is to fear and anxiety. The letter emphasizes that the debtor will experience a loss of good will and there is a threat of other action. But the specific action is left vague.

> PAST DUE BALANCE: $_____
>
> Dear _____:
>
> Why have you ignored our many requests for payment of your past due balance? In doing so, you must know you are forcing us to consider other action.
>
> When we take other action to collect the dollars you owe, both of us lose. We, for example, lose a customer.
>
> And you lose a supplier who means to do well by you.
>
> Please don't force us to take other action—which we must do, if your check in full is not received here within a week.
>
> Don't lose another minute. Please. Do mail your check today.

Other preliminary demand letters may explain in more detail about the past problem, noting that the creditor has tried so hard to settle the situation, but the debtor hasn't responded, leaving the creditor little choice:

> Dear _____:
>
> A letter like this is not one we like to write. But we have asked you again and again to pay your long-overdue bill of $500, and you have not responded, though we have made every attempt to try to work things out.
>
> It seems our only alternative is to take further action and turn your account over to our attorney for collection. We don't like to do this since we have had a good business relationship for many years, and we don't like ending a relationship with a lawsuit.
>
> Also, a lawsuit can be quite expensive for you since you will have to not only pay our bill, but court costs, too.
>
> This is why we'd like to give you at least one last chance to contact us and settle this matter. Please send your check or write or call us immediately. Please do it today.

Usually, at this final demand stage, it's more appropriate to send a letter, and it's helpful to have a copy you can use to describe and support your case if you go to court. Or if you have known the debtor for sometime, perhaps a personal phone call with the same serious, urgent tone might be in order. Your letter or call might sound something like the letter below:

> Dear Mr. Smith:
>
> You know, I'm really disappointed you've been ignoring my many requests to settle your debt. We've talked about this so many times, and I've made every attempt to work with you. But the money is still overdue.
>
> I'm beginning to feel the only way to resolve this is to take further legal action, though I would prefer not to do this since we've known each other so long. Thus, I thought I'd write and give you another chance to settle the matter.
>
> Can you send in your check today and let's get this resolved, so I don't have to turn the amount over for collection?

The Collection Message or Memo. Another possibility is the short collection message or memo which states how much is due and urges the debtor to contact you quickly before you take further action. You can write these messages yourself or obtain pre-printed ones at a stationery store. You need only type the pertinent information once and update the balance on these ready-made form letters.

The message on the Final Notice part reads:

> YOUR ACCOUNT IS NOW SERIOUSLY OVERDUE!
>
> You have apparently ignored our repeated requests for payment. Unless we receive your payment within the next 10 days, we will be forced to take immediate action. Avoid trouble and expense by completing this form and returning it along with your check at once!

Another collection message example is as follows:

> Dear _____:
>
> In spite of numerous requests for payment, we still have not received your check. We have tried to be fair and have extended credit far beyond our usual terms. Now we must insist on a check or reason for non-payment by return mail, to prevent drastic collection efforts.

If you wish, include a reply form to make it easy for the debtor to respond or include space for the debtor to note a reply on your letter. For instance, a typical reply section might look like the following:

```
_____  I am enclosing payment
_____  I made payment on _____
_____  My check number was _____
Additional comments:
_____
_____
_____
```

The Telegram or Mailgram. Still another type of preliminary demand is the brief telegram or mailgram to make the debtor pay more attention. It's like the final demand telegram or mailgram, except you don't set the date when you will act. For example:

```
YOUR ACCOUNT FOR $500 WILL BE REFERRED TO OUR
ATTORNEY FOR COLLECTIONS UNLESS YOU REMIT PAYMENT
IN FULL. PLEASE SEND IT TODAY.
```

or:

```
CALL US IMMEDIATELY ABOUT YOUR LONG OVERDUE DEBT
FOR $500. OTHERWISE WE WILL BE ASSIGNING YOUR
ACCOUNT FOR OUTSIDE COLLECTIONS.
```

After you send out your preliminary demand, wait two weeks (at most), and follow up with either one last even more sharply worded preliminary demand; or, as I prefer, go immediately into your final pitch. The matter is seeming more and more hopeless, so why wait?

The Final Demand

Finally, whether you have attempted a preliminary demand or not, you have given up on appealing to the debtor. Now it's time for your last demand to let the debtor know this is it!

Tell the debtor he or she has exactly 5 (or 10 days at most) to get payment to you, or you will take the promised action. And this time, specify what you plan to do. Also, make this last push in writing—even if you know the debtor. And, send it via certified mail. This will give the debtor even more indication that you're serious, and it's proof, if you need it in court, that the debtor has received your letter and knows you have demanded the debt.

Depending on circumstances, there are four types of final demand letters:

(1) **The Complete Letter.** This is most appropriate if you haven't previously outlined your case to the debtor. Essentially, you explain the situation, as if you were making a preliminary demand. But then, you sound even tougher at the end by stating the kind of action you plan to take, if payment isn't received or the matter satisfactorily disposed of by a certain date. An example is as follows:

```
Dear _____:

Your account of $250 is still overdue after 6
months, despite all my efforts to extend you every
courtesy in settling the matter. You have
acknowledged the debt, agreed to send the money,
but then, over and over again, no payment.

Under the circumstances, I can't wait any longer,
and as much as I don't like to do this, I will be
filing suit in small claims court on September 5,
if I don't receive your payment in full by then.

As you may be aware, if I am forced to do this,
your costs can increase considerably, since once a
judgment is rendered against you, you become liable
for court costs and additional interest and
collection expenses.

I hope I will not have to take this action, but if
I don't have your payment by September 5, this is
what I intend to do.
```

Note that the debtor still has an out—by paying. And, if appropriate, you can give the debtor an option of working out extended payments or another settlement with you. But he or she must respond, or you take the action you threaten.

(2) **The Referral Letter.** Use this type of final demand if an associate, assistant, or separate department in your company has been in touch with the debtor.

The advantage of sending this kind of letter after someone else has dealt with the debtor is that it shows you consider the matter serious enough to give it extra personal attention, such as the example on the following page shows:

> Dear _____:
>
> Your overdue account for $250 has just been referred to me, marked "final action."
>
> Since we like to give our clients every courtesy and extend the benefit of the doubt if there's a problem, I am sending you this letter as a last resort.
>
> Since you have not responded to previous requests, this is our last communication to you. Will you please send me your check for $250 or call me personally, so we can work out some mutually satisfactory arrangement to settle this debt.
>
> I will hold your account for 10 days (until December 10) in the hope we can amicably resolve this matter. If not, I will have no alternative but to turn your account over to our attorney for collection.
>
> Hopefully, it will not be necessary to do this, for as you know, an assignment for collection can seriously damage your credit reputation.

(3) **The Brief Letter.** This letter assumes the debtor is well aware of the situation and merely needs to know you have lost patience and will take a specified action if you aren't paid by a certain date:

Example 1:

> If your check for $250 is not in this office by September 15, we will refer your account to a collection agency.

Example 2:

> Your long overdue balance is for $250.
>
> We have held up legal proceedings to avoid the added costs of a court action. This letter is to advise you that we can wait no longer and will take legal action for payment in full, unless payment is received within 7 days from the date of this letter.
>
> This is our last request. You will receive no further notices from us about this matter.

Example 3 (with a headline):

```
           WE CAN'T WAIT ANY LONGER
We've tried to be patient and reasonable about the
$250 you owe us, but you have ignored all our
requests.
Thus, if you don't send your check to us by
September 15, WE'LL HAVE TO TAKE MORE DRASTIC
ACTION AND REFER YOUR ACCOUNT TO COLLECTIONS.
```

(4) **The Final Telegram or Mailgram.** With this method, a few lines will do, such as the following:

```
THIS IS A FINAL NOTICE. YOUR ACCOUNT OF $500 IS
BEING REFERRED TO AN OUTSIDE COLLECTION AGENCY
UNLESS WE RECEIVE YOUR PAYMENT BY SEPTEMBER 15.
SEND IT TODAY.
```

Waiting for the Debtor's Response

After you send out your final demand, it's up to the debtor. Don't get impatient and call to find out if the debtor received your letter or ask about his or her reaction. Your call will only defuse the urgency of your letter.

Just wait. Your last pitch may bring in some money. But often, when a debt problem has gotten this far, a final demand is largely a formality to show the courts you have formally demanded your money and got no response.

If the debtor does finally pay at this point and appeals to you to do further business together, that's up to you. But ask yourself: If you've had so much difficulty collecting this time, do you want to keep the door open for further problems or has the debtor satisfied you sufficiently that it won't happen again?

Conversely, if the debtor doesn't respond, do exactly what you said—refer the debt to a lawyer or collection agency, go to court yourself, or if it's not worth it, write it off.

Getting Outside Assistance

At some point, you will decide that dealing with the debtor yourself isn't working, and you need outside assistance to get your money back. This section describes the factors to consider in deciding when to get tough and your four major options:

(1) Using pre-collection letters;

(2) Hiring an attorney;

(3) Going to a collection agency; or

(4) Taking the matter to small claims (and sometimes municipal) court yourself.

When to make the move

The following factors will help you decide when to make the move yourself. Consider them along with your own personal style, and do what feels comfortable for you. (For instance, some creditors short circuit the appeals stage and take immediate strong action when they sense the debtor is likely to skip town or that his or her business is about to go bust.)

(1) **Size of the Debt.** If it's a big debt, you'll reduce your risks of losing big if you move faster and more aggressively than with a small debt.

(2) **The Age of the Debt and Common Payment Patterns.** How old is the debt? Is it owed to you by an individual or a business? And what is the payment agreement? If the debt is with an individual client or customer, you typically want to step up the pressure sooner—say after 60 or 75 days—since individuals are commonly expected to pay upon billing. On the other hand, if the debt is with a stable, solid business, the debt collection process can be drawn out longer without a similar cause for alarm, since the business may have a relatively slow pay cycle, and if you wait a few months to get tough, the business will still be around. Also, when you deal with a business, there can be many extenuating circumstances that drag on the process—like seasonal or temporary slumps, changes in management, and problems with recordkeeping.

(3) **The Debtor's Situation.** Ask yourself these questions to assess the situation: Is the debtor solvent or teetering on the verge of bankruptcy? Is any financial problem temporary or seasonal, or is it apt to continue? Is the debtor likely to receive a substantial amount of money soon—and how certain is this? Is your debt with an individual or a business? Such factors make a big difference in deciding what to do.

If there is a possibility of bankruptcy with a business, you typically want to move in quickly (preferably, three months or more before the bankruptcy petition is filed) to secure your assets and possibly make an early partial settlement or affirm your debt with a judgment, since the entire business gets liquidated in a bankruptcy. But if you are dealing with an individual, you may want to wait things out, if pressure from you may force a bankruptcy, since a bankrupt person has about $8,000 in exemptions, and there may be little or nothing left for creditors.

(4) **The Power and Status of the Debtor.** This factor can work both ways. For example, a high-status powerful debtor who is especially concerned about reputation may ignore routine requests. Yet, once you get serious, he or she may respond fearing your actions may leave the blot of a judgment or negative credit report on his or her record. On the other hand, if the debtor is powerful in your community or industry, there may be negative fallout if the debtor decides to become vindictive and spreads disparaging comments, whether true or not about you.

(5) **Your Relationship with the Debtor.** Is the debtor a stranger? A business associate? Or someone you know personally? How much do you value keeping the debtor's good will? Once you get tough, you are likely to break up your relationship permanently. Thus, the more you want to keep good will and the longer you are willing to give the debtor the benefit of the doubt, the longer you should try to resolve matters through appeals. But once you decide you don't care, feel free to get tough.

(6) **The Attitude of the Debtor.** Do you feel the debtor sincerely acknowledges the debt and is having trouble paying? Is there a dispute to work out? Or does the debtor seem to be stalling and giving excuses? Obviously, if you feel the debtor is stalling to avoid the debt, crack down sooner. Otherwise, perhaps continue the reminder/appeals process a little longer before getting tough.

(7) **Your Own Financial Situation.** Another issue may be how long you can carry the debt. The better your financial position or the larger your company, the longer you can probably carry the debt, because your cash flow position is stronger. Alternatively, if you have a small business, you may not be able to continue the process so long because you need the money to survive.

(8) **Your Own Time and Inclination to Follow Through Yourself.** Going after hard-core debtors can become wearing. And, after a point, it may make more financial sense to turn the matter over to someone else rather than investing your energy or that of others in your company in trying to collect. After all, if you can make more money pursuing your own business, why play bill collector? And, often you may not like doing this; few people do. So, you may want to get tough sooner so you don't continue to handle the problem yourself.

(9) **Your Own Attitude to the Debtor.** Besides your attitude towards debtors in general, you may have feelings about a particular debtor that push you towards leniency or getting tough. For example, you may genuinely like one debtor and want to maintain the relationship even though he or she owes you money and makes one excuse after another for not paying. But in another case, you may consider the debtor a jerk or a deadbeat and get angry just talking to the debtor; so you don't care if you ever do any business or talk to each other again. Thus, consider your feelings; though still weigh them along with the other factors that help you make a good cost-effective business decision.

Besides the nine major factors described above, there may be special factors that are important to you; take them into consideration when you decide. There are no absolute rules in deciding when to get tough—only guidelines for choosing what's best for you. Everyone has a personal style; some people prefer to give others more chances and promote good will—others think more about the bottom line or like to act more firmly, quickly, and decisively from the start.

Deciding which option to take

Once you decide you can no longer handle collecting a debt yourself, you have to determine which option would be best for you—and that option depends on the type of case, size of debt, type of debtor, and debtor's likely response. You may also want to use a combination of options, though you only use them in sequence, one at a time. Here we will give you a brief overview of your options and, in later sections, explain how to go about each one.

(1) **The Pre-Collection Letter Overview**

The pre-collection letter approach involves sending out a series of letters of increasing intensity asking for the money and threatening legal action if the money isn't paid. This effort is much like what you probably have already done. However, the difference is that these letters come from someone else, so the debtor takes them more seriously. He or she can see that you have taken another step in collecting your money and may go further if you still don't get it.

There are two types of pre-collection letter services. In the first type, independent companies simply sell you a series of two to three letters and send them out for you at specified intervals (usually every 7 to 10 days) until the complete letter series has been sent or until you get your money. Normally, you have to buy a minimum number of letter series (generally 25 or more) to sign up with this service. The price usually ranges from $7 to $9 per debtor to be contacted through a letter series. You get to keep everything that comes in; the money is mailed directly to you. Since you have a minimum commitment of letters, figure your initial investment at around $200 to start with one of these services.

The other type of pre-collection program is offered through a collection agency and is sometimes called a free demand service. Typically, the agency sends out one or two letters—much like the independent company does, charges about $8 for the service, and the debtor is directed to send the full amount to you.

But the difference is that if the debtor doesn't respond within a specified time limit—typically 10 days from the final notice, the collection agency transfers the debtor into "hard-core" status and then collects for you using its usual collection procedures and contract arrangements. Again, you may have to agree to a minimum commitment of letter sets (whether or not you actually need to use them all right away), although the agency usually asks for less (commonly about 10) than a letter service that only sends letters.

This is because the agency will get additional business from you if the letters don't work. Thus, if you go the agency pre-collection route, your investment will be about $80 for the letters, plus perhaps a small agency set-up fee of $40 to 50 to put you on the books or the computer if you are a small account.

Using this kind of service makes the most sense when you have these kind of collection problems:

- A number of small debts, including bad checks, where it is not worth the effort to make a lot of follow-up phone calls yourself. A percentage of these debtors will pay up if they get these letters.

- A debt that has dragged on with a normally solid, reputable individual or company, and the main problem is slow payment. This individual or company will probably pay you eventually, but needs more prodding than you can give yourself to motivate payment. For example, at the first sign of trouble that might result in a damaged credit reputation, this debtor will pay. Thus, an outside collection letter is all this individual or company needs to be motivated to write that check.

By contrast, if the debt is large and the debtor has financial problems or is trying to get out of paying, you don't want this kind of service. It will only prolong the process. Also, a savvy debtor will not be impressed since he or she already knows what to expect, having received similar letters before. So, the debtor just lets the letters run their course, and figures he or she has an extra 30 to 60 days before having to deal with the debt seriously.

(2) **The Attorney Overview**

An attorney packs more clout than collection letters or a collection agency, since after a letter or two, he or she can take the case directly to court, whereas the letters or agency only warn about turning over the matter for legal action. Also, an attorney's letter may get more attention from many debtors, since they are afraid of being hauled into court and figure such a letter means the attorney is getting ready to file suit.

However, face it: unless the debt is large enough, it doesn't make sense to hire an attorney. If it's less than $1,000 to 1,500, forget it, because you can handle the matter more quickly and economically in small claims court; and even if the debt is a little higher than the small claims limit and you have to shave off some of it to go to court yourself, you'll get back as much or more than you would with an attorney.

Typically, an experienced attorney won't touch a case on consignment that's less than $3,000—and only then, if he or she thinks it's an easy win. On the other hand, if the lawyer does agree to take your case on a fee basis, there are still no guarantees you'll collect, and you'll have additional lawyer bills besides.

You can figure on about $75 to 150 an hour for the average lawyer, plus out-of-pocket expenses for filing fees and court costs. You'll get your court costs added on to your judgment if you win, but you probably won't get lawyer's fees, unless your agreement with the debtor says so. And then, of course, you still have to collect—and that's another story.

There's only one possible exception to the general rule of not using a lawyer on a small case—find an attorney willing to make a few calls or write a letter or two for you, if you can find one to do it for a small charge. For example, a recently graduated attorney just starting a practice might be an ideal candidate to write such a letter on his or her letterhead, since he or she is eager for business and won't charge much. In turn, since the debtor won't know that the lawyer isn't planning to follow through or how experienced he or she is, it doesn't matter what attorney you use. He or she just needs a lawyerly-looking and -sounding letter and a good address. Your cost might range between $7 to $50.

Alternatively, some lawyers might be willing to make a phone call or write a letter or two for a percentage if you collect anything within 10 to 15 days after the letter. For example, one attorney agreed to do this for me for 15% of whatever he collected—about $75 on a $500 case.

However, while lawyers can be of some limited use for small accounts, in general, I feel you are better off letting a collection agency or letter service send out your letters. In fact, some collection agencies affiliated with lawyers can send out a letter under their attorney's name, and if they send it as part of a pre-collection package, it will only cost you about $8 for the letters versus $25 or more if you go to an attorney.

By contrast, when your debt is substantial—say $5,000 or more—and isn't likely to be settled by mediation (which is where agencies are good), I would go right to an attorney. The reason is that you'll get much speedier action. After a letter or phone call or two, the attorney can take the debtor right to court—and if there's any chance of the debtor getting rid of or hiding assets, a good lawyer can initiate attachment proceedings to prevent your assets from disappearing. Hire an attorney who has credit and collection experience. Check the attorney's references.

(3) **The Collection Agency Overview**

The collection agency will use some of the same strategies you have—letters and phone calls appealing to the debtor. But a key difference is the agency is a third party, so the debtor takes the contact more seriously. Also, agency collectors are generally trained pros, who have learned the most effective psychological phone techniques to get payment. Then, too, collectors can make some appeals you can't, because you are directly involved in the case and the debtor may have some feelings of hostility or resentment toward you getting in the way of paying. However, a third party caller may be able to persuade the debtor to put such feelings aside to acknowledge he or she does owe that debt and to recognize the possible consequences if it isn't paid.

Another advantage of collection agencies is they are normally more systematic than you (or an attorney) at following up on an account because this is their business. And, if you haven't been able to mediate a dispute yourself, they are very good at this. For instance, if there is a dispute, they can often get payment for the non-disputed amount while a conflict is being settled, whereas the debtor may want to resolve the dispute with you first.

An agency can also be helpful if you have problems locating a debtor, because of their skip-tracing services. Also, their access to credit information through credit reporting bureaus can help determine the debtor's real financial situation. Plus, some agencies can report your problems with the debtor to the credit bureaus, which can be a powerful tool in getting debtors who fear a bad credit record to pay.

Most collection agencies won't charge you anything either unless they collect, since they work on a commission basis. As one agency described its services, "If there's no collection, there's no fee," although some agencies may charge clients with only a few small bills such as a small set-up fee, perhaps $40 to 50. Typically, agency fees range between 25% for large volume commercial accounts to 50% for most individual assignments. The agency determines its fee based on a number of factors, including the size of the debt, how old it is, how collectible the agency considers it, and the number of accounts you are assigning. The age of the account is often a factor.

Many agencies also offer a pre-collection or free demand service, whereby they send out one or two letters, as previously described, advising the debtor that the account will be assigned to a collection agency or that further more drastic collection activities will occur unless he or she pays the creditor. Then, if the creditor doesn't receive payment by a certain date, usually 10 days, the agency gives the account the usual treatment.

Using a collection agency is most appropriate under these circumstances:

- You have small debts from consumers, clients, or business deals, which are too small for an attorney, and you don't want to take them to small claims court yourself.

- You have a debt that probably can be settled if you work out a dispute with the debtor, but you are unable to resolve it yourself. While you have the option of going to court, it may be better to use a collection agency first, because:
  — You may not have the time or interest in going to small claims court yourself; and if the dispute is confused, who knows what will happen in court.
  — Even if the case is large enough for an attorney, it may be better to let a collection agency mediate it, because an attorney tends to take a more adversary approach, which might interfere with a settlement, while a collector is trained to work with the debtor to resolve the problem.

- You feel you may need an attorney eventually for a large debt, but you don't know a good collection lawyer. In this case, advise the agency that you think legal action will probably be necessary to be sure you choose an agency willing to aggressively pursue legal means, if needed. Such an agency will work with a lawyer who specializes in collections—and since it's in the business—will usually know the best collection lawyers.

Use care when selecting a collection agency. As with any other type of business, there are reputable agencies and some that are not so reputable.

(4) **The Small Claims Court Overview**

If the amount of money owed to you is small and you want to try for the total due yourself, your option now is small claims court. Rules differ from state to state, but generally you can file claims for up to $1,000, and up to $1,500 in certain states like New York and California. If the amount owed is more, you can still file in small claims court; but you have to waive anything over the limit—unless you can find a way to legitimately split up your claim and file separate suits.

For example, if you made two different sales or loans to a person and can show these were two separate transactions, not part of a single agreement, that can qualify you for a separate suit. Or if you have billed someone separately for different products or services (say one bill for reimbursements, another for services, a third for commissions on sales), this might qualify for separate suits.

It is also possible to go to a municipal court yourself without an attorney if the case is over the small claims limit and is relatively simple. However, you'll have to become familiar with the procedures in your state., And since few creditors use this option, so we won't cover this here.

In either case, be prepared to spend some money and some time, though you'll get back the money if you win and collect. The advantage of small claims court is it's quick and easy. You file for a few dollars, set a court date, and barring problems in service or changes in the court date by the defendant, you can be in court in a month or two. Also, the judges are prepared to deal with defendants who aren't lawyers, so you present your case by simply describing your side of the story. Next the defendant, if there, gets to present the other side. And finally, the judge may ask some questions, and you each have a chance to rebut what the other said. The whole presentation usually takes a few minutes.

Then, the judge will often give you a decision on the spot, or if the case is complicated or the decision may create hostile feelings, the judge will take the matter under advisement, and you will get the decision by mail in the next day or two. If the debtor doesn't show up—and many don't (after all, the debtor has already been trying to evade you for months), you only need to show enough documents to indicate you have a case, and then you'll get a default judgment in your favor. Although there is an appeals process for losing defendants, normally you don't have to worry about that. Very few debtors bother to appeal—they know they owe the debt.

In municipal court, the process can potentially go as quickly, if the debtor doesn't bother to respond—and many won't. You write up a formal complaint describing your causes of action and request the money due, along with court costs, punitive damages, and other costs deemed proper by the court. After you have the defendant served, he or she has a limited time (usually 30 days) in which to file an answer. If so, a court date is set, and you will have to settle or go to court, which can drag on. However, if the defendant doesn't reply, you can ask for a default judgment. Since many debtors will be intimidated by the complaint, not know what they need to do to answer it, or realize they owe you the money, they won't respond. So again, this can be a quick and easy way of getting justice. It will cost you more to file in municipal than in small claims court—typically about $40, but you'll get it back if you win your judgment (and collect).

You have to decide, though, if it's worth the time and effort to go to court. Even if the debtor doesn't respond, you (or an employee who is directly involved with the debt, such as your bookkeeper) has to appear in court. And, of course, you have to take the time to file the action and prepare the case. So, consider whether it's worthwhile to try to collect yourself, when you deduct out the costs for your time and effort. If the debt is under $100, probably not. Even if the debt is sizable, would it be more cost effective to use a collection agency or attorney and get about 50 to 60%?

Then, too, consider if you can collect after you win. How hard is that going to be? Unless the debtor has assets or is likely to get them in the near future, and you can find them, you are not going to be able to collect for a while. Yet, the judgment is good for 10 years, so if you are willing to be patient, you may be able to collect down the road.

In brief, the most appropriate times to go to small claims court yourself are when the following occur:

- The debt is large enough to take the time and effort to go to court yourself, but too small to interest an attorney. (Remember, you do have the option of going to a municipal court if the debt is over the small claims limit and the case is simple enough that you don't need an attorney—however, it is not recommended.)

- You have given up on your attempts to collect and mediate the case, and are willing to take the chance of irrevocably terminating the relationship by filing suit.

- You are willing to invest your energy in preparing for and going to court.

- You want to act quickly, rather than trying an interim strategy like pre-collection letters or using a collection agency.

- You feel the chance to collect the full amount yourself is worth the effort, rather than turning the matter over to a collection agency or attorney and getting much less.

Final thoughts

- Be careful of what you put in writing, and have all letters reviewed by a competent collection attorney.

- Sending three demand letters is usually sufficient; if the debtor does not respond to the third letter, sending a fourth letter will probably be a lost cause. Telephone calls are often more effective in this instance.

- Collection agencies often have an in-house attorney who can pursue legal action for you. Also, using a collection agency can help you avoid the substantial investment of time and energy involved in pursuing a debt.

Bear in mind, however, that collection agencies will only do what you have already done: send letters and make telephone calls. And attorneys are not always the answer. Some attorneys cannot collect money, while others may give up the collection effort if they feel collection is not worth their time.

Going through with it

Now, that you know the pros and cons of each of the options, decide which course is more suitable to your situation and go with it. The next two chapters explain in detail what you have to go through in each process and what to expect.

Chapter 8

Pre-Collection Letters, Attorneys And Collection Agencies

Using Pre-Collection Letters

If you decide on a pre-collection letter approach, you have two options. You can make arrangements with a company that specializes in sending out letters and decide what to do next if the debtor still doesn't pay. Or you can use a pre-collection service offered by a collection agency and assign the account if unpaid to that agency after a pre-determined time period.

In either case, the letters direct the debtor to pay the money directly to you, or the debtor should advise the company sending the letters of any dispute within 30 days and seek to resolve the problem with you. Then, if the dispute is not resolved and you still claim the money is owed, the company will continue to send out letters.

Both approaches work best when the debt is more recent, for the longer you wait, the harder it is to collect. Since many creditors delay turning a debt over to a third party because of the high percentage fees charged by agencies and attorneys, they may end up with a debt which is very difficult to collect because of its age. For example, national estimates show that the rate of collections drops from about 79% collectable at 60 days to 74% at 90 days; 66% at 120 days, 57% at 6 months; and 44% on older accounts.

Thus, after about two months, if reminders and appeals haven't worked, the pre-collection letter can be an inexpensive way to persuade the slow payer to pay, rather than going to hard-core collection efforts immediately or letting your own appeals process drag on.

The following describes these two types of services, and then describes how to respond if debtors should call you in response to getting a letter.

Using an independent letter service

A number of companies specialize in sending out collection letters and all of them are, by law, registered and licensed as collection agencies and subject to the federal laws regarding sending letters to debtors. For example, the envelope can't indicate that the letter comes from a collection agency; and the company must stop sending letters if the debtor asks it to stop.

Also, because of these regulations, you can't create a letterhead and pretend to be a collection agency to send out your own pre-collection letters and avoid the fees. If you are found out—perhaps reported by the debtor, you've violated the laws prohibiting non-licensed collection agencies and will be subject to the corresponding penalties.

How the service works

The way the service works is that the company offers three types of letters and you select which series you want sent out—depending on whether this is an unpaid account or bad check—and the amount of pressure you want to exert on the debtor. The company sends out up to five letters in each series, with the final letter being a notice that legal action may be taken unless the debtor pays immediately.

The three types of letters are the diplomatic, intensive pressure, and bad check series. In each letter series, the debtor is at first informed that the creditor has asked Credit Network to contact him or her, and the letter ends with instructions to "immediately make payment or arrangements with:" followed by the name and address of the creditor. Also, the first letter of each series includes an important message that the validity of the debt is assumed unless contested:

```
"This debt or any portion thereof shall be assumed
valid unless disputed in writing within 30 days
after receipt of this notice. If disputed, this
office will provide verification of this claim or a
copy of the judgment against you."
```

Diplomatic letters

In the diplomatic series, the emphasis is on being gentle and respectful to the debtor. Thus, the first letter begins by suggesting that the overdue payment may be due to the debtor's oversight rather than to a willful disregard of obligation. Or if some legitimate misunderstanding exists about the debt, the debtor is urged to contact the creditor to discuss it. Finally, the letter concludes by advising the debtor he or she can make further collection action unnecessary by mailing in a full payment or making arrangements with the creditor.

The second letter, sent after 30 days, advises the debtor that no payment has been received and since he or she has not contacted the creditor to make payment arrangements or dispute the claim, the debt is assumed to be valid. So again, the debtor is asked (though diplomatically) to pay immediately. Perhaps the debtor overlooked this matter, the letter suggests, because of an unusually busy period or some other situation. But if he or she acts now this will prevent this matter from becoming a problem.

The third letter, sent about two weeks later, uses the appeal of fairness. When the debtor wanted credit, the creditor extended it; so now it isn't fair to ignore the creditor's request. The creditor would still like to settle the claim in a friendly way, but to do so, the debtor must cooperate by sending payment or contacting the creditor without delay.

Finally, a letter comes from an attorney advising the debtor that he represents Credit Network and would like the debtor to review the matter, assess the merits of the claim, and then pay in full, work out payment arrangements, or discuss the matter with the creditor to avoid a possible lawsuit and judgment.

Intensive pressure letters

The tone of the intensive pressure letters is quite different, although the final letter from the attorney is the same. The first letter starts off warning: "URGENT", advises the debtor that his or her account has been referred for immediate collection, and threatens that if the matter has not been settled in 30 days, the Credit Network has been authorized to pursue every possible remedy short of going to court. Thus, the debtor should immediately pay or make arrangements with the creditor.

The second letter announces that the "30 DAY GRACE PERIOD HAS EXPIRED!" without the debtor paying or contacting the creditor to make payment arrangements or dispute the claim. Thus, since the debt is assumed to be valid, the debtor should pay at once. Also, the letter warns that if the matter goes to court and a judgment is obtained, every major credit reporting agency may pick up and disseminate this information, which may impair the debtor's credit rating. So again, the debtor should pay at once.

The third letter is even more urgent. The debtor is warned at the outset: "COURT ACTION CONTEMPLATED!" Since he or she hasn't paid, the only alternative left is suggesting the creditor contact his or her local attorney to file a complaint for the principal, interest, and costs. Further, the debtor is warned that if any action brought isn't defended at his or her own expense, the result may be a default judgment, and any property or bank accounts might be seized by the county marshal or sheriff. Thus, it is to the debtor's advantage to settle now.

Then, comes the attorney's letter already described.

Bad check letters

The bad check series assumes that the check might be an oversight; it asks the debtor to send the creditor a money order or certified check to correct this and the original check will be returned.

However, if the debtor ignores this, a stern letter is sent 30 days later. It warns that although the debtor may have issued the check in good faith, he or she should know that intentionally issuing a check without sufficient funds may be a violation of state law and could lead to serious consequences. The letter also asks the debtor to pay by money order or certified check as soon as possible.

The last bad check letter warns that court action is contemplated and outlines what may happen if the debtor gets a judgment against him or her. It is illegal in most states to knowingly write a bad check.

The final written communication

Finally, if all of the letters in each of these series have gone out to no avail, one last letter announces that it will be the FINAL WRITTEN COMMUNICATION! the debtor receives. And, since he or she still hasn't paid, Credit Network will recommend that the creditor contact his or her attorney to proceed with court action. The letter also reviews what may happen if a judgment is received. Though it is up to the creditor to decide what to do, by paying now, the debtor can avoid the possible legal action.

The Effectiveness of These Letters

Though the company sending these letters does nothing more than send letters, such letters are a powerful tool in persuading some debtors to pay—most notably, the debtor who is basically honorable and wants to preserve a good business or personal relationship with you or keep a good credit record. In fact, Credit Network reports that approximately 56% of the debtors receiving these letters do pay, at a cost of about 7 cents on the dollar collected.

If these letters don't work, your next step is going to an attorney, filing suit yourself, or writing it off. Though the option is still open, it doesn't make sense to go to a collection agency now, since your last letters have talked of an attorney or legal action, so that's the alternative you should use. If you go to a collection agency now, it's like taking a step backwards in the process and giving the debtor more chances to delay when the collectors call. Take that ultimate step, if you do anything.

Using a pre-collection service with an agency

If you expect to assign your uncollected accounts to a collection agency if your pre-collection letters don't work, rather than using an attorney or going to court yourself, then it makes sense to use a pre-collection service operated by the agency you plan to use. (If the agency doesn't have a pre-collection service and you want to use one, choose another agency.)

This agency-run pre-collection service is much shorter and speedier than the one described above, since it is designed to extract the debtors who are ready to pay with one last push before assigning the rest to "hard-core." Thus, there is one or at most two letters, which talk vaguely of further action unless the debtor responds.

One form of pre-collection letter is the free demand service which some agencies do for free. According to this arrangement, the creditor sends a form letter from the collection agency to the debtor, stating that at the end of a certain time period (usually 10 days), he or she will turn the account over for collections if the debtor doesn't pay or make satisfactory arrangements. Thereafter, the agency will be authorized to take any actions it deems necessary to get the money.

The creditor sends a copy of this letter to the agency and keeps one for him or herself. If the creditor receives the money in the allotted time period, he or she notifies the agency immediately so the agency will make no further effort to collect, and the creditor is home free. He or she has the money and owes the agency nothing. But if the money doesn't arrive, the collection agency immediately activates the account and it goes into regular collections.

The other arrangement some agencies use is sending out two pre-collection letters on their own letterhead advising the debtor to pay the creditor the total indicated. Normally, there is a small charge for this—about $4 for a series of two letters, and some agencies have a minimum requirement that the creditor must contract for a minimum number of letters (commonly 10).

By the time these letters go out, the agency has already assigned an account number and a collector's desk number, so the agency can quickly begin acting if the creditor gets no response. Besides listing the name of the creditor and the amount due, this letter contains the usual disclaimer stating that disputes regarding the balance must be made in writing to the collection agency within 30 days, and the agency will, on request, send verification of the debt. Otherwise, the debt will be assumed to be valid.

In a typical first letter, the agency notes that according to its records, the account is critically past due, and therefore, it is asking the debtor to pay in full within 10 days or the agency will take further action. The debtor should send any payment directly to the creditor whose name is listed in the letter, and if he or she has already paid the full amount, he or she should disregard this notice.

The second letter, which goes out after 10 days, has a much tougher tone. It advises the debtor that he or she has failed to pay or make suitable arrangements with the creditor, and (like some of the later pre-collection letters previously described), it talks of a possible judgment against the debtor leading to a levy against his or her wages, automobile, or property, plus court costs and attorney fees. Finally, the letter reminds the debtor of the serious consequences of this situation, and urges payment directly to the creditor within the next five days; otherwise a lawsuit may be filed. Should the debtor want to discuss the matter, he or she should write or phone the creditor directly.

This approach is definitely firmer than the extended pre-collection strategy, but then, it's designed for a different purpose—to get the responsible debtors to pay up quickly and assign the rest to regular collections. Typically, depending on the type of debt and debtor, about 10 to 50% will respond to this kind of letter. Then, the rest are assigned to a collector who immediately follows up by phone.

Responding to the debtor's call after a pre-collection letter

There are special ways to respond if you get a call or letter from a debtor who is disturbed that you have turned your account over to an agency, or if the debtor sends in a partial payment, which you don't feel is enough. To respond most effectively, be prepared, so you know what to say, or prepare whoever will be dealing with these calls to do the same.

Responding to indignant debtors

The way to respond depends on whether you want to keep the debtor's business. If you don't care and just want your money, you can be tougher than if preserving good will is a priority. Yet, taking a no-nonsense approach, you can still combine firmness with an attempt to soothe the debtor's feelings. For example, you might say something like the following:

> *"Well, I'm really sorry the letter disturbed you, but we've had to tighten up our credit policies, so we've started referring all our accounts over 60 days due to an outside agency for collections. And now it's out of our hands. So, I would suggest you pay the bill, and that will be the end of the matter."*

If the debtor says he or she can't pay the whole thing now, you might come back with the following:

> *"Well, if you can set up a regular payment plan with us, we can ask the agency to hold off on further collection efforts. I would suggest ... (then propose an arrangement)."*

On the other hand, if you want to keep doing business with the debtor, and he or she threatens to end the relationship, you can be extra reassuring and play down the letter, though remain firm in asking for the payment now. For example, one approach recommended by the Credit Network people is to act surprised and dismayed when the debtor complains about the collection letter and ask him or her to read it over the phone. Then, remembering, you might explain the following:

> *"Oh, that's due to our new accounts receivable control system. We've had to tighten up on our past due accounts because the increase in interest rates has made it so expensive for us to borrow money. So we're referring all our overdue accounts out for collections automatically."*

Finally, you should try to shift any hostility the debtor may feel away from you by saying the collection process is out of your hands now. For example, tell the debtor:

> *"Please don't take the matter personally. But now that the account has been referred, it's an automatic system, and the only way I can stop the agency from continuing their collection efforts is to have the account paid in full. So, if you can send your check in today ..."*

Or if the account is relatively large, perhaps arrange to pick up a check. Take the approach that since you've got the debtor on the phone, you want to get him or her to take some action now.

Responding to partial payments

When you get a partial payment, there are two ways to handle this, depending on whether you feel the payment is large enough to warrant suspending outside collection efforts or not.

If you feel the partial payment is a sign of good faith, by all means ask the pre-collection service to hold off sending any further letters, and also ask the debtor to work out payment arrangements with you for the balance, so further collection activities won't be necessary. For instance, using an approach recommended by Credit Network, you might write the debtor a letter that follows along this line:

```
Dear _____:
Thank you for your partial payment of $____ on
your account. We have accordingly asked our
collection agency, _____, to suspend further
collection action. However, please contact us
within the next 7 days, so we can work out definite
payment arrangements for the balance and will not
have to refer this matter back to the agency for
collection.
I will look forward to hearing from you in the next
few days.
```

Conversely, if you don't feel the amount is enough, advise the debtor that the payment will be credited to his or her account, but collection activities will continue (unless the debtor contacts you in the next few days to work out a satisfactory payment arrangement). An example of this sort is below:

```
Dear _____:
Thank you for your partial payment of $_____ on
your account. Unfortunately, this amount is not
enough for us to recall your account from our
collection agency. However, if you contact us
within the next week to work out a satisfactory
payment arrangement, we will recall your account.
```

Smoothing over your relationship with the debtor after getting paid

Having an outside agency send out letters for you may strain a business relationship, so it's helpful to try to smooth things over again after you get paid. Although some agencies will send out a thank you letter in your name as part of their service, your own letter adds a personal touch. In either case, you acknowledge that the account is now paid, and you look forward to doing business again in the future. For example:

```
Dear _____:
Thank you for your payment of $_____. Your account
with us is now up to date.
We'll look forward to working with you again in the
near future.
```

Using An Attorney

Making sure you have a good case

If your account is fairly substantial and you are considering going directly to an attorney rather than a collection agency or going to court yourself, ask yourself the same questions a lawyer might ask to find out if you are likely to get a lawyer to take the case. You need to be able to answer "yes" to each question or few attorneys will handle your case. The key questions are as follows:

(1) **Is the Case Profitable Enough?**

To determine this, look beyond the dollar amount owed, although this provides a starting point for analyzing the bottom line. Some other issues the attorney will consider are the following:

- Will there be any problems in locating the debtor or the debtor's assets? If so, this could be a long, drawn-out, time-consuming case, so that even if you win and eventually collect, taking the case can become unprofitable.

- Will the case be lengthy, complicated, or difficult? If so, the amount of money involved should justify spending the amount of time for preparation.

- Do you have a contract with the debtor providing that the debtor will pay attorney's fees if you prevail in a suit? If not, all attorney's fees have to come out of the principal due. Accordingly, the attorney has to determine if the commission will be sufficient to justify the efforts.

- Is the case likely to result in a default judgment or in the debtor settling before going to court? Or might a single letter produce a settlement? If the lawyer thinks any of these things might happen, that's a plus, because such a case is much easier and less expensive to pursue.

- Is there any chance the debtor might file a counterclaim which you will have to defend? This could be costly, even if you prevail—and an attorney may want to avoid such a case or may ask you to pay these costs yourself, though he or she agrees to take the basic case on contingency.

Think about these issues before you see an attorney, and try to have the answers before you go. For example, if you know where a debtor is and some assets are located, that's an advantage. And if you can show that the case will be relatively easy to settle, that helps, too.

(2) **Can You Prove the Debtor Owes You the Money?**

The lawyer will want to see documents (such as bills, contracts, and promissory notes) to support your case. If you only have an oral contract, that's perfectly valid, but it's hard to prove in court; and some oral agreements have to be put down in writing to be considered legally binding.

If you have a series of bills or letters to the debtor about the debt, that helps. However, the best thing is to have a signed contract, promissory note, or letter from the debtor about the debt (either signed or on the debtor's letterhead). In this way, the debtor can't dispute your bills.

If the debtor doesn't want to put the oral agreement in writing, another alternative that others use is to record a conversation with the debtor on tape. The recording will most likely be refused as evidence in court, but it may help convince your lawyer to take the case.

If there is a dispute, be sure to let your prospective attorney know, and present the arguments you think the debtor might use. Then, by looking at your documents and hearing your side of the story, the attorney can decide if your case seems strong enough to prevail.

Although you may be tempted to play down any negatives to get an attorney to take your case, don't. After all, you want your attorney to know all he or she needs to mount a strong case, and you don't want to hire an attorney who finds it difficult to handle any problems that are likely to come up.

Moreover, if there is a possibility that the case will be expensive or difficult to win, it should be considered before taking on the case. The reason is that even if the attorney takes your case on a percentage, you usually have to advance the court costs yourself. And, if it looks like it may be difficult to win, you have to consider a counterclaim by the debtor which, if successful, may turn the tables on you where you end up paying the other side.

Choosing a good attorney

If your account is worth going to an attorney, then choose a good collections lawyer. Although almost any attorney can send out a collections letter and draw up a complaint, you will often need more than that to collect in a collections case, particularly if you have a dispute or a debtor who tries to hide his or her assets.

Thus, your attorney needs to be well-versed in collections—not just an everyday business or general practice attorney. And if he or she specializes as a collection attorney, so much the better. Ideally, such an attorney should be a member of the Commercial Law League, which is the national association of collection attorneys, and should be handling collection referrals from the larger collection agencies on a regular basis.

The advantages of a collection attorney, as Arnold S. Goldstein described in his book, *Getting Paid*, include:

- The collection attorney is in a better position to find out information on the debtor, since he or she is part of a network of other collection lawyers who exchange information, much the same as merchants do when they join together to form a credit association.

- The collection lawyer is set up to handle collections cases on a systematic, efficient basis. As a result, he or she can zero in on the problem and select the most productive strategies to use, whether it's letters, phone calls, or meetings with the debtor, or filing the necessary documents at court.

- The collection lawyer knows a number of techniques to protect the creditor's interest which another lawyer may not know. For example, before the case even comes to court, he or she may try to obtain some collateral from the debtor as security or perhaps go for a pre-trial attachment. Or if the debtor is on the verge of going bankrupt, the lawyer may be able to get some goods returned to the creditor, or perhaps arrange for a sale of the business, which will bring in more money than if the business were to be liquidated in a bankruptcy. Further, if the debtor goes bankrupt, the lawyer can help protect the debtor with remedies other lawyers may now know about.

- Through practice, the collection lawyer has gained a valuable understanding of the debtor's psychology and an ability to be a good negotiator using this information. Thus, he or she knows how to negotiate and what to negotiate for.

In short, as a result of this background, the collection lawyer is in a good position to keep the case moving ahead quickly, whereas an attorney who is inexperienced in this area can easily let it bog down when the debtor puts up legal obstacles. And, of course, another advantage is that when an experienced lawyer writes or speaks with the debtor, the message will carry real clout—it won't be just another threatening letter or call with little to back it up.

Where to find a good collections attorney

To find a good collections attorney, check with the three main sources below:

(1) **The Commercial Law League.** This is the national association of collection attorneys, and it has a roster of members all over the country. You can find a copy of this directory at most law libraries, and many business libraries have it, too. Or write to the Commercial Law League, 150 North Michigan Ave., Suite 600, Chicago, IL 60601 for a copy of the directory.

(2) **A Good Local Collection Agency.** Since agencies refer their uncollected claims to attorneys, you can find out the name of the lawyer who handles their cases in your area. An advantage of using a referral is that if the attorney is used by an agency, you can be sure he or she is good.

(3) **Friends or Business Associates.** You may have friends or associates who have used an attorney for collections or know people who have.

Working out fee arrangements with your attorney

Attorneys work under a number of fee arrangements, depending on their assessment of the case, i.e. the size of the debt, how much work they'll have to do, etc. Also, the number of cases you are assigning can make a difference— the more cases, the more willing the attorney will be to work out a lower percentage fee.

The usual commission rate, if the attorney takes the case on speculation, is 33% to 40%, with the creditor paying any out-of-pocket costs for filings, depositions, long-distance phone calls, summons, levies, and the like. And when you take a case to municipal or supreme court, these costs can be significant. So be prepared to pay up to at least $70 merely to file and serve your suit, plus another $100 or so for routine costs—much more if the defendant puts on an active defense.

If you can, work out a staggered commission arrangement, based on what the attorney has to do to collect your debt. Some attorneys may even suggest this. This way, if the attorney can settle the case with a single letter or phone call, you pay much less; or if he or she can work out a negotiated settlement, your commission rate is a little lower than if you have to go to court. Examples of common commission arrangements include the following:

(1) Making a collection after an initial phone call or letter   10% to 15%

(2) Resolving the case through negotiation before filing suit   35%

(3) Settling the case after filing in court   40%

If you are in a strong position because the debt is large, easily proved, and the case is likely to be settled quickly either out of court or through a default judgment—you might try negotiating for a lower rate than the lawyer originally suggests. But otherwise, it's probably best to accept the lawyer's original offer, because you want the lawyer to feel your case is profitable and be motivated to pursue it. If you try bargaining too hard and cut down the lawyer's profit too much, the case may end up on the lawyer's back burner, or he or she may not want to take it at all.

Also, be sure to ask your lawyer what he or she will do about fees in the case of a countersuit by the debtor. Many creditors forget to ask about this, assuming the lawyer will do whatever is necessary to handle that, too. But not all lawyers will. Instead, they will charge you their usual fees to handle the defense, and that could get very expensive. Thus, before you sign on with an attorney, be sure you have reached an understanding about this point, and preferably get the attorney to agree to handle your defense at no extra charge. Point out that it is in his or her interest to do so, since if you get a judgment, the amount due on a counterclaim may be deducted from what you win.

In working out an agreement with your attorney, consider the likelihood that the debtor will countersue, and assess how seriously he or she may prosecute this claim. If you have a fairly open-and-shut case, or the debtor has been trying to avoid you, you probably don't have to worry about such a suit. But if you expect a dispute or a difficult defendant, discuss this with your attorney, so you can work out a reasonable arrangement to handle the problem if it occurs.

Mostly, you'll find that attorneys take collection cases on a commission basis, but in some cases, the attorney may ask for a fee.

If the lawyer wants fees up front, you have to decide if the case is worth pursuing. My recommendation is no, because you could easily end up spending more on legal expenses than the debtor owes and have little hope of getting any of it back, since you don't get your legal expenses back in court, unless the debtor has signed an agreement to pay legal costs if you win. Also, if an attorney will only work for a fee, this suggests that you may not have a very strong or economically profitable case.

In any event, in discussing fees and commissions with the attorney, raise these issues, listen to what he or she says, and then decide.

Have an agreement that the attorney will appear in court on the court date. Some attorneys will simply file and not appear.

Using a Collection Agency

Using a collection agency is most appropriate when you've given up on collecting the debt yourself and the debt is small—say, under $2,000. You think the debt can probably be mediated, and you don't care if you don't continue your relationship with the debtor. Turning your account over to an agency is likely to disrupt and possibly end your relationship with the debtor permanently. In short, using an agency is a serious step, much like going to court.

What collection agencies can do for you

An agency can't do much more for you than you can for yourself. The advantage of an agency is that it can do it better, because that's their business. Also, if you have trouble locating the debtor, the collection agency, with its skip tracing abilities, can help. Then, too, bringing in a third party debt collector may suddenly make the debtor, who has been ignoring your efforts, take notice. For now the debtor knows you are really serious, and if a credit rating is valued, the bill will probably be paid.

In any case, if you're on the verge of giving up on an account, you can't lose, even if you have to give the agency as much as 50%, because if you don't do anything or can't collect yourself, 100% of nothing is nothing. But if the agency collects, at least you'll get 50% or more of what it gets. And, if the agency doesn't succeed, it doesn't charge you (except sometimes a small set-up fee on small accounts).

Typically, when an agency takes your account, a collector sends out a letter or two letting the debtor know a collection agency has taken over an account and gives him or her up to 30 days to contest the validity of the debt or the agency will assume it is valid. If the debtor doesn't respond, there is usually one more letter, advising him or her to pay the debt (within 5 to 10 days) or further collection activity will occur.

In many agencies, this initial contact is set up as a pre-collection letter or free demand service, so you only pay for the cost of sending out the letters. Sometimes, you may even pay nothing if the debtor pays within the specified time. After that period, the account goes into "hard core" collections, and the collector makes more further contacts by phone. An example of a typical letter sent out by an agency is shown on the following page.

When the collector calls, he or she will use the kinds of appeals described earlier, which you can use, too. But the collector is highly trained in using these techniques, so he or she may be more effective than you in motivating the debtor to pay. Then, too, the collectors in most modern agencies have access to continually updated computerized information on the debtor, so they can easily find out the location, credit status, and assets—information you are less likely to know.

Another reason an agency may be more effective is the collector's persistence. Once assigned an account, the collector will follow up on a regular basis to variously remind and appeal to the debtor and confront him or her about missed payments and broken promises.

SAMPLE COLLECTION LETTER

COLLECTIONS UNLIMITED
100 State Street
San Francisco, CA   94100
(415) 321-1234

Re: _____   Balance: $ _____

Your account has been listed with this agency for immediate collection. Time is of the essence. Therefore, it is important that payment in full be made today.

Payment in full should be mailed by check, cash, or money order immediately upon receipt of this letter, or you can come into our office in person ... before we release your account for further collection activity.

If you have any questions, you may call this office at (415) 321-1234 for prompt assistance.

Unless you notify this office within thirty (30) days after receiving this notice that you dispute the validity of the debt or any portion thereof, this office will assume this debt is valid.

If you notify this office in writing within thirty (30) days from receiving this notice, this office will obtain verification of the debt or obtain a copy of the judgment against you and mail you a copy of such judgment or verification.

If you request this office in writing within thirty (30) days after receiving this notice, this office will provide you with the name and address of the original creditor, if different from the current creditor.

Unresolved questions regarding collection agency law or practice may be sent to the Bureau of Collection and Investigative Services, State Department of Consumer Affairs, 1430 Howe Avenue, Sacramento, CA 95825.

Contact: _____
         (415) 321-1234

With a hard-core, resistant debtor, you may get worn down by the process, but the collection pro is trained to keep after the debtor, knowing that some debtors, realizing they owe the money, will eventually give in when they see that the collection agency won't give up. In fact, some debtors may become so anxious about calls from collectors that they stop answering the phone or have others answer for them until finally, they pay what they owe, just to stop the process.

Some accounts given to collection agencies aren't worked very hard. Many experienced collectors will only work the "gravy accounts"—those large balance accounts that will pay in full within 30 days. They do this primarily because they are usually paid on a commission basis.

Your likelihood of recovery

Once a collection agency goes to work, how likely are you to get back at least some of your money? It depends on where the debtor is located, the type of debt, whether the debtor has any money, and other considerations.

Agencies are usually loathe to give out recovery rates, because so many factors are involved; but in general, agencies collect about one-third to one-half of the accounts assigned to them. However, these figures vary widely. For example, an agency collecting from debtors who live in a fairly affluent suburban area is likely to collect perhaps 70% of the money assigned to it; whereas if the debtors come from a low-income area, recovery rates run about 15 to 20%. Also, recovery rates for the debts of existing businesses tend to be in the 50% range, while rates for individual customers and clients tend to be lower—perhaps 20% to 40% overall.

Thus, when you turn over an account, be realistic and don't expect miracles. If you are dealing with a solid citizen or business that hasn't paid you, you probably have a fair chance of collecting once the agency sets to work, since the involvement of a third party is likely to spur some action. But if the individual or business seems financially shaky or irresponsible, recognize that the agency will have a tough going just like you. Using a professional can increase the odds of collecting something—but there are no guarantees.

The process starts when you assign your account to the agency. Collection agencies have outside salespeople, who regularly call on large companies to persuade them to assign their account to the agency. But if you're a small business or have a few personal debts to collect, you'll normally have to find an agency to handle your account yourself.

Once you decide on an agency, assign your account exclusively to that agency until you or the agency cancel this arrangement with the appropriate notice. This exclusive policy makes sense for several reasons. First, you don't want several different collectors descending on the debtor; you might run afoul of federal laws about harassing the debtor. At the same time, the agency doesn't want to spend its time on an account if there's no exclusivity.

To turn over an account, you simply fill out an agreement of assignment or write a letter to the agency assigning the account. Commonly, the agency has its own form in which you fill out as much as you know about the debtor. A typical form looks something like the example shown on the following page. The agency uses this data to evaluate the accounts you are turning over and to determine if it can handle them and what the commission fee will be.

Alternatively, if you have a large number of accounts, the salesperson may make an assessment during the sales call by asking questions about the accounts, such as how many there are and their average size and type of debt, to determine how collectible and profitable they are likely to be. Then, the salesperson will set the fee and afterward ask you to fill out the forms.

Generally, the agency will decide whether to take the account and for what fee based on the following five factors:

- **The size of the account** (The bigger, the more profitable to the agency.)
- **The nature of the debt** (If it's with a business, it will probably be easier to collect than from an individual.)
- **How long the debt is overdue** (The less time the debt is past due—or the shorter its aging period—the more likely the agency can collect.)
- **The type of debtor** (Is he or she a responsible, stable individual with roots in the community and easy-to-get-at assets—or is the person likely to be a problem?)
- **The likelihood of collection and the expected cost of collection, taking into account the other factors.**

Based on past experience, the salesperson or agency head will have a fairly good idea of whether your account is likely to be profitable by weighing the amount due and how difficult or costly it will be to collect. Then, if the agency decides to take your account, it will propose a commission fee.

Normally, the proposed commission will be 50% unless you represent a large company with many accounts or have a few large accounts that are only a few months overdue. If the account is quite small, or perhaps the agency has to do some skip tracing, the agency will ask for a small set up fee—commonly about $40 to 50—in addition to its 50% commission.

Also, the agency will usually establish higher fee arrangements if it has to turn the account over to an attorney or use its own legal department, since the agency not only incurs legal costs but has to pay a percentage of its commission to the attorney—typically the attorney takes two-thirds; leaving only one-third for the agency. For example, if the original percentage was 40%, you may now have to pay a 50% commission. Or the agency may ask you to front the legal fees, in addition to paying a commission.

If you feel there are special circumstances that make your accounts particularly desirable—like a large easily collectible account or a large volume of business, by all means, try to negotiate the fee, since fees can range anywhere from about 25 to 50%. But if not, it's probably best to accept what the agency offers, so it will give your account full attention.

FORM 4

1. Debtor's full name	Spouse	Amount due $
Last Address	ZIP	Phone	Date last charge

Occupation and employer _____ Date last payment _____

References _____ Bank and auto info: _____

S.S. No. _____ Drivers license no. _____ Your file or acct no. _____

Remarks _____ Check if mail returned _____

2. Debtor's full name	Spouse	Amount due $
Last Address	ZIP	Phone	Date last charge

Occupation and employer _____ Date last payment _____

References _____ Bank and auto info: _____

S.S. No. _____ Drivers license no. _____ Your file or acct no. _____

Remarks _____ Check if mail returned _____

3. Debtor's full name	Spouse	Amount due $
Last Address	ZIP	Phone	Date last charge

Occupation and employer _____ Date last payment _____

References _____ Bank and auto info: _____

S.S. No. _____ Drivers license no. _____ Your file or acct no. _____

Remarks _____ Check if mail returned _____

The parties above are indebted to the undersigned in the sums set opposite their names, the validity being capable of legal proof.

The undersigned agrees to report promptly ANY PAYMENT or communication received from any of the debtors, and to remit to any and all fees due; and further agrees that may retain any interest collected, unless otherwise specified in writing

_____ agrees to remit (less commissions, and interest collected) on or before the 12th of every month.

The above accounts are hereby assigned to:

* Name of creditor: _____

Signature and title _____

Date _____

Address _____
_____

Type of business _____

Phone _____

* IF CORPORATION OR PARTNERSHIP, (PLEASE STATE)

An example of how third party collectors are paid

Based on a hypothetical original bill of $1,000.00—if paid in full—the collection agency would receive $500.00 (assuming the agency took the account on a 50% contingency basis).

Of the $500.00 received by the agency, the collector will generally receive 20%, or $166.50.

The amount paid to the collector will not reduce the $500 you receive.[1]

Patience pays off

In some cases, an agency will ask for a contract assigning the account to it for a minimum period of time—commonly 6 months to a year. But many agencies don't believe in long-term contracts, so you can cancel at any time with a 30- to 60-day written notice.

But even if the agency gives you a short-term cancellation option, don't be impatient. Only about 10% of the debtors respond to the first couple of letters; most require some consistent follow-up, often for several months until the collection process wears down the debtor.

So, don't expect miracles. Just turn your account over to the agency and wait. If you have chosen a good agency, the collectors will follow up regularly and will do their best to collect in a professional way.

How collectors work your account

Once your account is assigned, the agency will either set it up for pre-collection or turn it over to a collector directly. If it goes through pre-collection, the pre-collection or free demand letters will go out first. Then, if the debtor doesn't respond, a collector will get it.

As soon as your account goes into regular collections, the collector or clerk at the agency will make out a work card to keep track of the debtor, using the information from your account assignment form or letter.

An example of what a typical work card looks like is shown on the next page.

If a pre-collection letter hasn't already been sent, the collector will normally start with a reminder letter or two, before making calls. Generally, these initial letters draw about a 15 to 20% response rate.

As the collector works an account, he or she will make continuing notes on the work card about the date of each contact and what the debtor said. Then, the collector will file the card according to what additional action is needed and when to take the action. For example, if the collector can't reach a debtor, he or she will file the card a few days ahead as a signal to call again. Or if the debtor promises to make a payment or call by a certain date, the collector will make a note of this and file the card according to when the contact is expected. Then, if the debtor doesn't follow through—as often occurs—the collector can immediately see this and re-contact the debtor to find out what happened and appeal for payment again.

When any payments are received, they go in a trust account maintained by the agency. Once they clear, the agency takes out its commission and sends the rest to you.

If the agency decides the only way to collect is to sue, the collector will let you know. Often the agency will advance any money needed to pursue the suit through its own legal department or an affiliated attorney, though some agencies may ask you to cover some or all of its court costs, just as an attorney would, particularly if the agency is skeptical of its ability to sue successfully.

DEBTOR'S WORK CARD

Client _____ Clt. # _____ Recv. _____
Name _____ Date of Last Payment _____

Principal _____

Spouse _____

Date of Last Charge _____

Charge _____

Address _____

TOTAL: _____

Phone _____

	Amount paid		
Date	To Client	To Us	Balance Due

Debtor's Employment

Spouse's Employment

Comments/Previous Communication

Additional Info. & Follow-Up

In some cases, an agency may recommend settling for only a partial payment on the debt. If so, the agency will let you know, and the final decision is up to you. But usually, when an agency recommends this, it's because the collector is convinced the debtor can't or won't pay and this is the best he or she can do, short of going to court and then having more problems trying to collect.

Should the agency decide that collecting on your account is hopeless, it will advise you, too. Then, if you agree, you can write it off, or try another agency. You'll find that one agency might collect where another can't for all sorts of reasons (a different collector's style; a better ability to skip trace and find the person; a more persistent collector; or maybe the debtor has just come into some money).

In any case, after a certain point, if an agency hasn't collected, doesn't plan to sue, or asks you to cover court costs, consider whether to go to court yourself or drop the matter. You have to make this choice because, after a certain time, if you don't sue, the debt becomes legally uncollectable because of the statute of limitations—two years if you have a verbal agreement, even though it may be evidenced by your own bills and letters; four years if the debtor has agreed to the debt in writing.

Restrictions on collectors

When a collector goes to work on your account, he or she has to be businesslike and professional, not only because that increases the likelihood of collections, but because federal and state laws place all sorts of restrictions on collectors. Some of these restrictions were listed earlier in describing the limitations on anyone trying to collect a debt; other rules apply specifically to professional or third party collectors.

The purpose of these restrictions is to protect the debtor from abusive, harassing practices and from attempts to defame his or her character as a result of the debt. Since many collectors at one time did engage in such practices, state and federal laws were passed to restrain the collectors.

Keeping you posted

Some agencies, particularly those which are computerized, will keep you posted on the status of your accounts. There is usually no extra charge for this service. In some cases, the agency will automatically send you a printout on your accounts every two or three months; though usually this service is for clients with a number of accounts with the agency.

You can also call the agency for an update. However, don't call too frequently—no more than once a month; every two or three months is probably better. The agency can't spend too much time fielding questions from its clients, or this will disrupt the collectors from their main purpose—getting on the phone and calling debtors.

If your agency offers a computer printout, it will look something like the sample below—listing the account number and name of the debtor, the status of the account as of the last contact (i.e., whether it's still active, paid in full, debtor skipped, made a payment, broke a promise to pay, etc.), the original amount assigned and that date, the amount collected, and the balance due.

More and more agencies are computerized and can easily provide this data. But if not, the collector can simply check the file cards and tell you about the status of each account.

DEBTOR STATUS REPORT

Your Name Your ID Code
Your Address

Collections Unlimited — (555) 321-1234

DEBTOR CODE NO.	NAME OF DEBTOR	STATUS OF DEBT	DATE ACCT ASSIGNED	TOTAL AMT ASSIGNED	AMT COLLECTED	BALANCE DUE	DATE OF LAST PAYMENT
032134-AB	Able, Dick	Act	2/04/93	$200.00	$50.00	$150.00	4/07/93
034572-CD	Bowers, Tom	Skn	3/03/93	300.00	--	300.00	3/10/93
035489-EF	Canford, Sue	PIF	1/13/93	250.00	250.00	--	3/08/93
049583-AG	Davis, Pam	Ban	4/07/93	125.00	--	125.00	--
109846-TW	Edwards, Sam	Pay	4/30/93	465.00	200.00	265.00	5/07/93
108594-GF	Franklin, Paul	Act	3/06/93	85.00	--	85.00	--
119706-SS	Graves, Nancy	PIF	4/16/93	150.00	150.00	--	5/01/93

Choosing the right agency

Today, there are about 5,000 or 6,000 collection agencies in the United States, ranging from the small neighborhood agency with perhaps three or four people in the office, to the huge agency, such as Payco, which is part of a national chain of agencies, with several hundred people in a single office.

How do you decide which one is best for you? There are a number of factors to take into consideration.

- **The agency should be professional.** It should use professional, business-like practices in collecting your account, as most agencies do, and it should have fully trained collectors working in the agency. You don't want to retain an agency that uses overly vigorous methods, which border on being illegal and may negatively affect your reputation. Also, you want to avoid an agency that's financially shaky, or you may end up having to collect from the collector. Thus, do a little checking before you decide to assign your account. For example:

    Ask how long the agency has been in business (5 years or more is a good sign).

    Ask to see a list of names of clients, or ask for some names of past or current clients you can contact. (If the company is big, allows you to see a printout on some clients, or shows you client letters, it's probably okay. Or check a few references to be sure.)

You might also call the Better Business Bureau or Chamber of Commerce about a small local agency. If the agency is a member or if there have been no complaints, that's a good sign.

The agency should be licensed and bonded. Ask to see credentials if you're not sure.

- **The agency should make you feel comfortable working with it.** You should feel comfortable with the people at the agency and the approach they plan to use. Often you can get this feeling by talking to the salesperson or head of the agency, but if you still have questions, perhaps ask to look at their collection letters or listen in to a few of their telephone calls. Some agencies will be glad to accommodate you.

  Use a small local agency if there is a good one in your area. The reason is a local agency will tend to be more energetic and persistent than the large agency, which is more apt to depend on letters and the power of its name. As a result, the local agency's collectors will be more likely to call debtors more and provide more personalized service, which increases the likelihood of collecting the money. Also, since the agency is local, you will be able to check on it more easily before hiring and also after it collects for you.

  Furthermore, if the debtor lives in another area or moves away during the collection process, a good local agency will have reciprocal arrangements with agencies in other parts of the country and can work out arrangements with them better than you can directly. If they do refer the account, you still pay a single commission, and the two agencies split the fee.

- **The agency should specialize in your type of account.** In this, way their collectors will be more trained in what to say to these debtors. The three major types of accounts are commercial and industrial, involving business-to-business dealings; retail, involving collecting from customers; and professional and medical, involving debts from patients and clients. Some agencies handle all types of accounts; but others predominantly deal with one or two categories. Also, some agencies specialize even further in having a large number of accounts from a particular industry (such as banks or insurance agencies). In general, you'll do best to select your agency accordingly.

- **The agency should be agreeable to the specific guidelines you set.** For example, you might want the agency to ask your permission before starting legal action.

- **The agency should have a skip tracing department, if needed.** If you think any debtors are likely to skip, choose an agency with a skip tracing department. Otherwise, the agency will probably give up on your account or only follow through half-heartedly, since collectors tend to follow the path of least resistance and work the easiest accounts which bring the greatest return—and therefore the largest commissions. By contrast, some agencies pride themselves on handling the difficult skip cases, and if that's your problem, it pays to use them.

- **The agency should have its own legal department.** The presence of an attorney confers more clout, even if there is no need to sue. For example, an agency with its own attorney, can say: "We'll turn this account over to our legal department" or "We'll take legal action, if you don't pay." But an agency without a lawyer can't imply it has one or intends to take action itself unless it can.

- **The agency should be computerized.** It's a big plus if an agency is computerized, and increasingly, agencies are. The advantages of the computer are many. Collectors can make a daily update of all collections activity. The agency can more easily do skip tracing and locate the debtor's assets. Also, the agency can more easily locate debtors by matching up the debtor's name, address, social security number, driver's license, and other information.

- **If possible, the agency should have a direct computer link to the major credit bureaus.** This is another plus, especially if it's linked to TRW, Trans-Union, and CBI. In this way, the agency can get a report on the credit status of each debtor in seconds. Also, if the agency can report the names of all debtors to these bureaus (unless you ask them not to do so), this is a powerful incentive to get debtors to pay off your debt. Many collection agencies still can't do this.

- **The agency should be local.** The collection agency should be located near the person or the company that owes the debt.

- **The agency should have connections with the collection industry as a whole.** For example, the agency may be a member of the American Collectors Association and the National Collectors Association. And, it will have associations with other agencies and credit bureaus all over the country.

- **The agency should not require you to sign any longterm contract.** In this way, you can assign the account for as long as you feel the agency is providing you good service—and many good agencies agree. They don't feel a contract is necessary, because they believe the client will want to continue working with them since they are doing all they can to collect.

- **The agency should offer a pre-collection or free demand service.** In this way, you only have to pay a small amount, or even nothing, if it can collect right away.

- **Avoid shady agencies.** This includes agencies which have a reputation for being too rough and irresponsible or which use a misleading name in its title, such as "federal," "national," or "United States"—a sign the agency may be engaged in deceptive practices. Likewise, if the agency's initials spell out CIA, FBI, or acronyms identical or very similar to those of other government agencies, that's another clue to watch out.

Footnotes

[1] John J. Harrison, *It's A New Day For Consumers*, Toledo, Ohio.

Chapter 9

Deciding To Go To A Small Claims Court

This chapter and the next chapter discuss some basic procedures of the Small Claims Court process. The specific details will vary from state to state, but this will give you a general idea of what to expect. You always have the option of going to municipal court on your own (with a good chance of winning if the case is relatively clear-cut), but few creditors take this alternative.

The basic procedures for initiating a small claims action are relatively simple—but at each stage, you can run into complications if you make a procedural error, or if the defendant decides to fight back. Most of the time, you'll find the debtor doesn't do anything—or even show, so you'll probably win by default. But, just in case, be prepared. There's an excellent book on the ins and outs of putting on a small claims case published by Nolo Press in Berkeley, California: *Everybody's Guide to Small Claims Court* by Ralph Warner.

The Advantages of Going to a Small Claims Court

When you are owed a small amount, there are numerous advantages of going to a small claims court:

- **There is No Need for a Lawyer.** You don't have to pay a lawyer to represent you, so if you win, you keep everything. Besides, if the amount is small, most attorneys won't take the case on contingency (which means you have to pay an hourly fee, in addition to the cost of filing in municipal court). Unless your agreement says so, you won't get back your legal fees even if you win. Thus, given what lawyers charge, you may end up paying more than your claim is worth.

- **The Process is Simple.** The small claims process is extremely simple, compared to the much more complex legal forms and procedures in municipal court. You merely write out a few lines describing why you feel you have a valid claim when you file your case. Then, when you appear in court, briefly describe your side of the case to the judge. Present any documents or witnesses in an informal way. You don't have to know all the procedures lawyers do when they argue a case in a higher court.

- **The Process Doesn't Take Long.** In municipal court, a difficult defendant can delay a case for months or years. But in small claims court, your case will normally be heard in a month or two, and the defendant only has a limited power of delay. When you appear, the judge usually hears the case in a few minutes and makes a decision quickly, based on what you and the defendant (if present) say in court. Then, you may find out the results on the spot, or you'll learn them in a few days by mail if the judge takes the case on submission to look at the facts more closely or avoid any problems due to announcing the verdict in court (like an angry defendant).

An Overview of the Small Claims Court Process

Determining the validity of your case

Before deciding to sue, determine if you have a valid case—and, if you can prove it in court. The key issues to consider are the following:

1. **The Question of Liability and Proof**

   When you claim a debtor owes you money in court, you must be able to prove the person or his or her business is liable for the money you claim. There are two main grounds for a claim; one is you have a written, verbal, or implied contract, whereby you agreed to do something in exchange for payment. The other is that a person's intentional or negligent behavior caused you to suffer monetary damage—or damages which can be translated into a monetary value.

   You have to think through the strengths and weaknesses of your particular case. If you have a signed contract for the amount owed, that's usually easy. But even so, if the debtor decides to defend, you'll have to show that it was the debtor who broke the contract and not you. Other complications include the debtor claiming you only fulfilled part of the contract (so he or she just owes you for that); the debtor arguing that he or she suffered damages (because the contract wasn't carried out); or the debtor even questioning the legitimacy of the contract itself.

   Likewise, oral or implied contracts are binding in court. But in this case, you have to prove you had a contract, as well as showing that you carried it out, while the debtor broke it. A series of bills to the debtor can be one way to show there was a contract; and evidence of work you performed based on this contract can be another source of proof. But again, imagine how a debtor might try to refute you in court if he or she shows up. For instance, the debtor might dispute the amount of the bill or say you didn't perform the work up to standards.

If you are claiming a person's intentional or negligent behavior caused you monetary damages, be aware of what the other person might say to claim he or she didn't do anything intentionally or negligently.

In many cases, the issue will be very clear cut: the debtor acknowledges owing the money, claims he or she can't pay and probably won't show up at court. But if the debtor has disputed your claim before, be prepared for a defense in court and consider the matter objectively. Is your evidence good enough to outweigh any arguments the debtor might raise? Or is there any chance the debtor might countersue, claiming damages from you (and even possibly win)? If so, it may be better to drop the case.

If you're not sure, this is a good time to see the small claims legal advisor and describe the facts of your case. He or she can advise you if you seem to have a sound case and good chance to prevail, or if you don't.

2. **How Much Can You Sue For?**

   Once you've decided you have a valid case worth pursuing in court, the next question is how much to sue for. In general, according to a popular guide to suing, *Everybody's Guide to Small Claims Court,*[1] if in doubt, sue a little on the high side because the judge can't give you more than you request, even if he or she feels you deserve it; he or she, however, can award you less than you ask for.

   Keep your claim, however, within reasonable limits and be prepared to explain (with evidence) why you are asking for a particular amount. In this way, your case is treated more seriously by the judge with a better chance of settling with the debtor. Conversely, if your claim is way out of line, you may have problems. For instance, if you have a $500 claim and sue for $1,500, you may make the debtor very angry, ruin your chances for settling out of court, and lose the respect and sympathy of the judge.[2]

   To figure out the amount due in an ordinary contract case (where you've done work for someone, sold a product, made a loan, etc.), simply subtract anything you received from the amount you believe you were supposed to receive, and that's the balance due. If the case involves damaged property due to someone's intentional or negligent act, the amount due is usually the cost of fixing the item, unless this cost is more than the item's cash market value. Then the amount due is generally limited to the item's fair market value—or what you could have sold it for—before the damage occurred.

   Normally, you can only ask for the principal due, unless you have an agreement entitling you to interest or other fees from the date due, can show damages, or there is some law covering the matter.

Getting Interest. If your contract does entitle you to interest, be sure to ask for it when you sue, because the judge can only award you what you sue for (although sometimes a sympathetic judge may allow you to amend your claim, and continue the case to another date, but don't count on this. Ask for everything you want in the beginning.)

And, even if your contract doesn't specify this or you have no written contract, you can ask for interest anyway. Some judges will be lenient and give it, others won't; but it doesn't hurt to try.

Getting Damages. Though you may be tempted to add in damages for the hassle of going to court, you won't get it. You only get damages for actual money losses or injuries suffered, not for what you have to do to try to recover.

In fact, the whole area of damages and remedies can get tricky, so if you're claiming damages, it may be good to get legal advice. In general, you need to prove you really were damaged to the extent claimed and were not able to protect yourself against these damages. This is because of a legal doctrine known as "mitigation of damages," which means that a person who is suing over a broken contract matter must take reasonable steps to limit the amount of damages he suffers.[3] For example, if someone hires you for a five-day project and decides not to have you work on the project after you do one day's work, you may not be able to collect the total due, unless you can show you couldn't get other work, though you made reasonable efforts to do so.

Similarly, no matter how upset or angry you are that a person hasn't paid you, you usually can't claim emotional or other damages, since this is normally a financial matter, and you shouldn't let yourself get unduly upset by it. But if there are special considerations—for example, you went into partnership with a friend who agreed to finance the business and claimed to make much more than he or she did—then, you have a possible basis for claiming extra damages.

In any event, if you feel you can back up your damage claims, it doesn't hurt to throw them in, as long as you keep them reasonable. The judge can always throw them out. The problem with making claims that are too outrageous is the judge may not only look at them dubiously, but they may lead the judge to raise questions about your suit as a whole.

The other advantage of including damage claims is they can sometimes inspire a reaction from the defendant and encourage a settlement, whereas the defendant might ignore the suit if you were only asking for the exact amount of the money due. The defendant might ignore this, since he or she feels the money is due anyway—and by not responding, he or she can prolong the time for you to collect. On the other hand, if you ask for much more, the debtor might get nervous that you can get a much higher judgment than owed and will want to settle. However, some debtors may react in the opposite way, so if you ask for outrageous damages, you might spur the debtor to fight back on general principles and thereby eliminate any chances for settlement. Yet as long as you can justify the extra charges, you can probably spark a settlement.

Filing More Than One Suit. If your claim is over the small claims limit, you normally have to give up the excess and sue for that limit. Unless you have a basis for bringing different claims against the same person, you can only file one suit and can't split up your claim into two or more lawsuits.

If you have grounds for arguing that the debt involves two or more separate contracts or incidents resulting in damages, you can try dividing this up. At worst, the judge will advise you to either take your claim to municipal court or combine the suits into one claim subject to the limits of small claims court.

However, one strategy may increase your chances of having your two claims considered as separate cases, suggested by *Everybody's Guide to Small Claims Court*[4]. You can file your actions a few days apart, so they will be heard on different days, and in most cities, by different judges. Then, unless the defendant appears and argues you have split your claim, you are likely to win both judgments without any problem.

But, there is one possible drawback. If you bring your claims on the same day, and the judge feels they are one claim, he or she will give you a choice of waiving the excess over $1,500 or going to municipal court. But if you go to court on different days, and the judge questions your split claims on the second or third day and decides you shouldn't have done this, he or she will have to throw out your additional claims. This is because once you have sued someone and won, you cannot sue the person again for the same claim.

3. **Who Can You Sue?**

    Before filing suit, determine exactly who is liable and how to name the appropriate parties in your suit. When in doubt, sue as many people or businesses as you logically can connect to your suit. That way, if it's difficult to collect from one debtor, you can always go after another.

    However, avoid including people for frivolous grounds even though the judge can eliminate any parties you have included incorrectly and you are probably safe from a legal countersuit for malicious prosecution in Small Claims Court; there can still be adverse consequences, depending on what the defendant decides to do.

    Who to Name in Your Suit. If you are suing a single individual, it's easy to decide who to name. You simply name that person and use the most complete name you have.

    If the person owns a business and was acting on behalf of the business when the debt occurred, things get a little trickier. Or if the person worked for the business as an employee, agent, sales rep, or independent contractor, you have to determine the right person to sue.

    In general, if the person is both the business owner and the person who owes you the debt, you probably want to do the following:

- Sue the person if he or she is a sole proprietor doing business under a fictitious name. In that case, he or she has all liability for whatever the business does.

- Sue the person and any partners if the business is a partnership, since all partners are individually responsible for the acts of a business, unless they are specifically excepted as limited partners, who have no financial responsibility.

- Sue the business if it is a corporation and the person was acting in his or her role as a corporate officer, because in most cases, the owners of the corporation are not liable for the business debts, since they have limited liability. However, if it appears that the person was acting outside of this role or if you question the validity of the corporation, sue the individual as well as the business.

If the person was an employee, agent, sales rep, or independent contractor of the business, you have to consider the circumstances. For instance:

- If the debtor is an independent contractor referred to you by a business, and not an employee, you probably should sue the debtor only, unless you believe the business was negligent in making the referral or received some compensation for making it.

- If the individual is an employee, the business is normally responsible for its employees' acts, so sue both the individual and the business.

- If the debtor was acting outside of his or her normal role as an employee (for example, doing you a special favor or using equipment borrowed from his or her employer), then probably only the debtor has liability.

- If you are suing an independent contractor for any work you feel was done improperly or not at all, and that contractor is bonded by a surety or guaranty company, then you have to sue the company that holds this bond.

There are also times where you can sue the individual's spouse, if you entered into an agreement with both of them jointly, or if they are jointly responsible for any damages.

If in doubt, talk to an attorney, and if you have questions about the type of business or the debtor's relationship to the business, ask. If you can't get the debtor to tell you, maybe someone else in the business will.

Filling Out the Documents. If you sue more than one person, you must list and serve each person or business entity sued to bring them before the court. Typically, if you are suing an individual involved in a business dealing, list that person by name, followed by the abbreviation: Ind. ("individual") and/or DBA ("doing business as"). For example: Jack Smith, ind/dba, Corona Brake Systems. Then, if you are suing the business as well, list the name of the company or the company owner separately. Be sure you have the proper name of the owner, because that's who you have to sue.

If you do make a mistake, all is not lost, because you can take steps to substitute the correct name either at the court hearing or after winning judgment. But it's better to know the correct name in advance to avoid the hassle of revising the records.

Finding Out the Correct Name. If you aren't sure of the debtor's personal or business name and can't find out from the debtor or the business, there are several reference sources which may have this information. You can check with the Business Tax and License Office where the business is located, since this office keeps a list of the owners of all businesses paying taxes in the city. Alternatively, try the County Clerk's Office in the counties where the business operates, since the office keeps a file of Fictitious Business Names, and corporations, as well as individuals, can use fictitious names.

Also, the Secretary of State's office located in the state capitol has a list of both corporations registered with the state and of out-of-state corporations qualified to do business in the state. Finally, there are special state offices that handle licensing individuals in certain types of businesses where licenses or registration is required (e.g., architects, certified public accountants, and contractors).

4. **Is There Still Time to Sue?**

   Another important consideration before you sue is whether your suit is still timely. You have to sue before the statute of limitations runs out. These time limits vary from state to state and for different types of cases, but some common time frames are the following:

   - If the debt is based on an *oral contract*, you have *two years* from the day the contract was broken to sue.

   - If the debt is based on a *written contract*, you have *four years* to sue.

   - If the debt derives from *damage to personal or real property*, you have *three years* from the date the damage occurs.

   - If the debt was incurred due to *fraud*, you have *three years* from the date you discover the fraud.

   - If the debt derives from a *personal injury*, you have *one year* from the injury or from the date when you discovered it.

   In some cases, you may think your contract is only oral. But if you have some documentation signed by the debtor, or an agreement prepared on the debtor's letterhead and signed by you—that turns your oral agreement into a written contract. For example, if you verbally agree to something and the debtor sends you a signed letter or memorandum confirming your arrangement, that's a written agreement. On the other hand, when you send out a confirming letter and sign it, without a signed document (or memo on the debtor's letterhead), you only have evidence of an oral agreement, since the written agreement must be written by the person who owes the debt. In fact, you may have to prove that you did, in fact, write the letter when you said you did—and that the debtor received it.

To determine if there is still time to sue, count from the day the debtor failed to carry out the agreed upon contract, or if the debtor missed a payment on an installment contract, start with that. In the case of personal injury or personal damage, start with the day any injury occurred.[5]

It doesn't matter if you are able to serve the debtor or have the trial before the statute of limitations runs out. But you have to file suit in some court to be able to sue.

If the time limit is up, get the debtor to reaffirm the debt, and then, if he or she doesn't pay, you have new grounds to sue. For example, if the debtor hasn't paid you for over two years on an oral contract, suddenly comes into money, and starts paying you again, this doesn't initiate a new starting date for the statute of limitations. The only way to start the time clock going again is to get the debtor to sign a new written agreement to pay you, thus reaffirming the debt.

Or if the debtor asks you for more time to pay or wants lower payments, one way to protect yourself should you later want to sue is to ask the debtor to either sign a note waiving the statute of limitations or reaffirming the bill. Then, you get an extra four years in which to sue.

5. **Where Can You Sue?**

    You can only sue in the Small Claims Court district for a city, group of cities, or a county, where you can establish jurisdiction, based on one of the following grounds:

    - At least one defendant lives there; then, once you establish jurisdiction, you can sue the other defendants in this district, even though they live elsewhere.

    - A personal injury or damage to personal property occurred there.

    - The defendant entered into a contract there, which does not involve a retail installment account or auto sales contract.

    - The defendant agreed to perform the obligation or contract in this district, and this agreement does not involve a retail installment account, auto sale, or furnishing goods, services, or loans primarily for personal, family, or household use.

    - If a retail installment contract or auto sale is involved, you can sue in the jurisdiction where the buyer signed the contract, resided when the contract was signed, or now resides; or where the vehicle or goods are permanently kept.

    - You can sue an out-of-state business if it sells its products in the district where you are suing, although in most cases you can't bring a person who lives or does business in another state into a small claims court out of that state.

- If you can show that an out-of-state business is regularly doing business in your state—through either sales in stores or mail deliveries—then by all means, try to claim local jurisdiction.

In the case of mail or telephone orders, things aren't all that clear. But generally, to establish jurisdiction, use these guidelines, based on the fact that a contract requires both an offer and an acceptance to exist:

- If the debtor calls or writes you to place an order and you accept it, the contract was probably entered into in your location.

- Conversely, if you call or write the debtor to place an order, he/she accepts it, and you send money, but he or she never fills the order or sends you damaged goods, probably the contract was entered into where the debtor is located.

In short, since there are many grounds on which you can establish jurisdiction, there are many places where you can sue. From these alternatives, choose the location that's most convenient to you. The worst that can happen is that the judge or court clerk will tell you to start again in another jurisdiction or will transfer your case to that location. And, sometimes, even if you have claimed the wrong jurisdiction, and the debtor doesn't show up or write to protest, the judge will go ahead with the case anyway.

6. **Have You Tried to Settle with the Debtor?**

    Before you sue, you should make a final attempt to settle, if you haven't already done so. In fact, many state courts require you to make this demand before filing suit, and many judges believe this should be in the form of a letter. However, the courts tend to be fairly loose about this requirement.

    In any case, whether or not this part of the process is required, it makes sense to make one last attempt, before going to the expense and effort of going to court. Thus, be sure to send the debtor a final demand letter or make a last phone call to work out a settlement before going to court.

    If the case involves a business dealing where you have had some past phone contact, by all means phone. Even if you're angry with the person or the business, it's usually better to try to smooth things over and work them out.

    If you offer a compromise, either verbally or in writing, you are not bound to it if the debtor doesn't accept it. You can still sue for the full amount. If the call does result in some agreement, write it now—or you may find you and the debtor disputing the terms of the agreement later. Then, sign it and send a copy to the debtor. (Ideally, get the debtor's signature, too.)

    The advantage of this written agreement is that it provides proof of what has been agreed, and you can use the agreement like a contract, promissory note, or supporting evidence in court if the debtor breaks the agreement (depending on whether the debtor signed it).

    One good approach if the new agreement represents a compromise is to state that if the debtor breaks it, you will go back to your original agreement, and the full amount of the debt will immediately become due. If the debtor resists signing, point out that if he or she keeps this new agreement, there's no reason to worry, and emphasize that it represents a new concession by you to settle the matter.

Thus, it's only right to go back to the full amount if this settlement doesn't hold, for why should you, the creditor, have to go through the same hassle to collect as before, but now for less? Anyway, a debtor who sincerely wants to resolve things, will probably sign. If not, you can always go right to court and sue for the full amount.

Should your efforts to work out a settlement through discussion fail—or you feel it's not appropriate to try (for example, you are dealing with a business across the country), send your final demand letter. If this is a straight business debt, the letter can be relatively straightforward, as previously discussed.

Below is an example of this type of letter:

```
Dear Mr. Jones:
After 6 months, your bill of $500 is still
outstanding. Since you have raised no complaint in
response to our many requests for this sum, we have
to assume this debt is valid, and this is our last
request. Please send it within 5 days, or we will
be initiating legal action to collect this money.
```

Or, if the matter is somewhat complex, the letter should describe the circumstances and your reasons for taking action if not paid. The letter can be useful in settling your case, or if it doesn't work you can use the letter to present your case to the judge in a clear, easy to understand way. To make sure the judge will read it, keep your letter relatively short and to the point. Also, be sure your letter sounds respectful and polite, so it won't antagonize the debtor and the judge will read it sympathetically.[6]

7. **Can You Collect If You Win—Now or in the Future?**

The final consideration before you sue is whether you think you can collect now—or eventually. To collect, the person or business has to have some assets—and you have to be able to find them. The most likely ways to collect are the following:

- The person or business pays you voluntarily.

- The person has a job, so you may be able to garnish his or her wages.

- The person or business has other assets you may be able to attach, such as a bank account, car, real estate, stocks and bonds, expensive jewelry or art work, payments from others, etc.

If you think the person or business you may sue is having financial problems or will make it difficult for you to collect for other reasons, ask yourself some questions to decide if it is worth it to sue.

After all, it doesn't make sense to go to a lot of trouble and expense to sue if you don't think you can ever collect. So, if you have a debtor who is struggling to make it on welfare, Social Security, unemployment, a pension, or disability check, that's a danger signal the judgment may be uncollectable, unless the person has other assets. Or if a debtor makes most income from free-lance work as an independent contractor, that can be a problem, too, unless there are sufficient assets.

Still, even if you can't collect now, it might be worth it to sue anyway, before the statute of limitations runs out, since a judgment is good for at least 10 years (in most states), and can usually be renewed for an additional 10 years. And much can happen in that time. For example, a struggling debtor can get a good job; a low-income free-lancer can suddenly turn a corner and achieve success; a business having hard times can pull out of it to become another IBM.

So my attitude is to sue anyway, if you're willing to take the chance and wait it out. You may not collect on everything. But the accounts you collect on may make it worth the small court fees and limited time involved to pursue most small claims cases.

On the other hand, if a person or a business is on the verge of bankruptcy and plans to list you as a creditor, it may not make sense to sue. In this case, a judgment only serves as proof of your claim and gives you no special priority when the debtor lists you along with other creditors. Whatever you recover, if anything, will be decided by the bankruptcy trustee—a percentage of all the assets divided up among listed general creditors. So, the amount you get will be the same whether or not you have a judgment.

Thus, before you sue, decide on your likelihood of collecting now or in the future, and if you are not likely to collect now, decide if you want to take a chance and wait. If so—go ahead and sue. If not, write it off and chalk it up to another experience.

Filing your case

After determining who to sue, where, and for how much, your next step is filing your case in court. The procedures in small claims court are relatively simple, and you can fill out the necessary forms in about 10 minutes. Also, costs are low; much less than trying a case in Municipal Court. For example, in some states, the cost to file in small claims court is about $6 if you have less than 12 cases in a district or $12 if you use the small claims court a lot (12 or more cases); in Municipal Court, it costs about $35 to file your first complaint.

To get started, ask the clerk for a form entitled *Plaintiff's Statement* (see the example on the following page), and if you have any trouble filling out the papers, the clerks will help, although they cannot give legal advice (like how much to sue for or what to claim as your cause of action). But they will tell you what to fill in where or explain any instructions that seem unclear.

PLAINTIFF'S STATEMENT

1. State your name and residence address, and the name and address of any other person joining with you in this action. If this claim arises from a business transaction, give the name and address of your business and complete a fictitious business name declaration on back of this form if applicable.

   a. Name _____
      Address _____ Phone No. _____
              Street
              _____
              City   State   Zip

   b. Name _____
      Address _____ Phone No. _____
              Street
              _____
              City   State   Zip

2. State the name and address of each person or business firm you are suing. See "Information to Plaintiff".
   If you are suing one or more individuals, give full name of each.
   IF YOU ARE SUING A BUSINESS OWNED BY AN INDIVIDUAL, GIVE THE NAME OF THE OWNER AND THE NAME OF THE BUSINESS HE/SHE OWNS. YOU MUST STATE IF YOU WANT TO SUE THE INDIVIDUAL AS WELL AS THE BUSINESS.
   If you are suing a partnership, give the name of the partners and the name of the partnership.
   If you are suing a corporation, give the corporations full name, and the name and title of an officer.
   If your claim arises out of a vehicle accident, the driver and the registered owner of the other vehicle must be named.

   a. Name _____
      Address _____ Phone No. _____
              Street
              _____
              City   State   Zip

   b. Name _____
      Address _____ Phone No. _____
              Street
              _____
              City   State   Zip

   c. Name _____
      Address _____ Phone No. _____
              Street
              _____
              City   State   Zip

3. State the amount you are claiming. $_____ (Do not include court costs)
4. Describe **briefly** the nature of your claim and **date** it happened:
   _____
   _____

5. ☐ I have asked defendant to pay this money, but it has not been paid.
   ☐ I have NOT asked defendant to pay this money because **(explain briefly)**: _____

6. From venue table on reverse side select the reason why this is the proper court for your case.
   ☐ Place appropriate letter in box. If you select D, E, or F, specify additional facts below:
   _____

7. I _____ previously filed a claim against this party. Case No. _____ Where _____
      have/have not

8. **IF YOUR CLAIM DOES NOT ARISE OUT OF A VEHICLE ACCIDENT**, give address below where obligation was entered into or was to be performed or where injury was incurred.
   _____ _____
   (Street address)   (City or locality)

9. If your claim **DOES** arise out of a vehicle accident, fill out this section:
   a. Date on which accident occurred: _____, 19____.
   b. Street or intersection and city or locality where accident occurred:
      _____
   c. If you are claiming damages to a vehicle, were you on the date of the accident the registered owner of that vehicle?
      ☐ Yes ☐ No (Place X in one box)

10. I have received and read the form entitled "Information to Plaintiff" and understand **I HAVE NO RIGHT OF APPEAL ON MY CLAIM.**

Date _____ Signature _____

PLAINTIFF'S STATEMENT   SMALL CLAIMS
(SEE REVERSE)

Form No. 214-127 (REV. 9/93)

Each judicial district has its own form, and there are some differences from district to district, but essentially, the statement will ask you to list the following information:

- Your name as the plaintiff, and the name of anyone else joining you as a plaintiff in the suit;

- The name of the defendant or defendants;

- The address of each person or business suing;

- The address of each person or business being sued. (If you aren't certain of the true name or correct address of the person or business, see the section on locating the debtor and his or her assets. Also, you can leave the issue open by listing the defendants whose name you aren't sure about as John Doe's I, II, III . . . . Then, you can fill in the missing information at court.);

- The amount being claimed;

- The nature of or reasons for the claim;

- The address where the contract was to be entered into or was to be performed, or the location where the injury occurred;

- The date or location when any vehicle accident occurred, and a statement indicating whether you were the registered owner if you are claiming any damages;

- The number of small claims cases you have filed in that judicial district in the past year;

- The reason you believe this court is the proper court to hear your case (because at least one defendant lives or does business there; because the injury or damage occurred there; etc.). You choose the appropriate reason from a list.;

Also, some *Plaintiff's Statements* will ask you to indicate whether you have demanded payment or not; whether the defendant has refused to pay or not; and whether you have previously filed a claim against this party and if so where and what case number.

Finally, the statement asks you to acknowledge that you have read and understand about small claim procedures and realize you cannot appeal any judgment.

After you fill out your *Plaintiff's Statement*, give it to the clerk, who will review it to make sure it is complete. If so, he or she will use this form as a guide to type out a *Claim of Plaintiff* form for you, and will assign you a case number. An example of a *Claim of Plaintiff* form is shown on the following page.

SMALL CLAIMS CASE NO.

– NOTICE TO DEFENDANT – YOU ARE BEING SUED BY PLAINTIFF To protect your rights, you must appear in this court on the trial date shown in the table below. You may lose the case if you do not appear. The court may award the plaintiff the amount of the claim and the costs. Your wages, money, and property may be taken without further warning from the court.	– AVISO AL DEMANDADO – A USTED LO ESTAN DEMANDANDO Para proteger sus derechos, usted debe presentarse ante esta corte en la fecha del juicio indicada en el cuadro que aparece a continuación. Si no se presenta, puede perder el caso. La corte puede decidir en favor del demandante por la cantidad del reclamo y los costos. A usted le pueden quitar su salario, su dinero, y otras cosas de su propiedad, sin aviso adicional por parte de esta corte.

PLAINTIFF/DEMANDANTE (Name, address, and telephone number of each):   DEFENDANT/DEMANDADO (Name, address, and telephone number of each):

Telephone No.:   Telephone No.:

Telephone No.:   Telephone No.:

Fict. Bus. Name Stmt. No.   Expires: ☐ See attached sheet for additional plaintiffs and defendants

PLAINTIFF'S CLAIM

1. Defendant owes me the sum of $_____, not including court costs, because *(describe claim and date)*:

2. a. ☐ I have asked defendant to pay this money, but it has not been paid.
   b. ☐ I have NOT asked defendant to pay this money because *(explain)*:
3. This court is the proper court for the trial because ☐ *(In the box at the left, insert one of the letters from the list marked "Venue Table" on the back of this sheet. If you select D, E, or F, specify additional facts in this space.)*

4. I ☐ have ☐ have not filed more than one other small claims action anywhere in California during this calendar year in which the amount demanded is more than $2,500.
5. I ☐ have ☐ have not filed more than 12 small claims in this court including this claim, during the previous 12 months.
6. I understand that
   a. I may talk to an attorney about this claim, but I cannot be represented by an attorney at the trial in the small claims court.
   b. I must appear at the time and place of trial and bring all witnesses, books, receipts, and other papers or things to prove my case.
   c. **I have no right of appeal on my claim,** but I may appeal a claim filed by the defendant in this case.
   d. If I cannot afford to pay the fees for filing or service by a sheriff, marshal, or constable, I may ask that the fees be waived.
7. I have received and read the information sheet explaining some important rights of plaintiffs in the small claims court.
   I declare under penalty of perjury under the laws of the State of California that the foregoing is true and correct.

_____   ▶ _____   _____
(TYPE OR PRINT NAME)   DATE   (SIGNATURE OF PLAINTIFF)

ORDER TO DEFENDANT
You must appear in this court on the trial date and at the time LAST SHOWN IN THE BOX BELOW if you do not agree with the plaintiff's claim. Bring all witnesses, books, receipts, and other papers or things with you to support your case.

TRIAL DATE / FECHA DEL JUICIO	DATE	DAY	TIME	PLACE	COURT USE
1.					
2.					
3.					
4.					

Filed on *(date)*:   Clerk, by _____, Deputy

– The county provides small claims advisor services free of charge. Read the information on the reverse. –

PLAINTIFF'S CLAIM AND ORDER TO DEFENDANT

Rule 982.7

SMALL CLAIMS PACKET 170-128 (1-93)

1. **Setting a Hearing Date**

    Next, the clerk will ask you to choose a hearing date within certain time limits based on where the defendant lives or does business. Each state has its own regulations on the proper time for setting a hearing; however, in most states, the hearing should be held 10 to 40 days from the time you file the papers if the defendant lives or does business inside the county where you bring suit. Or if the defendant is outside the county, the case should be heard 30 to 70 days from the date of filing. If there is more than one defendant, and one lives or does business inside the county, the time limits for in-county defendants apply to everyone.

    Also, the clerk will set a time for your case. Usually small claims cases are heard for about two hours starting at 8:30 to 9:00 a.m. on workdays to make it convenient for everyone to get to work. However, larger districts with a big case load often schedule other times (for instance, in some cities, sessions are at 10:00 a.m. and 2:00 p.m., as well as 8:30 a.m.), and these larger districts are also required to have at least one evening or Saturday session per month.

    You can obtain a schedule of hearing times from the court clerk.

2. **Getting the Defendant Served on Time**

    When you set your hearing date, take into consideration that the defendant has to be properly served by a certain time for your case to be heard. The proof of proper service must be filed with the courts in a timely fashion. If you can't get the debtor served within these limits, you can continue the case to a later date. However, since resetting a case can be a hassle (making an extra trip to court and possibly waiting for unserved documents to be returned), it's better to set the hearing date a little later to increase your chances of serving the debtor or choosing a form of service that will speed up the process.

    The time limit varies depending on where the defendant is served. For example, in some states, if you serve the defendant in the same county, you must serve him or her at least five days before the hearing is scheduled. But if he or she is served out of county, service must be at least 15 days before the hearing. Furthermore, the proof that the defendant has been served must be in the county clerk's office at least 48 hours before the hearing. In counting the days, include both weekends and holidays and the date of the hearing, although not the day the papers were served. Check the court in your county as time restrictions may be different in your state.

    If you don't serve the defendant (or all defendants) in time, the case will be dropped from the calendar. You'll have to request a continuance and serve the debtor(s) again. Or, if some defendants in the case have been served, your claim against any unserved defendants will be dropped from the suit, until you properly serve that person for another court date. However, if an improperly served defendant does show up in court willing to defend the case and you are there, too, the judge will normally hear the case.

To reset a hearing if you haven't been able to serve a defendant in time, you must give the original documents to the clerk, so he or she can change the hearing date. In turn, you may have to wait a few days to get them back from the process server or by mail.

Occasionally, the original documents are lost; if this happens, you need a notarized statement from the process server attesting to the loss, or an indication that the certified letter has been lost by the post office, since the clerks aren't supposed to give you copies with a changed date without this.

3. **Choosing the Date**

Within these time limitations, you can set the case at your own convenience. If you can't get your court papers served in time, you can always continue the case and set a new date. You might as well make the case as convenient for yourself as possible, since about half the time, the defendant won't show up, and if you are filing several cases simultaneously, it's easier to set them for the same date.

If the defendant plans to show up and has any problem with the date, he or she can always ask to change it. The defendant does this by contacting you to work out a mutually convenient date or by writing directly to the court. In the latter case, if you don't like the new date the defendant has obtained, you can always ask to change the hearing, too.

If you can work out a mutually convenient date, just write a brief letter to the clerk of the court, noting the case number and title, and indicating that you wish to postpone the case to a specific date or to a date after a certain time. If you request a specific date, it's best to give a few alternative possibilities in case your preference isn't available because the calendar is already full. For example, you might send in a letter like the following:

```
Clerk of the Small Claims Court
600 Washington Street
Oakland, CA 94604

Re: SC 61333 Plaintiff vs. Defendant

I have discussed the date for this case with Mr.
Defendant, and we are both agreeable to setting
another court date. We would like to postpone this
case to Thursday, August 25 at 8:45 a.m. if
possible. But if that isn't convenient, we would
like to make it either Thursday, August 25 at 5:00
p.m. or Friday, August 26 at 8:45 a.m.


                              _____
                              Pam Plaintiff


                              _____
                              Dan Defendant
```

If you can't work out a mutually agreeable change or don't want to contact the defendant, send your own letter to the presiding judge of the court. Explain why you can't make the date presently scheduled and ask for an alternate date. Note that in the previous situation, the court clerk handles the change, because it is a procedural matter in which you and the defendant agree. But if only one of you requests the change, then a judge must decide, and he or she must feel you have a good reason for wanting to change, though usually, any reasonable excuse will do.

Generally, the courts automatically grant the first two or three requests for change as a courtesy to the parties involved in the suit. But the courts have their limits. After a certain point, if it looks like you and the defendant are playing hopscotch with the dates, the court will send out a final notice saying, in effect, this is it and there will be no more change.

Thus, if it looks like you and the defendant are having problems setting an agreeable date, call and try to work something out to everyone's satisfaction. It may be difficult if you are barely speaking, but do so anyway or have a friend or business associate call for you. Point out to the debtor that it makes more sense to get something convenient for both of you, since the hearing will be held regardless.

Most of the time this problem won't occur, since most debtors won't show up, and many others will feel they have to keep to your date, since they don't know they can change it. Then, too, you may be able to work out a settlement before this date. But if this problem with dates occurs, try to resolve it early and effectively by talking to the defendant.

After you select a hearing date, the clerk will type the relevant information on the form (time, date, and location) which you both will sign.

Getting ready to serve your papers

Now you have to decide how to serve the documents. You have two options: mail or personal service.

If you opt for mail service, the clerk will send your papers by certified mail and add the cost of mailing (about $3 in most states) to your original filing fee. Alternatively, you can take the papers with you and arrange for your own type of personal service—through the county sheriff or marshal where the debtor is located, through a private process server, or through a personal acquaintance, business associate, or friend. There are pros and cons to each type of service—and you may have to try more than one strategy with a defendant who's hard to serve.

Also, be aware that the service you choose can affect when you set your hearing. For example, if you choose mail service you typically have to set your hearing date further off to provide enough time for getting back service; the time difference can be substantial. The specifics depend on how close the defendant is—in county, out-of-county but in the area, or outside your region or state. Check with your court clerk for specifics.

Normally, any costs you incur for serving the defendant will be added on to the judgment, although some jurisdictions have special policies. For example, some judges usually require that you use the cheaper certified mail service first (before using a more expensive method) to get reimbursed for your costs of service. Conversely, in jurisdictions where there is a high rate of no-serves on certified mail (because defendants don't sign), there is no such policy.

Choose the most suitable type of service, depending on whether you think the defendant is likely to accept certified mail and how soon you want to try your case. Since serving the defendant can be a major problem in some cases, your choice of method may make a difference in whether the defendant gets served.

The following discussion describes the pros, cons, and procedures of each method.

1. **Using Certified Mails**

    The certified mail method is the cheapest and easiest way to serve a defendant. So as long as you think the defendant is likely to sign for the letter (which is what's required for proof of service), it's a good way to start. Moreover, as noted, some judges won't reimburse you for a more expensive service, unless you try this and fail.

    In dealing with businesses and well-established individuals, you are almost certain to get a signature, since the employees or officers at most established businesses routinely sign for these letters, and many individuals will, too. On the other hand, some people, particularly those who are struggling financially and know they have creditors after them, won't sign. They can guess what an envelope from the courts is likely to contain and don't want to see it.

    Thus, if you believe the service by mail method won't work or want to have the defendant served right away, use one of the personal methods.

    On the other hand, if you think the debtor is likely to evade process servers, use the mail method first, even though it's likely to fail. The reason for this is there's a last resort you can use if you can show the courts you have tried every strategy and still haven't been able to serve the defendant—service by publication. Using the mail service first helps bolster your case of diligently attempting but failing to serve the defendant.

    When you use this mail approach, the court will send you a notice if the papers are returned unserved because the defendant didn't sign for or refused them. Then, you can pick up the documents at court for personal service.

    Yet, even if you don't get this notice, that's still not a guarantee the papers were served properly and the case is on. It could be that the proof of service did come back, but the defendant didn't sign for the papers soon enough to meet the deadline for an appropriate service. Then, too, the papers should be signed for by the defendant him or herself, not someone else at that address, though sometimes a judge will let this requirement go.

Check with the courts a few days before the hearing to make sure the debtor was served and the proof of service came back in time. It's important to check because if the papers were not properly served, the case will be dropped from the court calendar, and you'll have to serve the person again.

2. **Using Personal Service**

To speed up the serving process or to serve a defendant who doesn't want to be served, use personal service. Personal service can offer a certain dramatic impact that getting a letter in the mail lacks.

Another advantage of personal service with a debtor trying to evade process servers is you don't have to serve the debtor directly in many states. Instead, if a process server can't serve the debtor after making a reasonably diligent attempt to do so (usually interpreted as three unsuccessful tries to serve the debtor personally), he or she can use substitute service, which means giving the papers to an appropriate member of the debtor's household or to a person in charge of the debtor's office.

Anyone 18 years or older, other than the plaintiff, can serve the papers, either personally or through substitute service, where permissible, as long as he or she follows the correct procedures and is not a party to the action. (For example, you can't have a witness serve the papers.) So, depending on what seems best for you, you can hire the county sheriff or marshal, sign up a private process server, or enlist a friend, relative, or business associate. We'll discuss the advantages of each after describing the procedures for personal and substitute service.

3. **Procedures for Personal and Substitute Service**

There are certain basic procedures all process servers have to follow to make a legally valid service, plus the professionals have developed a variety of tricks and strategies to locate, identify, and serve the difficult debtor. Thus, if you ask a friend or associate to serve your papers, and they have never served anyone before, be sure they know what to do. Here are the basics and some common process server techniques.

For a Valid Personal Service

- The process server must personally hand the documents to the defendant. He or she can't put them in the mailbox or leave them at the person's home or job. So this means the process server must arrange to stop by the defendant's home or work when he or she will be there.

  Thus, if you know the debtor's habits, you can help by giving the process server this information (e.g., "Mr. Eckert leaves his house around 8:00 a.m. to go to work, and he's usually home after 8:00 p.m.").

  Or if the person is hard to reach at home or work, and you know what he or she does for recreation, that can help the process server, too (e.g., "John's hard to find at home, but he usually hangs out at the Pines Bowling Alley every night").

If you have the phone number of the defendant's neighbors or work place, this can also help the process server, for he or she can call first to make sure the debtor is there before going out to serve the papers.

- **The process server has to make sure the right person is being served by identifying the defendant correctly.**

Again, this can be a tricky area, when the process server doesn't already know the defendant, as is usually the case. Normally, when you ask someone "Are you John Jones?", the person will readily tell you yes or no. But some debtors, on the alert for bill collectors and process servers, aren't about to admit anything about their identity if they don't have to.

You can help the process server make the identification by giving as complete a description as you have of the debtor (e.g., "He's 47, graying hair, about 5'10", medium build"). And if you have a photograph, so much the better.

- **The process server has to get close enough to the debtor to make personal contact.** This means he or she must actually see the debtor and be able to talk to him or her, whether or not the debtor is willing to take the papers.

For example, if the process server is sure a debtor is home, but is not answering the door, the process server has to do something to make the debtor either answer it or come to the window and identify him or herself.

- **Once the process server sees the debtor, makes personal identification, and is close enough to make the service, it doesn't matter if the debtor refuses to take the papers, gets angry, or tries to run away.** The process server can still make a valid service by dropping the paper near the debtor, and telling the debtor, "This is for you," or "You've been served." The process server shouldn't try to force the debtor to take the papers, and, of course, there is no need to do so. Leaving them in front of or near the debtor is a valid service.

- **Finally, once the process server gives or leaves the papers with the debtor, he or she shouldn't touch them again, or the service will be invalidated.** Thus, after serving the papers, the process server should leave immediately.

For a Valid Substitute Service

In some states, a process server who can't serve the defendant personally can make a substitute service. An example of how the process works is described below:

First, if the debtor is a private individual, the process server must show he or she used "reasonable diligence" in trying to serve the person, which usually means making three attempts without success. Afterwards, the process server can serve the person by giving a copy of the complaint to another member of that person's household who is at least 18 years of age.

In handing over the documents, the process server must also tell the person what the documents are all about.

If the individual owns a business, the process server, after three attempts, can leave the papers with an employee who is apparently in charge of the office, and must likewise say what the documents are.

Finally, if the suit is against a corporation, three attempts are not necessary. The process server can leave the papers with someone in charge of the office the first time.

In all cases of substitute service, however, the process server must mail another copy of the complaint to the person to be served at that address by first class mail. Then, after 10 days, service is considered to be completed.

4. **Filing a Proof of Service with the Court**

    To validate any service, whether personal or by mail, a proof of service must be filed with the courts. In the case of service by mail the proof of service is filed with the courts automatically, when the certified notice from the post office comes in.

    However, in the case of personal service, the affidavit of your process server stating when and where the defendant or other party was served must be delivered to the court. Also, this form indicates the fee charged for service so you can be reimbursed (usually) by the court. The process server can either use the small proof of service section at the bottom of the *Claim of Plaintiff* or a separate form with the same information.

    Once the proof of service is signed and dated by the process server, he or she can mail or deliver it to the court directly, or give it to you to get to court. In either case, it has to be in the clerk's office not less than 48 hours before trial—or your service will not be considered timely.

5. **Deciding Which Type of Personal Service to Use**

    There are three types of personal service: (1) sheriff, marshal, or constable; (2) private process server; or (3) friend, relative, or business associate. For paid service, the going rate is about $10 to 25 for each paper served, depending on how far the process server has to go to make the service. Process servers commonly ask for up to three weeks, though quicker service is possible, and difficult cases can take much longer.

    Beside cost considerations, these are the pros and cons for each method.

    - **Using Your County Sheriff, Marshal, or Constable**

        A uniformed county officer appearing at the debtor's home or business can definitely have an impact. Also, in most cases, the sheriff, marshal, or constable charges less than a private process server, (for example, in some states, it's $14, compared to $20 to 25 for a private agency).

        However, there are some limitations on when, where, and how these officers can serve the papers, making them most appropriate for certain situations.

One limitation is they can only serve papers in their own county. In some jurisdictions, they only serve papers during normal business hours, while others work evenings and weekends, too. So check on the times covered by the agency where the debtor lives or works.

If the agency is restricted to business hours, it will be able to serve a debtor who is usually at home or at work during the day, or a business, where it can perform substituted service on the person in charge. But if the debtor is likely to be hard to find, preferably use another form of personal service. And if the debtor's address is a mail drop, forget the sheriff, marshal, or constable, because they can't serve the debtor or use substitute service at a mail drop (whereas a private server may push the regulations a little, if someone at the mail drop will take the letter for substitute service).

Another limitation is the sheriff, marshal, or constable could be a little slower than a private agency, since the officers will serve papers as the occasion arises while they are taking care of other regular activities, most of which have a higher priority. So if they are having a busy week, serving your papers could take a little longer.

But a big plus when you use these officers is you can be sure your service is good, for as an arm of the county legal system, they are careful to follow correct procedures. Then, when they have served the debtor, they send a form directly to the court, or if they can't serve the paper, they'll send it back to you.

The court clerk can tell you where to find the local county officer's office. Or if you are serving a debtor in another county, contact the sheriff, marshal, or constable in that county. Either go there yourself, or if you are too far away, call to find out the cost, and send a check or money order along with the documents you want served.

■ **Using a Private Process Server**

Since private process servers work around the clock and can cross county lines, they may be more appropriate for serving papers on some debtors. Also, since this is their business, they place a priority on getting your papers served, and they are good at using various tricks to find and serve evasive debtors, as described earlier.

Some agencies may try a little harder, too, than the sheriff, marshal, or constable, before giving up on serving your debtor. For example, some law agencies normally make only three tries, and then, if you request it, attempt substitute service. But some private agencies have their process servers make up to 10 attempts. Also, some agencies will notify you by phone after they serve the defendant and will send a copy of their affidavit of service to you as well as to the court. By contrast, the county officers usually only notify you if they can't serve the debtor. The private process server may find a way to deliver to a mail drop, where a county officer won't.

The main problem you may run into with some process servers is the validity of your service. The reason is that private process servers get paid when they make a service, not by the hour, like the sheriff, marshal, or constable. Thus, if a debtor is hard to serve, they have an incentive to short-circuit some required procedures or to claim they made a personal service, when they did not actually serve the person—strategy sometimes called "sewer service," when the process server throws the documents away.

More common, though, are the shortcuts. For instance, the process server uses substituted service, after making less than three attempts; leaves the documents with an unauthorized person; or perhaps wrongly claims he or she saw the debtor at a window before leaving some papers at the door. Frequently, since a difficult debtor won't show up or contest the service, the error or deception is overlooked. But if a debtor decides to protest, you can have problems.

Most private agencies try to police their people closely to avoid such difficulties, and you probably won't have any problem with an established agency. But since there is a high turnover of employees in this field, this problem can readily develop. In any case, if you decide to hire a private agency, check the yellow pages. You'll find many of them located near your local courthouse, too.

Some of the larger agencies have branches in other cities, so they can transfer your papers to the agency nearest to where the defendant is located. Others may charge you an extra $5 or $10 to cover the additional costs of having a process server handle the matter out of the local office. Or if the defendant lives or works quite far away, it may be more efficient to locate an agency based in that area; mail the documents with payment.

If you want to check out the agency, ask a few key questions: How long have they been in business? How many process servers do they have? Do they have more than one office? How many attempts do they make to serve the debtor? Do they notify you when they make service? Some agencies will also be glad to give you referrals—usually local attorneys who assign them papers to deliver.

Then, once you've selected an agency that appears reputable, sit back and relax. They'll do what they can, and you may be pleasantly surprised by how quickly they act.

■ **Using a Friend, Relative, or Business Associate**

At times, friends, relatives, and business associates can serve a suit. In most cases, they may even be ideal for serving your claim, and often they will do so without charge as a favor to you. In fact, sometimes a person you know can get into the right place to serve the debtor whereas a professional process server cannot.

However, before you immediately go after the people you know, there are some important issues to consider, because you don't want to impose on them, and in some cases they will be at a disadvantage as a non-professional, because they don't know how to deal with the wiles of a reluctant defendant.

Probably the best time to ask a personal contact to help is when you think the debtor will be easy to serve, because he or she is usually at home or work at certain times, and because he or she lives or works near the person. Then, your friend or associate won't have to go far and is likely to serve the debtor the first time.

Also, when you ask a contact to participate, the situation should be one where you feel he or she won't encounter any special problems, such as a dangerous or hostile debtor. Professional process servers are already trained and prepared to deal with difficult situations; but your associate probably won't know how to respond and may find the experience unnerving.

Finally, your friend or associate should feel comfortable about serving someone for you. He or she shouldn't be put in a potentially embarrassing situation, because he or she knows the debtor, or perhaps they have mutual friends. Then, too, if the person is involved in the case in any way (say as a co-plaintiff or witness), he or she cannot legally serve the papers.

But, taking these considerations into account, your personal contact can make an ideal process server, especially if a friend lives nearby the debtor or a business associate works in the same building as the debtor and is glad to drop off the papers on his lunch hour. In such situations, it's very easy, convenient, and safe to serve the debtor.

In short, in some situations you have a greater flexibility with friends than with private process servers, and it may cost you less. But in other cases, you're probably better off with a pro.

Getting ready to respond to the debtor

Once you file your papers, be prepared to respond to what the debtor is likely to do before you go to court, if at all. The debtor has a number of options which include:

- **No Response.** About half of the debtors don't respond, and most of these won't show up in court either.

  When the debtor doesn't respond at all before your court date, you can usually figure on an easy day in court, so a limited amount of preparation is usually enough. You have to show the judge enough to indicate you have a case, and normally then you will win.

- **An Offer to Settle.** Often such an offer will come at the last minute, after you think the debtor isn't going to respond. Commonly, in this case, the debtor knows he or she owes you the money; is afraid of going to court; is concerned about paying more than the original debt, if you are asking for damages; or hopes you will settle for less.

In this case, use your best negotiating skills to get as much as you can. But if at all possible, settle if you feel the debtor has made a reasonable offer (the usual rule of thumb in the collections/credit business is about 75% to 80% of the principal). It's probably worth it to take what you can get now, rather than hoping the person has money and you can find it later.

If you can work out details easily on the phone, fine. If not, sit down and talk with the debtor. Try to find out what the debtor wants or suggests to facilitate settlement. Often, the debtor will want to save face, as well as settle for as little as possible. After all, if the debtor has been trying to avoid you, he or she may feel guilty, hurt, or embarrassed. Or the debtor may want to justify not paying if a minor grievance is used as an excuse to avoid the debt. So, make it easy for the debtor to apologize and you'll make it easier for him or her to pay, too.

If you do work out a settlement, the defendant may ask you to sign something agreeing to drop the suit in return for the settlement. Or perhaps you might suggest writing up something, stating what you both agree. For example, you might say that as part of this settlement you agree to drop the lawsuit and will take no other court action. In turn, the defendant agrees to make no further claims against you on this matter. The following is an example:

```
This is to indicate that Dan Defendant has paid me
$500 in settlement of my Small Claims lawsuit SC
12345 filed in San Francisco, on December 1, 1984
(P. Plaintiff vs. D. Defendant).

In return for this settlement, I agree I will
dismiss the suit now pending and take no further
action in this matter. Also, Dan Defendant agrees
not to take any further action regarding this
matter.
```

Preferably, arrange for the debtor to pay the settlement with a money order or cash, so you are certain the matter is closed and you won't have to pursue the debtor again for a bad check. If the debtor agrees, you can either sign a *Dismissal of Action* form for the court clerk—or don't show up for the hearing and the case will automatically be dismissed. In fact, you might use this as an argument in getting the matter settled—if you can work out a settlement, and the debtor pays you cash now, the matter can be dismissed without a judgment being filed.

However, if the defendant agrees to settle but claims he or she can't get a money order or cash to you right away, I would suggest accepting a check on a provisional basis, so you will consider the matter settled if the check is good. But in case it is not, tell the debtor you plan to go to court and get your judgment, based on either the settlement amount or what you originally sued for. Then, if the check is good, file the *Satisfaction of Judgment*.

- **Debtor Changes the Dates.** In this case, you can figure that the debtor is planning to show up, and depending on the circumstances, will probably do one of two things, and possibly both:

    (1) Dispute the case or give an explanation to reduce the amount claimed;

    (2) Ask to pay the judgment over time, whether acknowledging the debt or trying to fight it.

    If the new date is convenient for you, it's probably best to go to court then. This will save you a lot of back-and-forth hassle with the debtor. But if you can't make it, you can change the date as previously discussed.

    Also, plan to do some careful preparation for this case, on the assumption the debtor will appear, and plan for the arguments or excuses the debtor is likely to make.

- **The Debtor Files a Claim of Defendant.** When a debtor files such a claim, sometimes changing the dates as well, expect a serious defense to your suit, and be prepared to argue against the defendant's claim, too.

    A *Claim of Defendant* is much like a *Claim of Plaintiff* in asserting the other party owes a debt for a certain reason. The only difference is that the claim is filed by the original defendant in the case. Importantly, the *Claim of Defendant* must be based on the same incident for which the *Claim of Plaintiff* was filed. If a defendant believes you owe him or her money because of a different situation, a separate case must be filed.

    Normally, when you start a small claims action and the defendant files such a claim, it will be in small claims court, too. But the defendant can claim a larger amount and transfer the case into municipal or superior court, depending on the amount. (For example, in some states, municipal court is for cases up to $15,000; superior court for those over $15,000.)

    If a *Claim of Defendant* is served on you by mail, by all means sign for it. If you don't, the defendant can hire a process server to serve you personally and you may have to pay for this. Also, the defendant can use your failure to sign as a basis for writing to the court to request a later court date to allow more time to serve you; or he or she can show up in court to ask for a continuance.

    So, to avoid prolonging the court process, simply accept this counterclaim, and prepare a defense accordingly. Typically, the *Claim of Defendant* will be tried at the same time as your suit against the defendant, and if the defendant is successful, the results may affect your own judgment, as would a successful defense. (For example, if you sue a defendant for $600, and he claims you owe him $150, your own judgment might be reduced to $450, if the judge finds for you both.)

    However, sometimes the judge won't consider a *Claim of Defendant* until after the original suit has been heard, and then only if you lose or aren't granted your full judgment. For example, if the defendant sues you for damages for bringing your case, the judge won't consider this claim, unless he or she decides against you, and even then, you usually don't have to worry about a *Claim of Defendant* based on damages for bringing your suit, since the courts don't want people to be afraid to use the legal system when they feel they have a valid case. Thus, as long as you can show you have sufficient grounds to believe you have a valid case, whether or not you do, and are acting in good faith, you are usually safe from a damage suit based on malicious prosecution or misuse of legal process.

Footnotes

[1] Ralph Warner, *Everybody's Guide to Small Claims Court*, Berkeley, California: Nolo Press, 1983, p. 37.

[2] *Ibid.*

[3] *Ibid*, p. 39.

[4] *Ibid*, p. 37.

[5] *Ibid*, p. 53.

[6] *Ibid*, pp. 59-60.

Chapter 10

Preparing Your Case And Appearing In A Small Claims Court

Preparing Your Case

In deciding how extensively to prepare your case, you can use the likely or actual response of the debtor as a guide. You probably need to do only a little to support your claim if the matter is relatively open and shut, as many claims against debtors tend to be; if you have received no response from the debtor; or if you don't think the debtor is likely to show up. And, of course, if you have managed to settle for a money order or cash, you don't have to do any preparation at all, unless the debtor wants to see your records before agreeing to a settlement.

On the other hand, if the debtor asks for a change of dates, is likely to show up in court to raise a dispute, or files a *Claim of Defendant* against you, you better do all you can to bolster your case and defend yourself from any legal attacks.

Handling the basics

In most simple debtor cases, where the debtor doesn't show up or appears primarily to give an excuse or ask for an extended payment plan, you don't have to do much to prove your case. Essentially, all you need to do is show the judge a copy of your original agreement or bills or letters or both to the debtor stating the amount of the debt. Normally, the judge will take your word for it, and you don't need any witnesses or extensive documentation to support you.

Commonly, the judge simply glances at your court file to see that everything is in order (e.g., the service has been properly filed and the reason for your complaint is clearly stated); scans the documents you have presented; and assumes, based on your word, that these records are valid. Then, the judge will usually give you a judgment for the full amount of your claim, unless you have asked for something inappropriate (such as interest or damages to which the judge doesn't feel you are entitled).

The whole process takes only a minute or two, and frequently, the court will try the uncontested cases first to get them quickly out of the way.

Handling a more difficult case

If you think the defendant might show up with a spirited defense or claim against you, do some extra preparation. Not only have the basic evidence to prove your case (such as a written agreement, letters, and bills), but have additional supporting evidence to back up your side and break down the defendant's defense or counter claim. It helps to think in advance about the arguments the defendant is likely to bring up as to why he or she doesn't owe the money and how you can counteract them.

Getting Documents and Witnesses

If appropriate, use additional documents or witnesses to bolster your claim. Many of these documents will already be in your own possession (i.e., letters, phone bills, and memos) or you can get them from your associates. If you need documents from a source that won't release them on your request alone, you have the power to subpoena documents.

People rarely subpoena documents to go to small claims court. But if you do need records from the police department, phone company, hospital, corporation, or other sources, you can prepare a *Subpoena Duces Tecum*, obtainable from the court clerk. On this form, you have to indicate the correct person who is in charge of the documents (usually the person in charge of the department where the records are kept, not the person in charge of the whole organization).

Additionally, you must describe the documents you want, attach a declaration indicating why you need this material, make three copies, and ask the clerk to issue the subpoena. Then, you must have the papers served via personal service. If you are getting records from a large organization, it's a good idea to check to make sure you have the name of the correct person to serve with the subpoena; otherwise you won't get the records.

If you need witnesses, you can often get them to appear voluntarily without a subpoena. This is preferable, unless a witness needs a subpoena to take some time off from work. After all, it doesn't make sense to subpoena an unwilling witness to testify in your behalf; if unwilling, he or she will probably not help your case.

When you do have a witness, make sure the witness understands what the case is about and is aware of your position, how your opponent is likely to respond, and what you would like him or her to testify about. Of course, you can't invent a story for the witness—but you can discuss the matter so your witness brings up the points you want to emphasize (for example: "I was present when Dan Defendant asked Pam Plaintiff to do the work, agreed to pay, and seemed satisfied with the work when it was completed"). In short, if you bring in a witness, it's crucial that the witness is prepared, that you know what the witness will say, and that the witness has agreed to testify.

It's preferable if your witness isn't a close friend or relative, since the judge may give their testimony less weight than a person you are not close to, on the grounds they may be biased in your favor. But, if this person is an important witness in a close case, by all means, have that person testify.

If you need to subpoena a witness, you can get a *Civil Subpoena* form from the court clerk. (See the example on the following page.) Again, you must have the person personally served, with the proof of service returned to the clerk's office in a timely manner. While some witnesses may agree to testify without a fee, if the person does request a fee, they are entitled to the amount set by the court. (In some states, it's about $35 plus $.40 a mile for a regular citizen who must live in the state to be subpoenaed; it's quite a bit more for a police officer—about $125 payable in advance to the county clerk, although you may get a refund if the police officer only has to spend a limited time in court.)

An alternative to having a witness appear personally is to get a notarized statement from the witness, which is a good substitute, if it is very inconvenient or impossible for the person to appear.

One other alternative when a witness can't attend for a good reason (such as being ill, out-of-state, or unable to get off work) is to ask the court clerk or the judge if you can set up a conference call, so your witness can testify over the phone. If you feel such a call is necessary, ask the clerk or send a request letter to the presiding judge, and if you are turned down, ask again when you go to court. To help increase your chances of the judge saying yes, ask the witness to write a letter to the judge outlining what might be said and why he or she can't be present to say it. In some cases, the judge may feel the letter itself is enough to accept the testimony of your witness—or the judge may decide to speak to the witness by phone.

Below is an example of a typical letter:

```
To the Presiding Judge:

On December 1, 1983, I was present as an employee
for ABC Travel when Dan Defendant and Pam Plaintiff
signed an agreement for Pam to do art work for the
firm. Then, again, on December 15, 1983, I saw Pam
give the work to Dan Defendant, and he subsequently
used this in a brochure.

Pam Plaintiff has asked me to come to court to
testify about this, but I have a new job about 30
miles away from the courthouse and it will not be
possible for me to appear.

However, if you would like to call me during the
trial, I would be glad to testify on the phone. You
can call me at the above number, and I will be
there at the time the case is being heard.

Sincerely,
```

ATTORNEY OR PARTY WITHOUT ATTORNEY (Name and Address):	TELEPHONE NO.	FOR COURT USE ONLY
ATTORNEY FOR (Name):		

NAME OF COURT:
STREET ADDRESS:
MAILING ADDRESS:
CITY AND ZIP CODE:
BRANCH NAME:

PLAINTIFF/PETITIONER:

DEFENDANT/RESPONDENT:

CIVIL SUBPENA
☐ **Duces Tecum**

CASE NUMBER:

THE PEOPLE OF THE STATE OF CALIFORNIA, TO (NAME):

1. **YOU ARE ORDERED TO APPEAR AS A WITNESS** in this action at the date, time, and place shown in the box below UNLESS you make a special agreement with the person named in item 3:

   a. Date: Time: ☐ Dept.:   ☐ Div.:   ☐ Room:
   b. Address:

2. AND YOU ARE
   a. ☐ ordered to appear in person.
   b. ☐ not required to appear in person if you produce the records described in the accompanying affidavit and a completed declaration of custodian of records in compliance with Evidence Code sections 1560, 1561, 1562, and 1271. (1) Place a copy of the records in an envelope (or other wrapper). Enclose your original declaration with the records. Seal them. (2) Attach a copy of this subpena to the envelope or write on the envelope the case name and number, your name and date, time, and place from item 1 (the box above). (3) Place this first envelope in an outer envelope, seal it, and mail it to the clerk of the court at the address in item 1. (4) Mail a copy of your declaration to the attorney or party shown at the top of this form.
   c. ☐ ordered to appear in person and to produce the records described in the accompanying affidavit. The **personal attendance** of the custodian or other qualified witness and the production of the original records **is required** by this subpena. The procedure authorized by subdivision (b) of section 1560, and sections 1561 and 1562, of the Evidence Code will not be deemed sufficient compliance with this subpena.

3. IF YOU HAVE ANY QUESTIONS ABOUT THE TIME OR DATE FOR YOU TO APPEAR, OR IF YOU WANT TO BE CERTAIN THAT YOUR PRESENCE IS REQUIRED, CONTACT THE FOLLOWING PERSON BEFORE THE DATE ON WHICH YOU ARE TO APPEAR:
   a. Name: b. Telephone number:

4. **Witness Fees:** You are entitled to witness fees and mileage actually traveled both ways, as provided by law, if you request them at the time of service. You may request them before your scheduled appearance from the person named in item 3.

DISOBEDIENCE OF THIS SUBPENA MAY BE PUNISHED AS CONTEMPT BY THIS COURT. YOU WILL ALSO BE LIABLE FOR THE SUM OF FIVE HUNDRED DOLLARS AND ALL DAMAGES RESULTING FROM YOUR FAILURE TO OBEY.

Date issued:

_____   ▶   _____
(TYPE OR PRINT NAME)   (SIGNATURE OF PERSON ISSUING SUBPENA)

                                          _____
                                          (TITLE)

(See reverse for proof of service)

Form Adopted by Rule 982
Judicial Council of California
982(a)(15) [Rev. January 1, 1991]
Martin Dean's Essential Forms TM

CIVIL SUBPENA

Code of Civil Procedure, §§ 1985, 1986, 1987

Getting Reimbursed for Your Subpoena and Witness Fees

When you do have to subpoena witnesses or documents, or pay fees to witnesses to testify, getting reimbursed is often difficult. So take that into consideration in deciding how important it is to have that witness or document there.

It's up to the judge to decide. Some judges are liberal and will give you back these fees if you win. Others are more conservative and will only reimburse you if they feel the documents or witnesses were essential to your case. If they feel your case was strong enough without the witnesses or documents, you'll have to pay all or part of the fees yourself.

Also, remember that even if the judge decides to reimburse you, you still have to collect from the debtor, along with any other money owed.

What Types of Supporting Evidence to Get

The type of evidence to obtain depends on the nature of the case and the arguments the defendant is likely to bring up about not paying. Without going into specifics, some of the evidence you might use include the following:

- **Your Date Book.** Useful for backing you up on the times and dates when you had meetings to discuss the contract, perform the work, etc.

- **Phone Records.** Use these to show when you spoke to the defendant or to others involved in the case. If you initiated many of the calls, your own records are probably sufficient; if not, you can subpoena the appropriate documents from the defendant or the phone company.

- **Letters and Bills.** Your own letters and invoices will help to present your side of the story. If you have letters or paid invoices from the defendant which support your story—so much the better.

- **Signed Agreements, Contracts, or Promissory Notes.** Ideal for establishing a debt. But be prepared to have other evidence showing you carried out your part of the agreement.

- **Witnesses.** They can testify you made the agreement or carried out your part of it satisfactorily. (For example: they can state you did the work, produced a good product, shipped the product properly and on time, the defendant appeared satisfied with what you did, etc.)

- **An Itemized Sequence of Events.** Making this record takes some work on your part, but it can be useful if the activities related to the debt occurred over some time, and can be better understood if you prepare a chronology, rather than just presenting your date book, phone records, letters, and other documents separately, which might be confusing. In fact, organizing this material will help you sort out the case in your own mind and will definitely impress the judge.

- **Samples of Your Product of Work Done for the Defendant.** If the defendant is questioning the value of the product you produced or the work you did, it can help to have the product or a sample of the work there, as well as other evidence to show you performed to the defendant's satisfaction.

- **Books or Papers Dealing with the Legal Principles You Want to Establish.** Normally, you won't tell the judge anything he or she doesn't already know, but you will show the judge you are familiar with the law and have really done your homework in preparing your case.

- **Notarized Letters From Your Witnesses.** These are useful if you can't get a witness to come in personally. I have also used unnotarized letters from witnesses written on their own letterhead; but preferably, have your witnesses get their letters notarized. Then, the judge is not likely to question the validity of your evidence.

Frequently, you won't need to present all or most of this evidence, because the average small claims case lasts only a few minutes and even contested cases are often resolved in 10 to 15 minutes. However, if you have gone through the process of collecting this material, you will be more assured when you present your case.

Getting Advice

Although you can't bring a lawyer into Small Claims Court (unless the lawyer is a co-plaintiff or is testifying as a witness), you can consult a lawyer for advice. You won't be reimbursed for any legal fees unless your agreement with the defendant entitles you to legal costs if you win. But you can usually get free Small Claims advice provided by the county.

For example, in some states, each county is required to provide assistance to small claims litigants either in person or by phone or letter, and depending on the county, this assistance is more or less comprehensive. In some counties, there are regular times each week when you can consult with the Small Claims Advisor—usually a law student, paralegal, or new lawyer.

These assistants can be quite helpful. They can advise you on whether you have a good case, what evidence you need, and how to file (or they will direct you to the county clerk to handle routine procedures). They will also go over the steps on how to collect. And, they will evaluate letters, agreement forms, or documents which you aren't sure about.

Thus, though you still have to be prepared for uncertainties when you go to court, getting some advice beforehand can be reassuring in a case where you think the defendant is going to fight. You have a better idea of the strength of your position and what to emphasize; and by being more confident and knowledgeable, you'll present a better case.

Appearing in Court

When it's finally time to go to court and it's your first time, the prospect may seem a bit awesome. But be assured, the judges and court clerk at Small Claims Court are very understanding. and in some courts, the clerk takes a few minutes at the beginning of each session to describe what will happen and how to present your case.

Assuming you've prepared properly, you should feel confident you know what to say. When your case is called, present your side of the story simply and honestly, and be yourself. Then, be prepared to answer the judge's questions, if any. If the defendant is present, take notes if he or she says anything you want to respond to. Then, tell it to the judge. In Small Claims Court, you don't talk to the defendant—just to the judge—so forget the dramatics of playing lawyer. You'll get further with a cool, reasoned, respectful presentation to the judge.

Getting there

Before you appear in court, it's wise to make sure your case is on. Call the court a day or two before it is scheduled to make sure everything is set; in that way, you don't waste a trip to the courthouse. You want to be sure your proof of service has been received successfully and that the case hasn't been continued at the last moment because the defendant came up with an excuse to postpone it.

The clerk can easily check the calendar to be sure your case is still scheduled. (If not, find out why, and take it from there.)

It's important to arrive at the courthouse on time—unless you have suddenly contracted a serious malady or there's a real emergency. The reason is that if you aren't there and the defendant is, the judge may ask to hear the defendant's side of the case and he or she may win. Or at best, the judge will drop the case from the calendar, and you'll have to start again. Alternatively, if neither you or the defendant are there, the whole matter will be dismissed; so you're back on square one.

In some jurisdictions, it's common practice to require the litigants arrive early, followed by a wait of about 30 to 45 minutes—so that everyone is sure to be there when the judge arrives. But in other jurisdictions, court starts promptly on time, unless delayed by an earlier court session that lasts longer than usual.

Presenting your case

Now, you are ready to present your case. But before you do, here are a few key pointers: First, be brief and get to the point quickly. Present only relevant information. You'll make your case much stronger if you're succinct and don't ramble or digress.

Secondly, talk naturally, comfortably, and sincerely. Be yourself. The judge doesn't expect you to be a lawyer. So, don't be nervous. Speak clearly and calmly as you present your case, as if you were telling your story to another person you know.

Also, even if you're not that comfortable with public speaking, don't read your statement. It's not only dull for the judge to listen to this, it's also less convincing when you read something than when you say it yourself. If it helps, write some notes to yourself on an outline card to remind yourself what to say, but limit these notes to the main topics you want to talk about; use an outline form listing everything you want to talk about in the correct order. Then, as you speak, glance at your notes to jog your memory, but be sure to look at the judge frequently and talk in a conversational way.

If you feel it's difficult to explain any part of your presentation, you can use examples or illustrations as exhibits to support your case. For instance, bring in canceled checks, photographs, or samples of merchandise to support your point. If you do hand over any materials to the judge, they will all be mailed back to you after the case is over.

Presenting a Non-Contested Case

If the defendant isn't there, your job is easy. You merely have to show the judge you have enough to make a case and normally you will get a default judgment. Before you start, the judge will review the case file to make sure the defendant was properly served and everything looks in order. Then, the judge will ask you to present the facts of your case. Since your opponent isn't there, the judge won't expect you to say very much—probably you can summarize the whole matter in a minute or so.

Then, the judge will commonly ask to see any supporting documents (such as bills, contracts, or letters) which you can pass on to the clerk who will hand them to the judge. Also, the judge may have a question or two if anything needs to be clarified. (For example, if the original agreement dates back a year or two, the judge may want to know why you waited so long.) And, usually that's it—you win by default, and the judge will likely announce the amount on the spot, plus your costs. As long as you have sufficiently documented what you are asking for, you will probably get a judgment for the entire amount.

However, at times, you may get a judge who is especially concerned about being absolutely fair or wants to give the debtor every possible consideration, even though not present, so he or she may hesitate before making a decision or may reduce your award.

Presenting a Contested Case

If the case is contested, normally you as the plaintiff get to present your side of the story first. Then, the debtor relates his or her position, and you have a chance to speak again, as does the debtor. And, should you or the debtor have more to say, usually the judge will let you.

Remember, whatever you say, speak directly to the judge. Don't talk to the defendant, even when you want to disagree; the judge will make sure you direct all comments directly to the bench. The rationale is to keep the discussion about the case orderly. Otherwise, a direct confrontation of the creditor and debtor might easily turn into a hostile shouting match.

In presenting a contested case, you can go into more detail than if the defendant wasn't there. Begin by describing what the case is about, why there is a dispute, and what your position is in the matter. For example, if the debtor hasn't paid because he or she has expressed dissatisfaction with something, you might start off saying something like:

> "This case involves some merchandise I sold to the defendant. Mr. Smith received it from me about six months ago and didn't pay the bills I sent for three months. Then, when I sent him a letter telling him I expected payment or would take some legal action, he called me for the first time claiming that there was some problem with the shipment. But he never said anything before this to indicate he was dissatisfied in any way. So, my position is that he owes me the money."

After you describe the situation, pass any papers or other supporting evidence to the clerk, indicating what they are as you hand them over. If you have brought any witnesses, be sure to tell the judge they are present now.

Don't worry about the debtor interrupting you (which may happen if something you say gets him or her angry), and he or she starts protesting. At this point, the judge will intervene and tell the defendant to be quiet and wait to present his or her side of the case.

Once you finish your initial presentation, it is up to the judge to decide what to do next—ask you questions, review your documents, ask your witnesses to step forward, or ask the defendant to speak immediately. However the judge handles it, eventually the defendant will have a chance to speak. As stated before, take notes so if you disagree with anything the debtor says, you can counter it when the judge asks if you want to reply or add anything.

For example, suppose a debtor claims he was dissatisfied with your product comments:

> "I didn't say anything right away because I was out of the country on vacation when the merchandise arrived, and the plaintiff knew this. Then, when I got back, I left a message for the plaintiff to call me because I wanted to complain. But instead, I simply kept getting these bills."

You might note this as the defendant talks, and then reply:

> "I did return the defendant's call. I left a message with his secretary, but he didn't call back. Then, when I sent the first bill, it said on it very clearly: 'All complaints or adjustments should be made within 30 days.' Mr. Smith had plenty of time to respond, and he could have called me again to complain if there was any problem because our policy is to make anything good, if that is the case."

When the defendant speaks, whatever you do, don't interrupt and similarly stay silent while any witnesses testify, even if you think they are completely wrong. You'll only get an admonition from the judge to wait your turn, and possibly anger the judge, if you try to interrupt.

Concluding Your Presentation with a Request for Costs

Often you'll get your costs added automatically, as indicated in your file; but just to be sure, ask for them if the judge awards you a judgment in the courtroom and doesn't specifically acknowledge them. Or if the judge says the case will be taken under submission, remind the judge about your costs, too.

You can't recover for your expenses in preparing your case or appearing at your hearing, which might include expenses like consulting an attorney, making copies, taking time off from work, or your own hourly charges for preparation time. Also, you can't add on any interest charges, unless you asked for them in your suit. And you can't collect your expenses for unnecessary witnesses or documents. What you can recover for are the following:

(1) Your fee for filing;

(2) Your costs for serving the suit (though in some jurisdictions you won't get reimbursed for a private process server, unless you have tried certified mail first or have a good reason for using an individual rather than the mails);

(3) Your costs for subpoenaed witnesses (if the judge feels they are necessary for your case);

(4) Your costs for necessary documents (such as corporation papers listing the officers of a corporation you want to serve);

Finding out the judgment

Frequently, the judge will announce the verdict in the courtroom, and in the case of a default, will almost always do so. Many judges like to explain their reasons if they can come to a decision in court, so the plaintiff, defendant, or both understand why the judge made that decision, and see it as fair, even if they may not like it. Also, this way, the parties to the action know where they stand when they leave.

However, if the judge feels the case is complex or feels announcing the verdict may result in angry, possibly violent, losers, he or she will probably take the case under advisement, or send the decision by mail, or both. If the judge does take the case for further consideration, he or she may ask you or the defendant to leave some documents. However, when you get the decision by mail, you will get your papers back.

Even though the judge takes the case on advisement, this doesn't mean the case is still open for further evidence. You had your chance in court, so forget about suddenly discovering extra documents and asking the clerk to give them to the judge. The judge won't look at them, and you may not get them back.

Judgments Involving Time Payments

Normally, a judgment will be for a certain amount, payable once the judgment is affirmed. However, after defending a case and losing, some debtors may request time payments—or if the judge feels a debtor may have difficulty paying, the judge will suggest this, knowing that a debtor who can't pay is more likely to ignore the judgment.

In fact, some debtors may appear in court who acknowledge they owe the debt or have no real defense, simply because they want to request time to pay. Others may put on a defense, but then ask the judge for time payments if they lose. In turn, judges commonly try to be fairly sympathetic to debtors as long as they have a convincing story,

If the judgment does permit time payments (in what's called a stipulated judgment), an additional amount will be added to cover the interest over this time period (now about 10%). Also, the judgment will indicate that if the debtor misses a payment, the entire sum will become due immediately (though, of course, you still have to collect!).

What happens next?

What happens next depends on the verdict, though whatever the verdict, the court clerk will mail you and any other parties to the case the official notification in the next day or so.

If you lose, it's all over, since you have no appeals from a small claims decision—unless the defendant has filed a *Claim of Defendant* and you lose. Then, you can appeal that to Superior Court by paying the required fees. But otherwise the case is closed.

If you win the judgment, there's a slim chance the debtor might pay right away. Or possibly the debtor might pay voluntarily after receiving a notice of judgment in the mail. But in most cases, it will take some time to collect, since most debtors won't pay up without some enforcement efforts by you. Also, you have to wait before seeking payment until the appeals period is over and the judgment affirmed (20 to 30 days, depending on the state) to give the debtor time to appeal. In most cases, the debtor is not likely to do anything. But you still have to wait.

Things the debtor may do may include the following:

(1) If the debtor has forgotten to ask for time payments in court, he or she may decide to request them. If so, the debtor may call you first to see if you are agreeable to such an arrangement. If this happens, it may be good to agree, if you feel the debtor is having financial problems, or if you think maintaining good will may help you get your money, since the alternative is chasing after the debtor's assets to collect. Should you make such an agreement, write up a statement of this agreement and both sign it, indicating that you both have voluntarily agreed to monthly payments, but if the debtor doesn't pay as agreed, the entire debt will become due. (Essentially, you are creating a private stipulated judgment.)

Whether or not the debtor contacts you, the debtor can contact the court clerk and ask to have the case brought before a judge to set up a formal payment schedule.

(2) If the defendant has appeared to argue the case and loses, he or she can appeal to Superior Court by filing the necessary fees, currently about $35.

The defendant has 20 days to do this from the date the judgment was entered. If so, you will receive a notice in the mail stating that an appeal has been filed against you. Then, it will take about 2 to 6 months before you are notified of the court date. There is no charge to argue against this appeal, although you are entitled to hire an attorney, as is the defendant. However, since the appeal is handled informally as was your small claims case, you probably don't need an attorney, and the debtor is unlikely to have one.

(3) If the defendant has defaulted by being a no-show, he or she has 30 days in which to file a motion to set aside the default. However, a very good reason is needed to succeed. The defendant usually has a better chance of success if a motion is filed within a few days of receiving the notice of judgment.

Some good excuses might be "I wasn't served correctly, so I didn't know about the hearing," or "I had a sudden death, illness or other emergency in the family and couldn't appear or notify the court about this."

If the judge sets the judgment aside, the case can be reopened, which means you have to set a new hearing date and present your case again.

Very few defendants actually do try to overturn a default, and judges tend to turn down such requests, unless the defendant has an extremely powerful case. This usually isn't a serious worry. But still you have to wait.

Waiting it Out

During this waiting period (in some states, it's 20 days if the debtor appeared in court; 30 days if you have won through a default), I would recommend being very quiet. Don't even contact the debtor unless, of course, it's someone you normally happen to see. The reason for this is you don't want to remind the debtor about the judgment because that might inspire him or her to file an appeal.

If the debtor does nothing during this waiting period to challenge your judgment, you have finally won ... with one slight exception which rarely occurs. Although the debtor can no longer appeal the verdict, a debtor can in some instances attempt to vacate the results for up to six months from the judgment date on the grounds of not being able to defend the case due to special circumstances (e.g., a serious illness or accident after being served). If so, the debtor has to ask for a new hearing within a certain time period (10 to 20 days in some states). But normally, the debtor won't do this, since he or she must appear at a hearing.

However, now comes what is often the biggest challenge—trying to collect!

Part IV

Collecting What You Win In Court

Chapter 11

What To Do After You Win— Your Alternatives

Once you win your judgment, you still have to collect. Sometimes this can be the hardest part. The key to collecting is knowing your options, deciding the best ones to take, and following through.

At times, a debtor who appears in court will pay you on the spot when you win. Or a conscientious debtor, whether present or not, will voluntarily send you a check.

But commonly, you have to make some effort to collect. You'll find some debtors much easier to collect from than others. Probably the easiest ones are respectable businesses, organizations, and members of the community. A phone call or a note will remind them to pay.

But other debtors will do everything possible to avoid paying, particularly if they disputed your debt in the first place, are having financial difficulties, or are just unwilling to pay. So, with them you'll have to use various strategies, ranging from reminders, appeals, and threats about what you can do, to actually employing one or more of the legal weapons now available to you. Yes, sometimes a consumer will dispute an account, even after a legal judgment. Remind the consumer that a judge has declared the debt valid and owed.

Your strategy and the debtor's likely response depend on the debtor's attitude, financial status, position in the community, and your relationship with the debtor.

The following sections describe the basic procedures. You need to know them if the debtor decides to be difficult, because then you have to make a serious effort to collect. The courts don't enforce your judgment for you. You have to do it yourself.

Yet, if you're willing to seriously invest the time and energy, you can probably collect on your own and save on legal fees. However, if things start to get complicated (for example, the debtor moves out of state or has hard-to-reach assets) and the stakes are high enough (say, $1,500 or more), you may do better assigning your case to a collections lawyer who specializes in collecting on judgments. You'll give up 30% to 40%, but the lawyer will know what to do and will act accordingly. In addition, you should plan on paying other monies up front for such actions as garnishment of the debtor's wages or assets.

A collection agency is probably not the best resource for collecting judgments unless your main problem is finding the debtor or any assets, since some agencies have good skip tracing departments. But otherwise, you will usually end up paying more to an agency than a lawyer for much the same result. The reason is that agencies usually require a 50% commission on judgments, and most agencies don't like judgments anyway, since the techniques they are good at—making telephone appeals—usually don't work, which is why you had to get a judgment. Then, once these agencies make a few attempts, they usually have to bring in an attorney anyway and turn over much of their fee to the lawyer. Thus, if you give up collecting your judgment yourself—you might as well go straight to a lawyer.

However, before you give up, there's plenty you can do on your own, if you plan your strategy effectively and are willing to persist to show the debtor you mean business and expect to collect.

Deciding to Collect On Your Own

Before you proceed to collect, wait until your judgment has been properly entered in the court records (commonly a day or two) by the clerk and, then, if necessary, wait for the appeals period to end, so that you're sure the debtor isn't going to either make an appeal or file a motion to vacate the trial proceedings if he or she didn't appear.

There are two major problems with acting too quickly. First, you may remind the debtor he or she has an option to retry the case. Secondly, if you start enforcement procedures too quickly, they are invalid, and the debtor has a potential cause of action against you to set these procedures aside and can even sue you for damages for their inappropriate use.

So, check the applicable waiting period in your state. For example, in some states, a Municipal or Superior Court judgment is valid as soon as it is entered, meaning that the court clerk has recorded or docketed it in the county's docket of judgments—a routine procedure that usually occurs a day or so after the judgment is granted.

However, in Small Claims Court, you usually have to wait 20 days after the verdict for the judgment to be affirmed if the debtor shows up in court or 30 days if the debtor has defaulted. The waiting period is to give the debtor (who has appeared and lost) the opportunity to appeal to Superior Court, while the debtor who hasn't shown up can either move to vacate the results and set a new hearing date or can file an appeal.

Once this waiting period is over, you can start your efforts to collect. However, the debtor who has defaulted may have up to six months to file a motion for a new hearing (in some states) if he or she has a very good excuse as to why he or she didn't appear at the original hearing (such as "I was unemployed and in the hospital" or "I was in jail and my life was falling apart").

Most debtors won't try to appeal, particularly when the amount involved is small or they clearly owe you the money but don't want to or can't pay. Thus, unless you suspect an appeal is likely, once the judgment is affirmed, start your efforts to collect.

Knowing your options

Your judgment gives you a variety of options for collecting, and you can pursue any number of them simultaneously until you get paid.

To be in the best position to collect, you should have a general idea of what they are. Then, you can use this knowledge for these two key purposes:

(1) To choose the major legal alternative (or alternatives) most likely to get your money;

(2) To tell the debtor what you can do to enforce your judgment to persuade the debtor to pay you voluntarily, so you don't have to use these procedures.

The major legal alternatives

Your first option is to choose the major legal alternative (or alternatives) most likely to get your money. Legally, the debtor has three types of assets:

(1) Real property, including a private residence, rental property, land, and other real estate holdings;

(2) Personal property or chattels, which includes any tangible items the person owns, such as a car, equipment, furniture, inventory, stocks, bank accounts, documents, instruments, mortgages, etc.

(3) Intangibles, technically called "choses in action," which include monies owed or paid to the debtor by third parties, such as an employer, consumers, or the debtor's debtors.

If the money is owed by a corporation, any of these items are fair game. However, if you are collecting from an individual or small solely- or jointly-owned business, the debtor can claim various exemptions. For example, you can only collect up to 25% of the debtor's wages, and the debtor may be able to claim a substantial homestead exemption on a home (up to $45,000 in some states) if the debtor or a member of the family lives there. Also, there are exemptions on personal property (for instance, up to $2,500 on a car used for business purposes or up to $8,000 for miscellaneous personal items.)

Then, too, other creditors may have previous claims on the debtor's assets. For instance, secured creditors may already have rights to specific items of property; and other creditors may have placed liens on the debtor's real property, which will take priority over anything you try to do. Or perhaps another creditor has previously garnished a part of the debtor's wages.

Thus, before you use the available legal remedies, it's a good idea to learn not only what assets the debtor has, but what obligations he or she already has, too, so you know what assets are actually available. You may not be able to find out everything precisely—but at least have a general idea. As we'll discuss, you can obtain this information either from the debtor directly or from the public record, as well as by doing some private digging on your own.

The major legal remedies

You will use certain legal remedies, depending on which assets you decide to go after. The specific procedures vary from state to state, so check with your local Small Claims Legal Advisor or look up the relevant civil procedure codes for your state. In general, though, the following basic procedures, used in California, are the same as or similar to procedures in other states.

(1) **Going After the Debtor's Real Property.** To go after the debtor's real property, you can do either or both of the following:

- Get a judgment lien attached to the property by filing an *Abstract of Judgment* with the county recorder's office, in the county where the debtor owns this property. This judgment lien doesn't get you paid directly, but it does place an encumbrance on the property and it establishes the priority of your claim, so that when the proceeds of a sale are distributed to creditors, you are paid off based on the seniority of your claim. So as long as there is money, each creditor in line will get paid off. Also, if the property is transferred or conveyed to someone else, your lien stays on it; so if you haven't already been paid off by the debtor through some other means, you may still get your money from a subsequent owner. You will usually not get paid until the property is sold.

- Get a *Writ of Execution* to force a sale of the property. By forcing a sale, you may be able to get your money from the property at once. But you must know what you are doing and have enough money to cover the costs of the sale, or this can be a very costly adventure. This is because when you force a sale, you must put up a large deposit to cover the costs of the sale. Then, if the sale goes through, the proceeds go first to the sheriff, marshal, or constable to cover the costs of the sale (as much as a few thousand dollars), and then they are distributed to pay off any mortgages, exemptions, and senior liens on the property before yours. Thus, if a sale isn't likely to bring in enough so there's money left to pay you, there's no point in forcing a sale. Also, if you don't get the minimum bid needed to cover expenses, you'll end up footing the bill. Thus, be very cautious before trying to force a sale. It may be wiser to simply get your lien and wait until the debtor sells the property or someone else forces a sale.

(2) **Going After the Debtor's Real Property.** To go after the debtor's personal property, you need to get a *Writ of Execution* and give it to the sheriff, marshal, or constable to levy on the property. Also, you need to include a letter of instructions which specifies very clearly what this property is and where the officer can find it. For example, if it's a bank account, you need to specify the bank, branch, and account number. If it's a car, you need to specify the make, license number, and where the car is located. If it's equipment, furniture, or inventory, you have to describe it in detail. Or if it's cash or checks the debtor will be receiving while operating a going business, you must state this, too.

Then, if the officer has obtained cash or checks, he or she will deduct the fee first from your deposit, and the rest will go to you. Or if the officer has collected specific items of property, he will hold an auction sale (subject to various procedures, including notifying the debtor, so the debtor has a chance to file for exemptions or protest the sale). When the sale is over, the deputy takes the fees off the top, and you get the rest.

Also, in the case of certain types of personal property, you have another way to protect yourself in some states, though this method is not often used by individual creditors. You can put a judgment lien on the property, which attaches like a lien does to real estate. This way you preserve your rights in this property prior to its sale. Primarily, this lien is used for the type of property involved in running a business—such as accounts receivable, equipment, farm products, inventory, negotiable documents, and chattel paper. You create this lien by filing a *Notice of Judgment Lien* in the office of the Secretary of State.

(3) **Going after the money due a debtor from third parties.** To go after the money due a debtor from third parties, including employers, you have to use garnishment procedures. These procedures require the person who owes the debtor money to pay over a certain amount to you, rather than to the debtor. If you are garnishing money from an employer, you can get up to 25%. In other third party actions, you can generally get it all. Then, if the other party doesn't pay you without a good reason (for example, an employer claims the debtor no longer works there), that person becomes liable for the amount garnished and you can obtain a judgment against that person.

An example of the 25% garnishment: A debtor who earns $1,000 per paycheck has his or her wages garnished. You can collect $250 per paycheck (the law may be different in some states, and you may only be able to collect the $250 once a month). The garnishment continues until the judgment is satisfied.

To garnish a person's wages, use a *Writ of Execution* and write your instructions on an *Application for Earnings Withholding Order*. Or to collect money owed the debtor by other third party debtors, you also use a

Writ plus garnishment instructions. As with writs for other purposes, you obtain and file them in the court where the judgment was issued. Then, you take them to the sheriff, marshal, or constable in the county where the garnishment is to occur for execution.

The costs of these remedies and getting back your costs

All of these remedies cost money, although you will generally get everything back if you collect from the debtor.

The expenses you can get back from the debtor include the costs of the following:

(1) Filing legal papers

(2) Serving the papers

(3) Having an officer execute a levy to collect money

(4) Having an officer seize and store property or execute a sale. Also, you can add on the interest which has accumulated since your judgment at the going rate in your state. However, you can't normally collect for any lawyer's fees involved in collections.

Some of these fees can be relatively nominal. For instance, it's about $3 to 4 to file papers and $14 for the sheriff, marshal, or constable to serve them. But if you want an officer to spend a day collecting money, that will be about $50, and if the officer starts seizing property and storing it, the costs can mount up. You have to cover those costs in advance. For instance, to have a sheriff seize a car, you have to come up with about $300 ($400 for a truck.)

Weigh the remedies you choose against the likelihood of collecting and getting back your costs. If you incur costs in excess of what seems reasonable to the courts, you may not get everything back, if the debtor challenges the costs you have added. For example, if you have a sale and it is unsuccessful, you may not be able to get back your costs of having the sale. Or if you repeatedly send the sheriff to collect from a business or bank account which has no money, the court may consider your collection costs excessive and throw them out.

In order to get back your expenses, you have to file a memorandum of costs with the courts. (It may have a different name such as a *Memorandum of Credits, Accrued Interest and Costs After Judgment*.) This indicates how much the debtor has paid you and you deduct this from the amount owed. Then you add on your various fees for filings, notary fees, serving supplementary papers, and fees to the sheriff, marshal, or constable. Unless the debtor questions these figures, they are added on to the judgment.

The importance of accuracy in using legal remedies

Once you start using these legal remedies, be careful to be accurate in giving instructions to the levying officer. If you make a mistake, act quickly to correct it. Otherwise, you may not only end up not getting back your costs due to errors, you may also end up paying additional money to the debtor for overzealous collection activities or to others from whom you have mistakenly tried to collect.

For example, if you send over the sheriff to pick up some property at the debtor's place of business, be sure the debtor owns it or there's a high probability of this. Generally, you can go on the assumption that any property in a place under the control of the debtor is also owned or controlled by the debtor. But if the debtor presents documents indicates that someone else owns the property, the sheriff either won't take it, or subsequently, you have to give it back.

As long as you make an error in good faith or make a mistake a reasonable person might make, you can usually rectify the error without any serious consequences. You may not be able to get back your costs, but by putting things right, you don't have to worry about damages.

However, if you don't correct an error in time, watch out. Either the debtor or the person you incorrectly tried to collect from can sue you for damages. For example, suppose you have the sheriff pick up a car you think belongs to the debtor, but the person merely has the same name and files a statement saying he is not the debtor within the required 10-day response period. You must return the car. If you don't, and the sheriff goes ahead and sells it, you not only owe the person for the car, you can also be sued for damages.

Similarly, find out and follow all the legal procedures in your jurisdiction exactly. If there's a requirement to notify the debtor by personal service at least 10 days before a sale, be sure you so direct the levying officer to notify the debtor. And, if any third parties are involved that need to be notified, be sure they are notified, too. The reason for following these procedures religiously is that if anything is even the slightest degree out of order—and the courts can be real sticklers for rules and procedures—the debtor or an involved third party has grounds for invalidating the whole collection process. That can result in a variety of untoward results—you can not only fail to collect what you intended, but you may have to give back what you already collected. Furthermore, the debtor may be able to sue you for damages for the abuse or misuse of the collection process.

Conversely, if you don't act in a timely fashion, you may lose the power of the remedies you have. For instance, if you don't get a *Writ of Execution* to act on a judgment in some states within a certain time from the date of judgment, the judgment becomes inactive, and you have to revive or renew it by filing an application or initiating a court action for a summary judgment lien based on the original judgment. Or if you don't renew a judgment lien on personal or real property in time, it will lose its force, too.

In short, once you make a decision to use the legal remedies available to you, know how to use them, and be prepared to follow through appropriately to collect.

Choosing the best remedy to collect

As we'll discuss later, the best remedy is to try to avoid using a legal remedy by working something out with the debtor.

But, if you can't do that, the following are some of the easiest remedies you can use yourself, depending on the types of assets the debtor has. Subsequent sections will describe how to use each of these remedies, which include the following:

(1) Garnishing the wages of a debtor who works at a regular job. (Bear in mind, however, that wages paid at the federal minimum rate cannot be garnished.) In addition, the debtor will receive a 15-day notice before the garnishment. This will allow the debtor to pay in a cooperative manner, without a garnishment.

(2) Levying against the debtor's bank account (assuming it has a substantial amount of money in it).

(3) Arranging for a sheriff, marshal, or constable to be a keeper in a going business and collect any receipts that come in (sometimes known as a "till tap").

(4) Levying against some major items of personal property (like a car, expensive computer or video system) and directing the levying officer to conduct an execution sale (assuming the value of the property is more than any exemptions and the cost of conducting the sale.)

(5) Placing a judgment lien on some real property the debtor owns (as long as the debtor's equity in the property is more than the outstanding liens, mortgages, and exemptions, so there's something left to collect).

Other complications

Usually, with some persistence, you'll find the legal collection process fairly routine. However, things can get complicated under a number of circumstances. If so, you'll have to do more to collect. For example, you may need to do additional research to find the debtor's assets and determine how to get at them, and at a certain point, you may need an attorney to proceed. Some of these complications may include the following:

(1) The debtor or the business goes bankrupt.

(2) The debtor has concealed most of his or her assets through various business entities and fronts.

(3) The debtor has enlisted a number of friends and relatives to hide his or her property from creditors.

(4) The debtor has left town and is difficult to find.

(5) The debtor has moved to the other end of the state—or has moved to another state or country.

(6) The debtor gets divorced, and it's hard to determine what property still belongs to the debtor.

(7) The debtor dies and the estate goes into probate.

(8) The debtor is resisting your collection efforts by filing a variety of claims—for exemptions, for improper service, for misuse or abuse of legal process, etc.

Getting the debtor to pay voluntarily

Your second option in collecting is to get the debtor to pay voluntarily. It's less expensive and time consuming than legal procedures, and it makes it easier than collecting from an unwilling debtor.

Thus, if the debtor doesn't pay within a week or so of being notified of the judgment by the court, try to work things out with the debtor. To do so, start with a modified version of the appeals process to motivate the debtor. Begin with a reminder, and, then, if necessary, follow up with a few appeals before you begin legal enforcement procedures. In the process, you may have to negotiate and be willing to settle for less than the full amount—but it may be worth it, compared to the hassle involved in getting the whole thing.

Reminding the Debtor

Depending on circumstances, you can remind the debtor with a phone call or brief letter. A phone call works well if you know the debtor and he or she is local. If the debtor lives out of the area or is a business contact, send a letter.

Most likely, the debtor already knows about the judgment, since he or she has been in court or has received a formal notification in the mail. However, your reminder does two important things:

(1) It lets the debtor know you are serious in your efforts to collect.

(2) It opens up a channel of communication with the debtor, so you can try to work something out without using legal enforcement procedures.

Don't have overly high expectations that the reminder will produce immediate results. Commonly, it's best to view the reminder as simply the first step—your opening gambit—in the after-judgment negotiation process. Through the reminder, you are notifying the debtor that you would like to work out a payment arrangement and plan to proceed further if you can't get a voluntary agreement.

Then, wait for the debtor's response to decide what to do (e.g., expect the full payment to arrive soon, accept a series of installment payments, or mention some legal remedies you might use if the debtor doesn't pay).

If you prefer to write, you might combine your reminder with a statement that you'd like to settle this amicably and close with a brief mention of what you can do legally if the debtor isn't responsive. Possibly, too, if you are aware the debtor is having problems making an immediate payment difficult, you might mention you are willing to take this into consideration in the arrangements you work out.

In short, your strategy at this point is to suggest you would like to work things out in a spirit of good will—yet you are prepared to be firm.

The following sample letter (on the following page) illustrates this approach. It combines a reminder with a mention of possible legal remedies and expresses a hope not to use them. It also takes into account the financial difficulties the debtor has been experiencing.

However, whether you write or phone, be prepared for the debtor to evade or ignore your request. For example, when you phone, the debtor may give you reasons why he or she can't pay now or make promises to pay which may be broken. If you do get excuses, be prepared to come back with a counteroffer—such as "Well, what about in two weeks?" or "How about a $100 payment each month?" Or maybe stress why it is urgent to pay you now, even though the debtor would prefer to spend the money on something else. For example, say something like:

> *"Well, I'd really like to be able to wait, but I have my own financial problems, too. And, that's why I went to court. As you know, I have various ways to enforce collection, though I'd prefer not to use them. So, I hope we could work things out. And, that will save you any additional expenses of my having to enforce the judgment."*

On the other hand, when you write, the debtor may not answer your first letter, much less send a payment. So, be ready in about 10 days to write again, this time with stronger language about what you can do.

Appealing to the debtor

If your reminder doesn't work, be ready to follow up quickly with a series of appeals in writing. The reason for writing now, if you didn't before, is to underline your seriousness of purpose and to describe in more powerful detail exactly what you can do that will be detrimental to the debtor if he or she doesn't pay.

6537 Chabot Road
Oakland, CA 94618

July 12, 1984

Mr. Jack Smith
1234 Andrews Place
San Francisco, CA 94121

Dear Jack:

As you know, I received a judgment for $1301.26 from the Oakland courts against you for reimbursements, commissions, and other work done for you. Since your answering service indicates you haven't been getting your mail there, I am enclosing my last correspondence to you from April prior to filing suit as a courtesy. It describes how I arrived at this bill.

Since your shows were canceled and a number of people around the country apparently let you down, I am aware you have been through some difficult times.

Accordingly, I would be open to a regular payment plan to take care of this matter over the next few months and then clear the judgment from your credit records. Also, since I feel our difficulty in getting together to resolve this matter prior to this judgment was due to many of these other problems you had, I would be open to discussing future projects, once the present matter is resolved.

I would hope this still can be handled amicably, and I will look forward to hearing from you in the next 10 days—by July 22, before I take further action. As you may know, if I have to take measures to enforce this judgment, these costs will be added on to the original judgment, and I would prefer not to have to effect a levy.

I hope to hear from you soon.

Sincerely,

Gini Graham Scott

GGS:aj

If appropriate, mention some positive benefits of the debtor paying you now (such as an ability to get back in your good graces or do business again). However, your main emphasis should be on the problems which not paying will cause the debtor. After all, the debtor hasn't paid, even in response to a judgment.

Thus, this appeals process is quite different than making pre-judgment appeals, where your emphasis was on motivating the debtor to pay while keeping good will. In the past, the good will and rewards approach didn't work, so now your appeals should stress the possible difficulties or penalties to the debtor.

In turn, these difficulties or penalties will come from the legal arsenal of weapons you now have to use against the debtor. Tell the debtor what you can do, and your knowledge about your legal rights will help to impress and motivate the debtor.

One problem many creditors with small debts have is the debtor knows the creditor can't do anything, unless he or she actively enforces the judgment. So, the debtor guesses the creditor will give up, ignores the creditor's requests, and soon the creditor in frustration goes on to other things. But if you show the debtor you do, in fact, know exactly what to do to collect, he or she will be aware you are not making idle threats, but really intend to act. In this case, the debtor is more likely to pay or contact you to try to work something out.

Thus, after taking into consideration the debtor's assets and work situation, indicate the specific legal actions you may take if the debtor doesn't pay. And to give your message even further urgency, perhaps start your letter off with the words: FINAL NOTICE. Then, go into the details, though, remember to stick with the legal remedies. You don't want to come across like the Mafia and end up being charged with making threats, character assassination, or extortion.

Discussing the situation and working things out with the debtor

In some cases, an effective reminder or appeals will bring in a payment. In other cases, you may get a phone call or letter from the debtor offering to work something out.

Now you have to use your best abilities as a negotiator to finalize the arrangements. Sometimes, the debtor may mainly want you to listen, so use your judgment in assessing what the debtor tells you.

Some debtors will seek to work out payment arrangements. They will claim they can't pay the amount due now or will ask for installments. Or they may describe their dire financial straits, perhaps hoping you will drop the matter. Then it's up to you to suggest a way they can pay.

Do you think the debtor really is having financial difficulties? Or is he or she trying to delay the time of reckoning? Is the debtor sincere in offering to pay you if you will wait a few weeks or accept payments on time? Or is this likely to be a broken promise?

If you feel the debtor is sincere and has some financial problems, then of course, agree to wait, and point out that you are doing so as a courtesy to the debtor.

Again, not every debtor will keep such a promise, so you're taking a calculated risk in letting up on the pressure. But consider the alternative. You then have to use your legal remedies to collect, which can be an expensive hassle. But if you take a chance, you may not need to use them if the debtor pays. Or, if the debtor doesn't pay, you can still use these remedies a few weeks later. Thus, taking a chance with a debtor's offer is worth the risk, unless there is some pressing reason why you need to act immediately (such as, the debtor is about to move).

For the same reason, it's worth it to agree to a reasonable installment plan, whereby the debtor arranges to pay on a regular and voluntary basis. If the debtor breaks the agreement, you can always proceed legally to collect the remaining balance. (You might want to check, however, with the debtor first to find out why the installment is late. Maybe the debtor hit another financial snag, but intends to pay if you will wait a few weeks. So, again, try to work things out with the debtor on a voluntary basis before you act.)

Another possibility, if the debtor is experiencing major financial problems, is to find a non-monetary solution, if the debtor is willing and has something which you want. For example, maybe the debtor could perform a service for you, or give you some products or property to pay off all or part of the debt. Sometimes the debtor may suggest this, or if you seem to be stalemated in working out an arrangement, maybe propose this yourself.

In short, use your creativity to think up ways to get payments short of going through the courts.

And, if the debtor counters with an offer to pay you part of the debt to satisfy the whole judgment, consider the offer seriously. Perhaps seek to negotiate the amount upwards as much as you can, but realize that in the long run, it may be worth it to take less. Even though the debtor may be legally responsible for the whole amount, it may be better to settle for a smaller amount to resolve the situation. At least you will have something, whereas if you hold out for everything that's due, you may find you either can't collect, or if you do, the effort required to collect the whole amount may outweigh the gain of obtaining it.

One alternative is the "shotgun" or "blanket" garnishment. A creditor selects a number of places (for example, three banks) where the debtor may have assets. The "shotgun" or "blanket" garnishment allows the creditor to collect from any of the three banks where the debtor holds assets. It is a costly procedure, but it does have a relatively high rate of success.

Another alternative is the "debtor's exam," usually performed by an attorney. This is a process of asking the debtor (under oath) about his or her financial status. The debtor is required to truthfully disclose his or her employment status and earnings, location and amount of assets, and other pertinent information.

Chapter 12

Finding The Debtor And Any Assets Through Public And Private Records

If you aren't able to work out a voluntary payment arrangement with the debtor and decide to proceed legally, you have to locate the debtor's assets in order to levy against them, and to do that, you usually need to know where the debtor is. In some cases, you can locate assets where the debtor is living or working—or if you know the debtor's location, you can serve him or her with papers to appear for questioning about any assets.

Some collection agencies and attorneys are already set up for finding debtors and their assets through their skip tracing departments or their link-up with computer banks and credit exchanges, which have data on individuals all over the country. So, if you are trying to collect from a particularly difficult and evasive debtor, you may need to take your judgment to one of these services.

However, barring a complicated case, there is much you can do to locate the debtor or any assets yourself using relatively accessible public records and some personal ingenuity.

What to Look For and How to Find It

As you seek out information on the debtor and any assets, keep in mind that your objective is to find the assets which you can most easily turn into cash. In fact, as you proceed and the debtor sees you are serious, you may find the formerly reluctant debtor suddenly decides to work out a voluntary payment arrangement with you. If so, try to work out a settlement with the debtor. It will be less expensive and time consuming for everyone concerned.

Realistically, it makes sense to first go after the assets which are easiest to reach and least expensive and complicated to obtain. In general, you might consider going after the assets in the following order, depending on which assets the debtor has:

(1) Bank account (if you can find it);

(2) Wages (if the debtor works for an employer);

(3) Receipts from a going business (if the debtor is a business owner);

(4) Major items of personal property (such as a car, truck, boat, or expensive jewelry, video, stereo, or camera equipment);

(5) Business equipment and inventory;

(6) Money owed to the debtor by the debtor's debtors (including customers and clients); or

(7) Real property (if the debtor owns a home, other buildings, or land).

We'll discuss how to reach these assets in a later section. First we'll focus on how to find them.

Getting ready to find the debtor and any assets

To find the above assets requires organization to get together all the information you currently know about the debtor, decide what additional information is most important to gather first, and then note the records and people to contact for the information you need.

Probably the most efficient way to do this is the method skip tracers use. Start by making a worksheet, on which you write down everything you know now and leave blanks to fill in data as you collect it. This list should include the following:

- Debtor's full name
- Former names or nicknames
- Date of birth
- Social Security number
- Address (including postal addresses or box numbers)
- Previous addresses
- Current job or business address
- Previous jobs
- Home phone number
- Work number

Also, you may find it useful to list the names and addresses of people the debtor knows. You may want to contact them about where the debtor lives, works, or about his or her assets. For example, some of these people may include the following:

(1) Landlord (may have information on employment, bank account. To find out the name of the landlord, contact the county recorder's office. Give the address of the property and ask for the name of the property owner);

(2) Nearby neighbors (may know where the debtor works, when likely to be home);

(3) People at work (may know where the debtor lives, activities the debtor is involved in);

(4) Friends and associates (may know where the debtor lives or works, activities involved in, etc.);

Also, as you get information from public and private records, fill this in, too, such as the following:

(1) Bank account number;

(2) Car or other vehicle ownership and license number;

(3) Real property ownership, location, amount of equity;

(4) Major items of personal property;

(5) Customers of clients owing the debtor money.

Frequently, some information will lead you to other sources of data. So, keep filling in the blanks as you learn more, until you have the information you need to enforce your judgment.

You can use the form in this chapter to help you gather information.

The Major Sources of Information

There are three major sources of information about the debtor:

(1) Public and private records;

(2) Information given voluntarily by the debtor and his or her personal contacts;

(3) Information obtained from the debtor or his or her personal contacts as a result of court proceedings (such as an *Order of Examination*; a *Subpoena Duces Tecum*, or Interrogatories).

If possible, it is easier and less expensive to get information from the records or from the debtor and personal contacts without going through the courts. So we'll discuss those procedures first. But if you have to, use the courts.

A checklist of some of the major sources follows the Debtor Information Sheet.

Form 5

Information on the Debtor and Any Assets

Name of Debtor _____

Previous Names/Nicknames _____

Date of Birth _____ Social Security Number _____

Home Address _____

Home Phone Number _____

Current Job or Business Address _____

Business Phone Number _____

Postal Address or Box Holder _____

Previous Home Addresses _____
_____

Previous Job or Business Addresses _____
_____

Names of Personal Contacts:

Landlord's Name _____ Phone Number _____
Address _____

Neighbor's Name _____ Phone Number _____
Address _____

Friend's Name _____ Phone Number _____
Address _____

Relative's Name _____ Phone Number _____
Address _____

Associate's Name _____ Phone Number _____
Address _____

Checklist of Sources for Locating Debtor and Any Assets

Public records:
- ☐ County tax assessor
- ☐ Voter registration records
- ☐ Post Office
- ☐ Motor vehicle registration dept.
- ☐ Court records
- ☐ Municipal water district

Private records:
- ☐ Telephone company
- ☐ Criss-Cross directories
- ☐ Gas and electric company
- ☐ Collection agencies
- ☐ Credit bureaus

Personal contacts:
- ☐ Friends/relatives
- ☐ Neighbors/former neighbors
- ☐ Employers/former employers
- ☐ Work and business associates
- ☐ Leaders of membership groups

Court procedures:
- ☐ Order of Examination (to examine debtor)
- ☐ *Subpoena Duces Tecum* (to get records)
- ☐ Interrogatories (to examine debtor in writing if debtor lives too far away to come to court)

To find out where debtor works:
- ☐ Friends, acquaintances, neighbors
- ☐ Landlord
- ☐ Work and business associates
- ☐ Trade associations and unions
- ☐ Leaders of membership groups
- ☐ Credit bureau data

To find out debtor's bank acc't:
- ☐ Friends and acquaintances
- ☐ Work and business associates
- ☐ Landlord
- ☐ Customers and clients
- ☐ Calling banks in area where debtor lives or works

To find out name of debtor's landlord if he or she rents:
- ☐ County Tax Assessor's Office
- ☐ Haines or Polk directory for that city
- ☐ Land title/title insurance company
- ☐ Neighbors
- ☐ State list of property owners

To find out if debtor owns home or other real property and where located:
- ☐ County Tax Assessor's office
- ☐ Land title/title insurance company
- ☐ State list of property owners

To find out ownership of car or other vehicle:
- ☐ Motor vehicle registration dept.
- ☐ Friends, neighbors, acquaintances
- ☐ Work and business associates

To find out about other major items of personal property:
- ☐ Friends and acquaintances
- ☐ Work and business associates
- ☐ Visiting debtor's home, place of business

To find out about customers or clients owing the debtor money:
- ☐ Work and business associates

When to Use the Different Sources

The following listing details the major sources to use (besides asking the debtor) for specific types of information. A detailed discussion on using each of these sources follows in this and the next section.

To find out where the debtor is living you should check the following:

- Telephone directory or information;
- Motor vehicle registration department
- Post Office (if debtor has mailbox and has a business in his or her home);
- Trade associations and unions;
- Credit bureau data;
- Work associates;
- Friends and acquaintances;
- Organizations the debtor belongs to;

Using Public and Private Records for Information

Since most people leave an extensive paper trail about themselves in both public and private records, these records are often a useful source of information.

Most public records are fully open to the public. You merely have to write, call, or visit the appropriate office. Many privately organized records, like criss-cross telephone directories, are also readily available, at no charge. In other cases, you may be able to get private records by making a special request or serving a subpoena (ask the court clerk for a *Subpoena Duces Tecum*). Or you may gain access for a small charge (for instance, to make a credit bureau inquiry). The following section describes the major public and private records you are likely to use and where to find them.

Telephone Information

- **Criss-Cross Directories.** The two major criss-cross directories are the Polk Directory and the Haines Directory, which are available for most major metropolitan areas. These directories give you information on the debtor's address, phone number, and neighbors, which is unavailable from the usual alphabetical listing. Also, these directories may include names of people not in the regular phone directory, since these listings are compiled by reps going door to door getting information.

If you only know the street where the debtor lives, you can pinpoint the debtor's exact address (unless the debtor isn't listed) by going down all the listings for that street until you find the debtor. Also, once you have the debtor's address, you can obtain his or her phone number, since the directory lists the phone number for each address.

Conversely, since the directory lists each phone number in numerical order followed by the owner's name and address, you can find out how the debtor is listed and an address, if you only have his or her phone number (unless, of course, the number is unlisted). Then, too, you can use the street listing to get the names, addresses, and phone numbers of the debtor's neighbors.

In addition, the Polk Directory gives the occupation, if known, of each person listed. And it has a business section, with the names of companies and ads for them by type of business.

One or both of these directories may be found at major public and business libraries, the County Tax Assessor's or Recorder's Office, other government offices; and title companies.

County Tax Assessor's Office

The tax assessor has a printout of every property owner and piece of property in the county listed by name and by street address. So, if you have the debtor's correct name, you can locate any property he or she owns in the county. Or if you have the address of that property, you can find out the name of the owner—who may be the debtor, a spouse or business associate, or the landlord. Furthermore, this printout will include the mailing address where the assessor sends tax bills to the owner. Some assessor's offices will give out this information by phone, or you can go to the office yourself or write the tax assessor.

County Recorder's Office

Once you know the person has property in the county, you can determine if this property has any value as an asset by doing a title search.

To do this, look up the lot and block number of the property to find the appropriate file. This will tell you the current value of the property. Then, to find out the owner's net equity, look back in the records up to 10 years to see if there are any outstanding liens, mortgages, or deeds of trust on the house. These will be listed according to the date they were filed against the property or when last renewed. Since all of these existing encumbrances will be senior to yours (unless an earlier lien should lapse), you can determine if the debtor has enough remaining equity in the property by deducting the total of these encumbrances and any exemptions the debtor is entitled to (such as a homestead exemption, which is

$30,000 or $45,000 in California). Then, if anything is left, you can decide if it's enough to make it worthwhile to go after this property.

State List of Property Owners

Another source of information on real property, besides the county tax assessor's office, is the statewide alphabetical list of property owners, available at some title company offices. The list will tell you if the debtor owns anything anywhere in the state. To find out if he or she is listed, call a local title company to ask if they have a list and are willing to check. These companies are in the yellow pages.

Voter Registration Records

You'll find these records in city hall. If the debtor is a voter, the listing will include the debtor's name, address, phone number, birth date, party affiliation (if any), and date of registration. Even if the debtor isn't a voter, these records may be useful for finding out the names, addresses, and phone numbers of relatives with the same last name as the debtor (as long as the name isn't too common like Smith).

Post Office

If the debtor has a post office box and this box is listed in the name of a business, the post office will release the address and phone number. You merely have to call the post office and a clerk will tell you over the phone. You don't have to even explain why you want the number.

However, if the address is a private residence, the post office won't normally give out the address, with one exception. If a process server gives the post office a certified statement indicating that the name, address, and telephone number of the current box holder are required to serve legal papers in a currently pending proceeding, the post office can give out any names, addresses, and numbers. (See the example on the following page.)

Motor Vehicle Registration Agency

If the debtor owns a car, truck, RV, large boat, or plane, you can use the motor vehicle records to find out the address of the debtor and information on the vehicle (including license number, vehicle ID number, and other data). To obtain these records, you must have a valid reason for requesting the data (having a legal matter pending or collecting a judgment is a good reason) and include the required fee (check with the agency first) with your request. Note that the agency will send the person you are asking about the name, address, and phone number of the person requesting information.

EXAMPLE OF POST OFFICE FORM

Post Office Box Clerk: Date: _____

_____   Re: P.O. Box No. ____

_____

Pursuant to the United States Post Office Administrative Support Manual Sect. 353.323(g) the undersigned herewith certifies that he is impowered by law to serve legal process and that the name(s), address(es) and telephone numbers of the current tenant of the above-numbered box are required to effect services of legal process in a currently pending proceeding.

The Administrative Support Manual Section 353.323(g) is reprinted below for your convenience.

UNITED STATES POSTAL SERVICE

g. Process Servers. The name or address of an individual post office boxholder may be furnished to a person empowered by law to serve legal process, upon written certification that the information is required to effect service in a currently pending proceeding.

Please reply to my attention certified by: _____

Please enter your reply here: _____ Box No. _____

Is held by: _____   Address: _____

       Home telephone _____ Work telephone _____

and _____   Address: _____

       Home telephone _____ Work telephone _____

Date: _____

To submit a request, obtain an official request form from your state agency, and fill in the required information about yourself or whoever else is making the request for you. Usually, for the agency to search the records, you must list either the license or identification number of the vehicle or the owner's first and last name, along with as much other information as you have on the owner's last known address, city, or region, and the make and year of the car. (See an example of a request form on the following page.)

Then, submit the request to your local office or mail it with the required fee to the appropriate DMV main office. In a few weeks, you'll get a printout with information on the vehicle or on the car licenses and vehicles listed to any owners with the same name in the city or region you have indicated. For example:

```
B 3P SMITH JOHN
A681
C2][
DATE: 07/19/84 TIME: 09:50
MATCHED ON: *L/N*F/N* Z
NAME:SMITH JOHN ADD:166 CTY:SUNNYVALE
VR#:1HAL1 FC:L YR:82 MK:BMW
NAME:SMITH JOHN H. ADD:166 CITY:SUNNYVALE
VR#: 469RNE FC:A YR:77 MK:FORD
ANI END
```

Once you have a license number, you can get more detailed information on the owner's address and clarify the ownership status of the vehicle. For example, you can find out if the debtor is the legal owner as well as the registered owner, and if there are any liens or loans out on the car. This information is important, because the debtor must be the legal owner for you to consider this one of the debtor's assets, and the debtor must have enough equity in the vehicle after outstanding encumbrances are deducted for this asset to be worth pursuing.

Court Records

If the debtor has been involved in any legal actions—whether as a defendant or plaintiff—the records from Small Claims, Municipal, or Superior Court can be a fertile source of information. You'll find out any previous legal suits the debtor has been involved in, the results, and importantly, the current address of the debtor at the time of the suit and the name and address of any attorneys representing the debtor or the opposing party.

If an attorney is listed, you can contact him or her to help you locate the debtor. Or possibly, if the plaintiff's attorney is still trying to collect a judgment, he or she may be open to sharing information with you. Then, too, if things get difficult, you might turn your own judgment over to that attorney for collection.

EXAMPLE OF REQUEST FORM FROM MOTOR VEHICLE DEPT.

DMV — *A Public Service Agency*

Driver License/Identification Card or Vehicle/Vessel Registration Information Request
(For Requesting the Record of Someone Other Than Yourself.)

COMPLETE ONE FORM FOR EACH REQUEST

FOR DMV USE ONLY
NAME
STREET
CITY   STATE   ZIP CODE

Notice to Individual Information Requesters
Requests for driver license/ID or vehicle/vessel records are subject to review and approval by the Department. A (10) day delay for notification to the subject of record is required unless you are requesting information on yourself, spouse or minor residing at your address. The subject of record will receive the second page of this request for review and has the right to object the release of the information requested. After the (10) day delay notification period and an objection is not received the record will be released. If an objection is received a letter of explanation will be mailed. The service fee will not be refunded.

INSTRUCTIONS: Your local field office will not process your record request unless it is for your own record (or that of your spouse or minor child at your address). Please mail this form to the address shown at bottom of form. Complete Parts A, B, C, and D for all information requests. *(Print carefully.).*

PART A: *REQUESTER:*

YOUR NAME   AREA CODE   TELEPHONE
BUSINESS ADDRESS   CITY   STATE   ZIP CODE

PART B: *INFORMATION REQUESTED* — Check ONE box *(Fee must be paid by check or money order payable to DMV)*

DRIVER LICENSE/IDENTIFICATION — Enter either the driver license/ID number and full name OR full name and birthdate.

TYPE OF RECORD	INFO REQUEST/FEES (NON-REFUNDABLE)	CERTIFY RECORD (NO FEE)
☐ Current Record	$ 5.00	☐ Yes ☐ No
☐ Copy DL/ID Photo Document (Subject picture not available)	$20.00	☐ Yes ☐ No
☐ Copy DL 44-Application for DL/ID (Includes guarantor signature for minors)	$20.00	☐ Yes ☐ No

VEHICLE VESSEL REGISTRATION — Enter either the license plate/CF number OR the full name and complete address of the individual.

TYPE OF RECORD	INFO REQUEST/FEES (NON-REFUNDABLE)	CERTIFY RECORD (NO FEE)
☐ Current Record	$ 5.00	☐ Yes ☐ No
☐ Automated Computer History Year(s) _____ *(Please indicate)*	$ 5.00	☐ Yes ☐ No
☐ Owner as of ___/___/___	$ 5.00	☐ Yes ☐ No
☐ Photo Copy Year(s) _____ *(Please indicate)*	$20.00	☐ Yes ☐ No

NAME (LAST)   (FIRST)   (MIDDLE)   BIRTHDATE
ADDRESS   (CITY)   (STATE)   (ZIP CODE)   CALIFORNIA DRIVER LICENSE/ID NO.
VEHICLE/VESSEL IDENTIFICATION NO.   VEHICLE/VESSEL MAKE   YEAR MODEL

PART C: *REASON FOR REQUESTING INFORMATION AND THE INTENDED USE*
> **NOTE:** For verification purposes, this section must be complete or your request will be refused.

(THE SPECIFIC NEED FOR THE INFORMATION MUST BE STATED—INCLUDE DATES, ADDRESS, COURT CASE NUMBER, LOCATION, ETC. RELATED TO YOUR REQUEST). IF REQUESTING RESIDENCE ADDRESS INFORMATION, INCLUDE FEDERAL OR STATE STATUTE, IDENTIFIED BY CODE NAME AND SECTION NUMBER, WHICH REQUIRES USE OF RESIDENCE ADDRESS INFORMATION.

Executed at _____ CITY COUNTY STATE   on _____ DATE

I certify under penalty of perjury that the information given in this request is true, correct and factual. The information received will be used for any unlawful purpose.

I understand that I may be subject to prosecution for perjury (Penal Code Section 118) and false representation (California Vehicle Code Section 1808.45). These are misdemeanors and punishable by a fine not exceeding five thousand dollars ($5,000) or by imprisonment in the county jail not exceeding one year, or both fine and imprisonment for each offense.

X _____
SIGNATURE OF REQUESTER   DRIVER LICENSE OR ID NO.

DMV USE ONLY
OFFICE NO.   DATE   INITIALS

Driver license or ID number must match that of requester or information will not be released.

PART D: This section of your request will be detached and returned to you along with the information you requested.

Send information to *(Print carefully)*
Name _____
Address _____ STREET
_____ CITY   STATE   ZIP CODE

Send your request to:
DEPARTMENT OF MOTOR VEHICLES
P. O. Box 944247 — Mail Sta C198
Sacramento, CA 94244-2470

INF 70 (REV. 12/92)

These court records can also be useful in giving you the names and possibly addresses of the debtor's relatives and associates. For example, a divorce or child support action will include information on the debtor's ex-spouse, and possibly involved relatives will be named. Similarly, a business dispute may list names and addresses of former business partners and co-workers.

You can obtain these records by asking to see them at the recorder's office associated with the appropriate court. In many courts, the latest records are on a computer printout or microfiche, so they're especially easy to use. In using the printouts, just look under the alphabetical listings for both the defendant and plaintiff by year (or by month for the more recent cases) to see if the debtor is listed. (And if the debtor is in business, check under both the debtor's name and the name of the business.) With older cases, you'll have to look through the handwritten record books, where the names are listed under broad alphabetical categories (such as A–Ag and Ah–Am).

If you find the debtor's name, the full listing will include the name of the opposing party in the case followed by the court docket or case number. Write down this number and give it to the court clerk to obtain the case file. You'll be able to review everything on it—except for occasional sealed documents—and you can ask the clerk to copy anything available for public viewing (there is usually a cost for this service).

Utility Company Records

These include records from the municipal or county water district and the gas and electric company where the debtor lives. If you haven't found out the debtor's current mailing address or phone number from other sources, you may be able to obtain them from these records, since these companies need the address to send out the bills.

To learn the company's policies on giving out records, call the customer service department. Some companies will give out information if you have a good reason or tell them about the court judgment. In other cases, you will be required to subpoena these records with a court order (a *Subpoena Duces Tecum*). Should you decide to do this, get the name of the appropriate person in charge of the records you want. You have to name the correct person to get the records.

Business and Professional Licenses and Records

Another way to locate a debtor who has a business or is in a licensed profession, is through the licensing agencies that handle that occupation. The person will have a registration or license on file, which will include the debtor name, latest address, and phone number. For example, some of the licensing agencies to check include the following:

- **State Sales Tax Agency.** A source of information on companies involved in retail or mail order sales since they are supposed to have a resale permit issued by this agency and to pay sales tax to this agency. The company's current address should be listed on the license. To get this information, call the accounts references department at your state agency.

- **Business License Board or Business Tax Collector.** Many communities require each business to be licensed by the city or county each year. If the debtor's business is registered, this license or certificate will have the debtor's latest address. However, whether the debtor is registered will depend on the city, debtor's line of business, size of the business, and whether the debtor chooses to register. Many cities require all businesses to register; some only certain categories of businesses. Also, size may be a factor in whether the city requires registration or whether the debtor registers. (Some small businesses go along for some time without such agencies knowing the business exists—or without the owner knowing he or she should register.)

    In any case, if the debtor has registered, you can find out from the county or city clerk, though policies differ on how this information is organized and whether you can get it by phone or have to come in. In some offices, the file will list all the debtors with licenses by the business name, followed by the address, owner's name, and account number. In others, the businesses are listed by address, followed by ownership information and a phone number. Check on the procedures in your area.

- **Fictitious Business Name Records.** Another possible way to locate a debtor with a business is through the list of fictitious business names usually found in the county clerk's office. If the debtor is using a made-up name, the business should be on file, and the listing will include the company's address and the owner's home address. However, not all states require registration of fictitious business names. Any business operating under the owner's name and many corporations will not be on record.

- **Secretary of State's Office.** If the debtor's business is a corporation, a listing will be on file with the Secretary of State and will include the name of the agent for service of process (usually the chief executive officer or president of the corporation), the current address of the company, and the number of shares of stock issued.

- **Securities and Exchange Commission.** Another source to check if the debtor's business has issued any stocks or securities. This listing will include information on the location of the company, key officials, and the amount of stock issued.

- **Occupational and Business Licenses.** Many occupations and businesses require licenses, and if the debtor is currently active in that occupation, he or she should have a license on file with the appropriate state licensing board or other governmental agency. By contacting the governing agency, you can find out if the person is currently licensed and his or her last known business or home address.

    You can learn what occupations need licenses and what agency handles them by calling your state department of consumer affairs or local consumer representative, sometimes called a consumer complaint and protection coordinator. They're listed in the phone book, and this consumer listing also includes a list of those occupations and businesses covered by some sort of licensing requirement or watchdog agency. Some of the occupations requiring licenses include the following:

Accountants
Advertising agencies
Automobile dealers, salesmen, and repair services
Barbers, beauty salons, and cosmetologists
Contractors
Dance studios
Day care centers

Dentists, doctors, and nurses
Employment agencies
Many health professionals
Insurance adjusters and sales representatives
Landscape architects
Marriage and family counselors
Real estate agents and brokers
and many others

If you believe the debtor may be in a particular occupation, simply call or write to the agency (check to see which is the appropriate procedure) requesting information on whether the person is currently licensed and his or her last known home and business address. (For an example, see the sample real estate inquiry form on the following page.)

Trade Associations and Unions

To find debtors who are involved in unionized work, contact the local union. Or if the debtor is involved in a job with a trade association, he or she may be a member of that. The union or association can tell if the person is a current member, and if so, where the person currently works. If the rep asks why you want to know, have a good reason. Possibly say you are trying to contact the person about employment. Or maybe you previously worked with the person and just got back into town.

You'll find a list of the labor unions and trade associations in your phone book under "Labor Organizations." Some of the occupations which are unionized or have associations include the following:

Airline pilots
Bakers
Carpenters
Clothing and textile workers
Department store employees
Goverment employees
Hospital workers
Hotel and restaurant employees and bartenders
Laundry workers
Longshoremen

Machinists
Painters
Plumbers
Postal workers
Printers
Retail clerks
Teachers
Transit workers
Transport workers
Truck drivers
Waiters and waitresses

If you think the person might work for the state, call your state personnel agency.

FORM 6

REAL ESTATE INQUIRY FORM

Date _____

From: _____
_____

To: Department of Real Estate
_____
_____

Please advise me if the following party, _____ ,
is currently licensed as a:

Salesperson _____ No _____ Yes Expiration date _____

Broker _____ No _____ Yes Expiration date _____

If not a currently licensed salesperson or broker, does this person have a license that expired?

_____ Yes, as a broker _____ Yes, as a salesperson

_____ No   If yes, expiration date: _____

The person's last known business address is:
_____
_____
_____

The person's last known home address is:
_____
_____
_____

Thank you for your assistance,

_____

In the Military

You can locate debtors in the military, too, by contacting the appropriating branch, as follows:

- Army—Office of the Adjutant General, Department of the Army, Washington, DC 20025
- Marines—Commandant of the Marine Corps, MMSRB, Washington, DC 20380
- Navy—Chief of Naval Personnel, Navy Department, Washington, DC 20025
- Air Force—Air Adjutant General, Department of the Air Force, Washington, DC 20025
- Coast Guard—U.S. Coast Guard, 500 7th Street NW, Washington, DC 20590

Credit Bureau Information

Even if you don't belong to a credit bureau like CBI, Equifax, TRW or Trans Union, you may be able to get a member of a credit bureau to run the file of a debtor for you. As previously discussed, a credit bureau file can quickly give you much of the information you need—such as the person's most recent address and employment. Also, it lists the names of other creditors who might be willing to share information about the debtor. And, it indicates any legal actions involving the debtor, so you can go to the appropriate courthouse and get the file if you want.

Probably the credit bureau members who are most likely to do a run for you are collection agencies and auto repossessors, though other likely members of credit bureaus include landlords, property managers, and large store owners. Commonly, you can expect to pay about $10 to 20 for a run; the credit bureau member pays about $2 to 3 for each inquiry.

If you have the debtor's Social Security number, include that when you ask for a run, because then you are certain to get information on the right person. If you don't have it, the bureau will give you the nearest matches, based on the debtor's name and address or general location. In this case, however, make sure you have information on the right person before you start to collect, so you don't have problems by trying to collect from the wrong person. One way to check is to get the person's Social Security number from an independent source. If it matches the number in the credit bureau's file, you know you are correct. (Though if it doesn't, this could still be the same person, since some people have gotten more than one I.D. number. So, if uncertain, do some additional checking.)

Examining the Debtor Through the Courts

If you can't readily find out about the debtor's assets through other methods, you can attempt to examine the debtor through the discovery procedures available through the courts.

Theoretically, the discovery process is supposed to start when the debtor gets a first notice of judgment from the courts, since a *Judgment Debtor's Statement of Assets* (see example in this chapter) is enclosed with this notice. The debtor is supposed to fill this out and list various information to help the creditor collect, such as occupation, name and address of employer, amount of pay, bank accounts and balance in the account, vehicles, and other personal property. Then, the debtor is supposed to mail it to you, as the person who won the case, within 35 days, unless the debtor appeals the judgment or files a motion to vacate.

However, commonly debtors don't fill this out, even though the form warns in large letters that the debtor may have to go to court to answer questions or the court can impose penalties if he or she doesn't comply. But then, why should the debtor take this warning seriously? After all, if the debtor doesn't pay you voluntarily after receiving the notice of judgment—why should he or she want to give you information so you can readily collect?

Thus, to initiate this discovery process, you usually have to take further steps to get the debtor to come to court, supply records, or answer your questions under penalty of law.

The usual procedure used is the *Order of Examination*, which requires the debtor to appear with you in court to answer questions, under the supervision of a referee or judge. You can additionally require the debtor to bring needed records to court by filing a *Subpoena Duces Tecum*, along with an affidavit that these records are necessary to your inquiry.

Or, as an alternative (usually used if you can't get the debtor to come to court), you can use two other major forms of discovery:

(1) Serving the debtor with interrogatories—questions he or she must answer;

(2) Requesting permission to inspect the land or other property owned by the debtor.

Using the order of examination

There are two steps to examining the debtor in court:

(1) Filing and serving the *Order of Examination* on the debtor, who lives or works in the jurisdiction of the court of examination, and

(2) Actually examining the debtor.

If you can't find out what you need in one examination, or if the debtor doesn't have enough money at this time to settle the judgment, you can legally call the debtor in for an additional examination after a specified waiting period (check time limits in your state). In fact, you can set up additional examinations, until the judgment is satisfied, assuming you have the patience to continue the process.

If the debtor doesn't show up—and many won't—you have the power to ask the court to issue a bench warrant for the arrest of the debtor (about $14 for service), and later you can normally add this to the fees due you from the debtor. After the judge issues the warrant, noting this on the case records, it is sent to the sheriff, marshal, or constable in the jurisdiction where the debtor lives or works for service for the life of the warrant (about three months). Some judges will issue a warrant the first time the debtor doesn't show; though sometimes the judge will give the debtor another chance, so you'll have to reschedule another hearing; and then, if the debtor doesn't appear, the judge will agree to the warrant.

Although some officers will act on such a warrant immediately, especially if it is for a large amount (say over $1,000), in most jurisdictions, this warrant will be treated as an inactive bench warrant, particularly if it involves a small judgment, so the officer won't immediately go after the debtor to bring him or her in. However, the warrant will be out there, so if the debtor should have any encounter with the law (such as a traffic stop), a search of the records will bring up the warrant, and now the debtor will be subject to arrest unless he or she immediately pays the amount due on it.

Typically, in acting on the warrant, the officer will arrest the debtor, unless the debtor pays, and then the debtor will have to go to jail, post bail, and appear before a judge, who will ask why he or she didn't appear and set up another hearing date. In some cases, before arranging for another hearing, the judge may try to persuade the debtor to settle or call the plaintiff to see if the plaintiff and debtor can work out an agreeable payment plan, or if not, at least arrange a mutually agreeable hearing time.

If a judge sets up a new hearing date which isn't convenient for you, you can always write to the courts to request a change, as in the case of any hearing. And, if the debtor doesn't show up again you can always request another warrant—though normally, after an encounter with the arrest powers of the courts, the debtor will show up. If the time limit on an issued bench warrant expires without being served, you can request another warrant, too—and, usually the judge will issue this as a matter of course.

Transferring the order of examination procedure to another court

In order to use the *Order of Examination* procedure, the debtor usually must live or work within a certain distance of the place of examination (for example, 150 miles). If the court where the judgment was originally issued is beyond this limit, you probably will have to either use another procedure to examine the debtor or transfer the matter to another court in the county where the debtor lives.

To make the transfer, get an *Abstract of Judgment* and an affidavit form from the court of judgment (usually for a small fee) and then take or mail this to the small claims court in the county where the debtor lives. On this affidavit you must state that the person lives or works in this county, and this is why you wish to transfer the matter to this court. Also, you must include a request that this new court issue an Order of Examination and enclose the required fee (about $12).

Filing and serving the order of examination and other documents

To start the process, ask the small claims court clerk for an *Order to Appear for Examination* form. It lists the name of the court and the address where the examination is to occur, and the clerk will type in the other requested information (such as the case number and the name of the person required to appear).

Also, the clerk will assign you a time of appearance. In each court, there are only certain days and times when these examinations occur, and you will have to set the hearing accordingly, allowing enough time for the defendant to be served with the papers. (For example, in some states, the defendant must have at least 10 days notice—and you should allow 2 to 4 weeks for service.)

Besides requiring the debtor to appear, you can also require the debtor to bring in specified records (such as bank statements, checkbooks, and stock certificates) by filing and serving a *Civil Subpoena Duces Tecum* on the debtor; and you can have this served along with the *Order of Examination*. One advantage of doing this is you don't end up with a debtor in court who repeatedly says to you: "I don't know," and can't give you any account numbers because he or she left the records at home.

To use this procedure, get a *Subpoena Duces Tecum* form from the court and specify on it the time and place the person must appear with the records (as on the *Order of Examination*). Also, obtain an affidavit form (called a *Declaration for Subpoena Duces Tecum*) from the court, and indicate on it the exact items you want the debtor to produce in court (e.g., current checkbooks, savings account passbooks, driver's license, automobile registration, records of stocks and bonds, last year's income tax form, business licenses, etc.). Finally, you must explain on this form why you need this material. (See the example of a *Subpoena Duces Tecum* in this chapter.)

Unless you have to transfer the examination to another court, there's no charge for issuing an *Order of Examination* or a *Subpoena Duces Tecum*. However, you have to arrange for personal service, and usually, that will cost about $15 to 25 for each document, unless you can find someone to serve the papers for you without charge (such as a friend, associate, or even the debtor's lawyer). You can choose any type of personal service, including the local sheriff, marshal, or constable; a registered process server; or designate a specially appointed person. But you can't use the mails.

If you will incur some charges for using this procedure or if interest has been accumulating for a few months, file a *Memorandum of Costs* with the court at this time, too. Then, you can add your additional costs onto the original judgment.

Examining the debtor

Before you appear at the examination, make sure the debtor has been served properly and the examination is still set to go at the scheduled time. You don't want to waste time appearing if the matter has been dropped from the calendar, since you'll have to reset it and serve the debtor again.

But assuming everything is set to go, be sure to appear. And, come prepared with a list of questions to ask about the information you want.

Commonly, the examination will occur like this. You will be directed to a regular courtroom, where a referee or judge is present, along with a bailiff. Then, the referee or judge will help you get started and will be available in case you have any questions or problems.

If the debtor isn't there, you can request that the judge or referee find the debtor in contempt of court and issue a warrant. Then, it's up to the judge to decide. Some may find the debtor in contempt on the first non-appearance; others may want to wait until you try to examine the debtor again and fail, to give the debtor the benefit of the doubt.

However, if the debtor is present, a good starting point is the questions the debtor didn't answer on the *Judgment Debtor's Statement of Assets*. Also, some courts in some states provide a list of suggested questions, such as the *Examination in Supplementary Proceedings* form from the Small Claims Court. An example of the *Examination in Supplementary Proceedings* form is included in this chapter.

Probably, the best strategy is to go through these questions, decide which ones are appropriate to ask given the debtor's circumstances, and add any additional questions that might be important.

In court, you'll ask the debtor the questions yourself, while a referee or judge sits in attendance, in case you have any problems. Mostly, some assistance from the referee or judge is sufficient to get the debtor to cooperate. But, if the debtor still doesn't comply, the referee or judge can find him or her in contempt, so you do have the power of the court behind you in getting the debtor to answer your questions and give you the information you want.

Another key tip that can bring you instant cash: while conducting the examination, ask the debtor to hand over any cash or checks to him or herself, which he or she has brought to the hearing. And if the debtor resists, get the referee or judge to assist. In particular, ask the debtor to open up a change purse or wallet or empty out any pockets. The reason this technique is often effective is because many debtors don't realize you have this power to take any cash or checks on their person and so may come to court with a substantial amount of money. You can take it all, though you might be nice and leave the debtor with enough for a phone call and car fare to get home.

Finding The Debtor And Any Assets Through Public And Private Records 237

SUBPOENA DUCES TECUM EXAMPLE

Name and Address of Court:

SMALL CLAIMS CASE NO.

PLAINTIFF/DEMANDANTE (Name, address, and telephone number of each):

DEFENDANT/DEMANDADO (Name, address, and telephone number of each):

Telephone No.:

Telephone No.:

Telephone No.:

Telephone No.:

☐ See attached sheet for additional plaintiffs and defendants.

DECLARATION FOR SUBPENA DUCES TECUM

1. I, the undersigned, declare I am the ☐ plaintiff ☐ defendant ☐ judgment creditor ☐ other (specify): in the above entitled action.
2. This action has been set for hearing on (date): at (time): in the above named court.
3. (Name): has in his or her possession or under his or her control the following documents relating to (name of party):
   a. ☐ Payroll receipts, stubs, and other records concerning employment of the party. Receipts, invoices, documents, and other papers or records concerning any and all accounts receivable of the party.
   b. ☐ Bank account statements, cancelled checks, and check registers from any and all bank accounts in which the party has an interest.
   c. ☐ Savings account passbooks and statements, savings and loan account passbooks and statements, and credit union share account passbooks and statements of the party.
   d. ☐ Stock certificates, bonds, money market certificates, and any other records, documents, or papers concerning all investments of the party.
   e. ☐ California registration certificates and ownership certificates for all vehicles registered to the party.
   f. ☐ Deeds to any and all real property owned or being purchased by the party.
   g. ☐ Other (specify):

These documents are material to the issues involved in this case for the following reasons (specify):

I declare under penalty of perjury under the laws of the State of California that the foregoing is true and correct.
Date:

_____ ▶ _____
(TYPE OR PRINT NAME)   (SIGNATURE OF JUDGMENT CREDITOR)

Form Approved by the
Judicial Council of California
SC-107 [New January 1, 1992]

DECLARATION FOR SUBPENA DUCES TECUM
(Small Claims)

Code of Civil Procedure, §§ 1985-1987.5

EXAMPLE OF JUDGMENT DEBTOR'S STATEMENT OF ASSETS

MAIL TO THE JUDGMENT CREDITOR
DO NOT FILE WITH THE COURT

TO JUDGMENT CREDITOR *(fill in name of judgment creditor)*:

FROM JUDGMENT DEBTOR *(fill in your name)*:

SMALL CLAIMS CASE NO.

JUDGMENT DEBTOR'S STATEMENT OF ASSETS

The **judgment debtor** in this small claims case is the person (or business) who lost the case and owes the money. The person who won the case is the **judgment creditor**.

TO THE JUDGMENT DEBTOR:
The small claims court has ruled that you owe money to the judgment creditor.

1. You may appeal a judgment against you only on the other party's claim. You may **not** appeal a judgment against you on **your** claim.
    a. If you appeared at the trial and you want to appeal, you must file a Notice of Appeal within 30 days after the date of mailing on the Notice of Entry of Judgment or the date you received it in court.
    b. If you did not appear at the trial, before you can appeal, you must first file a **Motion to Vacate the Judgment** within 30 days from the date the Notice of Entry of Judgment was mailed or delivered to you, and the judgment cannot be collected until the motion is decided. If your motion is denied, you then have 10 days from the date the notice of denial was mailed to file your appeal.

2. Unless you pay, appeal, or move to vacate, you must fill out this form and send it to the person who won the case within **30 days** after the Notice of Entry of Judgment is mailed to you by the clerk.

3. If you file an appeal or a Motion to Vacate, you do not need to fill out this form unless you lose your appeal or motion to vacate. Then you will have **30 days** to pay or complete this form and deliver it to the judgment creditor.

If you fail to follow these instructions you may have to go to court to answer questions or the court can impose penalties on you.	Si usted no sigue estas instrucciones es posible que tenga que presentarse ante la corte para contestar preguntas, o la corte puede imponerle multas.

If you were sued as an individual skip this box and begin with no. 1 below. Otherwise, check the applicable box, attach the documents indicated, and complete no. 12 on the reverse.
   a. ☐ (Corporation or partnership) Attached to this form is a statement describing the nature, value and exact location of all assets of the corporation or the partners, and a statement showing that the person signing this form is authorized to submit this form on behalf of the corporation or partnership.
   b. ☐ (Governmental agency) Attached to this form is the statement of an authorized representative of the agency as to when the agency will pay the judgment and any reasons for its failure to do so.

EMPLOYMENT

1. What is your occupation? *(Please provide job title and name of division or office in which you work.)*

2. Name and address of your business or employer *(include address of your payroll or human resources department, if different)*:

3. How often are you paid?
    a. ☐ daily ☐ every two weeks ☐ monthly
       ☐ weekly ☐ twice a month ☐ other *(explain)*:

4. What is your gross pay each pay period?
   $

5. What is your take home pay each pay period?
   $

6. If your wife or husband earns any income give the name and address of the business or employer, job title, and division or office:

(Continued on reverse)

Form Approved by the
Judicial Council of California
SC-133 [Rev. January 1, 1992]

JUDGMENT DEBTOR'S STATEMENT OF ASSETS
(Small Claims)

Rule 982.7

EXAMPLE OF JUDGMENT DEBTOR'S STATEMENT OF ASSETS
(Reverse Side)

CASH, BANK DEPOSITS

7. How much money do you have in cash? .... $ _____

8. How much other money do you have in banks, savings and loans, credit unions, and other financial institutions either in your own name or jointly *(list)*:

Name and address of financial institution	Account number	Individual or joint?	Balance
a.			$
b.			$
c.			$

PROPERTY

9. List all automobiles, other vehicles, and boats owned in your name or jointly:

Make and year	Value	Legal owner if different from registered owner	Amount owed
a.	$		$
b.	$		$
c.	$		$
d.	$		$

10. List all real estate owned in your name or jointly:

Address of real estate	Fair market value		Amount owed
a.	$		$
b.	$		$

OTHER PERSONAL PROPERTY *[Do not list household furniture and furnishings, appliances, or clothing.]*

11. List anything of value not listed above owned in your name or jointly:

Description	Value	Address where property is located
a.	$	
b.	$	
c.	$	
d.	$	
e.	$	
f.	$	
g.	$	
h.	$	
i.	$	
j.	$	

12. I declare under penalty of perjury under the laws of the State of California that the foregoing is true and correct.

Date: _____

.... ▶ _____
(TYPE OR PRINT NAME)   (SIGNATURE)

Mail or deliver this completed form to the judgment creditor at the address shown on the Notice of Entry of Judgment form.

SC-133 [Rev. January 1, 1992]   **JUDGMENT DEBTOR'S STATEMENT OF ASSETS**   Page two
                                          (Small Claims)

240 Collection Techniques For A Small Business

EXAMPLE OF ORDER TO APPEAR FOR EXAMINATION

214-033 (Rev. 11/87)

ATTORNEY OR PARTY WITHOUT ATTORNEY *(Name and Address):*   TELEPHONE NO.:

FOR COURT USE ONLY

ATTORNEY FOR *(Name):*

NAME OF COURT:
STREET ADDRESS: **OAKLAND-PIEDMONT-EMERYVILLE JUDICIAL DISTRICT**
MAILING ADDRESS: **600 WASHINGTON STREET**
CITY AND ZIP CODE: **OAKLAND, CALIFORNIA 94607-3997**
BRANCH NAME:

PLAINTIFF:

DEFENDANT:

APPLICATION AND ORDER FOR APPEARANCE AND EXAMINATION
☐ ENFORCEMENT OF JUDGMENT   ☐ ATTACHMENT (Third Person)
☐ Judgment Debtor   ☐ Third Person

CASE NUMBER:

ORDER TO APPEAR FOR EXAMINATION

1. TO *(name):*
2. YOU ARE ORDERED TO APPEAR personally before this court, or before a referee appointed by the court, to
   a. ☐ furnish information to aid in enforcement of a money judgment against you.
   b. ☐ answer concerning property of the judgment debtor in your possession or control or concerning a debt you owe the judgment debtor.
   c. ☐ answer concerning property of the defendant in your possession or control or concerning a debt you owe the defendant that is subject to attachment.

Date: Time: Dept. or Div.:   Rm.:
Address of Court ☐ shown above ☐ is:

3. This order may be served by a sheriff, marshal, constable, registered process server, **or** the following specially appointed person *(name):*

Date: _____   ▶ _____
(SIGNATURE OF JUDGE OR REFEREE)

This order must be served not less than 10 days before the date set for the examination.

IMPORTANT NOTICES ON REVERSE

APPLICATION FOR ORDER TO APPEAR FOR EXAMINATION

1. ☐ Judgment creditor   ☐ Assignee of record   ☐ Plaintiff who has a right to attach order
   applies for an order requiring *(name):*
   to aid in enforcement of the money judgment or to answer concerning property or debt.
2. The person to be examine is
   ☐ the judgment debtor
   ☐ a third person (1) who has possession or control of property belonging to the judgment debtor or the defendant or (2) who owes the judgment debtor or the defendant more than $250. An affidavit supporting this application under CCP §491.110 or §708.120 is attached.
3. The person to be examined resides or has a place of business in this county or within 150 miles of the place of examination.
4. ☐ This court is **not** the court in which the money judgment is entered or *(attachment only)* the court that issued the writ of attachment. An affidavit supporting an application under CCP §491.150 or §708.160 is attached.
5. ☐ The judgment debtor has been examined within the past 120 days. An affidavit showing good cause for another examination is attached.

I declare under penalty of perjury under the laws of the State of California that the foregoing is true and correct.
Date:

▶ _____
(TYPE OR PRINT NAME)   (SIGNATURE OF DECLARANT)

Form Approved by the
Judicial Council of California
AT-138, EJ-125 [New July 1, 1984]

APPLICATION AND ORDER FOR APPEARANCE AND EXAMINATION
(Attachment—Enforcement of Judgment)

CCP 491.110, 708.110, 708.120

FORM 7
EXAMINATION IN SUPPLEMENTARY PROCEEDINGS EXAMPLE

Name _____ Spouse _____

Address _____ How long _____ Phone _____

Number of dependents and relationships _____

Employed by _____ Occupation _____ How long _____

Salary $ _____ per _____ How paid _____ When _____

Employer of spouse _____ Occupation _____ How long _____

Salary $ _____ per _____ How paid _____ When _____

Interest in any business _____

Other income _____

Own home _____ Value $ _____ Mortgages $ ____ Equity $ ___

Homestead date _____ Mortgagee _____ Payments $ _____ When _____

Rent _____ Amount $ _____ per month Date due _____

Landlord's name and address _____

Interest in other real estate _____ Encumbered? ____ Description _____

Bank _____ In whose name _____

Checking or savings _____ Last bank account _____ Closed _____

Safe deposit box _____ Where _____

Cash on person $ _____ Cash elsewhere _____

Stocks, bonds, securities _____

Life insurance co. _____ Amount $ _____ Annual premium $ ___

Jewelry _____ Interest to date _____

Auto or interest therein _____

Registered owner _____ Legal owner & address _____

Value $ _____ Payments $ _____ per _____ Unpaid balance $ _____

Other vehicles _____

Ever file for bankruptcy? _____ If so, when? _____ Where ? _____

Property pledged or pawned? _____

Debts owed to debtor _____

Name of parents _____ Address _____ Phone _____

Name of relatives or friends _____ Address _____ Phone _____

Promise to pay _____

Remarks _____

Serving interrogatories on the debtor

If you find it inconvenient to examine the debtor in court, of if the debtor lives too far away for you to require an appearance, you can require the debtor to answer written interrogatories.

Although you can write up your own questions, you can also use the *Judgment Debtor's Statement of Assets* or the *Examination in Supplementary Proceedings* form provided by some courts. This is different from the *Statement of Assets* form in that you are serving the debtor with these or other questions to fill out using the sheriff, marshal, or another process server to personally serve them on the debtor. Thus, your request for an answer now acquires the force of law—so if the debtor doesn't respond or doesn't answer truthfully, you have the power to ask the judge to order the debtor to respond appropriately. This time, if the debtor doesn't respond, you can ask the judge to hold the debtor in contempt of court.

The interrogatories process takes much longer than the *Order of Examination* procedure, since you are using the mails. Thus, this is an ideal time to try to persuade the debtor to pay you now, so you don't have to use the process, by sending the debtor a letter describing exactly what you intend to do and the costs to the debtor if you do it. Perhaps even enclose a copy of some of the legal documents you might use such as the *Writ* or *Subpoena Duces Tecum*, though stress how you really don't want to use them, and you may not have to.

Then if the debtor doesn't respond to your letter, go ahead with the interrogatories procedures. It's a hassle and expensive, but when you eventually find the debtor's assets, the debtor will have to pay these costs. Also, should the debtor try to avoid responding to your interrogatories, you can use your correspondence to help persuade a judge to issue a contempt finding against the debtor, since your letter shows your efforts to try to settle outside of court.

To serve your interrogatories, send them to the sheriff, marshal, or constable in the county where the person lives—or use a regular process server (though it's probably easier to use the county officer since the debtor is out of town). Call the appropriate law enforcement office in the area to find out the current fee and who should receive your interrogatories—or get this information from your local court clerk or from the state directory listing court districts, officers, and fees. Then, send your interrogatories with the required fees.

Once the debtor is served with these questions, he or she has 30 days to respond, and must do so by having a process server serve the papers on you.

What to do when the debtor responds— or doesn't respond

If the debtor responds adequately to your interrogatories, you're probably home free with the information you need to collect, unless the debtor is broke. Or perhaps you may get a phone call offering to pay. If so, you can short-circuit the process and simply collect the debt (though do add on your costs for serving the interrogatories).

But what if the debtor doesn't respond at all or doesn't give responsive answers? Then you can take steps to require the debtor to respond or face the penalties in court. The following sections describe some steps you can take.

If the debtor doesn't answer at all, you can file a motion with the courts within a certain time of the debtor's failure to respond (about 45 days, depending on the state). Then, the court will issue an order that the debtor must respond under penalty of law.

To write up a motion, get some legal paper, write at the top: *Motion for an Order Compelling an Answer for Interrogatories*; and include the following information from your judgment: the case number, the name of the court, and the names and addresses of the parties to the action. Next, skip a few lines and explain the reason(s) you are filing this motion—because the debtor refused to respond to your written interrogatories and you would like the court to issue an order requiring a response to your questions.

However, before you actually write and file this motion, send the debtor a letter stating that he or she has 10 days to send you the answers or you will file a motion. The reason for doing this is this letter serves as a notice of your motion, so you don't have to formally serve the debtor with a notice of motion by the courts.

Then, if you hear nothing in 10 days, go ahead and write up and file your motion with the court clerk. The clerk will give this motion to the judge, who will issue an order that the debtor must respond. You, in turn, can mail a copy of this motion to the debtor, as long as you have previously sent a letter of notice. Otherwise, the debtor must be formally served.

If, after another 30 days, the debtor hasn't responded, you can file another motion asking the judge to hold him or her in contempt of court for violating a court order. Entitle this one *Motion for Contempt of Court*.

This time, the judge will order the debtor to appear for a hearing on this motion, and again you have to arrange to have the debtor served with this order. Now if the debtor doesn't show up, he or she will be held in contempt and a bench warrant issued for his or her arrest to require an appearance on the contempt charges. Then, depending on what happens, this can lead to another order to respond to the interrogatories or perhaps some time in jail, unless the debtor arranges to pay what he or she owes.

When the debtor's responses are non-responsive

You know the debtor's responses are non-responsive when you get "I don't know's" to questions the debtor obviously should know, or if you get a response you know to be incorrect.

If you do get non-responsive answers, you should also file a motion in the courts within a certain time of receiving these answers (about 45 days). Then, once again, the court will issue an order requiring the debtor to make further responses, or if you have a good reason, you can persuade the judge to require the debtor to appear in court for a hearing.

Again, advise the debtor in writing that he or she has 10 days to send you adequate answers or you will file the motion, so you don't need to serve the debtor with a notice.

This time, entitle your motion something like *Motion for an Order to Compel Further Responses to Interrogatories*. Then, as before, include the relevant information about the case (e.g., the case number, court, and the names and addresses of the plaintiff and defendant) and explain your reasons: for instance, the debtor didn't give appropriate answers or tell the truth, and you would like the court to issue an order requiring the defendant to submit proper answers or to appear at a hearing to answer personally.

If the debtor is required to respond, he or she has 30 days, and if the judge has set a hearing, this will be indicated in the order.

In either case, if the debtor doesn't respond, responds inadequately again, or fails to appear at the hearing, you can request that he or she be held in contempt of court. If the debtor doesn't send in any answers, you can make this request in the form of a motion; or if he or she doesn't appear for a hearing, simply explain the situation and ask the judge to make such an order.

In either case, if the judge does hold the debtor in contempt, a bench warrant will be issued for the debtor's appearance on contempt charges, with the outcome depending on the debtor's response (perhaps another order to respond if the debtor has a good explanation or maybe jail if the debtor doesn't cooperate or arrange to pay.)

Your Cost of Using Interrogatories

The main costs of using the interrogatories process comes from serving the debtor. There's no charge to write up the interrogatories or file a motion to compel a response or request a hearing if you do it yourself. But each time you formally serve the debtor, it will cost you about $15 to 25 in service fees.

However, since these are costs you can charge to the debtor, you might keep him or her advised about these mounting costs (either with letters of advance warning or with the official cost memorandums as costs go up) to persuade the debtor to pay you now. Otherwise, not only will your own costs be added to the judgment, but when the debtor responds, he or she will have additional fees for serving you.

Similarly, let the debtor know about the possible penalties for non-response and non-compliance to encourage payment, too.

In other words, the advantage of knowing the process, costs, and penalties, and letting the debtor know you know the process and will use it unless the debtor cooperates, is that you may not need to use it. Just like a lawyer, your best strategy in using interrogatories as in any other legal process is to do what you can in advance to settle rather than using the courts. It's much less expensive and time consuming this way.

Skip Tracing

Basic skip tracing requires more than a lot of work—it also requires a strong desire to find your debtor. The amount of time involved to track down a debtor may be greater than you have or wish to expend. In these cases, it may be best to find someone else to do the tracing for you.

If you choose to do the skip tracing yourself, here are some tips to increase your odds of locating the debtor.

- Call Directory Assistance and have the operator try to find the debtor's phone number. This step is as effective as it is simple. And in some areas, the operator will check the entire area code, not just a specific city.

  Always have the invoice and the amount owed in front of you, in case you are successful in obtaining the debtor's phone number.

- Refer to the completed New Client Questionnaire (see page 3). Call friends and relatives and ask for the debtor's current address and phone number. Never state the real reason for the call; explain only that you are trying to contact the individual. If they will not give you that information, leave your name and phone number and ask that your call be returned.

- Use the Polk Directory or other criss-cross directories to obtain the names and phone numbers of neighbors. Call and ask if they have a forwarding address for the debtor. Again, do not disclose the debt as the reason for trying to contact the individual.

- Contact the post office and ask for the debtor's forwarding address. This request must be made to the specific post office where the debtor formerly received mail. There may be a small charge for this.

- Contact former employers and ask if they know where the individual is now working.

- Contact the landlord. It is always possible that the landlord will know where the tenant has moved to. On the other hand, it is also possible that the tenant left town owing back rent.

- Contact a credit bureau. Using information on the debtor's credit report, contact other creditors who show good pay records, or look for recent inquiries or requests for credit. The more recent the inquiry or request, the greater the chances of obtaining the debtor's new address or phone number.

Chapter 13

Using the Legal Process to Collect

Once you locate the debtor's assets, you can use various remedies provided by the courts to collect.

Though some of the specific procedures and names vary from state to state, there are several basic tools to use in collecting your judgment. Some or all of them are available in the different states:

The Tools to Collect Your Judgment

(1) **Writ of Execution, Possession or Sale**—used to levy against the debtor's assets, so you can take those assets or sell them to get your money (See Page 249 and 250 for an example of the form);

(2) **An Order to Withhold (or Garnish) Wages**—used in some jurisdictions, in addition to a *Writ of Execution*, to garnish the wages of a debtor from an employer, who becomes the garnishee. (See Page 269.)

(3) **Memorandum of Costs (sometimes called a Memorandum of Accrued Credits, Costs, and Interest)**—This is used to keep a running total of your additional costs after judgment, including costs for filing and serving writs, orders of examination, interrogatories, and abstracts of judgment; for executing sales; and interest. (See Page 253 and 254.)

(4) **Sheriff, Marshal, or Constable**—acts as your agent in enforcing the *Writ of Execution* and any garnishment proceedings. Per your instructions, he or she takes assets into custody, turns any cash or checks over to you; sells

property in an execution sale; and serves notices and court orders for you. They can often prior to taking any legal action if the debt involves bad checks or more than $500 in fraudulent action.

(5) **Abstract of Judgment**—used to record your judgment in any county where the debtor has real or personal property, so you can attach a judgment lien to it. This establishes the priority of your claim to the property, so you are in a better position to collect when the property is sold (or you force a property sale). An example of the form is shown later in this chapter.

(6) **Complaint for Renewal or Application for Revival of a Judgment**—used to extend the life of your judgment beyond a 10-year enforcement period, as long as you file suit to renew or apply to revive the judgment before the period ends.

It is crucial to use the tools of the court correctly, efficiently, and effectively in the four key ways noted below to avoid possible legal problems.

(1) **Follow the specified procedures, using the right tools to achieve the intended result.** For example, if your jurisdiction requires you to use an *Order to Withhold Wages* to garnish an employee's earnings, don't try to do this with just a letter of instructions and the usual writ. The sheriff either won't be able to execute your order; or if he or she mistakenly tries, the person against whom an execution is attempted can refuse to obey because the process is invalid, later seek a return of funds inappropriately collected, or perhaps even attempt to sue for misuse of legal process.

(2) **Use these procedures in a timely fashion.** By acting quickly, you increase your chances of collecting before changes in the debtor's situation make it more difficult to collect (e.g., he or she moves, goes bankrupt, gets divorced, or dies). Secondly, acting in a timely manner is important, because there are time restrictions on when you have to act to enforce your judgment.

(3) **Take into consideration the exemptions to which the debtor is entitled, before you seek to enforce a judgment, because you can't collect on exempt assets.** As a result, if you try to levy against them or garnish exempt wages, the debtor can simply file a claim of exemption and get back any exempt money or property. In turn, you may not be able to get back the money you expended in trying to get exempt assets.

(4) **Make sure you have correct and complete information about the debtor, location of assets, and type of assets to be collected.** You need to be able to give this information to the sheriff, marshal, or constable who acts for you, and if your information is incorrect or incomplete, you are responsible for whatever happens in an incorrect levy—and, this could create some legal problems for you.

In short, when you do use these court procedures yourself, know what you are doing before you act to use the proper procedures at the proper time to collect the proper assets from the proper person at the proper place. The levying officer will act for you—but he or she will do exactly as you instruct on the legal papers you fill out. So, make sure your instructions are correct to get

Using The Legal Process To Collect 249

WRIT OF EXECUTION EXAMPLE

ATTORNEY OR PARTY WITHOUT ATTORNEY *(Name and Address)*:   TELEPHONE NO.:

☐ Recording requested by and return to:

FOR RECORDER'S USE ONLY

☐ ATTORNEY FOR   ☐ JUDGMENT CREDITOR   ☐ ASSIGNEE OF RECORD

NAME OF COURT:
STREET ADDRESS:
MAILING ADDRESS:
CITY AND ZIP CODE:
BRANCH NAME:

PLAINTIFF:

DEFENDANT:

WRIT OF
☐ EXECUTION (Money Judgment)
☐ POSSESSION OF ☐ Personal Property
☐ SALE ☐ Real Property

CASE NUMBER:

FOR COURT USE ONLY

1. **To the Sheriff or any Marshal or Constable of the County of:**

   You are directed to enforce the judgment described below with daily interest and your costs as provided by law.

2. **To any registered process server:** You are authorized to serve this writ only in accord with CCP 699.080 or CCP 715.040.

3. *(Name)*:

   is the ☐ judgment creditor ☐ assignee of record whose address is shown on this form above the court's name.

4. **Judgment debtor** *(name and last known address)*:

   ☐ additional judgment debtors on reverse

5. **Judgment entered** on *(date)*:

6. ☐ **Judgment renewed** on *(dates)*:

7. **Notice of sale** under this writ
   a. ☐ has not been requested
   b. ☐ has been requested *(see reverse)*.

8. ☐ Joint debtor information on reverse.

[SEAL]

9. ☐ See reverse for information on real or personal property to be delivered under a writ of possession or sold under a writ of sale.
10. ☐ This writ is issued on a sister-state judgment.
11. Total judgment.. $
12. Costs after judgment (per filed order or memo CCP 685.090)............... $
13. Subtotal *(add 11 and 12)*................... $
14. Credits... $
15. Subtotal *(subtract 14 from 13)*........... $
16. Interest after judgment (per filed affidavit CCP 685.050)...................... $
17. Fee for issuance of writ........................ $
18. **Total** *(add 15, 16, and 17)*................ $
19. Levying officer: Add daily interest from date of writ *(at the legal rate on 15)* of.. $
20. ☐ The amounts called for in items 11-19 are different for each debtor. These amounts are stated for each debtor on Attachment 20.

Issued on *(date)*:   Clerk, by _____, Deputy

- NOTICE TO PERSON SERVED: SEE REVERSE FOR IMPORTANT INFORMATION -

(Continued on reverse)

Form Approved by the Judicial Council of California
EJ-130 [Rev. September 30, 1991*]
Martin Dean's Essential Forms ™

WRIT OF EXECUTION

Code of Civil Procedure, §§ 699.520, 712.010, 715.010
*See note on reverse.

WRIT OF EXECUTION EXAMPLE
(Reverse side)

SHORT TITLE:

CASE NUMBER:

Items continued from the first page:

4. ☐ **Additional judgment debtor** *(name and last known address)*:

7. ☐ **Notice of sale** has been requested by *(name and address)*:

8. ☐ **Joint debtor** was declared bound by the judgment (CCP 989-994)
    a. on *(date)*:
    b. name and address of joint debtor:

    a. on *(date)*:
    b. name and address of joint debtor:

    c. ☐ additional costs against certain joint debtors *(itemize)*:

9. ☐ *(Writ of Possession or Writ of Sale)* **Judgment** was entered for the following:
    a. ☐ Possession of real property. The complaint was filed on *(date)*:   ***(Check (1) or (2))***:
        (1) ☐ The Prejudgment Claim of Right to Possession was served in compliance with CCP 415.46.
            The judgment includes all tenants, subtenants, named claimants, and other occupants of the premises.
        (2) ☐ The Prejudgment Claim of Right to Possession was NOT served in compliance with CCP 415.46.
            (a) $ was the daily rental value on the date the complaint was filed.
            (b) The court will hear objections to enforcement of the judgment under CCP 1174.3 on the following dates *(specify)*:
    b. ☐ Possession of personal property
        ☐ If delivery cannot be had, then for the value *(itemize in 9e)* specified in the judgment or supplemental order.
    c. ☐ Sale of personal property
    d. ☐ Sale of real property
    e. Description of property:

- NOTICE TO PERSON SERVED -

WRIT OF EXECUTION OR SALE. Your rights and duties are indicated on the accompanying Notice of Levy.

WRIT OF POSSESSION OF PERSONAL PROPERTY. If the levying officer is not able to take custody of the property, the levying officer will make a demand upon you for the property. If custody is not obtained following demand, the judgment may be enforced as a money judgment for the value of the property specified in the judgment or in a supplemental order.

WRIT OF POSSESSION OF REAL PROPERTY. If the premises are not vacated within five days after the date of service on the occupant or, if service is by posting, within five days after service on you, the levying officer will remove the occupants from the real property and place the judgment creditor in possession of the property. Personal property remaining on the premises will be sold or otherwise disposed of in accordance with CCP 1174 unless you or the owner of the property pays the judgment creditor the reasonable cost of storage and takes possession of the personal property not later than 15 days after the time the judgment creditor takes possession of the premises.

▶ *A Claim of Right to Possession form accompanies this writ (unless the Summons was served in compliance with CCP 415.46).*

*NOTE: Continued use of form EJ-130 (Rev. Jan. 1, 1989) is authorized until June 30, 1992, except if used as a Writ of Possession of Real Property.

EJ-130 [Rev. September 30, 1991*]
Martin Dean's Essential Forms ™

WRIT OF EXECUTION

Page two

Using The Legal Process To Collect 251

the results you want. You can check with your local small claims legal advisor, court clerk, or county law enforcement office to be sure.

Using the Writ of Execution and Memorandum of Costs

- **Filling Out the Writ.** The *Writ of Execution* is your key tool for enforcing a money judgment, whether you are going after real or personal property, collecting money owed to a debtor by a third party, or garnishing wages. (See the example on Page 249 and 250.)

    Give this writ to the sheriff, marshal, or constable in the area where the debtor or any assets are located, and include with it very precise instructions describing what you want the officer to do.

    To fill out the writ, indicate that you are the judgment creditor and, where requested, include your name and address and list the plaintiff, defendant, and case number. Also, indicate that you have a money judgment, unless your judgment specifies that you are entitled to the possession or sale of personal or real property. Also, indicate the last known address for all judgment debtors to be affected by the writ, and your costs after judgment (to be explained in more detail).

    Then, on a separate sheet of paper or your own letterhead, write down your instructions very clearly. In some jurisdictions, if you are seeking to garnish wages, use a *Wage Garnishment* form for your instructions (sometimes called an *Application for Earnings Withholding Order*). Be very accurate in describing these assets and where they are because the levying officer will follow your instructions exactly.

    For example, if you want to levy against a person's bank account you should indicate the name of the person's bank, where it is located, and the account name and number. To have the officer take the person's car, indicate the name of the person, license number, and address where the car is likely to be located during the day when the officer carries out the levy. To get the receipts of a going business, arrange for an 8-hour keeper and indicate the name and address of the business and the hours you want the keeper there. To seize personal property, give the officer specific instructions on what to seize and sell, though be sure the property to be seized belongs to the debtor, is not exempt, and is worth enough for a sale, or you'll have problems when the debtor seeks the return of the property or when you discover the value of the property sold isn't enough to pay for the cost of a sale.

- **Preparing the Memorandum of Costs.** When you prepare the writ, also fill out a *Memorandum of Credits, Accrued Interest and Costs After Judgment*. Include your fees to the sheriff or other officer for levying on this Writ, and add any other fees you have not yet recorded for other court actions (such as serving the debtor to be examined in court or filling out interrogatories).

There's an example of how to fill out the writ, write instructions, and prepare the *Memorandum of Costs* on Page 253 and 254 using a bank account levy to illustrate. The cost of this levy goes on the *Memorandum of Costs*, and it is recorded again on the writ as one of the "Costs After Judgment." Your additional costs for getting the writ and any interest to date are entered directly on the writ.

- **Arranging to Have the Writ Served.** Once the writ and instructions are prepared, send or preferably take them to the sheriff, marshal, or constable's office in the county where the levy is occurring, with the appropriate fees for the action requested. (Usually, the levying officer will want an original and three copies.)

Then, the officer will use the writ and instructions to fill out a *Notice of Levy* which he or she will serve personally or by mail on the debtor, employer, bank official, or other person in charge of the debtor's assets. If someone other than the debtor is in charge of these assets, the debtor gets a notice, too. In the event that more than one debtor is bound by the judgment, each will receive a separate *Notice of Levy*, although all of them are listed on the same writ.

The *Notice of Levy* names the person being served, the property to be levied upon, and the amount necessary to satisfy the judgment. Also, it advises the debtor or other person in charge of the assets that he or she has up to 10 days to seek an exemption if the notice was personally served, or up to 15 days after it was mailed, by filing a claim of exemption. Or if the debtor wishes to get the property back, he or she can do so by paying the full amount of the judgment.

If you want the officer to take more than one action against a particular debtor, you need a separate writ, Instructions, and *Notice of Levy* for each action. (For instance, you can collect part of the debt from the debtor's bank account and have to levy on the receipts of the business to get the rest.) Just be aware that you can't collect more than the balance due with these levies. Thus, use the fewest number of levies you need to collect. It's more efficient and it keeps costs down, so there is more money left from what you seize for you. For an example of a *Notice of Levy*, see Page 258.

The role of the sheriff, marshal, or constable

After the sheriff, marshal, or constable gets the *Writ* and instructions from you and prepares the *Notice of Levy*, an officer will serve this Notice on the specified party (e.g., the debtor, third party creditor, employer, or bank officer) advising them that the specified assets are being levied against, and the debtor has up to 10 or 15 days to respond to either pay off the debt or claim the assets are exempt. If any sale is contemplated, the officer will also send notices to you and the debtor and will post notices in several public places (such as the sheriff's office, public library, and local Department of Vehicles).

EXAMPLE OF MEMORANDUM OF CREDITS, ACCRUED INTEREST AND COSTS AFTER JUDGMENT

214-21 (Rev. 1/91) Name, Address and Telephone No. of Attorney

Space Below for Use of Court Clerk Only

Attorney(s) for

**MUNICIPAL COURT FOR THE OAKLAND-PIEDMONT-EMERYVILLE JUDICIAL DISTRICT
COUNTY OF ALAMEDA, STATE OF CALIFORNIA**

_____ Plaintiff(s)

vs.

_____ Defendant(s)
(Abbreviated Title)

No._____

**MEMORANDUM OF CREDITS,
ACCRUED INTEREST AND
COSTS AFTER JUDGMENT**

MEMORANDUM OF CREDITS

CREDIT for payments and partial satisfaction of judgment, including direct payments and executions partially satisfied:
$... .
(if none, state none)

INTEREST ACCRUING AFTER JUDGMENT

INTEREST ACCRUING AFTER JUDGMENT at 10% from date of judgment on balances due after dates of payments or credits acknowledged above: $.. .

MEMORANDUM OF COSTS AFTER JUDGMENT

1 COSTS AFTER JUDGMENT CLAIMED ON MEMORANDUM FILED HERETOFORE:............... $............
2 CLERK'S FEES... $............
3 .... $............
4 SHERIFF OR MARSHAL'S FEES: .... $............
5 .... $............
6 SERVING SUPPLEMENTARY PROCEEDINGS:... $............
7 .... $............
8 NOTARY FEES: .... $............
9 .... $............
10 .... $............
11 .... $............
12 .... $............
13 .... $............
                                                                              TOTAL $............

I, the undersigned, say: I am ....
the attorney(s) for the ....
in the above entitled action, that, to the best of my knowledge and belief, the items in the within memorandum are correct and that the said disbursements have been necessarily incurred in said action.
I declare under penalty of perjury that the foregoing is true and correct.

Executed on........................at......................................., California

....
Signature

NOTE: A notice of motion to tax costs shall specify the items of the cost bill to which objection is made. The fees sought under this memorandum may be disallowed by a court upon a motion to tax filed by the debtor notwithstanding the fees having been included in the writ of execution.

Code of Civ. Proc. Sec. 682:2, 1033.7, 2015.5
Rule 503(d) California Rules of Court.

**MEMORANDUM OF CREDITS, ACCRUED INTEREST
AND COSTS AFTER JUDGMENT**

EXAMPLE OF MEMORANDUM OF CREDITS, ACCRUED INTEREST AND COSTS AFTER JUDGMENT (Reverse side)

DECLARATION OF CERTIFICATE OF SERVICE BY MAIL

.... C.C.P. Sec. 1010, et seq. 2015.5

DECLARATION OF SERVICE BY MAIL

My.......................... address is ....
    (business/residence)

I am, and was at the time the herein mentioned mailing took place, a citizen of the United States, ...
                                                                                                                                                                            (employed/resident)

in the County where said mailing occurred, over the age of eighteen years and not a party of the above-entitled cause.

On.., I served the foregoing Memorandum of Costs by depositing a copy thereof, enclosed in separate, sealed envelope, with the postage thereon fully prepaid, in the United States mail at

.... County of................................., California,
   (city or postal area)

each of which envelopes was addressed respectively as follows:

Executed on..............................., at................................., California.
                 (date)   (place)

I declare under penalty of perjury that the foregoing is true and correct.

....
(Signature of Declarant)

ATTORNEY'S CERTIFICATE OF SERVICE

I, the undersigned, certify: that I am an active member of the State Bar of California and not a party to the above-entitled cause,

and my business address is ....

...., California;

that on ....I served the foregoing Memorandum of Costs by depositing

a copy thereof, enclosed in separate, sealed envelope, with the postage thereon fully prepaid, in the United States mail at

..................................., at................................., California,
   (city or postal area)

each of which envelopes was addressed respectively as follows:

Name:.................................. Address:..................................

....
Attorney

ACKNOWLEDGEMENT OF SERVICE

Received copy of the foregoing Memorandum of Costs

on..............................,.............................., Attorney for ....

on..............................,.............................., Attorney for ....

SAMPLE LETTER OF INSTRUCTIONS

> 1234 North Street
>
> San Francisco, CA   94103
>
> November 4, 1993
>
> To the Sheriff, County of San Francisco
>
> Please serve this Writ and levy against the bank account of Dan Defendant. This account is at the National Bank of America, 567 Andrews Avenue, San Francisco. The account number is 034-7311078.
>
> Then, please send any funds collected to me at the above address.
>
> A check for your fee for a bank levy of $28 is enclosed.
>
> Sincerely,
>
> Pam Plaintiff

After this grace period, if the debtor does not pay or the assets are not exempt, the levy will go through. Conversely, if the debtor pays or any assets are exempt, they will be returned to the debtor.

When the debtor doesn't respond, different things happen, depending on the type of assets involved. For example, any non-exempt funds in the debtor's bank account are turned over to the levying officer, who will pay those funds to you. If the action is against wages, the employer has to start paying up to 25% of the debtor's wages to this officer, who will send it to you. Or, if property is involved, the officer is free to sell it and turn over the proceeds, less any storage and sale expenses, to you.

Alternatively, if the officer is unable to carry out the levy within a certain time period (up to 180 days in some states), he or she will return the *Writ* to the court, and the court will send you notice of its return. Then, you have the option of seeking another Writ to try a levy again.

Though an officer may have up to six months to act on a *Writ*, more typically, the sheriff, marshal, or constable will take some action within a week or so and will let you know much sooner than this time limit if an officer hasn't been able to make a levy. For example in some jurisdictions, the sheriff's office will only hold a *Writ of Execution* against an auto for up to two months. And, if you are seeking the assets of a going business, the sheriff will expect to act within a few days.

Using an abstract of judgment

The primary purpose of using an *Abstract of Judgment* is to create a lien on real or personal property, and thereby establish the priority of your claim to it.

In addition, you can use the abstract to transfer the jurisdiction over a case to another court—such as when you want another court to issue an *Order of Examination*, so you can examine the debtor there, rather than in the court which originally rendered the verdict.

You get the abstract from the court which tried the case, and there is usually a small fee (about $3 to 4) to have it issued. Then, after you record the usual information about the judgment (including the name of the plaintiff, defendant, case number, and any data on the debtor's driver's license or social security number—see the example on Page 259 and 260), file the *Abstract* with the agency that handles what you want to do.

For example, to attach a lien to real property, send or take the abstract to be recorded at the county recorder's office in the county where the debtor owns property. To put a lien on personal property (such as inventory or equipment), file this *Abstract* with the secretary of state in the state where this property is located. Or to have another court assume jurisdiction, send or take an abstract to that court, along with instructions on what that court should do. And, of course, include the required fees for whatever action you take.

Using a Memorandum of Credits, Interests, and Costs After Judgment

Use the *Memorandum of Credits, Accrued Interest, and Costs After Judgment* to add additional expenses onto your judgment, and deduct any payments the debtor makes. Besides filling this out when you obtain a Writ of Execution, you should fill it out when you use any other court procedures that cost money, such as examining the debtor in court, serving interrogatories, recording an *Abstract of Judgment*, or having an officer execute a sale. Also, if it has been some time since you have taken any action, use this memorandum to add on your interest.

After you fill out this form, file one copy with the court clerk and have another copy served on the debtor. (You can use any kind of personal service—a county officer, a private process server, or a friend). The reason for serving it on the debtor is to give the debtor a chance to protest your accumulating costs by filing the appropriate forms with the court, though most likely, the debtor won't.

Getting the Debtor's Assets

Now that you know about the legal process and tools available, you're ready to go after the debtor's assets. Keep in mind, though, that many of the debtor's personal assets may be exempt, and if there are other creditors stalking the debtor, you may have to get there before them to collect. (Also, note that it's easier to go after the debtor's more readily accessible assets first—like a bank account, wages, and receipts from a going business. So, save the harder-to-reach assets which you have to sell for later—like personal property, equipment, inventory, and stocks and bonds.) But, first, we'll discuss exemptions since you want to avoid property that might be exempt.

Knowing what property is exempt

When you're trying to collect from an individual or small business run by a sole proprietor, you run into the problem of exemptions. It's not normally an issue when you are collecting from an established going business or from someone with numerous assets. But state and federal law has created numerous exemptions from debt collectors to protect the individual from losing so much that he or she can't make a fresh start. In this case, an attachment of the business checking account is best.

In fact, you'll find some low income people are "judgment proof," because they don't have enough personal property to take and because their income is too low or comes from exempt sources (such as welfare or disability payments). Since circumstances always change, it's wise to monitor the situation from time to time to see if there are improvements. But otherwise, don't waste time going after any assets, since there's nothing to collect. Everything is exempt.

However, with most other individual wage earners and small business owners, you'll find some assets are exempt while others are not. By knowing the difference, you can avoid spending time or money trying to collect exempt assets.

While specifics differ from state to state, in general, the following assets are exempt:

- **Wages.** If the person is only receiving the minimum wage as provided by law, all wages are exempt; or up to 75% of all wages as long as the person is left with at least this minimum. Therefore, you can only garnish up to 25% of the person's wages, and if another creditor has already garnished them, you have to wait until that order runs out.

- **Personal and household property.** All personal and household property is exempt, up to a limit set by the federal government or the state. Since this limit can go up to about $8,000, this means that usually you can forget about taking any of the debtor's personal effects or furniture, unless the debtor has much more than $8,000 in personal property and the items you are taking are non-essential or high-value luxury items (like expensive jewelry, antiques or cameras).

- **The value of a motor vehicle.** Up to a certain amount (approximately $1,200 in some states), the value of a motor vehicle is exempt. This means that you can't take a car worth less than $1,200, and if it is worth more, and the car is sold at an execution sale, you only get back what's left after the debtor receives the value of the exemption in cash. Also, any costs of the sale and storage are deducted (around $200 to 400). Trying to take a car, however, is often not a good idea because of the likelihood that the bank will have a lien on the automobile.

EXAMPLE OF NOTICE OF LEVY

| ATTORNEY OR PARTY WITHOUT ATTORNEY (Name and Address): | TELEPHONE NO.: | FOR RECORDER'S USE ONLY |

☐ Recording requested by and return to:

ATTORNEY FOR (Name):
NAME OF COURT:
STREET ADDRESS:
MAILING ADDRESS:
CITY AND ZIP CODE:
BRANCH NAME:

PLAINTIFF:

DEFENDANT:

NOTICE OF LEVY
under Writ of ☐ Execution (Money Judgment) ☐ Sale

LEVYING OFFICER (Name and Address):

TO THE PERSON NOTIFIED (name):

| LEVYING OFFICER FILE NO. | COURT CASE NO: |

1. The judgment creditor seeks to levy upon property in which the judgment debtor has an interest and apply it to the satisfaction of a judgment as follows:
    a. judgment debtor (name):
    b. the property to be levied upon is described
        ☐ in the accompanying writ of possession or writ of sale.
        ☐ as follows:

2. The amount necessary to satisfy the judgment creditor's judgment is (specify total amount due under the writ less partial satisfactions plus daily interest from the date of the writ until the date of levy):
    $

3. You are notified as
    a. ☐ a judgment debtor.
    b. ☐ a person other than the judgment debtor (state capacity in which person is notified):

(Read Information for Judgment Debtor or Information for Person Other Than Judgment Debtor on reverse.)

Notice of Levy was
☐ mailed on (date):
☐ delivered on (date):
☐ posted on (date):
☐ filed on (date):
☐ recorded on (date):

Signed by:

☐ Levying officer ☐ Registered process server

(Continued on reverse)

Form Approved by the
Judicial Council of California
EJ-150 [Rev. January 1, 1985]
Martin Dean's Essential Forms ™

NOTICE OF LEVY
(Enforcement of Judgment)

CCP 699.540

EXAMPLE OF ABSTRACT OF JUDGMENT

ATTORNEY OR PARTY WITHOUT ATTORNEY (Name and Address):	TELEPHONE NO.:	FOR RECORDER'S USE ONLY
☐ Recording requested by and return to:		
☐ ATTORNEY FOR ☐ JUDGMENT CREDITOR ☐ ASSIGNEE OF RECORD		
NAME OF COURT: OAKLAND-PIEDMONT-EMERYVILLE JUDICIAL DISTRICT		
STREET ADDRESS: 600 WASHINGTON STREET		
MAILING ADDRESS:		
CITY AND ZIP CODE: OAKLAND, CALIFORNIA 94607-3997		
BRANCH NAME:		
PLAINTIFF:		
DEFENDANT:		
ABSTRACT OF JUDGMENT	CASE NUMBER:	FOR COURT USE ONLY

1. The ☐ judgment creditor ☐ assignee of record
   applies for an abstract of judgment and represents the following:
   a. Judgment debtor's
      Name and last known address

   b. Driver's license No. and state: ☐ Unknown
   c. Social Security No.: ☐ Unknown
   d. Summons or notice of entry of sister-state judgment was personally served or mailed to (name and address):

   e. ☐ Additional judgment debtors are shown on reverse.
   Date:

   ....(TYPE OR PRINT NAME).. ▶ _____(SIGNATURE OF APPLICANT OR ATTORNEY)

2. a. ☐ I certify that the following is a true and correct abstract of the judgment entered in this action.
   b. ☐ A certified copy of the judgment is attached.
3. Judgment creditor (name):

   whose **address** appears on this form above the court's name.
4. Judgment debtor (full name as it appears in judgment):

[SEAL]

5. a. Judgment entered on (date):
   b. Renewal entered on (date):
   c. Renewal entered on (date):

   This abstract issued on (date):

6. Total amount of judgment as entered or last renewed:
   $
7. ☐ An ☐ execution ☐ attachment lien
   is endorsed on the judgment as follows:
   a. Amount: $
   b. In favor of (name and address):

8. A stay of enforcement has
   a. ☐ not been ordered by the court.
   b. ☐ been ordered by the court effective until (date):
9. ☐ This judgment is an installment judgment.

Clerk, by _____, Deputy

Form Adopted by Rule 982
Judicial Council of California
982(a)(1) [Rev. January 1, 1991]

ABSTRACT OF JUDGMENT
(CIVIL)

Code of Civil Procedure, §§ 488.480,
674, 700.190

EXAMPLE OF ABSTRACT OF JUDGMENT
(Reverse side)

PLAINTIFF:
DEFENDANT:

CASE NUMBER:

INFORMATION ON ADDITIONAL JUDGMENT DEBTORS

10. Name and last known address

Driver's license No. & state: ☐ Unknown
Social Security No.: ☐ Unknown
Summons was personally served at or mailed to (address):

14. Name and last known address

Driver's license No. & state: ☐ Unknown
Social Security No.: ☐ Unknown
Summons was personally served at or mailed to (address):

11. Name and last known address

Driver's license No. & state: ☐ Unknown
Social Security No.: ☐ Unknown
Summons was personally served at or mailed to (address):

15. Name and last known address

Driver's license No. & state: ☐ Unknown
Social Security No.: ☐ Unknown
Summons was personally served at or mailed to (address):

12. Name and last known address

Driver's license No. & state: ☐ Unknown
Social Security No.: ☐ Unknown
Summons was personally served at or mailed to (address):

16. Name and last known address

Driver's license No. & state: ☐ Unknown
Social Security No.: ☐ Unknown
Summons was personally served at or mailed to (address):

13. Name and last known address

Driver's license No. & state: ☐ Unknown
Social Security No.: ☐ Unknown
Summons was personally served at or mailed to (address):

17. Name and last known address

Driver's license No. & state: ☐ Unknown
Social Security No.: ☐ Unknown
Summons was personally served at or mailed to (address):

18. ☐ Continued on attachment 18.

982(a)(1) (Rev. January 1, 1991)

ABSTRACT OF JUDGMENT
(CIVIL)

Page two

- **The person's tools of the trade.** (Up to a certain value, usually about $2,500.) This includes tools, equipment, instruments, materials, uniforms, furnishings, books, one motor vehicle, and other personal property used in the person's work or business. As in the case of the car, if there is an execution sale, you only get what is left over after the debtor gets the exemption and expenses of the sale are deducted.

- **Income received from various government benefit programs.** This includes Social Security payments, disability benefits, retirement income, and money from annuities, pensions, unemployment insurance and strike benefits.

- **Miscellaneous insurance benefits.** This includes unmatured life insurance, endowment, and annuities as well as any benefits paid from a matured policy, which are necessary to support the debtor, his or her spouse, and any dependent. Though you can attach the loan value of an unmatured policy, a certain amount of this value is exempt (usually about $4,000).

- **Various benefits due to legal claims are also exempt.** This includes personal injury settlements and workers' compensation claims to the extent they are necessary to support the debtor, spouse, and dependents.

- **The debtor's homestead.** This is defined as the principal dwelling where the debtor or his or her spouse lives. As long as debtor or the spouse lives there, the exemption remains. (It ranges from $30,000 for a single debtor to $45,000 for a debtor living with a spouse or child or for a debtor who is 65 or older, depending on the state.) Because of this homestead exemption, you get back only what is left after the debtor takes the exemption, and after any other encumbrances on the house are deducted, such as a mortgage and any prior liens placed on the house before your lien or execution sale.

- **Money in a person's bank account.** Since it can be traced to funds which would be exempt, money in a person's bank account is exempt. (For example, if a person deposits funds earned at a job, 75% of those funds would be exempt. Or if the person can show these earnings come from benefits and other earnings that would be exempt, they would be completely exempt.) Also exempt is money received from the government and deposited in a checking account.

Check with your local small claims legal advisor on the specific exemptions in your area.

What the Debtor Can Do to Protect Exempt Property

The reason you want to avoid trying to collect on exempt property is that the debtor can file a claim to get the property back. You may also not be able to collect your expenses for an unsuccessful and wrongful attempt to collect. In some cases, the expenses involved will be small and your expenses for such an attempt may not be questioned—such as when you try to levy on a bank account with exempt funds or seek to garnish wages when another creditor has already beat you to it. (As noted, these expenses will be about $30).

But if your expenses are high and you make a mistake, the costs may be questioned and denied. For example, if you try to sell off some of the debtor's furniture which can't be sold, you're looking at about $400 or more in expenses to arrange for a 48-hour keeper to take the property into custody and store it. Or if you try to levy on an auto which is exempt, that's about $200 in expenses. In turn, you may not be able to get back such costs, because presumably you should do some checking before incurring major expenses to make sure the assets are ones you can collect.

Since not all debtors know how to protect themselves or act quickly enough to claim an exemption, you may sometimes end up with exempt property you should not normally be able to collect. But, if the debtor does know, he or she can act to void your collection efforts—though you can still try to counter those efforts with an appeal.

Finding out about other creditors

Besides making sure the assets aren't exempt, the other important thing to do before going after the debtor's assets is to check that other creditors with judgments or secured property interests haven't already gone after the same assets, so you know if there is likely to be something left to attach.

Depending on the type of assets involved, there are four sources to check for information on other creditors (unless you can get this information from the debtor).

- **County Recorder.** This is the source to check by doing a title search, if you are considering putting a lien on the debtor's real property or forcing an execution sale. A title search will tell you whether the debtor is the sole owner or owns the property as community property (in which case all of it is subject to any liens and attachments) or owns only a share of it as a joint tenant or tenant-in-common (in which case, you want to determine what liens or encumbrances exist on the debtor's share of the property). Then, after you determine what the debtor owns, you can find out what's left after you deduct any homestead exemptions, mortgages, or liens, and decide if there's enough equity in the debtor's property to justify seeking a lien or perhaps initiating a sale. If you have trouble understanding the record, ask one of the clerks in the Recorder's Office for help.

- **Secretary of State.** Check these records if you are considering placing a lien on major items of personal or business property or asking a levying officer to take them into custody and sell them. These records will tell you if any secured creditors have filed a notice of their security with the secretary of state's office. If so, they have "perfected" their security interest, which means their interest will take priority to your attempts to attach that property and sell it. If you try to do so and the secured creditor learns about it, he or she can ask that any sale be set aside, because he or she already has a "perfected security interest" in that property.

- **County Clerk's Office.** This office has a record of any previous efforts by creditors to levy against the debtor's assets, since copies of writs issued and returned become part of the case files. You'll have to check the files on a case by case basis by looking up the cases where the debtor was a defendant. These records include information on both successful levies (which you can infer from any credits listed on the memorandum of costs and from the filing of a satisfaction of judgment if any) and on unsuccessful attempts (which result in the levying officer returning the writ to the court).

- **Office of the Sheriff, Marshal, or Constable Where the Debtor or Debtor's Assets are Located.** Since this is the office responsible for carrying out any levies against the debtor, this office will know if any creditors currently have *Writs of Execution* assigned for levy against a particular debtor's assets. It makes sense to find out if there are such creditors because the levying officers are supposed to levy upon the writs in the order in which they receive them. So this information can help you decide whether it's worth it to go after a particular asset or use another approach.

For example, since only one wage garnishment is permitted at a time, if one creditor is currently garnishing a debtor's wages, you know your own order will be returned and you'll have to file again. So, rather than waste the time and money on filing, you might wait for the current garnishment order to expire (it lasts for 90 days), and get your own order in on the expiration date, so you are likely to be the first in line to be the next garnisher. Alternatively, perhaps you might opt to go after a different asset, such as the bank account of the debtor. Or you might wait until the debtor gets a new job and try to be the first to file your order to attach wages. Similarly, if you learn the sheriff has already taken some property from a going business, you know that property is no longer available and you'll have to go after something else.

In short, find out as much as possible about the status of the debtor's assets before you file, so you don't end up trying to get unavailable assets, which are already in the hands of other creditors.

Levying on the debtor's bank accounts

The debtor's bank or savings account is probably the easiest asset from which to collect if you can find it and if it has any money in it. When you find it, you can readily determine how much money is in it by calling up the bank to find out if a check with a certain amount of money will clear. If yes, try a little later with a slightly higher check, until the check won't clear or you know there's enough to cover your judgment and levy. If you get a no, try a smaller check, until one will go through. Through a process of elimination, you'll get a rough idea of the balance in the account.

Obviously, there's no point in levying on the account if there's very little there. But in this case, you might try monitoring the account to see if the balance goes up substantially. Then try to time your levy for a time when there is more money in the bank—preferably enough to satisfy your full judgment, although be prepared for collecting only a partial payment. An excellent time to levy an account is soon after the debtor gets paid.

If the sheriff, marshal, or constable is willing, make an arrangement whereby the deputy serving the levy will wait for you to call in a request to serve it now, and will then serve it that day. (This way you can call the bank, and if the account has a high balance, call the officer.) Or alternatively, ask if you can specify the day and time in your instructions. (Then pick a time when you think there is likely to be more money in the account.)

After you levy on the debtor's funds, it's likely the debtor will open up another account or change banks. So, if you haven't satisfied your judgment completely, you'll have to find the debtor's accounts again, or levy against another asset.

To levy on an account, simply take or mail the original *Writ of Execution* (and commonly one copy) to the sheriff, marshal, or constable in the county where the bank is located. Include the current fee (about $28 depending on the state) and provide instructions indicating the name and location of the bank, name and number of the account, amount of the outstanding debt to collect, and other relevant information, such as when and how to serve the levy, if the officer is receptive to more specific instructions. For example, your letter of instructions might say the following:

```
"Please levy upon all funds up to $1,000 in the
checking (or savings) account of John Andrews,
account number 123-42-6089, located at the National
Bank of California, 124 South Street, San
Francisco."
```

If the account is in the debtor's name alone or held by a sole proprietorship, the whole account will be subject to your levy, and you don't need to post a special bond based on the amount of your levy. However, if the account is in the name of the debtor and someone else, you can only attach the debtor's share of the funds (normally an equal share), and you have to post a bond for twice the amount on which you are seeking to levy (though you'll get it back after the levy is carried out successfully).

Also, be aware that exemptions can affect your levy. For instance, if these funds represent wages and the debtor makes a claim showing this, you can only get up to 25% of those funds which come from wages. Similarly, if the source of the debtor's funds are fully exempt (such as welfare or disability payments) and the debtor claims this, you can't get anything from the bank.

In any event, once the levying officer serves the appropriate bank official, the bank will put a hold on the funds in the account at the time of the levy for the required 10 days, while the debtor has a chance to claim an exemption. If he or she doesn't, the bank will pay these funds over to you. Conversely, if the debtor does make a claim, any funds found exempt, either by statute or after a hearing, will be released back to the debtor, and the remainder, if anything, will go to you.

Levying on the debtor's wages

If the debtor is working, another relatively accessible source of funds is wages. However, the debtor must earn more than a minimum amount each week (30 times the current minimum wage) for you to garnish his or her wages. Then, you can garnish up to 25% of the wages, as long as the debtor is left with at least this minimum amount.

Also, be aware of a few other possible hurdles to collecting wages, though in most cases, garnishing wages is fairly routine:

- The debtor has a chance to show that any wages, even above the minimum, are subject to an exemption, if these are necessary to his or her own support of a spouse or children.

- You can't garnish wages if they have already been garnished by another creditor (the one exception is a former spouse seeking alimony or child support payments). Your order will be rejected and you will have to file again.

- You can't garnish the wages of a federal employee or person in the military, due to federal laws.

The garnishment procedures operates like this: You must obtain the usual *Writ of Execution*. Then, depending on the jurisdiction, you either write your instructions in a letter or use an *Application for Earnings Withholding Order*, previously described. In your letter or application, ask the sheriff, marshal, or constable in the county where the debtor works to issue an *Earnings Withholding Order* directing the employer to withhold the debtor's earnings for a specified garnishment period (up to 90 days). Also, this letter or application should include the names and addresses of the employer, debtor, and person to whom the money should be paid, the amount to be collected, and whether you have previously applied for an order.

Then, based on this information, the levying officer will prepare an *Earnings Withholding Order* (see the example in this chapter), and will serve it either personally or by mail on the employer or an agent in charge of the office or payroll. Also, along with this *Order*, the levying officer will delivery an *Employer's Return* form, and a notice with instructions about the garnishment for the employee.

The employer must then fill out the form and mail it back to the levying officer within 15 days. On this form, the employer has to correct any wrong information about the name and address of the employer or debtor; indicate whether the debtor is still employed, and if so, any earnings in the last pay period; and state how often the debtor is paid (daily, weekly, every two weeks, twice a month, monthly, or other).

Also, the return form instructs the employer how to handle the withholding, if he or she has previously received a wage garnishment order. For example, orders for support have first priority, then orders for taxes, and then previously received *Earnings Withholding Orders*. Should the employer get two orders on the same date, he or she should comply with the one with the earliest date of judgment; or if the judgment dates are the same, the employer can select which order to carry out.

By law, the employer is required to return these forms and carry out the order; and if the employer doesn't, you can bring an action against him or her to recover this amount, as well as attorney's fees. Also, an employer may be subject to criminal prosecution if he or she doesn't obey.

Finally, the employer must advise the debtor about the *Earnings Withholding Order*, so the debtor understands how much will be held for the garnishment period, and is aware that he or she has up to 10 days to see an attorney, work out an agreement with the creditor, or file a claim of exemption and a financial statement (as previously described) to show these earnings are needed for support. The procedures for filing this claim are included in this notice.

Then, after this waiting period, if you don't work out some other arrangement with the debtor or the debtor doesn't seek or obtain an exemption, the employer will begin sending a portion of the debtor's wages above the minimum to you each pay period, using a formula described on the *Earnings Withholding Order*.

If the debtor does seek an exemption, you have an opportunity to oppose it as described earlier, and if the exemption is denied, you'll start getting your money. The withholding period begins 10 days after the employer receives the order (unless the levy is turned down) and continues for up to 90 days.

However. this period may end sooner if you collect all your money before then or if the employer gets an order of higher priority (i.e., for support or taxes). Of course, if the debtor stops for this employer, the withholding period will stop. But if the debtor resumes working for the employer during this time, the withholding period starts again, too.

If the debtor still owes you money after the garnishment order expires or is terminated by the court, or if the first order was ineffective, you can apply for another order against the same employer, though you have to wait—10 days after an order expires; 60 to 100 days if the order is terminated by the court—perhaps because of an exemption. Or if you file against a new employer, you can do so immediately.

Although these procedures may seem somewhat torturous and involved, commonly you will find the employer complies and you will get regular payments for as long as the withholding period continues and the employee is employed. But should payments stop, check back with the employer or levying officer to make sure the arrangement is continuing as it should, so you get your money.

Levying on the receipts of a going business

Another relatively accessible source of assets, if you have a judgment against a corporation or individual with a small business, is to collect any cash on hand or any receipts that come in over an 8 to 48 hour period. All sales must be considered final, and any checks are considered the equivalent of cash. However, the levying officer will not take over any MasterCard, Visa, or other credit card purchases.

The way the levy works is this: You give the sheriff, marshal, or constable a *Writ of Execution* with instructions indicating when and where to go. Per your instructions, the levying officer goes to the business, informs the person in charge of your order, and proceeds to collect as instructed, up to the amount of your levy, plus the costs of collection.

You pay in advance for the cost of the levy, plus the amount of time the deputy spends at the business, figured at the daily rate (about $35 a day). You put up a deposit to cover the maximum costs of making the levy and get back a refund if the deputy doesn't stay that long. Of course, with a successful levy, these costs are passed on to the debtor.

You Have Several Different Options

(1) **A Till Tap.** The deputy makes a single trip to the business and picks up all the money currently in the cash register. Thus, if you know a company is likely to have a substantial amount of cash or checks on hand at a certain time, instruct the deputy to visit the business then. The advance fee is about $49; and you'll get back about $21 if the deputy can't collect for some reason (e.g., there's nothing in the till; the business is closed; or you sent the deputy to the wrong address).

(2) **An 8-Hour Keeper.** In this case, the deputy spends a day at the place of business and collects any funds that come in. This is a particularly good approach to use at a retail establishment, which will be getting cash and checks throughout the day. In fact, the presence of an officer who takes each bill or check as it goes into the cash box may be enough to induce the debtor to work out a settlement with you, so you won't need to send in another keeper to get the rest.

This is also a good approach to use to find out about the assets of the business, before taking other more expensive measures, since you can have a deputy take an inventory of any equipment, furniture, and merchandise. The advance fee for this is also about $49, with a refund of about $21 if the deputy doesn't spend the entire day. Also, you can arrange for the deputy to serve a *Subpoena Duces Tecum* along with your order to require the debtor to send you information on all sorts of business documents and records, as well as the company checkbook. Or, perhaps wait for the results of the keeper first, and then if you still need more information, arrange for a subpoena.

(3) **An 8- to 12-Hour Keeper or a 12- to 24-Hour Keeper.** The procedure is much the same as in the 8-hour keeper arrangement—the deputy just stays

longer, and it costs more. It may make sense to use this arrangement if you're dealing with a business that has unusually long hours or operates around the clock. The deposit is around $410 though you may get much of this back.

(4) **A 48-Hour Keeper.** Again, a deputy shows up at the business, this time for up to 48 hours. While this procedure can be used solely for collecting cash on hand and receipts as with the other keepers arrangements, this is also the procedure you need to use to take any personal property or inventory from the business, since the deputy needs this time to make moving and storage arrangements. This deposit is also about $410.

In any of these levies, the officer will stay up to the time instructed, or until he or she has collected the balance specified in your *Writ*, plus the amount needed to cover the costs of collection. After collecting and deducting the collection fee, the officer will pay any proceeds over to you. Then, you apply these to the total due on the judgment.

Normally, the officer will not have any problems taking charge of the business, but if the debtor objects, he or she has one option—to close the business. Otherwise, the deputy will stay, as requested in your order.

Taking the debtor's business property

As long as the debtor has a business establishment open to the public, such as a store, bar, grocery, or office, the levying officer can take any assets. Aside from any cash on hand or receipts obtained while the business is operating, the levying officer can (if he or she is there long enough) take inventory, furnishings, equipment, and other items, which are not previously claimed by a secured creditor who has "perfected" that claim by filing it with the secretary of state.

However, if the debtor is running the business from a home, you're probably out of luck, since the levying officer can't forcibly enter a dwelling to take anything without a court order, and judges are reluctant to issue such an order, since they consider a person's home his or her castle. So, unless you can show some pressing need to take property from the debtor's home—and there's a good chance you can't—you can't get the debtor's personal and business property this way.

Also, if the debtor is involved in a partnership, you can only go after the debtor's property or share of the business, unless your judgment is against everybody involved.

To get the property of a going business, you have to arrange for a 48-hour keeper, since the levying officer needs this time to take over the property. To make these arrangements, give the sheriff the usual *Writ of Execution*, along with a letter of instructions and the required deposit (about $410).

EXAMPLE OF EARNINGS WITHHOLDING ORDER

ATTORNEY OR PARTY WITHOUT ATTORNEY (Name and Address):	TELEPHONE NO.:	LEVYING OFFICER (Name and Address):
ATTORNEY FOR (Name):		
NAME OF COURT, JUDICIAL DISTRICT OR BRANCH COURT, IF ANY:		
PLAINTIFF:		
DEFENDANT:		

APPLICATION FOR EARNINGS WITHHOLDING ORDER (Wage Garnishment)	LEVYING OFFICER FILE NO.:	COURT CASE NO.:

TO THE SHERIFF OR ANY MARSHAL OR CONSTABLE OF THE COUNTY OF
OR ANY REGISTERED PROCESS SERVER

1. The judgment creditor *(name)*:

   requests issuance of an Earnings Withholding Order directing the employer to withhold the earnings of the judgment debtor (employee).
   Name and address of employer   Name and address of employee

   Social Security Number *(if known)*:

2. The amounts withheld are to be paid to
   a. ☐ The attorney (or party without an attorney) named at the top of this page.
   b. ☐ Other *(name, address, and telephone)*:

3. a. Judgment was entered on *(date)*:
   b. Collect the amount directed by the Writ of Execution unless a lesser amount is specified here:
   $

4. ☐ The Writ of Execution was issued to collect delinquent amounts payable for the **support** of a child, former spouse, or spouse of the employee.

5. ☐ Special instructions *(specify)*:

6. *(Check a or b)*
   a. ☐ I have not previously obtained an order directing this employer to withhold the earnings of this employee.
   -OR-
   b. ☐ I have previously obtained such an order, but that order *(check one)*:
      ☐ was terminated by a court order, but I am entitled to apply for another Earnings Withholding Order under the provisions of Code of Civil Procedure section 706.105(h).
      ☐ was ineffective.

   ▶
   _____   _____
   (TYPE OR PRINT NAME)   (SIGNATURE OF ATTORNEY OR PARTY WITHOUT ATTORNEY)

   I declare under penalty of perjury under the laws of the State of California that the foregoing is true and correct.

Date:
   ▶
   _____   _____
   (TYPE OR PRINT NAME)   (SIGNATURE OF DECLARANT)

Form Adopted by the
Judicial Council of California
982.5(1) [Rev. January 1, 1993]
Martin Dean's Essential Forms ™

APPLICATION FOR EARNINGS WITHHOLDING ORDER
(Wage Garnishment)

CCP 706.121

While you might mention the type of property the officer might find, you don't have to be too specific, since the keeper will typically take everything and close the business. Or if you have a relatively small judgment, the officer may use his or her own judgment to take into custody what appears necessary to gain the value of your judgment in an execution sale. Generally, in these sales, the value is about 10% on the dollar, depending on the state.

Although the debtor can close the business to prevent the officer from taking the ongoing receipts of the business (though the officer will still get any cash on hand), the debtor can't close up to avoid a levy on property. The officer has a court order to back up the levy, and if the debtor resists, the officer can make an arrest and take the debtor to jail.

In taking the property, the officer goes on the assumption that the debtor owns or is in charge of everything present, unless the debtor shows evidence that certain items of property do not belong to him or her or are the secured property of someone else. Later, if the debtor wants to get back any property or protest the levy, he or she has to file a *Claim of Exemption* with the levying officer within 10 days, stating these are necessary tools, materials, or equipment for the business (though this exemption only includes up to a certain amount— for example, $2,500, depending on the state). Then, the levying officer will notify the court, which will decide on the matter at a hearing (though you and the debtor needn't be present). Or perhaps the debtor may work out a settlement with you to pay off the judgment and costs; then you can authorize a release.

If the matter isn't settled otherwise in this 10-day period, the levying officer will hold an execution sale by notifying the debtor at least 10 days before the sale of its time and place, and posting other notices in the city or district where the sale will take place. Thereafter, if the debtor doesn't settle with you, the sale will occur.

After the sale, the officer will turn over any proceeds to you up to the balance of your judgment, less any fees for having the sale. If anything is left over, that will go to the debtor.

If you want, you can always go to the sale and bid yourself, and, of course, the debtor can attend and buy back property, too. But usually, such sales are rare, since they are so expensive and the returns so little. More commonly, the debtor will seek to work out a settlement with you get back the property without a sale.

Levying on the debtor's motor vehicles (cars, trucks, R.V.s, boats, etc.)

If the debtor has a valuable motor vehicle or more than one vehicle, this is another likely asset, although it's more difficult and expensive to get than money in the bank, wages, or business assets.

First, assuming you can find it, make sure the debtor owns the car or other vehicle and has enough equity in it to make it worth collecting and selling.

To determine ownership, you will probably need to complete a request form at the motor vehicle agency with the license number and a small fee (about $3 depending on the state) and ask for the name of the legal owner. The information you receive will probably also tell you whether there are any outstanding loans or liens on the car.

Then, to determine the debtor's equity, deduct the value of any outstanding loans, plus any exemptions (for example, in some states the debtor has a personal exemption of $1,200 or a business exemption of $2,500 if the vehicle is a tool of his or her trade). Or if the debtor has another similar vehicle, apply the exemptions first to that. Then, assuming the car will be sold for the going price, ask yourself if the amount left over after a sale is enough to attempt a levy, and if so, go ahead and do it.

You'll have to put up a substantial deposit (about $200) to cover the cost of taking, storing, and selling the car—but again, you will normally get it back from the proceeds of the sale.

As in the case of any sale, there's a notice of sale and the debtor has a chance to claim an exemption or settle with you before the sale. (See the discussion on selling the debtor's business property.) But, if the debtor doesn't, the sale is held and you, like the debtor, are free to attend and bid. Afterwards, after expenses are deducted from your deposit, any proceedings up to the value of your judgment go to you. and the remainder, including any exemptions, are returned to the debtor.

Again, give a *Writ of Execution* and letter of instructions to the levying officer. In this case, include key identifying information on the car or vehicle—such as color, make, license number—and most significantly, where and when the officer is likely to find it. The officer can't go into a private garage or warehouse to get it, unless the door is open or the owner voluntarily invites him or her in. But as long as the vehicle is parked on the street or in a public place, it's fair game.

Getting other personal property from the debtor

Although technically, you can levy against any personal property owned by the debtor if it's valuable enough, including expensive cameras, video equipment, stereos, jewelry, and the like, this is usually fairly difficult because, again, the levying officer cannot go into the person's home to collect a judgment without a court order, as previously noted.

Also, there are numerous exemptions on personal property in many states, so that the average items a person has in the house, such as furniture, clothing, and appliances, are likely to be covered by some exemption.

Thus, for all practical purposes, forget about going after everyday items of personal property, unless the debtor is in a strong financial position and has valuable assets.

Getting personal property from a private place

If you decide to go after the debtor's personal property and the debtor doesn't turn it over voluntarily, you can get it this way.

First, you need to be able to clearly identify the specific property you are after. For example, if you know the debtor has some expensive jewelry or video equipment at his or her home, you can levy on this if you can describe it in detail (e.g., instead of jewelry say "a pearl necklace," or "diamond ring"; instead of video equipment say "a Canon VHS video recorder and camera," etc.)

The process begins with the usual writ and letter of instructions, and then the levying officer goes to the debtor's house to ask for the property. If the debtor resists, the officer will advise the debtor that he or she may be liable for costs and attorney fees for any further proceedings to obtain the property. However, if the debtor still refuses to comply, the levying officer has to leave, since he or she can't enter a person's private dwelling without a court order.

After this happens, the officer will notify you of the failure to get the property, and to proceed you must make a motion to the court for a court order. In this motion, you have to describe the particular property you want to levy on, where it is to be found, and why you have a good reason to believe this property is located there. Additionally, to be convincing, explain why you need to get this property to satisfy your judgment, rather than satisfying it in another way, since the courts are normally reluctant to issue court orders permitting entry onto private property.

When you get this court order, the levying officer will return and make another request for the property, showing the court order. Now, if the debtor doesn't turn it over, the levying officer can actually force entry into the property, unless there is a substantial risk of death or serious bodily harm to anyone. If so, the levying officer will describe this situation to the court, and the court will decide what the officer should do (which could be anything from going back with additional help and possibly arresting the debtor if he or she resists again, to suggesting that you find another way to get your money.)

Levying on various money assets

Some debtors may have various types of money assets in the form of certificates, instruments, or documents. These includes stocks, bonds, securities, accounts receivables, chattel paper, items in a safe deposit box, negotiable documents of title, etc. To reach these, use the *Writ of Execution* and give the levying officer specific instructions on what these items are and where to find them. Then, the officer will ask the debtor to turn them over.

Since specifics differ depending on the items you want to reach, check with your local sheriff, marshal, or constable on what to do.

Levying on third persons who owe the debtor money

If you can't get your money directly from the debtor, you also have the alternative of going after the people who owe the debtor money or have property belonging to the debtor. The process is similar to garnishing the wages of an employer who owes the debtor wages, though these funds are due to the debtor for other reasons (for example, the debtor did some work as an independent contractor, sold some goods, or loaned some property or money to the person).

Once you have information about this person's obligation to the debtor, use the writ and levy procedure. Give the levying officer a *Writ of Execution* with instructions describing this person as a debtor of the debtor, and include the person's address and phone number. Then, the levying officer will serve this person with a copy of your writ and a *Notice of Levy*.

Now, unless this person has a good reason for refusing (such as he or she doesn't owe the debtor the money), he or she must pay the levying officer the amount due to the debtor or arrange to pay any amount that becomes due during the period the levy continues (it lasts for up to 2 years, depending on the state). Likewise, if the third party has any property belonging to the debtor and you have instructed the officer to collect it, he or she must turn it over to the officer along with any documents necessary to make the transfer.

If the person doesn't turn over the money or property sought in the *Writ*, he or she must explain the reasons for not doing so. And, if the person doesn't have a good reason for refusing, he or she becomes liable for the value of the judgment, until he or she complies with the levy or the judgment is satisfied.

To facilitate this process, a *Garnishee's Memorandum* (as it is called in some states) is used. The officer gives the debtor's debtor a copy of this memorandum, along with the *Writ* and *Notice of Levy*. Then, the person must fill this out within 10 days, with complete information about the nature of any obligation to the debtor and any reasons for not complying with the levy. If the garnishee doesn't send this memorandum to the officer or provide full information, or if you feel the reasons aren't good enough, you can take the person to court and seek a judgment requiring him or her to pay.

Generally, though, such a court action isn't necessary. Given the possible penalties, a debtor's debtor will pay after being notified of your original levy.

Collecting money from the debtor's real property

Another possible way to get your money is from the debtor's real property, although this is usually a long-term procedure. Also, if you are a small debtor (anything under $3,000 or so), you should probably limit your efforts to putting a lien on the property and waiting for someone else to sell it, which is when you may collect.

EXAMPLE OF CLAIM OF EXEMPTION
(Enforcement of Judgment)

[NOT FOR WAGE GARNISHMENT]
[RETURN TO LEVYING OFFICER. DO NOT FILE WITH COURT]

ATTORNEY OR PARTY WITHOUT ATTORNEY (Name and Address):	TELEPHONE NO.:	LEVYING OFFICER (Name and Address):

ATTORNEY FOR (Name):

NAME OF COURT, JUDICIAL DISTRICT OR BRANCH, IF ANY:

PLAINTIFF:

DEFENDANT:

CLAIM OF EXEMPTION (Enforcement of Judgment)	LEVYING OFFICER FILE NO.	COURT CASE NO.

Copy all the information required above (except the top left space) from the Notice of Levy. The top left space is for your name or your attorney's name and address. The original and one copy of this form must be filed with the levying officer. **DO NOT FILE WITH THE COURT.**

1. My name is (specify):
2. Papers should be sent to
   - [ ] me.
   - [ ] my attorney (I have filed with the court and served on the judgment creditor a request that papers be sent to my attorney and my attorney has consented in writing on the request to receive these papers.)
   - at the address [ ] shown above [ ] following (specify):
3. [ ] I am not the judgment debtor named in the notice of levy. The name and last known address of the judgment debtor is (specify):

4. The property I claim to be exempt is (describe):

5. The property is claimed to be exempt under the following code and section (specify):

6. The facts which support this claim are (specify):

7. [ ] The claim is made pursuant to a provision exempting property to the extent necessary for the support of the judgment debtor and the spouse and dependents of the judgment debtor. **A Financial Statement form is attached to this claim.**
8. [ ] The property claimed to be exempt is
   a. [ ] a motor vehicle, the proceeds of an execution sale of a motor vehicle, or the proceeds of insurance or other indemnification for the loss, damage, or destruction of a motor vehicle.
   b. [ ] tools, implements, materials, uniforms, furnishings, books, equipment, a commercial motor vehicle, a vessel, or other personal property used in the trade, business or profession of the judgment debtor or spouse.
   c. all other property of the same type owned by the judgment debtor, either alone or in combination with others, is (describe):

9. [ ] The property claimed to be exempt consists of the loan value of unmatured life insurance policies (including endowment and annuity policies) or benefits from matured life insurance policies (including endowment and annuity policies). All other property of the same type owned by the judgment debtor or the spouse of the judgment debtor, either alone or in combination with others, is (describe):

I declare under penalty of perjury under the laws of the State of California that the foregoing is true and correct.

Date:

_____ ▶ _____
(TYPE OR PRINT NAME)   (SIGNATURE OF CLAIMANT)

Form Approved by the
Judicial Council of California
EJ-160 [New July 1, 1983]
Martin Dean's Essential Forms ™

CLAIM OF EXEMPTION
(Enforcement of Judgment)

CCP 703.520

Using The Legal Process To Collect 275

EXAMPLE OF NOTICE OF OPPOSITION OF CLAIM OF EXEMPTION
(Enforcement of Judgment)

ATTORNEY OR PARTY WITHOUT ATTORNEY *(Name and Address)*:   TELEPHONE NO.:   **FOR COURT USE ONLY**

ATTORNEY FOR *(Name)*:

NAME OF COURT:
STREET ADDRESS:
MAILING ADDRESS:
CITY AND ZIP CODE:
BRANCH NAME:

OAKLAND-PIEDMONT-EMERYVILLE MUNICIPAL COURT
Small Claims Division – 3rd Floor
600 Washington Street
Oakland, CA 94607-3997

PLAINTIFF:

DEFENDANT:

LEVYING OFFICER FILE NO.:   COURT CASE NO.:

NOTICE OF OPPOSITION TO CLAIM OF EXEMPTION
(Enforcement of Judgment)

— *DO NOT USE THIS FORM FOR WAGE GARNISHMENTS* —

The original of this form and a Notice of Hearing on Claim of Exemption must be filed with the court.
A copy of this Notice of Opposition and the Notice of Hearing *must* be filed with the levying officer.
A copy of this Notice of Opposition and the Notice of Hearing must be served on the judgment debtor and other claimant at least 10 days *before* the hearing.

TO THE LEVYING OFFICER:

1. Name and address of judgment creditor   2. Name and address of judgment debtor

Social Security Number (if known):

3. ☐ Name and address of claimant *(if other than judgment debtor)*

4. The notice of filing claim of exemption states it was mailed on *(date)*:

5. The item or items claimed as exempt are
   a. ☐ not exempt under the statutes relied upon in the Claim of Exemption.
   b. ☐ not exempt because the judgment debtor's equity is greater than the amount provided in the exemption.
   c. ☐ other *(specify)*:

6. The facts necessary to support item 5 are
   ☐ continued on the attachment labeled Attachment 6.
   ☐ as follows:

I declare under penalty of perjury under the laws of the State of California that the foregoing is true and correct.

Date:

▶

_____   _____
(TYPE OR PRINT NAME)   (SIGNATURE OF DECLARANT)

Form Approved by the
Judicial Council of California
EJ-170 [New July 1, 1983]

NOTICE OF OPPOSITION TO CLAIM OF EXEMPTION
(Enforcement of Judgment)

CCP 703.550

EXAMPLE OF CLAIM OF EXEMPTION
(Wage Garnishment)

ATTORNEY OR PARTY WITHOUT ATTORNEY (Name and Address):	TELEPHONE NO.:	LEVYING OFFICER (Name and Address):
ATTORNEY FOR (Name):		

NAME OF COURT, JUDICIAL DISTRICT OR BRANCH COURT, IF ANY:

PLAINTIFF:

DEFENDANT:

CLAIM OF EXEMPTION (Wage Garnishment)	LEVYING OFFICER FILE NO.:	COURT CASE NO.:

- READ THE EMPLOYEE INSTRUCTIONS BEFORE COMPLETING THIS FORM -

Copy all the information required above (except the top left space) from the Earnings Withholding Order. The top left space is for your name or your attorney's name and address. The original and one copy of this form with the Financial Statement attached must be filed with the levying officer. DO NOT FILE WITH THE COURT.

1. I need the following earnings to support myself or my family (check a or b):
   a. ☐ All earnings.
   b. ☐ $ _____ each pay period.

2. Please send all papers to
   ☐ me.
   ☐ my attorney
   at the address ☐ shown above ☐ following (specify):

3. I am willing for the following amount to be withheld from my earnings **each pay period** during the withholding period. **I understand that the judgment creditor can accept this offer by not opposing the Claim of Exemption, which will result in the following sum being withheld each pay period** (check a or b):
   a. ☐ None
   b. ☐ Withhold $ _____ each pay period.

4. I am paid.
   ☐ daily   ☐ every two weeks   ☐ monthly
   ☐ weekly   ☐ twice a month   ☐ other (specify):

NOTE: *You must attach a properly completed Financial Statement form to this Claim of Exemption.*
The Financial Statement form is available without charge from the levying officer.

I declare under penalty of perjury under the laws of the State of California that the foregoing is true and correct.
Date:

▶

_____   _____
(TYPE OR PRINT NAME)   (SIGNATURE OF DECLARANT)

Form Adopted by the
Judicial Council of California
982.5(5) [Rev. July 1, 1983]
Martin Dean's Essential Forms ™

CLAIM OF EXEMPTION
(Wage Garnishment)

CCP 706.124

EXAMPLE OF FINANCIAL STATEMENT

SHORT TITLE:	LEVYING OFFICER FILE NO.:	COURT CASE NO.:

FINANCIAL STATEMENT
(Wage Garnishment - Enforcement of Judgment)

NOTE: If you are married, this form must be signed by your spouse unless you and your spouse are living separate and apart. If this form is not signed by your spouse, check the applicable box on the reverse in item 9.

1. The following persons other than myself depend, in whole or in part, on me or my spouse for support:

	NAME	AGE	RELATIONSHIP TO ME	MONTHLY TAKE-HOME INCOME & SOURCE
a.			Spouse	
b.				
c.				
d.				
e.				

2. **My monthly income**
   a. My gross monthly pay is: .... 2a. $ _____
   b. My payroll deductions are (specify **purpose** and **amount**):
      (1) Federal and state withholding, FICA, and SDI .... $ _____
      (2) _____ $ _____
      (3) _____ $ _____
      (4) _____ $ _____
      My TOTAL payroll deduction amount is (add (1) through (4)): .... b. $ _____
   c. My monthly take-home pay is (a minus b): .... c. $ _____
   d. Other money I get each month from (specify source):
      _____ is: .... d. $ _____

   e. **TOTAL MONTHLY INCOME** (c plus d): .... e. $ _____

3. I, my spouse, and my other dependents own the following property:
   a. Cash .... 3a. $ _____
   b. Checking, savings, and credit union accounts (list banks):
      (1) _____ $ _____
      (2) _____ $ _____
      (3) _____ $ _____ b. $ _____
   c. Cars, other vehicles, and boat equity (list make, year of each):
      (1) _____ $ _____
      (2) _____ $ _____
      (3) _____ $ _____ c. $ _____
   d. Real estate equity .... d. $ _____
   e. Other personal property (jewelry, furniture, furs, stocks, bonds, etc.) (list separately):

   e. $ _____

(Continued on reverse)

Form Adopted by the Judicial Council of California
982.5(5.5), EJ-165 [New July 1, 1983]
Martin Dean's Essential Forms ™

FINANCIAL STATEMENT
(Wage Garnishment - Enforcement of Judgment)

CCP 703.530
706.124

EXAMPLE OF FINANCIAL STATEMENT
(Reverse side)

SHORT TITLE:	LEVYING OFFICER FILE NO.:	COURT CASE NO.:

4. **The monthly expenses for me, my spouse, and my other dependants**

    a. Rent or house payment and maintenance .... 4a. $ _____
    b. Food and household supplies .... b. $ _____
    c. Utilities and telephone .... c. $ _____
    d. Clothing .... d. $ _____
    e. Medical and dental payments .... e. $ _____
    f. Insurance (life, health, accident, etc.) .... f. $ _____
    g. School, child care .... g. $ _____
    h. Child, spousal support (prior marriage) .... h. $ _____
    i. Transportation & auto expenses (insurance, gas, repair) *(list car payments in item 5)* .... i. $ _____
    j. Installment payments *(insert total and itemize below in item 5)* .... j. $ _____
    k. Laundry and cleaning .... k. $ _____
    l. Entertainment .... l. $ _____
    m. Other *(specify)*:

    m. $ _____

    n. **TOTAL MONTHLY EXPENSES** *(add a through m)*:   n. $ _____

5. I, my spouse, and my other dependents owe the following debts:

CREDITOR'S NAME	FOR	MO. PAYMENTS	BALANCE OWED	OWED BY *(State person's name)*

6. Other facts which support this Claim of Exemption (i.e., unusual medical needs, school tuition, expenses for recent family emergencies, or other unusual expenses to help your creditor and the judge understand your budget) *(describe)*: *(If more space is needed, attach page labeled Attachment 6.)*

7. ☐ An earnings withholding order is now in effect with respect to my earnings or those of my spouse or dependents named in item 1 *(specify each person's name and monthly amount)*:

8. ☐ A wage assignment for support is now in effect with respect to my earnings or those of my spouse or dependents named in item 1 *(specify each person's name and monthly amount)*:

9. ☐ My spouse has signed below.
    ☐ I have no spouse
    ☐ My spouse and I are living separate and apart.

I declare under penalty of perjury under the laws of the State of California that the foregoing is true and correct.

Date:

_____ ▶ _____
(TYPE OR PRINT NAME)   (SIGNATURE)

_____ ▶ _____
(TYPE OR PRINT NAME OF SPOUSE)   (SIGNATURE OF SPOUSE)

FINANCIAL STATEMENT
(Wage Garnishment - Enforcement of Judgment)

982.5(5.5), EJ-165 [New July 1, 1983]
Martin Dean's Essential Forms ™

EXAMPLE OF MEMORANDUM OF GARNISHEE

ATTORNEY OR PARTY WITHOUT ATTORNEY (Name and Address): TELEPHONE NO.:

☐ Recording requested by and return to:

ATTORNEY FOR (Name)
NAME OF COURT:
STREET ADDRESS:
MAILING ADDRESS:
CITY AND ZIP CODE:
BRANCH NAME:

PLAINTIFF:

DEFENDANT:

FOR RECORDER'S USE ONLY

LEVYING OFFICER (Name and Address):

MEMORANDUM OF GARNISHEE
(Attachment - Enforcement of Judgment)

NOTICE TO PERSON SERVED WITH WRIT AND NOTICE OF LEVY OR NOTICE OF ATTACHMENT: This memorandum must be completed and mailed or delivered to the levying officer within 10 days after service on you of the writ and notice of levy or attachment unless you have fully complied with the levy. Failure to complete and return this memorandum may render you liable for the costs and attorney fees incurred in obtaining the required information.
- RETURN ALL COPIES OF THIS MEMORANDUM TO THE LEVYING OFFICER -

LEVYING OFFICER FILE NO.: COURT CASE NO.:

This memorandum does not apply to garnishment of earnings

1. If you will not deliver to the levying officer any property levied upon, describe the property and the reason for not delivering it:

2. **For writ of execution only** Describe any property of the judgment debtor not levied upon that is in your possession or under your control:

3. If you owe money to the judgment debtor which you will not pay to the levying officer, describe the amount and terms of the obligation and the reason for not paying it to the levying officer:

(Continued on reverse)

Form Approved by the
Judicial Council of California
AT-167, EJ-152 [New July 1, 1983]
Martin Dean's Essential Forms ™

MEMORANDUM OF GARNISHEE
(Attachment - Enforcement of Judgment)

CCP 488.610
701.030

EXAMPLE OF MEMORANDUM OF GARNISHEE
(Reverse side)

SHORT TITLE:	LEVYING OFFICER FILE NO.:	COURT CASE NO.:

4. Describe the amount and terms of any obligation owed to the judgment debtor that is levied upon but is not yet due and payable:

5. **For writ of execution only** Describe the amount and terms of any obligation owed to the judgment debtor that is not levied upon:

6. Describe any claims and rights of other persons to the property or obligation levied upon that are known to you and the names and addresses of the other persons:

DECLARATION

I declare under penalty of perjury under the laws of the State of California that the foregoing is true and correct.
Date:

_____ ▶ _____
(TYPE OR PRINT NAME)   (SIGNATURE)

If you need more space to provide the information required by this memorandum, you may attach additional pages.
☐ Total number of pages attached:

AT-167, EJ-152 [New July 1, 1983]
Martin Dean's Essential Forms ™

MEMORANDUM OF GARNISHEE
(Attachment - Enforcement of Judgment)

Page two

EXAMPLE OF NOTICE OF HEARING ON CLAIM OF EXEMPTION

ATTORNEY OR PARTY WITHOUT ATTORNEY (Name and Address):   TELEPHONE NO.:   FOR COURT USE ONLY

ATTORNEY FOR (Name):

NAME OF COURT, JUDICIAL DISTRICT OR BRANCH COURT, IF ANY:

PLAINTIFF:

DEFENDANT:

NOTICE OF HEARING ON CLAIM OF EXEMPTION
(Wage Garnishment - Enforcement of Judgment)

LEVYING OFFICER FILE NO.:   COURT CASE NO.:

1. TO:
   Name and address of levying officer   Name and address of judgment debtor

   ☐ Claimant, if other than judgment debtor   ☐ Judgment debtor's attorney
     (name and address):   (name and address):

2. **A hearing to determine the claim of exemption of**
   ☐ judgment debtor
   ☐ other claimant
   will be held as follows:

   a. date: time: ☐ dept.:   ☐ div.:   ☐ rm.:

   b. address of court:

3. ☐ The judgment creditor will not appear at the hearing and submits the issue on the papers filed with the court.

Date:

_____   ▶ _____
(TYPE OR PRINT NAME)   (SIGNATURE OF JUDGMENT CREDITOR OR ATTORNEY)

If you do not attend the hearing, the court may determine your claim based on the Claim of Exemption, Financial Statement (when one is required), Notice of Opposition to Claim of Exemption, and other evidence that may be presented.

(Proof of service on reverse)

Form Adopted by the Judicial Council of California
982 5(8), EJ-175 [Rev. July 1, 1983]
Bancroft-Whitney Co. Laser Edition TM

NOTICE OF HEARING ON CLAIM OF EXEMPTION
(Wage Garnishment - Enforcement of Judgment)

CCP 703.550
706.105

EXAMPLE OF EMPLOYER'S RETURN
(Wage Garnishment)

ATTORNEY OR PARTY WITHOUT ATTORNEY (Name and Address):	TELEPHONE NO.:	LEVYING OFFICER (Name and Address):
ATTORNEY FOR (Name):		
NAME OF COURT, JUDICIAL DISTRICT OR BRANCH COURT, IF ANY:		
PLAINTIFF:		
DEFENDANT:		
EMPLOYER'S RETURN (Wage Garnishment)	LEVYING OFFICER FILE NO.:	COURT CASE NO.:

EMPLOYER: You must complete both copies of this form and mail them to the levying officer within 15 days. *Please correct any errors* in the mailing information above and provide any missing information, including the name of the person to whom notices should be directed.

FAILURE TO COMPLETE AND RETURN THESE FORMS MAY SUBJECT YOU TO PAYMENT OF ATTORNEY FEES AND OTHER CIVIL PENALTIES.

Name and address of employer

Name and address of employee

Attn: _____
(Insert name above)

Social Security Number (if known):

1. I received the Earnings Withholding Order on (date):

2. The employee is

   a. ☐ not employed by this employer *(if not employed, omit items 2b through 6 and proceed to item 7 on reverse).*

   b. ☐ now employed by this employer and in the last pay period had gross earnings of
   $

3. The employee's pay period is

   a. ☐ daily   b. ☐ weekly   c. ☐ every two weeks

   d. ☐ twice a month   e. ☐ monthly   f. ☐ other *(specify)*:

(IF YOU HAVE RECEIVED NO OTHER ORDERS THAT PRESENTLY AFFECT THIS EMPLOYEE'S EARNINGS, OMIT ITEMS 4, 5, AND 6, AND PROCEED TO ITEM 7 ON REVERSE.)

(Continued on reverse)

Form Adopted by the
Judicial Council of California
982.5(4) [Rev. January 1, 1993]
Martin Dean's Essential Forms ™

EMPLOYER'S RETURN
(Wage Garnishment)

Code Civ. Proc., § 706.126

The reason to take this approach is because it's incredibly complicated and expensive to force a sale of real property, and if the debtor is living on the property, there's probably a homestead exemption. Also, it takes months and months of notices to force a sale, and you have to put up a large bond as a deposit to cover these expenses, which can include assorted court proceedings if the debtor seeks to prevent a sale.

Thus, with small debts, it makes sense to try to collect from easier and more immediate avenues first. But, if you have problems collecting elsewhere and the debtor does own property, the sensible strategy is to get in line with a lien on the property as soon as you can, so you are more apt to get a share of the proceeds when the property is sold.

To obtain a lien, get an *Abstract of Judgment* from the court where you got your judgment, which briefly summarizes the main facts of the judgment (e.g., name of parties, case number, debtor's last known address; and current amount of the judgment). Then, take or mail this to the County Recorder's Office in any or all of the counties where the debtor owns real property. (There is usually a charge for the abstract and an additional charge to record it.)

Once the recorder receives your abstract, a judgment lien will be placed on the property that is good as long as your *Writ of Execution* remains valid (up to 10 years initially, and you can continue it in force by renewing your *Writ* and your lien—though hopefully, you will collect long before this.) As the value of your judgment increases due to interest and court costs, record an abstract with the new total to reflect this. Should you get a partial payment, your lien will be reduced accordingly, whether you record it or not.

Your judgment lien attaches in the order of filing to establish the priority of your claim. Then, when the property is sold, either by the debtor voluntarily or when another creditor forces a sale, you'll get your money under certain conditions.

Commonly, the debtor will pay you off if he or she sells the property, because most buyers don't want to purchase property which is encumbered by a lien, and your lien reduces the property's value by that amount. In the event the new buyer takes the property without the debtor paying you off, the property remains subject to your lien, and eventually you may get your money from that buyer.

When a forced execution sale occurs, you will get your money if your lien is high enough up in line and is senior to any lien held by the person forcing the sale, since the sale extinguishes all junior liens. After the sale, the proceeds are distributed in order of priority (first is expenses of the sale, then any homestead exemptions, then any tax liens, and then the lien creditors according to the rank of their lien. The most senior lienholder gets paid off first then the next senior lienholder, and so on down the line, to any lien held by the person forcing the sale, though if a creditor is paid off through other sources, that lien would be extinguished).

Commonly, the creditor who forces the sale has to get at least enough to pay off part or all of his or her own judgment, or the creditor can't sell the house. So, as long as your lien is senior to the creditor forcing the sale, you'll get paid. If you've got a junior lien, though, you're out of luck, since it's eliminated by the sale.

Thus, getting paid from real property can take some time, but if you're willing to wait for a long term payoff, it might be worth it to get your lien and wait. Alternatively, even if you don't plan to use the complicated sale procedures, it might help to know them because you can use them to convince the debtor you are going to initiate a sale. And, this might motivate the debtor to pay, particularly when he or she considers the benefits of paying off your small debt versus the problems of staving off a forced sale.

Again, check the specific procedures in your own state, county and city.

Chapter 14

Dealing With Complications

Usually, the basic procedures for collecting from an unwilling debtor just described will work under normal circumstances, but what if you run into complications?

Sometimes you can handle these complications yourself, if you are prepared. But often, this is the time to bring in an attorney, if the amount is large enough.

This section provides an overview of some major complications that may happen and how to deal with them.

Dealing With a Bankruptcy

The usual bankruptcy proceeding is a Chapter 7 action, as governed by the Federal Bankruptcy Reform Act, which is used to discharge the debtor's debts and liquidate non-exempt assets. The alternate procedures which are sometimes used are the Chapter 11 reorganizational plan for businesses and the Chapter 13 plan for individual wage earners, designed so the debtor can pay off debts on a long-term basis, without having to go through the usual liquidation.

Once the debtor files a bankruptcy petition—or is arranging to do so within the next 90 days—immediately stop any collection efforts, since on filing, all of the debtor's assets become part of an estate, which is administered by a trustee selected by the creditors or appointed by a district judge for the federal bankruptcy court.

Also, the filing creates an automatic stay on all legal actions against the debtor which is retroactive for the 90-day period before the filing except for small everyday business transactions. This stay is so the trustee can help the debtor resolve his or her affairs in an orderly way. Additionally, this stay is designed to keep the creditors from racing in once they suspect a bankruptcy may be imminent to collect what's left, since they might disrupt this orderly process, as well as drive the debtor into bankruptcy by their eagerness to collect.

Once a trustee arrangement is set up, the trustee will use a financial statement prepared by the debtor (or an attorney) to determine what assets the debtor has and what debts are owed to what creditors and to gather all of the assets into the debtor's estate. Then, if the debtor is an individual, the trustee will, in accordance with the applicable state or federal provisions where the debtor goes bankrupt, return some of the assets of the estate back to the debtor as exempt property. This individual exemption may be up to about $8,000, plus a homestead exemption, which is about $30,000 to 45,000, depending on the state.

Once any exemptions are deducted, the trustee will distribute the rest among the debtor's creditors in order of priority. First, any government tax liens are taken care of; then secured creditors; and finally general creditors, which includes creditors with judgments. Your major advantage in having a judgment compared to unsecured creditors without judgments is these represent proof the debtor owes you the money; you don't have to prove the validity of your claim.

The laws dealing with bankruptcy are extremely complex. The federal statute alone consists of about 300 pages of tightly packed prose. And, some states have their own bankruptcy system or offer the debtor a choice between the federal or state system. A general description of what happens follows.

The bankruptcy process

The debtor (either an individual or a business) starts the process by filling out a comprehensive form (commonly with the assistance of a bankruptcy lawyer), listing all current assets and all current debts the debtor knows about. Then, the debtor or the attorney files this form and a bankruptcy petition with the courts.

Once this petition is filed, all assets become part of the bankrupt estate. In addition, the trustee has the power to take back any major payments (about $100 or more) the debtor has made to creditors within 90 days of filing the petition and return these to the estate on the grounds that these represent a preferential transfer. Similarly, the trustee can take back any major items of property (including personal property, business equipment and inventory, and real estate) which the debtor has given to someone else on the grounds that these are a fraudulence conveyance. By the same token, if the debtor has assigned a security interest to a creditor which is "perfected" within this period (either by being recorded or given to that person), the trustee can set aside that transaction, too, as prejudicial to the other creditors.

After all these assets are collected, the trustee will return any exempted assets back to the individual debtor and will distribute whatever is left over to the listed creditors in a certain order, depending upon the state or federal bankruptcy plan selected. In general, though, the individual debtor will be able to keep between about $6,000 to 8,000 in assets as exempt, plus any homestead, on the grounds that the debtor should be left with something to make a new start.

If a business is undergoing a special Chapter 11 reorganization, it will be allowed to keep any assets considered necessary to keep the business running while paying off past creditors according to a special schedule.

By contrast, under the usual Chapter 7 liquidation, any company assets will be liquidated completely unless the business is an extension of an individual debtor who has a sole proprietorship to share in a small home-industry style partnership. Then, the bankruptcy laws affecting the individual debtor will apply.

In discharging the debts from the estate, the trustee uses the priority formula previously noted (first tax liens, then secured debts, then general creditors). If there's enough for the general creditors, these proceeds will be distributed on a proportional share basis to all listed creditors. So, depending on the number of creditors sharing in these proceeds and the relative size of your debt, you'll get a certain amount on the dollar owed. Often, however, this can be very little—sometimes as low as a few pennies on the dollar.

Meanwhile, once the petition is filed, the individual debtor can start to accumulate money again which is free of the claims of past creditors, whether they have been listed in the petition or not. By contrast, if a business has been liquidated in discharging its debts, rather than restructured under a reorganization plan, it's all over—the business is defunct.

What to do as a creditor

Under the circumstances, since a bankruptcy discharges all debts, whether listed or not, if you think a bankruptcy is pending or are aware that one has been filed, your best approach is to make sure you are accurately listed as a creditor. If the petition has been filed and the debtor has listed your debt, you should get a notice. Or if the bankruptcy is pending, remind the business owner or bookkeeping department to list you. In either case, make sure the amount of your debt has been or will be listed accurately.

In the event your debt is unlisted or there is some mistake, file a claim with the trustee against the estate. You can find out the details of with whom and how to file by contacting the debtor, lawyer handling the case, or the bankruptcy court in the debtor's jurisdiction. The reason you want to be properly listed is that only listed creditors will receive payments from the estate or through a business's or wage earners reorganization or payment plan. Unlisted creditors will get nothing.

If the debtor is an individual and you aren't fully paid off after the distribution of assets or aren't likely to be, there is one other strategy to try—either soon after the debtor files the petition or before the bankruptcy action is concluded with a discharge. You can ask the debtor to reaffirm the debt by writing up an agreement with your acknowledging the debt. Otherwise, it will be fully discharged, whatever you receive, by the bankruptcy.

The time when this strategy may work is when the debtor is someone you have known for some time or when you are someone the debtor may want to do business with again. In this case, the debtor may feel a moral obligation or feel he or she can benefit from a continued relationship; and so has a motivation to renew an obligation to you. If so, try asking for a reaffirmation, though be tactful and emphasize the benefits the debtor will get.

Although there's a good chance the debtor might still say no—after all, that's why the debtor went through bankruptcy: to discharge debts—on a selective basis, the debtor may still be open to making a reaffirmation if you can give the debtor a reason to say yes. Just be sure when you ask that you don't make the debtor feel threatened and don't harass the debtor with repeated requests—such acts are actually against the law and punishable by contempt of court. But, since you may be able to get the debtor to agree voluntarily, this approach is at least worth a try.

Then, if the debtor agrees, he or she must sign an agreement reaffirming the debt, along with an affidavit that he or she is entering freely into this agreement. Also, the debtor must file it with the bankruptcy court for its approval, since the court wants to make sure the debtor is knowledgeably and voluntarily making this commitment and it will not be harmful to the debtor.

Dealing With a Divorce

If the debtor should get divorced, you may have a problem in determining what still belongs to the debtor. With certain types of assets (such as earnings or a personal bank account), it may be quite clear what belongs to the debtor. But you can run into problems where the debtor and spouse have shared property (such as a joint bank account or a house they have bought together), or when it isn't clear who owns what (such as what furniture belongs to whom).

Before the divorce (in states recognizing community property), you may be able to collect any of these shared assets on the grounds that what belongs to one belongs to both. But when a divorce occurs, this community status is broken up, and the spouses go through the difficult process of assigning assets to one another.

Thus, in this situation, if you are uncertain about ownership, use an Order to Examination procedure to determine whether the debtor owns a particular asset, or perhaps wait a few months until things settle down, and it becomes clear who has taken over what property.

The obligation for a debtor to pay a creditor remains despite the fact that a divorce is taking place. If someone made a prior agreement to pay you, he or she still owes you, regardless of the divorce decree.

Collecting Assets From Another State

You may need to collect on out-of-state assets under two circumstances:

(1) A debtor who formerly lived in the state moves out of state, and takes all the property, too.

(2) A debtor who still lives in the state doesn't have enough to satisfy the judgment in the state, but has significant amounts of property elsewhere.

Depending on the state, you have to either apply for a sister-state judgment or file suit for a judgment based on your judgment, at a cost of about $100 to 200 (although, you'll get this back if you collect). While the procedure is fairly routine, and you'll usually get your new judgment automatically (and it will generally last as long as your original judgment is good), you or a representative have to be in the state to file. Furthermore, if the procedure involves filing suit, you have to serve the debtor just as you did in getting your original judgment. And, because you can't get a judgment on a judgment in a small claims court, you'll have to file in a superior court.

Thus, if the only way you can collect is from out-of-state assets, you probably have two major alternatives:

- Get a lawyer if the judgment is large enough (and retain a lawyer in the desired state if you can, since he or she is already there and may take a smaller percentage than a local lawyer who must refer the case for you.)

- Wait until the debtor returns to your state with assets (if this is likely).

Finally, if you find the debtor is especially unstable and is moving assets around from state to state, you probably have a no-win situation. It's usually too expensive (unless you have a huge judgment) to keep getting sister-state judgments. So, it may be best to file and forget.

Dealing With a Debtor Who Gives Property to Someone Else

If a debtor transfers property to someone else or puts it in someone else's name to avoid creditors, this is called a fraudulent conveyance, and you can set it aside to take that property. In fact, you can reach back up to three years to do so.

A typical situation might be when the debtor has a valuable piece of property, like some video equipment or extensive inventory and tries to hide it from creditors by storing it at someone else's home or business. Or perhaps the debtor puts the property in a friend's name, but continues to use it. (For example, the debtor turns over the title on a car to a friend, but continues to drive it; or continues to run a business under a friend's name.)

If the debtor sold this property to another person who bought it in good faith as a bona fide purchaser in the course of everyday trade, that's perfectly legal, because the purchaser has given and the debtor has received fair value for the item. So there's no fraud involved. But if the debtor simply turns over the property with no fair consideration in return, that's fraud—and you can set it aside.

The easiest way to get around this, if it seems obvious that a fraudulent conveyance is involved, is to simply disregard the conveyance and instruct the levying officer to levy against the property anyway. Then, if the debtor goes to court and tries to have the levy put aside in the 10-day period after the levy, you can oppose it on the grounds there was a fraudulent conveyance. As long as you can show this is the case, the debtor will lose the property. (You do this by showing the debtor is still in charge of or using the property on a regular basis or that the debtor gave it to the other person without getting anything in return.)

If you have any doubts about whether the property still belongs to the debtor or not and you want to avoid a suit for a wrongful attachment, you can initiate a suit against the debtor yourself to have the fraudulent conveyance set aside. Then, once you do, you can go after the property. However, it's much easier to simply seek a levy and place the burden of overturning the levy on the debtor.

In either case, check with your local small claims advisor on specific procedures.

Dealing With a Name Change

As in the fraudulent conveyance situation, if the debtor changes a name to evade creditors, with a little research, you can usually set the debtor's action aside and levy against the debtor's property anyway. The major requirement is that the new name is being used by the debtor personally or by a business which he or she owns as a sole proprietor or a partner. If the debtor has set up a corporation with a new name, you have a new legal entity, and it is more difficult to get at any assets which have been placed under a corporate umbrella, unless you show this corporate shell is really a legal fiction to protect the debtor or that the debtor is acting as an individual rather than as a representative of the corporation. (You might want see an attorney to do this if enough money is involved.)

However, if you're only trying to set aside a simple name change, you can probably do it yourself. The first step is to find out if the debtor has done anything to formalize the new name legally. If it's a business name, check at the county clerk's office, to see if the debtor has filed for a DBA—"doing business under a fictitious name." Or if the debtor has adopted a new personal name, check the change of name records at your local courthouse.

If there are no legal records showing the new name, and the assets in question are still under control of the debtor, just make a levy using the debtor's original name—and perhaps include the new name in parenthesis. On the other hand, if there are legal records, levy against the assets under the new name, and advise the levying officer about the name change in your instructions. Perhaps even include a copy of the legal papers showing the change. As long as you can connect the new name to the debtor, that's all you need.

Dealing With the Death of the Debtor

If the debtor dies, all of the debtor's property becomes part of the decedent's estate which is settled under probate. If you have previously placed a lien on any property belonging to the debtor, that lien will remain on the property when it passes to the new owner. But if the debtor dies before you have recorded a lien with the proper official (county recorder for real property; secretary of state for chattels and personal property), it's too late. The property no longer belongs to the debtor, but to the probate estate.

Accordingly, depending on whether you have an existing lien, you have one or two options:

- If you already have a lien, you may be able to get a payment from the heir to the property, who wants to get rid of the lien. Alternatively, after the property transfer is completed, you have the option of initiating an execution sale (though for reasons previously discussed, this is very expensive, and it is not normally a good idea unless you have a substantial judgment and are likely to get a sufficient bid to cover previous liens and exemptions and pay off your judgment).

- If you don't have a lien or aren't able to satisfy your judgment by collecting on it, file your claim with the administrator handling the decedent's estate. He or she will distribute the estate to the approved claimants, much like the bankruptcy trustee. As soon as you hear the debtor has died, find out from the debtor's relatives, business associates, or others, who is handling probate, and ask about the procedures for filing a claim. Then, file your claim as soon as possible for timely consideration. You have up to four months after the debtor dies to file a claim.

Renewing or Reviving a Judgment

Hopefully, you won't have to renew or revive a judgment. But if you haven't been able to collect after some years and still have hopes of collecting (e.g., the debtor may come into some money, or you want to keep a property lien alive until the property is sold), you have to take some action to keep your judgment alive. Otherwise, you will lose your power to collect, sometimes forever, sometimes until you revive the judgment, depending on circumstances.

Commonly, your original judgment lasts for 10 years. In some states, you don't have to do anything to keep it active during this 10-year period. But in other states, you must have a *Writ of Execution* issued on your judgment within a certain number of years (frequently after 5 to 7 years).

Likewise, procedures for renewing or reviving a judgment differ from state to state. While the renewal process involves creating a new judgment by suing on the old judgment, the revival process involves filing an application to keep the old judgment from expiring. And, while some states use the renewal process and others, the revival procedure, a few states give the creditor a choice.

There are some advantages to one procedure over another depending on your situation. For example, the renewal process is better if you are seeking a sister-state judgment on an extended or revived judgment because the statute of limitations has run out; though you can get it if you have a renewed judgment since this is considered a new judgment. On the other hand, a revived judgment is better if you want to extend the life of a property lien, since in this case, the original lien stays on the property and maintains the same position. But when you get a renewed judgment, this is considered a new judgment, so your lien drops down to a junior position.

In either case, though, it is important to file for renewal or revival before the end of the original judgment period. In fact, you probably should allow a sufficient grace period (about six months) so that the renewed or revived judgment will issue before the old judgment lapses. In this way, you don't have a gap that can cause enforcement problems. For instance, if you use the revival process and file in time to extend your judgment without a gap, you won't lose your current lien status on real or personal property. But if there is a gap, you will.

Again, check on the procedures in your own state with the court clerk or Small Claims advisor.

Chapter 15

A Few Final Words

In summary, the collection process can be a quick and easy one of reminding the debtor and getting paid, or it can drag on for a long time, through a series of increasingly intense appeals, followed by efforts to take the debtor to court and collect. The process depends both on the nature of the debtor and your skill in using techniques to collect.

One of the most important requirements to successful collection is a positive mental attitude (PMA). If you believe the debt is collectable, it usually is. However, it's important to temper your enthusiasm with common sense and a solid knowledge of collection laws and public relations.

In a sense, you might think of the collection process as a funnel. When you start, you have a large pool of people who owe you money, and your first efforts to collect with gentle reminders will bring in money from many of these people. Then, when you appeal to those who still haven't paid, many will pay at this point. After this, the process of getting tough and using a collection agency, lawyer, or threatening to go to Small Claims Court will bring in payments from a still smaller pool of people. And thereafter, getting a judgment will get others to pay.

Finally, you may be left with a small number of recalcitrant debtors, where you must use even more pressure with the help of the courts. And again, some will pay; but some may slip through for various reasons—they don't have any money; they are sufficiently evasive to elude you; or at some point, you decide the effort isn't worth it and give up.

Sound recordkeeping is essential. Taking notes — handwritten and stored in a file folder, or stored in a computer database — will help you keep track of past and current accounts, the status of the collection process, and the end result of your efforts. Use discretion in what you write down, however; your records can be subpoenaed if you are sued by the debtor.

In short, there are all sorts of debtors, and different techniques work with different ones. The key is to figure out the needs and motives of the debtor, and to apply these techniques as appropriate in a firm, persistent way. Offer to help the debtor whenever possible, such as an offer to settle for a lesser amount if they can pay within 30 days. You want to be sympathetic and supportive at first; but then gradually increase the pressure, all the while showing the debtor you are serious and intend to keep on until you get your money.

In most cases, you will. For collecting money is much like anything else in life: You'll succeed if you believe in yourself, so keep persisting until you reach your goal.

Remember, it's your money ... and you don't make money until you're paid. So go to it ... keep at it ... and good luck in your efforts to collect!

Bibliography

American Collectors Association. *Telephone Collectors Handbook, Advanced Telephone Collecting.*

American Entrepreneur Association. *Collection Agency,* AEA Business Manual No. X1207. Los Angeles: AEA, 1983.

Credit Network promotional materials, 1982. Credit Network, 210 Fifth Avenue, New York, NY.

Frailey, L. E. *Handbook of Business Letters.* Englewood Cliffs, New Jersey: Prentice-Hall, 1984.

Goldman, Bruce, & Pepper, Kenneth. *Your Check is in the Mail.* New York: Warner Books, 1984.

Goldstein, Arnold S. *Getting Paid.* New York: John Wiley & Sons, 1984.

Hardesty, T. Frank. *Collection Techniques for Accounts Receivable.* Fairfax, California: Dible Management Institute, Inc., 1982.

Harrison, John J. *It's A New Day for Consumers.* South Bend, Indiana, 1993.

Information Please Almanac, 1982.

King, Norman. *Past Due.* New York: Facts on File, 1983.

Little, John D. *Complete Credit and Collection Letter Book.* Englewood Cliffs, New Jersey: Prentice-Hall, 1964.

Paulson, Timothy R. *Collection Techniques for the Small Business.* Seattle: Self-Counsel Press, 1978.

Walker, Glen. *Credit Where Credit is Due.* New York: Holt, Rinehart and Winston, 1979.

Walker, Glen, & Clark, Cathy. *Credit!* Fountain Valley, California: Eden Press, 1982.

Warner, Ralph. *Everybody's Guide to Small Claims Court,* Berkeley, California: Nolo Press, 1983.

FORM 1

NEW CLIENT QUESTIONNAIRE

Name _____

Home Address _____

City _____ State _____ Zip _____

Business (if own business) _____

Employer (if employed)_____

Address _____

City _____ State _____ Zip _____

Phone _____ Can we call you at work? _____

Nearest relative for emergencies:

Name _____

Address _____

City _____ State ____ Zip _____ Phone _____

Nearest friend for emergencies:

Name _____

Address _____

City _____ State ____ Zip _____ Phone _____

Who referred you to us:

Name _____

City _____ State ____ Zip _____ Phone _____

Do you: ❏ Own Home ❏ Rent Other _____

How long at last address?_____

Previous address if there less than 2 years: _____

City _____ State _____ Zip _____

Bank Name:_____ Account # _____

If paying by charge card:

Charge Account Name _____ Account # _____

FORM 2
CHECK DEPOSIT RECORD

Date Deposited	Name on Check	Address	Phone Number	Bank Acct. #	Driver's License #	Credit Card #

FORM 3
PROMISSORY NOTE

Amount of Note: $_____   Date: _____

For value received, the undersigned promise(s) to pay to the order of
_____the sum of

   (1) $_____ (*amount of note*) as follows: paid herewith

   (2) $_____ (*down payment*) leaving a balance of

   (3) $_____ (*total financed*) plus finance charge of

   (4) $_____ (*finance charge*) for a total of payments of

   (5) $_____ (*total you will pay*)

The annual percentage rate is _____ per cent simple interest.

TERMS OF PAYMENT: $_____ payable on ___/___/___, and $_____ each thereafter, beginning on ___/___/___ with a final installment of $_____ for a total of _____ payments.

DEFAULT in the payment of any installment shall, at the option of _____, and without notice or demand, render the entire balance at once due and payable. Acceptance of any late payment shall not constitute a waiver of any subsequent payment when due.

IF SUIT is instituted to collect on this note, the undersigned promise(s) and agree(s) to pay the cost of such action, together with attorney fees in such amount as may be fixed by the court.

CONSIDERATION for this promissory note is: Forbearance of legal action in the matter of:_____ vs._____.

Signer: Co-Signer:

          x _____   x _____

Print names:

          _____   _____

Address:

          _____   _____

          _____   _____

This note signed at_____, (city)_____ (state)_____
on this date: _____ we received a copy of
this note:_____ (initial) _____ (initial)

Sign and return this note immediately upon receipt. Make all payments promptly. Payments are due in our office on the due dates indicated above. Late payments are subject to a $25.00 late charge. No statements will be sent. Your check is your receipt.

Payment is posted on the received business day, not the date mailed.

In addition to the late charge, interest will incur after late charge.

SAMPLE CREDIT RATING SCORING SYSTEM

Subject	Points
Telephone at home	2
Time on job	4
Years at residence	2
Checking/Savings	1
Total	9

Note: Financial institutions also use the "5 C's"— Character, Capacity, Capital, Conditions and Collateral to make a credit determination.

Source: *It's A New Day For Consumers*, by John J. Harrison

COLLECTIONS SYSTEM TIME LINE

Name of Stage	Length of Time for Stage	Time Elapsed Since Money First Due at Start of Process
Balance of Payment Becomes Due	--	0
Notification/Reminder Stage	30 days	5-30 days
First notification		5-30 days
Discussion Stage	15-45 days	35-60 days
Push or Firm Demand Stage	10 days	50-105 days
The Bitter End Stage	30-180 days	60-115 days
Going to a collection agency before you get the case back or the agency files suit	30 days-6 mo.	2-4 months
Hiring an attorney before filing suit	30-60 days	2-4 months
Filing for a Small Claims Court appearance and having a hearing	30-60 days	2-4 months
Filing a Municipal Court Action and getting a default judgment if the debtor doesn't answer (a contested case can take much longer)	30-60 days	2-4 months

FORM 4

| 1. Debtor's full name | Spouse | Amount due $ |

Last
Address _____ ZIP _____ Phone _____ Date last charge _____

Occupation
and employer _____ Date last payment _____

References _____ Bank and auto info: _____

S.S. No. _____ Drivers license no. _____ Your file or acct no. _____

Remarks _____ Check if mail returned _____

| 2. Debtor's full name | Spouse | Amount due $ |

Last
Address _____ ZIP _____ Phone _____ Date last charge _____

Occupation
and employer _____ Date last payment _____

References _____ Bank and auto info: _____

S.S. No. _____ Drivers license no. _____ Your file or acct no. _____

Remarks _____ Check if mail returned _____

| 3. Debtor's full name | Spouse | Amount due $ |

Last
Address _____ ZIP _____ Phone _____ Date last charge _____

Occupation
and employer _____ Date last payment _____

References _____ Bank and auto info: _____

S.S. No. _____ Drivers license no. _____ Your file or acct no. _____

Remarks _____ Check if mail returned _____

The parties above are indebted to the undersigned in the sums set opposite their names, the validity being capable of legal proof.

The undersigned agrees to report promptly ANY PAYMENT or communication received from any of the debtors, and to remit to any and all fees due; and further agrees that may retain any interest collected, unless otherwise specified in writing

_____ agrees to remit (less commissions, and interest collected) on or before the 12th of every month.

The above accounts are hereby assigned to:

* Name of creditor: _____

Signature
and title _____

Date _____

Address _____
_____

Type of business _____

Phone _____

* IF CORPORATION OR PARTNERSHIP, (PLEASE STATE)

Form 5

Information on the Debtor and Any Assets

Name of Debtor _____

Previous Names/Nicknames _____

Date of Birth _____ Social Security Number _____

Home Address _____

Home Phone Number _____

Current Job or Business Address _____

Business Phone Number _____

Postal Address or Box Holder _____

Previous Home Addresses _____
_____

Previous Job or Business Addresses _____
_____

Names of Personal Contacts:

Landlord's Name _____ Phone Number _____
Address _____

Neighbor's Name _____ Phone Number _____
Address _____

Friend's Name _____ Phone Number _____
Address _____

Relative's Name _____ Phone Number _____
Address _____

Associate's Name _____ Phone Number _____
Address _____

FORM 6

REAL ESTATE INQUIRY FORM

Date _____

From: _____
_____

To: Department of Real Estate
_____
_____

Please advise me if the following party, _____,
is currently licensed as a:

Salesperson _____ No _____ Yes Expiration date _____

Broker _____ No _____ Yes Expiration date _____

If not a currently licensed salesperson or broker, does this person have a license that expired?

_____ Yes, as a broker   _____ Yes, as a salesperson

_____ No   If yes, expiration date: _____

The person's last known business address is:
_____
_____
_____

The person's last known home address is:
_____
_____
_____

Thank you for your assistance,

_____

FORM 7
EXAMINATION IN SUPPLEMENTARY PROCEEDINGS EXAMPLE

Name _____ Spouse _____

Address _____ How long _____ Phone _____

Number of dependents and relationships _____

Employed by _____ Occupation _____ How long ____

Salary $ _____ per ____ How paid _____ When _____

Employer of spouse _____ Occupation _____ How long ____

Salary $ _____ per ____ How paid _____ When _____

Interest in any business _____

Other income _____

Own home _____ Value $ _____ Mortgages $ ____ Equity $ ___

Homestead date _____ Mortgagee _____ Payments $ ____ When ____

Rent _____ Amount $ ____ per month Date due _____

Landlord's name and address _____

Interest in other real estate _____ Encumbered? ____ Description ____

Bank _____ In whose name _____

Checking or savings _____ Last bank account _____ Closed ____

Safe deposit box _____ Where _____

Cash on person $ _____ Cash elsewhere _____

Stocks, bonds, securities _____

Life insurance co. _____ Amount $ _____ Annual premium $ ___

Jewelry _____ Interest to date _____

Auto or interest therein _____

Registered owner _____ Legal owner & address _____

Value $ _____ Payments $ ____ per ____ Unpaid balance $ _____

Other vehicles _____

Ever file for bankruptcy? _____ If so, when? _____ Where ? _____

Property pledged or pawned? _____

Debts owed to debtor _____

Name of parents _____ Address _____ Phone ____

Name of relatives or friends _____ Address _____ Phone ____

Promise to pay _____

Remarks _____

VERIFICATION

TO: The Tax Assessor for the County of _____

Please advise us who owns the following parcel: _____
_____

Please advise if, and at what street address, _____
_____
owns real property in your county.

Thank You,

Name of Requestor _____

Company _____

Address _____

City _____ State _____ Zip _____

If you have any questions, please call _____

BANK VERIFICATION FORM

Can you please provide us with the following information on the person listed below. We need it for verification purposes.

Name _____

Address _____

City _____ State _____ Zip _____

Checking Account Number: _____

Savings Account Number: _____

Name of Requestor _____

Company _____

Address _____

City _____ State _____ Zip _____

If you have any questions, please call _____

Index

Abstract of Judgment
....206,235,248,255-256,259-260,283
American Collectors Association ..85
*Application for Earnings Withholding
Order*.................................207,265
Attorney 127,129,144-148,215

Bad check letter...........................140
Bank account, debtor's...218,263-265
Bankruptcy...... 100-102,210,285-288
      chapter 7 285
      chapter 11...............................285
      chapter 13...............................285
      creditor's role 287-288
Better Business Bureau 36
Billing practices..................... 18-19
Business inventory, debtor's 218
Business license....................229-230
Business property, seizing............268
Business receipts, debtor's 218
      levying 267-268

Cash On Delivery (COD)......1,5,7,77
Check Deposit Record............. 13-14
"Choses in action" as asset...........205
Claim of Defendant 186-187,189,199
Claim of Exemption 270,274,276
Claim of Plaintiff.........................186
Collateral............................... 23-25
Collection agency . 127, 131, 148-159
Collection, do's and don'ts 51-54
      four stages of 46-48,55-77
      letter.......................................150
*Complaint for Renewal or Application
for Revival of Judgment* 249
Computers 50
Conditional sales 25-26
Consignments............................. 27
Contested case 196-198

Contracts, written....................19-22
Co-signers...................................25
County recorder...................223,262
Credit bureaus................. 33,221,232
Credit cards.............. 1,3-9,13,15,267
Credit rating...........................30-33
Credit references 37
Criss-Cross directories... 221-222,245

Debtor Information Sheet 219-220
Debtor, death of...................218-219
      locating...........................218-219
Debtor's exam 215
*Declaration for Subpoena Duces
Tecum* 235
Demand for payment 119
Demand letter......................120-126
Department of Motor Vehicles
.... 11,221-222,224,226-227,252
Dismissal of Action 185
Divorce 288

Earnings Withholding Order
.....................................265-266,269
Employer's Return 265,282
*Examination in Supplementary
Proceedings* 236,241,242
Exempt property..................257,262
Extending credit......................... 1-8

Fair Debt Collection Act................51
Federal Bankruptcy Reform Act ..285
Federal Trade Commission Act 51
Fictitious Business Name.............229
Financial statement 33,277-278
Fraudulent conveyance 289-290

Garnishment
.................207-208,210,215,248,251

Harassment 52
Interrogatories 219,221,242-244
Inventory, as security 25,28

Judgment, collecting 200,203-215
Judgment Debtor's Statement of Assets 233,236,238-239,242
Judgment, waiting period following 200

Labor organizations (unions) 230
Letter of Instructions 255,268
Letter services 138

Mail order 12
Mailgrams 65
Memorandum of Credits, Accrued Interest and Costs After Judgment 208,235,251-254,256
Memorandum of Garnishee 273,279-280
Money assets, levying 272
Motion for an Order Compelling an Answer for Interrogatories 243
Motion for an Order to Compel Further Response to Interrogatories 244
Motion for Contempt of Court 243
Motor vehicles, levying 270

Name change 290-291
National Association of Credit Management 35-36

Negotiation 105-115
New Client Questionnaire 2,3
Non-contested case 196
Non-payment, major reasons for 79-80
Non-sufficient funds (NSF) 10-12
Notice of Hearing on Claim of Exemption 281
Notice of Judgment Lien 207
Notice of Levy 252,258
Notice of Opposition of Claim of Exemption 275

Order of Examination 219,221,233-235,240,256
Order to Withhold Wages 248
Out-of-state assets, collecting 289
Overdue accounts, tracking 48-50

Personal property, debtor's 205,218
  seizing 271-272
Plaintiff Claim and Order to Defendant 174

Plaintiff's Statement 172
Post Office 221-222,224-225,245
Pre-collection letter. 127,129,137-144
Pre-collection service 141-142
Privacy, invasion of 54
Promissory notes 19-20,76
Public records 217-232

Real Estate Inquiry Form 231
Real property, debtor's 205,218
  forced sale of 273,283-284
  lien against 206,210
Reminders, written 56-59,61-64,211-214

Sales tax agency, state 228
Satisfaction of Judgment 185
Secretary of State 207,229,262
Securities and Exchange Commission (SEC) 229
Service, debtor response to 184-187
  for small claims court 175-184
  personal 179
  process 182
  substitute 180
  using friend or relative 183-184
  using law enforcement personnel 181,208,252,268,271-272
Skip tracing 245
Small Claims Court .... 127,133, ... 162-187,189-200,204,226,292-293
Small Claims Legal Advisor 206
Stalls, dealing with 85-96
"Starter" checks 10
Statement of Assets 242
Subpoena, Civil 191-192
Subpoena Duces Tecum 190,219,221-222,233,235,237,242
Superior Court 199,204,226

Tax assessor 221,223-224
Tax collector 229
Telegrams 65
Telephone calls 64-65
Trade associations 230

Uniform Commercial Code (UCC). 10

Wages, going after debtor's
  (See also Garnishment) 218
Witnesses 190-194
Writ of Execution ... 206-207,209,242,247,249-251,255, ... 264-265,267-268,271,273,283,292

ESTABLISH A FRAMEWORK
for excellence
WITH THE SUCCESSFUL BUSINESS LIBRARY

**The Oasis Press®
PSI Research**

P.O. Box 3727
Central Point, Oregon
97502-0032

Call Direct
1-800-228-2275

Fax Line
1-541-476-1479

Email Address
info@psi-research.com

Fastbreaking changes in technology and the global marketplace continue to create unprecedented opportunities for businesses through the '90s and into the new millennium. However with these opportunities will also come many new challenges. Today, more than ever, businesses, especially small businesses, need to excel in all areas of operation to complete and succeed in an ever-changing world.

The Successful Business Library takes you through the '90s and beyond, helping you solve the day-to-day problems you face now, and prepares you for the unexpected problems you may be facing down the road. With any of our products, you will receive up-to-date and practical business solutions, which are easy to use and easy to understand. No jargon or theories, just solid, nuts-and-bolts information.

Whether you are an entrepreneur going into business for the first time or an experienced consultant trying to keep up with the latest rules and regulations, The Successful Business Library provides you with the step-by-step guidance, and action-oriented plans you need to succeed in today's world. As an added benefit, PSI Research/The Oasis Press® unconditionally guarantees your satisfaction with the purchase of any book or software application in our catalog.

THE OASIS PRESS® ONLINE

More than a marketplace for our products, we actually provide something that many business Web sites tend to overlook... *...useful information.*

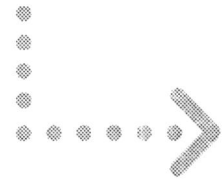

It's no mystery that the World Wide Web is a great way for businesses to promote their products, however most commercial sites stop there. We have always viewed our site's goals a little differently. For starters, we have applied our 25 years of experience providing hands-on information to small businesses directly to our Web site. We offer current information to help you start your own business, guidelines to keep it up and running, useful federal and state-specific information (including addresses and phone numbers to contact these resources), and a forum for business owners to communicate and network with others on the Internet. We would like to invite you to check out our Web site and discover the information that can assist you and your small business venture.

ALL MAJOR CREDIT CARDS ACCEPTED
CALL TO PLACE AN ORDER
— or —
TO RECEIVE A FREE CATALOG
1-800-228-2275

International Orders (541) 479-9464   *Fax Orders* (541) 476-1479
Web site http://www.psi-research.com   *Email* sales@psi-research.com

PSI Research P.O. Box 3727 Central Point, Oregon 97502 U.S.A.

The Oasis Press Online
http://www.psi-research.com

Where Business Talks To Business

Multipurpose Templates For Your Business

Financial Templates for Small Business includes 28 templates which cover everything from Annual Income to Variable Rate Loan Amortization, and the manual shows you how and where to use them in simple terms.

There are historical spreadsheets to help you analyze historical information, forecast spreadsheets to help you predict the future and a variety of other spreadsheets to aid you in evaluating your business and the proposed purchase of another's business. Whether your business is existing or not, these templates will help you plan for the future.

FINANCIAL TEMPLATES
for small business

These new *Financial Templates for Small Business* are sure to make an impact on the way you keep track of your business resources and will make a valuable addition to your business computer library.

Order Today:
Financial Templates
Available for IBM or MAC:
Price: **$69.95**
Catalog #: **FTMPSTMP3I (IBM)**
Catalog #: **FTMPSTMP3M (MAC)**
Call 1-800-228-2275 or
FAX 1-541-476-1479

THE OASIS PRESS BOOKS & SOFTWARE
For More Information Call Toll-Free 1-800-228-2275
PSI Research/The Oasis Press   P.O. Box 3727   Central Point, Oregon   97502-0032

NEW FROM THE OASIS PRESS

Let *SmartStart* pave your way through today's complex business environment.

You may be like more than 35 million other Americans — you dream of owning a business. In fact, there has never been a better time to start a small business. According to a recent research study by the Entrepreneurial Research Consortium, one out of three U.S. households has someone who is involved in a small business startup. With statistics like these, the odds seem to be in your favor... until you start dealing with the many regulations, laws, and financial requirements placed on 21st century business owners.

SmartStart Your (State*) Business goes a step beyond other business how-to books and provides you with:

✘ Each book is state specific, with information and resources that are unique. This gives you an advantage over other general business start-up books that have no way of providing current local information you will need;

✘ Quick reference to the most current mailing and Internet addresses and telephone numbers for the federal, state, local, and private agencies that will help get your business up and running;

✘ State population statistics, income and consumption rates, major industry trends, and overall business incentives to give you a better picture of doing business in your state; and

✘ Logical checklists, sample forms, and a complete sample business plan to assist you with the numerous start-up details.

SmartStart is your roadmap to avoid legal and financial pitfalls and direct you through the bureaucratic red tape that often entangles fledgling entrepreneurs. This is your all-in-one resource tool that will give you a jump start on planning for your business.

SmartStart Your (State) Business
$19.95, paperback
*When ordering, be sure to tell us which state you are interested in receiving

Order direct from The Oasis Press®

You can order any Successful Business Library title directly from The Oasis Press®. We would be happy to hear from you and assist you in finding the right titles for your small business needs at:

1-800-228-2275

Because *SmartStart* is a new state-specific series, new states are being released every month, please call to confirm a state's scheduled release date — or check with your favorite bookstore.

The Oasis Press®
The Leading Publisher of Small Business Information

A PERFECT COMPLIMENT TO ASSIST YOU IN CREATING A BUSINESS PLAN

The Successful Business Plan
Software for Windows

Rhonda M. Abrams' book *The Successful Business Plan: Secrets and Strategies* has what you need to get your idea or venture into a plan of action that sells. Now, Oasis Press Software has made it even easier to complete the actual creation of your business plan with *The Successful Business Plan software*. Offered as a Windows™ package or as template files. Whatever your needs are for developing a business plan of your own, The Oasis Press software can help make the job easier.

Runs on Windows 95™

This easy-to-use standalone program combines a versatile spreadsheet with a text processing program and an outline processor. With the outline processor you can manipulate the basic outline, creating any structure you prefer. The text editor allows you to enter and format the text associated with each topic in the outline. Several forms in *The Successful Business Plan* book, which require mathematical calculations are pre-formatted templates ready to enter your financials. Templates can be changed to modify formulas or the description of a category. *The Successful Business Plan* has been designed to conform to common Windows™ features.

The Successful Business Plan Software
Please specify choice:
Software only	$ 99.95
Software with paperback	$109.95
Software with Binder	$125.95

SYSTEM REQUIREMENTS WINDOWS VERSION:
IBM compatible with Windows 3.1 or later
4MB memory • 4MB hard disk memory
Graphics card & Monitor
Mouse and printer optional, but beneficial

Template Files

The Successful Business Plan Templates make it easy to complete the financial portion of your business plan. Financial calculations from the forms in the book are included. In addition, there are three loan amortization templates to make estimates of expenses easier to predict when considering real estate or capital equipment purchases. There are also spreadsheets for making projections, regardless if you are already in business or just starting up.

Successful Business Plan Templates
Templates Only	$69.95
Templates with paperback	$79.95
Templates with Binder	$89.95

SYSTEM REQUIREMENTS:
Fully functional with Lotus 1-2-3
(version 2.1 or later) or Excel 4.0
or a compatible spreadsheet program

CALL TO PLACE AN ORDER — or — **TO RECEIVE A FREE CATALOG** **1-800-228-2275**

International Orders (541) 479-9464   *Fax Orders* (541) 476-1479
Web site http://www.psi-research.com   *Email* sales@psi-research.com

PSI Research P.O. Box 3727 Central Point, Oregon 97502 U.S.A.

From The Leading Publisher of Small Business Information
Books that save you time and money.

This authoritative guide will transform the roles of administrators and improve effectiveness for corporate, nonprofit, and community organizations — many of which are over-managed but lack effective leadership. Its skills-oriented solutions teach managers to be effective leaders and train leaders to be better managers, a distinction often overlooked by other management guides. An excellent tool for new managers, Randall Ponder's *Leader's Guide* focuses on helping leaders hone in on their skills.

The Leader's Guide　　　　　　　　　　　　　　　　**Pages: 275**
Paperback: $19.95　　　　**ISBN: 1-55571-434-X**

This innovative book provides managers with an entirely new way of looking at information that can save time, money, headaches, and maybe even their jobs or companies. It provides cutting-edge principles and concepts that will help people work far more effectively and easily with all sorts of data.

Information Breakthrough　　　　　　　　　　　**Pages: 250**
Paperback: $22.95　　　　**ISBN: 1-55571-413-7**

This resource shows high-tech entrepreneurs how to access money to develop, produce, and market their products or services. Author Richard Manweller shares insider know-how on finding funding, making presentations, and crafting a business plan. Sample plans, proposals, agreements, and spreadsheets are all included in this useful and inspiring guide.

Funding High-Tech Ventures　　　　　　　　　　**Pages: 150**
Paperback: $21.95　　　　**ISBN: 1-55571-405-6**

With the immense popularity of the Internet, many businesses and organizations are feeling the pressure to establish some sort of Internet presence. *Connecting Online* cuts through the hype and shows you why it is essential to first establish a solid image and communicative environment with your key audiences on the Internet. This book is the definitive source for all of your image building strategies on the Internet, regardless of whether you are a seasoned professional or entirely new to the concept.

Connecting Online　　　　　　　　　　　　　　　**Pages: 470**
Paperback: $21.95　　　　**ISBN: 1-55571-403-X**

ALL MAJOR CREDIT CARDS ACCEPTED

CALL TO PLACE AN ORDER
— or —
TO RECEIVE A FREE CATALOG　　**1-800-228-2275**

International Orders (541) 479-9464　　*Fax Orders* (541) 476-1479
Web site http://www.psi-research.com　　*Email* sales@psi-research.com

PSI Research　P.O. Box 3727　Central Point, Oregon　97502　U.S.A.

From The Leading Publisher of Small Business Information
Books that save you time and money.

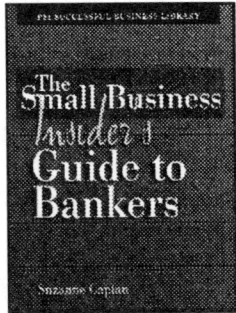

In business, the banker and the institution they represent are often perceived as opponents to your business' success. Shows why business owners should take a leading role in developing and nurturing a worthwhile and lasting partnership with their banker. This inside look will help new and seasoned business owners develop a functional understanding of how the banking industry operates, how to speak their language, and how to turn your banker into an advocate for the growth and success of your small business.

Small Business Insider's Guide to Bankers   **Pages: 176**
Paperback: $18.95   **ISBN: 1-55571-400-5**

Saves costly consultant or staff hours in creating company personnel policies. Provides over 70 model policies on topics such as employee safety, leave of absence, flex time, smoking, substance abuse, sexual harassment, performance improvement, and grievance procedures. For each subject, practical and legal ramifications are explained and a choice of alternate policies is presented.

Company Policy & Personnel Workbook   **Pages: 350**
Paperback: $29.95   **ISBN: 1-55571-365-3**
Binder: $49.95   **ISBN: 1-55571-364-5**

There are numerous intangible factors that influence the valuation of an enterprise, including asset variables, operating income, the buyer's income, and return on investment. *The Secrets to Buying and Selling a Business* approaches the transition from the viewpoints of both seller and buyer, giving you a very practical and balanced overview of the process. Covers financing, protecting investments, how to construct a deal, as well as other key points. Includes sample forms, checklists, and worksheets.

Secrets to Buying & Selling a Business   **Pages: 300**
Paperback: $24.95   **ISBN: 1-55571-398-X**

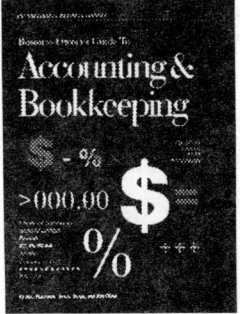

Makes understanding the economics of your business simple. Explains the basic accounting principles that relate to any business. Step-by-step instructions for generating accounting statements and interpreting them, spotting errors, and recognizing warning signs. Discusses how creditors view financial statements.

Business Owner's Guide to Accounting & Bookkeeping   **Pages: 172**
Paperback: $19.95   **ISBN: 1-55571-381-5**

ALL MAJOR CREDIT CARDS ACCEPTED

CALL TO PLACE AN ORDER
— or —
TO RECEIVE A FREE CATALOG
1-800-228-2275

International Orders (541) 479-9464   *Fax Orders* (541) 476-1479
Web site http://www.psi-research.com   *Email* sales@psi-research.com

PSI Research   P.O. Box 3727   Central Point, Oregon   97502   U.S.A.

From The Leading Publisher of Small Business Information
Books that save you time and money.

Written for managers and business owners, this book tells exactly where to draw the line in sexual harassment, and how to draw it firmly, so that employees understand and respect it. The book also clearly spells out the procedures that are most effective if a suit is lodged and gives tips on enlisting a good attorney.

Draw The Line: A Sexual Harassment Free Workplace **Pages: 172**
Paperback: $17.95   **ISBN: 1-55571-370-X**

Focuses on developing the art of working with people to maximize the productivity and satisfaction of both manager and employees. Discussions, exercises, and self-tests boost skill in communicating, delegating, motivating, developing teams, goal-setting, adapting to change, and coping with stress.

Managing People   **Pages: 260**
Paperback: $21.95   **ISBN: 1-55571-380-7**

The heart of customer service — the transaction between customer and service provider — is the focus of this book. Author Richard Gallagher demonstrates how the three secrets of customer service make these transactions satisfying and productive. An excellent follow-up to Stan Lindsay's *The Twenty-One Sales in a Sale!*

Smile Training Isn't Enough   **Pages: 200**
Paperback: $19.95   **ISBN: 1-55571-422-6**

Author Luigi Salvaneschi clearly shows how studying eight specific liberal arts principles can help nurture your own leadership skills within — and make you an asset for the business world of the 21st century. Each chapter leads you through his new concept in management thinking and tells how it applies to both the business world and your own personal life. Includes exercises to explore at home, work, and while traveling.

Renaissance 2000   **Pages: 345**
Paperback: $22.95   **ISBN: 1-55571-412-9**

ALL MAJOR CREDIT CARDS ACCEPTED

CALL TO PLACE AN ORDER
— or —
TO RECEIVE A FREE CATALOG
1-800-228-2275

International Orders (541) 479-9464   *Fax Orders* (541) 476-1479
Web site http://www.psi-research.com   *Email* sales@psi-research.com

PSI Research P.O. Box 3727 Central Point, Oregon 97502 U.S.A.

From The Leading Publisher of Small Business Information
Books that save you time and money.

Luigi Salvaneschi, the former President of Blockbuster Video, Senior Vice-President of Kentucky Fried Chicken, and member of the Board of Directors at McDonald's shares his vast knowledge about site relocation. Helps you identify and understand your retail trading zone and gives industry insights on using city layout and traffic patterns to your benefit. Also shows unique methods for analyzing your competitors to maximize your retail potential.
Location, Location, Location **Pages: 346**
Paperback: $19.95   ISBN: 1-55571-376-9

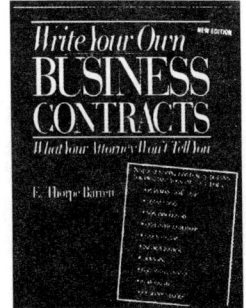

Explains the dos and don'ts of contract writing so any person in business can do the preparatory work in drafting contracts before hiring and attorney for final review. Provides a working knowledge of the various types of business agreements, plus tips on how to prepare for the unexpected.
Write Your Own Business Contracts **Pages: 340**
Paperback: $24.95   ISBN: 1-55571-170-7
Binder: $39.95   ISBN: 1-55571-196-0

An extensive summary of every imaginable tax break that is still available in today's reform tax environment. Goes beyond most tax guides on the market that focus on the tax season only, instead it provides you with year-round strategies to lower taxes and avoid common pitfalls. Identifies a wide assortment of tax deduction, fringe benefits, and tax deferrals. Includes a simplified checklist of recent tax law changes with an emphasis on tax breaks. Available in it 4th Edition!
Top Tax Saving Ideas for Today's Small Business **Pages: 336**
Paperback: $16.95   ISBN: 1-55571-379-3

Essential for the small business operator in search of capital, this helpful, hands-on guide simplifies the loan application process as never before. The Insider's Guide to Small Business Loans is an easy-to-follow road map designed to help you cut thought the red tape and show you how to prepare a successful loan application. Several chapters are devoted to helping you secure a loan guaranty from the Small Business Administration.
Insider's Guide to Small Business Loans **Pages: 260**
Paperback: $19.95   ISBN: 1-55571-373-4
Binder: $29.95   ISBN: 1-55571-378-5

ALL MAJOR CREDIT CARDS ACCEPTED

CALL TO PLACE AN ORDER
— or —
TO RECEIVE A FREE CATALOG
1-800-228-2275

International Orders (541) 479-9464   *Fax Orders* (541) 476-1479
Web site http://www.psi-research.com   *Email* sales@psi-research.com

PSI Research   P.O. Box 3727   Central Point, Oregon   97502   U.S.A.

Order Directly From The Oasis Press®

Call, Mail, Email, or Fax Your Order to: PSI Research, P.O. Box 3727, Central Point, OR 97502
Order Phone USA & Canada: +1 800 228-2275   Email: sales@psi-research.com   Fax: +1 541 476-1479

Includes Titles Through Winter 1999

TITLE	✔ BINDER	✔ PAPERBACK	QUANTITY	COST
Advertising Without An Agency: A Comprehensive Guide to Radio, Television, Print...		❏ $19.95		
Bottom Line Basics: Understand and Control Your Finances	❏ $39.95	❏ $19.95		
BusinessBasics: A Microbusiness Startup Guide		❏ $16.95		
The Business Environmental Handbook	❏ $39.95	❏ $19.95		
Business Owner's Guide to Accounting & Bookkeeping		❏ $19.95		
businessplan.com: how to write a web-woven strategic business plan		❏ $19.95		
Buyer's Guide to Business Insurance	❏ $39.95	❏ $19.95		
California Corporation Formation Package		❏ $29.95		
Collection Techniques for a Small Business	❏ $39.95	❏ $19.95		
A Company Policy and Personnel Workbook	❏ $49.95	❏ $29.95		
Company Relocation Handbook	❏ $39.95	❏ $19.95		
CompControl: The Secrets of Reducing Workers' Compensation Costs	❏ $39.95	❏ $19.95		
Complete Book of Business Forms		❏ $19.95		
Connecting Online: Creating a Successful Image on the Internet		❏ $21.95		
Customer Engineering: Cutting Edge Selling Strategies	❏ $39.95	❏ $19.95		
Develop & Market Your Creative Ideas		❏ $15.95		
Developing International Markets: Shaping Your Global Presence		❏ $19.95		
Doing Business in Russia: Basic Facts for the Pioneering Entrepreneur		❏ $19.95		
Draw The Line: A Sexual Harassment Free Workplace		❏ $17.95		
Entrepreneurial Decisionmaking: A Survival Manual for the Next Millennium		❏ $21.95		
The Essential Corporation Handbook		❏ $21.95		
The Essential Limited Liability Company Handbook	❏ $39.95	❏ $21.95		
Export Now: A Guide for Small Business	❏ $39.95	❏ $24.95		
Financial Decisionmaking: A CPA/Attorney's Perspective		❏ $19.95		
Financial Management Techniques for Small Business	❏ $39.95	❏ $19.95		
Financing Your Small Business: Techniques for Planning, Acquiring, & Managing Debt		❏ $19.95		
Franchise Bible: How to Buy a Franchise or Franchise Your Own Business	❏ $39.95	❏ $24.95		
Friendship Marketing: Growing Your Business by Cultivating Strategic Relationships		❏ $18.95		
Funding High-Tech Ventures		❏ $21.95		
Home Business Made Easy		❏ $19.95		
Information Breakthrough: How to Turn Mountains of Confusing Data into Gems of Useful Information		❏ $22.95		
Improving Staff Productivity: Ideas to Increase Profits		❏ $16.95		
The Insider's Guide to Small Business Loans		❏ $19.95		
InstaCorp – Incorporate In Any State (Book & Software)		❏ $29.95		
Joysticks, Blinking Lights and Thrills		❏ $18.95		
Keeping Score: An Inside Look at Sports Marketing		❏ $18.95		
Know Your Market: How to Do Low-Cost Market Research	❏ $39.95	❏ $19.95		
The Leader's Guide: 15 Essential Skills		❏ $19.95		
Legal Expense Defense: How to Control Your Business' Legal Costs and Problems	❏ $39.95	❏ $19.95		
Legal Road Map for Consultants		❏ $18.95		
Location, Location, Location: How to Select the Best Site for Your Business		❏ $19.95		
Mail Order Legal Guide	❏ $45.00	❏ $29.95		
Managing People: A Practical Guide		❏ $21.95		
Marketing for the New Millennium: Applying New Techniques		❏ $19.95		
Marketing Mastery: Your Seven Step Guide to Success	❏ $39.95	❏ $19.95		
The Money Connection: Where and How to Apply for Business Loans and Venture Capital	❏ $39.95	❏ $24.95		
Moonlighting: Earn a Second Income at Home		❏ $15.95		
Navigating the Marketplace: Growth Strategies For Your Business		❏ $21.95		
No Money Down Financing for Franchising		❏ $19.95		
People Investment: How to Make Your Hiring Decisions Pay Off For Everyone	❏ $39.95	❏ $19.95		
Power Marketing for Small Business	❏ $39.95	❏ $19.95		
Profit Power: 101 Pointers to Give Your Business a Competitive Edge		❏ $19.95		
Proposal Development: How to Respond and Win the Bid	❏ $39.95	❏ $21.95		
Public Relations Marketing: Making a Splash Without Much Cash		❏ $19.95		
Raising Capital: How to Write a Financing Proposal		❏ $19.95		
Renaissance 2000: Liberal Arts Essentials for Tomorrow's Leaders		❏ $22.95		
Retail in Detail: How to Start and Manage a Small Retail Business		❏ $15.95		
Secrets of High Ticket Selling		❏ $19.95		
Secrets to Buying and Selling a Business		❏ $24.95		
Secure Your Future: Financial Planning at Any Age	❏ $39.95	❏ $19.95		
Selling Services: A Guide for the Consulting Professional		❏ $18.95		
The Small Business Insider's Guide to Bankers		❏ $18.95		

BOOK SUB-TOTAL (Additional titles on other side)

TITLE	✔ BINDER	✔ PAPERBACK	QUANTITY	COST
SmartStart Your (State) Business... series		❏ $19.95		
Please specify which state(s) you would like:				
Smile Training Isn't Enough: The Three Secrets to Excellent Customer Service		❏ $19.95		
Start Your Business (Also available as a book and disk package, see below)		❏ $ 9.95 *(without disk)*		
Successful Business Plan: Secrets & Strategies	❏ $49.95	❏ $27.95		
Successful Network Marketing for The 21st Century		❏ $15.95		
Surviving Success: Managing the Challenges of Growth		❏ $19.95		
TargetSmart! Database Marketing for the Small Business		❏ $19.95		
Top Tax Saving Ideas for Today's Small Business		❏ $16.95		
Twenty-One Sales in a Sale: What Sales Are You Missing?		❏ $19.95		
Which Business? Help in Selecting Your New Venture		❏ $18.95		
Write Your Own Business Contracts		❏ $24.95		
BOOK SUB-TOTAL (Don't forget to include your amount from the previous side)				

OASIS SOFTWARE Please specify which computer operating system you use (DOS, Mac OS, or Windows)

TITLE	✔ Windows	✔ Mac OS	QUANTITY	COST
California Corporation Formation Package ASCII Software	❏ $ 39.95	❏ $ 39.95		
Company Policy & Personnel Software Text Files	❏ $ 49.95	❏ $ 49.95		
Financial Management Techniques (Full Standalone)	❏ $ 99.95			
Financial Templates	❏ $ 69.95	❏ $ 69.95		
The Insurance Assistant Software (Full Standalone)	❏ $ 29.95			
Start Your Business (Software for Windows™)	❏ $ 19.95			
Successful Business Plan (Software for Windows™)	❏ $ 99.95			
Successful Business Plan Templates	❏ $ 69.95	❏ $ 69.95		
The Survey Genie - Customer Edition (Full Standalone)	❏ $199.95 (WIN)	❏ $149.95 (DOS)		
The Survey Genie - Employee Edition (Full Standalone)	❏ $199.95 (WIN)	❏ $149.95 (DOS)		
Winning Business Plans in Color (MS Office Addition)	❏ $ 39.95			
SOFTWARE SUB-TOTAL				

BOOK & DISK PACKAGES Please specify which computer operating system you use (DOS, Mac OS, or Windows)

TITLE	✔ Windows	✔ MacOS	✔ Binder	✔ Paperback	QUANTITY	COST
The Buyer's Guide to Business Insurance w/ Insurance Assistant	❏		❏ $ 59.95	❏ $ 39.95		
California Corporation Formation Book & Text Files	❏	❏		❏ $ 59.95		
Company Policy & Personnel Book & Software Text Files	❏	❏	❏ $ 89.95	❏ $ 69.95		
Financial Management Techniques Book & Software	❏		❏ $129.95	❏ $119.95		
Start Your Business Paperback & Software (Software for Windows™)	❏			❏ $ 24.95		
Successful Business Plan Book & Software for Windows™	❏		❏ $125.95	❏ $109.95		
Successful Business Plan Book & Software Templates	❏	❏	❏ $109.95	❏ $ 89.95		
BOOK & DISK PACKAGE SUB-TOTAL						

SOLD TO: Please give street address for shipping.

Name:

Title:

Company:

Street Address:

City/State/Zip:

Daytime Phone: Email:

SHIP TO: If different than above, please give alternate street address

Name:

Company:

Street Address:

City/State/Zip:

Daytime Phone:

GRAND TOTAL

SUB-TOTALS *(from other side)* $

SUB-TOTALS *(from this side)* $

SHIPPING (see chart below) $

TOTAL ORDER $

If your purchase is:	Shipping costs within the USA:
$0 - $25	$5.00
$25.01 - $50	$6.00
$50.01 - $100	$7.00
$100.01 - $175	$9.00
$175.01 - $250	$13.00
$250.01 - $500	$18.00
$500.01 +	4% of total merchandise

You can also order online 24-hours a day and 7 days a week at http://www.psi-research.com

PAYMENT INFORMATION: *Rush service is available, call for details.*
International and Canadian Orders: *Please call 1-541-479-9464 for quote on shipping.*
Please indicate a method of payment below:

❏ **CHECK** *Enclosed, payable to PSI Research*   ❏ VISA   ❏ MASTERCARD   ❏ AMEX   ❏ DISCOVER

Card Number: Expires:

Signature: Name On Card:

Use this form to register for an advance notification of updates, new books and software releases, plus special customer discounts!

Please answer these questions to let us know how our products are working for you, and what we could do to serve you better.

Collection Techniques for a Small Business

Rate this product's overall quality of information:
- ☐ Excellent
- ☐ Good
- ☐ Fair
- ☐ Poor

Rate the quality of printed materials:
- ☐ Excellent
- ☐ Good
- ☐ Fair
- ☐ Poor

Rate the format:
- ☐ Excellent
- ☐ Good
- ☐ Fair
- ☐ Poor

Did the product provide what you needed?
- ☐ Yes ☐ No

If not, what should be added?
_____
_____
_____
_____
_____
_____

This product is:
- ☐ Clear and easy to follow
- ☐ Too complicated
- ☐ Too elementary

Were the worksheets easy to use?
- ☐ Yes ☐ No ☐ N/A

Should we include?
- ☐ More worksheets
- ☐ Fewer worksheets
- ☐ No worksheets

How do you feel about the price?
- ☐ Lower than expected
- ☐ About right
- ☐ Too expensive

How many employees are in your company?
- ☐ Under 10 employees
- ☐ 10 - 50 employees
- ☐ 51 - 99 employees
- ☐ 100 - 250 employees
- ☐ Over 250 employees

How many people in the city your company is in?
- ☐ 50,000 - 100,000
- ☐ 100,000 - 500,000
- ☐ 500,000 - 1,000,000
- ☐ Over 1,000,000
- ☐ Rural (Under 50,000)

What is your type of business?
- ☐ Retail
- ☐ Service
- ☐ Government
- ☐ Manufacturing
- ☐ Distributor
- ☐ Education

What types of products or services do you sell?
_____
_____

What is your position in the company?
(please check one)
- ☐ Owner
- ☐ Administrative
- ☐ Sales/Marketing
- ☐ Finance
- ☐ Human Resources
- ☐ Production
- ☐ Operations
- ☐ Computer/MIS

How did you learn about this product?
- ☐ Recommended by a friend
- ☐ Used in a seminar or class
- ☐ Have used other PSI products
- ☐ Received a mailing
- ☐ Saw in bookstore
- ☐ Saw in library
- ☐ Saw review in:
  - ☐ Newspaper
  - ☐ Magazine
  - ☐ Radio/TV

Where did you buy this product?
- ☐ Catalog
- ☐ Bookstore
- ☐ Office supply
- ☐ Consultant

Would you purchase other business tools from us?
- ☐ Yes ☐ No

If so, which products interest you?
- ☐ EXECARDS® Communications Cards
- ☐ Books for business
- ☐ Software

Would you recommend this product to a friend?
- ☐ Yes ☐ No

Do you use a personal computer?
- ☐ Yes ☐ No

If yes, which?
- ☐ Macintosh
- ☐ PC Compatible
- ☐ Other

Check all the ways you use computers?
- ☐ Word processing
- ☐ Accounting
- ☐ Spreadsheet
- ☐ Inventory
- ☐ Order processing
- ☐ Design/Graphics
- ☐ General Data Base
- ☐ Customer Information
- ☐ Scheduling
- ☐ Internet

May we call you to follow up on your comments?
- ☐ Yes ☐ No

May we add your name to our mailing list? ☐ Yes ☐ No

If you'd like us to send associates or friends a catalog, just list names and addresses on back.

Is there anything we should do to improve our products?
_____

Just fill in your name and address here, fold (see back) and mail.

Name _____
Title _____
Company _____
Phone _____
Address _____
City/State/Zip _____
Email Address (Home) _____ (Business) _____

PSI Research creates this family of fine products to help you more easily and effectively manage your business activities:
The Oasis Press®   PSI Successful Business Software
PSI Successful Business Library   EXECARDS® Communication Tools

04/98

If you have friends or associates who might appreciate receiving our catalogs, please list here. Thanks!

Name_____   Name_____

Title_____   Title_____

Company_____   Company_____

Phone_____   Phone_____

Address_____   Address_____

Address_____   Address_____

FOLD HERE FIRST

BUSINESS REPLY MAIL
FIRST CLASS MAIL PERMIT NO. 002 MERLIN, OREGON

POSTAGE WILL BE PAID BY ADDRESSEE

PSI Research
PO BOX 1414
Merlin OR 97532-9900

NO POSTAGE
NECESSARY
IF MAILED
IN THE
UNITED STATES

FOLD HERE SECOND, THEN TAPE TOGETHER

Please cut along this vertical line, fold twice, tape together and mail.